THE TEACHINGS

FOR THE FOURTH DENSITY AQUARIAN

by
Chief
Little
Summer

and
Warm
Night
Rain

VOLUME II

THE TEACHINGS

FOR THE FOURTH DENSITY AQUARIAN
Volume II

as revealed by
Chief Little Summer and Warm Night Rain

ISBN 1-880440-04-0
Library of Congress Catalog Card Number: 92-062028

Cover and Illustrations
Warm Night Rain

Typesetting
David Nielsen
Historical Publications
Austin, Texas

Graphics
Catherine Polito
Management by Design
Austin, Texas

Publisher
Piqua Press, Inc.
P.O. Box 202590
Austin, Texas 78720-2590
(512) 837-7171

First printing -- November 1992

This Volume is dedicated to all of our
Students who have reminded us of the things
that we must teach so that other Wanderers
might also understand and be about their Father's
business.
And
a very special thanks to Bill and Nancy
whose undaunted efforts have made
all things possible.
And
a wink and a nod
to
Our Beloved
World Teacher!

Table of Contents

Chapter	*Section Subject*	*Page*

V
The Tensor Concepts

VI
Conversations With The Chief

Preface

It is spring, 1992. We have been under the Fourth Density Vibration for a year now. There is a tremendous resistance to this vibration of Love and Understanding. The resisting force comes from the Americas, especially the United States of America.

You, our reader, are probably an American. It is not our intent to offend you, or promote ill will. It is our honor/duty to inform you and point out certain facts that have been carefully camouflaged, or disguised, by other names or deliberately hidden.

As always, you, dear reader, have the Divine Free Will to accept, or reject, anything we say — for any reason you so choose. It is our honor/duty to offer information and the product of our observations. Not to lead the masses in revolution.

We respectfully ask that the reader be apprised of this understanding, as the variety of the materials presented unfold. Note how the rising Fourth Density Vibration enhances certain things, while other aspects of the yet Third Density are becoming more restricting, even enslaving. The conflict, the struggle, is indeed upon us. Choices have been made. The courage of our convictions is being challenged. There is no escape.

May the sound vibration complexes, known as words, that we have strung together to attempt to convey a thought bring you a peace...through understanding.

The format for Volume II is the same as it was for Volume I. The Kundalini is rarely mentioned, but is expected that the reader/student will utilize this powerful meditation, as the thoughts within this book are translated into your own Mind/Body/Spirit Complex.

It is absolutely mandatory that you have a firm understanding of *The Teachings Volume I* before making any valid attempt to comprehend the material contained herein. This is the second book of a four Volume series. Each succeeding Volume will continuously refer to its predecessors. The completed series will form a large portion of the working/teaching factor of our new Fourth Density budding civilization.

The core or hub of *The Teachings* is the conscious contact with the Higher Self via the Kundalini Meditation. The succeeding Volumes, with their infinite variety of ancient wisdom/knowledge, are all spokes stemming from this Kundalini hub, reaching out to the rim of ultimate understanding of creation and basking in the Love of our One Infinite Creator as a full fledged Co-Creator.

It is our fervent hope and prayer that our words permit and encourage you to learn *to be,* and most of all - to enjoy our Creator's magnificent Universe!

Megwich!
(Our Thanks!)

We are . . . Chief Little Summer and Warm Night Rain

Note: As always, the reader may accept everything we say; accept part of what we say; or reject everything we say. This is your Free Will prerogative. We would have it no other way! Read on at your own risk!

Section I

The Rays

This section deals with the Rays, their respective and collective energies and the practical uses when properly applied.

Chapter 1

We greet you in the Light and Love of our One Infinite Creator. We are Chief Little Summer and Warm Night Rain.

Let us begin this section with the chant:

"I am that I am, A-yeh,
I am that I am, A-yeh,
I am that I am, A-yeh,
I am that I am, A-yeh,
I am that I am, A-yeh,
I am that I am, A-yeh,
I am that I am, A-yeh,
A-yeh,
A-yeh,
A-yeh,
A-yeh,
A-yeh."

(A-Yeh is pronounced — Ahhh-Yaaay)

Our Prayer of Protection: "In the Name of the Presence and the Power Universal, protect us from harm and all unenlightened spirits. May the Light of our Spirit Guides and the Light of our Higher Selves illuminate our thoughts, that we might reflect the Radiant Glory of ALL THAT IS."

* * *

Now, let us prepare to raise the Kundalini. You have been taught this procedure in Volume I of *The Teachings*. We must assume that you have mastered the practice by this time. The material contained in Volume I is essential to the understanding of the material following in Volume II.

Now, let us begin. Make yourself comfortable, back straight. Align and balance the chakras . . . awaken the Kundalini . . . activate the Red . . Orange . . Yellow . . Green . . Blue . . Indigo . . Violet . . With your consciousness attached, visualize the Kundalini bathing the lower half of the Golden Sphere, which is your Higher Self. The flowing Kundalini falls down all around your body, which is protected by the aura of seven domes. Firmly establish the contact with your Higher Self and, when you are ready, begin to read.

NOTES:

* * *

The Rays Are Light And Love

Light may be physical or non-physical. Rays consist of Non-Physical or Etheric Light. The source of Etheric Light is the Creator and it is found everywhere in Creation. The source of Physical Light is the Sun, or some type of device that delivers electrified "fire". Physical Light is found periodically throughout the Universe.

When Physical White Light is passed through a prism, the spectrum of rainbow colors are produced. When Etheric White Light is passed through an "Etheric Prism," the same phenomenon occurs. These colored Lights are the Rays. Even as the artist would use various colors to create a certain effect on canvas, the various Rays/Colors have specific uses and purposes. This is convenient for those of us in the Human form, dwelling on this yet Third Density Earth. If we were residing on a much higher realm of reality, then all of our environment would be "White Light." This would be appropriate, for all color is contained within the White. However, on this level of reality total White Light, physical and/or non-physical, would quickly become boring!

Fortunately, a prism of sorts was provided and our reality is indeed a universe of color. This color may be observed with the physical eyes and, with some training, may be seen with the Etheric Eye — sometimes referred to as the Third Eye. The use of etheric vision is not automatic with Third Density Human Beings, it must be developed. This can readily be accomplished as the apprentice develops and perfects his/her meditations. The Kundalini Meditation is an ideal tool to be employed for this purpose. Full instruction on the proper use of the Kundalini method of meditation may be found in Volume One of "*The Teachings for the Fourth Density Aquarian.*"

NOTES:

The Colors

The spectrum is White Light broken and segregated into seven colors. The seven colors are: Red, Orange, Yellow Green, Blue, Indigo, and Violet. Of these seven colors, three are considered to be "prime" colors, and they are: Red, Yellow, and Blue. The remaining four colors are classified as "basic colors." The vibration of the Red color is the coarsest. As one moves up the spectrum, the color's vibrations begin to refine until the apex (or Violet) is reached. The Violet is the most highly refined vibration of all colors that are indigenous to Planet Earth.

The artist would see the lower colors, Red, Orange, and Yellow, as "warm" colors. The Green, Blue, Indigo are often thought of as "cool" colors. The Violet is considered to be the "summation" of all color. Just as the accomplished artist might use a color to create a mood or convey a thought, the various individual Rays also perform this function to a high degree. Any given color is readily identifiable and is associated with specific things or purposes. Colors are like that, and the Rays are not exemptions.

It is wise to study the Rays and develop a working understanding of their function and use. The Rays are a source of energy provided by the One Infinite Creator, for your discovery and use. Each Ray performs a specific duty or duties, and when this is understood, accepted, and utilized, then the life of the seeker is truly enhanced. These seven sources of Divine Energy are available to one and all. Study, learning, and practice constitute the tuition fee for those who wish to partake of the Creator's bountiful Creation.

Reflecting Light-Relaying Love

The Rays are Light. Light is Intelligent Infinity. Light is the Second of the Four Creative Forces. The twin of Light is Love. Love is Intelligent Energy. It is the Third of the Four Creative Forces. The Rays are energy. Energy is intelligent. Intelligent Energy is Love. The Rays are: Light. The Rays are: Love. The twins Love and Light are Truth. The Rays are: Power Universal. These are available powers that are to be used by the

NOTES:

personality who skillfully taps into them. They cannot be generated. Love and Light are two of the four basic Creative Forces, and simply ARE! The personality may readily *reflect* the Light of the Creator, and *relay* the Infinite Love. As the reader begins to grasp the awesome and magnificent power that is incorporated within the Etheric Light of seven distinct colors, then the unlimited possibilities that this presents to the competent practitioner begin to unfold. As a bonafide member of Creation, these are our inherited tools!

We shall take an in-depth look at each individual Ray. Each Ray shall be defined as it relates to color, density, chakra/-body locations, and purpose. A review of Section Five, Volume One, of *The Teachings,* could be useful to the reader.

The Red Ray

Let us begin with the *Red Ray.* This is the Foundation Ray. It is the beginning or initial energy invoked by the One Infinite Creator via the Fourth Creative Force: Vibration. This Ray is the vibration of the mineral kingdom. In a physical-tangible universe, the Red Ray you have with you always. It is considered to be the First Density. The Red Ray is the Base Chakra of Second, Third, and Fourth Density Beings. It is associated with the genitals, and is the impetus of sexual energy. The Red is a prime color.

The Orange Ray

Above the Red, and somewhat refined, we find the *Orange Ray.* This Light Energy is the agent of growth and change. It is this Energy that is a prime-mover. The vibration of Orange is the specific Energy that permits Second Density, the plant and animal kingdoms, to flourish. This Energy does not permit self-awareness. Second Density Entities are not aware of themselves. They are aware of other-selves, but are not aware of self. This is the realm of the Group Soul: A school of fish is a typical example of this Group Soul activity. When a stimulus is presented to the school, all bodies respond as one, as though they had but one mind. Each fish experiences itself as a part of

NOTES:

the whole. The whole has many parts, or perhaps only a few parts. The fetus carried to term by a Third Density female is of the Orange Ray vibration. On the Human body, the chakra involved with the Orange Ray is in the area of the spleen and is located on the level of the navel. The Spleen Chakra is considered to be the power chakra of the lower body. The Orange Ray Energy stimulates growth/evolution in the Human Being.

The Yellow Ray

The next color Ray in the order of refinement is the *Yellow Ray.* The Yellow Ray is a prime color. This specific vibration is the life force that permits Third Density, the Human Being, to survive. It is this higher vibration that permits, for the first time, the awareness of self. This Yellow Chakra is located in the Human form, in the solar plexis area of the physical body. This vibration and color is the essence of the ego — the seat of emotions. Stimulated by the drive of the Red, spurred on by the need to grow from the Orange, the Yellow Ray, Third Density Human Being, conducts interaction with other selves to further promote his/her own individuality, independence, and awareness of self.

The Green Ray

The *Green Ray,* or the Emerald Green Ray, is next on our list. It is the Ray residing in the middle in our spectrum of seven Rays. The Emerald Green Ray is of Fourth Density. It is this vibration of reality where dwells MAN. MAN is the highest form of physical life in Creation. The Third Density Human Being is a sub-species of MAN. The Third Density Entity eventually becomes aware of self, and then polarizes; that is, he/she chooses one of the only two paths of evolution that permits an entrance into Fourth Density from Third Density. These paths are: (1) dedicated service to others or (2) dedicated service to self. The Density or Ray that is immediately above the current self is the "pulling" impetus that inspires the entity to evolve, to grow, to become. This Ray is most influential, as it draws upon the Human Being at this time.

NOTES:

The Emerald Green Ray's purpose is three fold. It is Love, it is Healing, it is Manifestation. This is the only Ray that is so divided. The Love/Compassion aspect embraces and personifies the Third Creative Force. Love is Intelligent Energy. The Green Ray is Love. This happy configuration permits manifestation to be achieved. The utilization of manifestation via the Green Ray functions in congruence with the Indigo Ray, which is the mentality. A thought form is visualized under the auspices of the Indigo Ray by the personality's focused thinking. This thought form is then saturated with the Green Ray of Manifestation, and using etheric materials, the thought form physically materializes. This method of producing desired items is a way of life for entities of Fourth Density and above. If a Human were to accomplish this, it would be considered a "miracle." The third and major aspect of the Green Ray is: Healing. It is our intent to devote the next section of this book to this very important subject. We shall therefore not expand on Healing at this time. The three-fold purpose of the Green Ray (Love, Healing, and Manifestation) is often associated with the three-fold flame: Love, Wisdom, and Power. This concept may then be amended to the three-fold aspect of the forthcoming New Dispensation, namely: Dignity, Integrity, and Compassion. This Green Ray, this Love, this Intelligent Energy is highly versatile!

The chakra that is identified with the Green Ray of Love is, of course, the Heart Chakra. This is the balancer, the one in the middle, number four. There are three chakras and Rays above the Heart Chakra and a like amount below. The three energies below make up the "lower body", while the three energies above the Green make up the "upper body." This balancing factor should not be understated. It is incredibly important in the stabilizing of the personality.

The Blue Ray

As we now rise to the realm of the upper body, we find the next color of the spectrum to be the *Blue Ray*. The Blue Ray is a prime color. This color is sometimes observed as sky blue,

NOTES:

while others are more comfortable seeing this Ray as royal blue. The Blue Ray is the color vibration associated with Fifth Density. It is within this Density that MAN evolves from physical to non-physical. Those entities inhabiting low Fifth Density do indeed wear physical bodies. Those entities in high Fifth Density almost always wear a body of "Light." Those ones in mid-Fifth Density vacillate from one to the other. This is often referred to as the Quasi Status. Like Fourth Density, these ones are highly mobile and are *very* active in their roles as Co-Creators.

The Blue Ray is associated with the Throat Chakra. This is the power chakra for the upper body even as the Orange Chakra is the Power Chakra for the lower body. The Blue Ray is the Ray of communication. This is the seat of the learning and teaching of spirituality. The Blue is often used to aid in the balancing of the Green Ray of Love with the Indigo Ray of Wisdom. All chakras are receivers of their respective Rays. Only the top three Rays are also transmitters. The Blue Ray is the first to fall into this category.

The Indigo Ray

The next Ray in refinement is that color known as *Indigo.* This is the vibration of color associated with Sixth Density. This Density consists entirely of Light . . . White Light. Within this White Light are *all* colors. The vibration of Indigo is the life force that unites those ones who reside in this exalted reality. This vibration is the home of the Social Memory Complex. Please refer to Section Three, Volume One of *The Teachings,* for more complete information.

The Indigo Ray is the energy that permits the Third Eye to function. This is the energy of the personality's mentality, the intellect. The Indigo Ray, via the Third Eye, is the gateway to Intelligent Infinity. This is the tool of the Adept, the Master. It is the thought that inspires the apprentice to become. The Indigo Ray is the builder of form . . . the thought form. All things first begin with a thought. It is the thought that is eternal. The Indigo

NOTES:

creates the thought — the Green creates the tangibility via Manifestation.

The penetration of Intelligent Infinity is the goal of the budding Adept, the Master. To attain conscious contact and access to all knowledge, information, and experience contained in the Universe is indeed an awesome goal. This is achieved via the Indigo Ray, as it is invoked with the Kundalini Meditation. Unlimited possibilities exist as one begins to use this most magnificent Ray. The Indigo Chakra is also a transmitter of energy.

The Violet Ray

The *Violet Ray* is the last color in our spectrum of White Light, as observed and understood on our Third Density illusion of reality. This vibration of color is of Seventh Density, and is considered to be the realm of our Radiant One, The One Infinite Creator. There is no information available in this Universe, or any Serial Universe, that affords an understanding of the activities that transpire on Seventh Density. All things begin and end in mystery. All things begin and end in the Creator!

The Violet Chakra is located in the crown of the head. It is considered to be the essence of the Creator. This Ray cannot be manipulated as the six Rays below it *can* be manipulated via their respective chakras. The energy of the Violet is the summation of the combined six energies below it. The Violet or Crown Chakra is also a transmitter. The personality may invoke the Violet Ray and respectfully use it. It is used mostly for protection.

This concludes the list and definitions of the seven Rays that are indigenous to Planet Earth. There are more than seven Rays in the Universe. Two more Rays of Light that may be called into the Earth Plane are the *Silver Ray* and the *Golden Ray*. The Silver Ray Energy is the essence that allows for the functioning of one's Prime Spirit Guide and the Sub-Guides. These ones dwell in this color and, through intuition, communicate with their charges. The Golden Ray is the energy that activates the Higher Self. This Ray is often referred to as the

NOTES:

Buddhic Ray. It is of an extremely high vibration. The higher Densities have a solid working relationship with these two Rays. Earthlings rarely tap into them and when they do, the result is minimal though experienced as fantastic.

Chapter 2

Energy Transfers

The energy of the Rays may be transferred or it may be projected. Via the lower four chakras, the Red, Orange, Yellow or Green energy may be transferred from one Human to another. These four chakras are incoming from one Human to another. These four chakras are incoming only and are not transmitters as are the top three, the Blue, Indigo, and Violet Rays. The Yellow is the most effective energy to transfer between Human Beings; the reason being that the Third Density Human operates in this particular vibration of energy. Fourth Density Entities would naturally be more compatible with the Green Ray energy exchange. It is possible for the Human to accomplish this transfer now; however, it is not so practical. The exception would be when those participating in the exchange are Wanderers or higher.

For sexual purposes, the Red Ray Energy may be transferred/exchanged by simply connecting the Base Chakras. This connecting is accomplished by both participants visualizing the chosen chakras gently touching each other. This is further simplified if the participants are seated, facing each other, knee to knee. Other positions/postures are also useful as long as the participants continue to face each other.

The Orange Ray energy exchange is useful in promoting the general health or well-being of another. The exchange of energy is a beautiful way of sharing self with another self. This is a Love Exchange regardless of which Ray is chosen.

For all intents and purposes, the connecting of the Blue, Indigo, and Violet Rays between Third Density entities will not result in any noticeable transfer, though it would not likely result in any harm. The three highest Rays deal with Fifth, Sixth, and Seventh Density entities and are non-physical. The Third Density entity utilizes these high realms as sources of information, knowledge, and guidance. The four lower Rays are all incorporated within physicalness and are utilized as such. The upper

NOTES:

three Rays deal strictly in the etheric, though all seven Rays are Etheric Light in their nature.

Man

Fourth Density MAN is physical, just as Third Density Human Beings are physical. If MAN were to offer an energy exchange with a Human, he would initiate the contact via the Yellow Ray. If the Human were to attempt an exchange of energy with MAN, he would have to do so via the Green Ray. This would be most difficult for the Third Density Human to achieve, though not impossible. MAN is Love. Compassion, which is a form of Love, is that energy which MAN bestows on men. Love has many forms and faces. Though MAN understands many aspects of Love, he certainly does not grasp them all. The Human's concept of the scope of Love is barely discernible. Precious few aspects of Love are perceived and practiced by men.

Balance

To be usable in a practical way, Love must be balanced with Wisdom. Third Density Entities would need to be highly enlightened in order to grasp this working. The higher divisions of Fourth Density begin to balance Love and Wisdom in respectable harmony. Love is Green Ray. Wisdom is Indigo Ray. Fifth Density Quasi MAN endeavors to balance Love and Light. Light is the totality of Wisdom. The Rays are the same. For as long as eternity lasts, entities shall find themselves attempting, ever struggling to balance something with something else. The Creator created Creation like that! The Orange Ray of change and growth provides the necessary impetus and motion that always stimulates this activity. True growth cannot be achieved without balance. Sixth Density is the collection and refinement of all that has preceded.

The Heart Chakra may be observed as having three parts. These parts are seen as three green balls in a horizontal line across the chest. Love/Compassion would be the center ball. Wisdom and Power would be the two outside balls. These may be substituted with Dignity and Integrity. In whatever form the

NOTES:

three-fold flame is divided, the parts in a Universal sense are: Love, Healing, and Manifestation. This is the Green Ray.

For those of you who choose to heal, be advised, this is your source of power. The effectiveness of the healing is directly proportionate to the balance and the will of the healer. As the healer establishes and maintains his energy centers as being aligned, balanced and crystal clear, then the desired results shall be forthcoming. The working Love energy is the color Green. It is in the center of the spectrum. The three colors above and the three colors below balance themselves on the three fold purpose of the magnificent Emerald Green Ray. Again we remind you that the Green Ray is Love; Love is Intelligent Energy!

The Four Basic Bodies

In esoteric teachings we find the Human body divided into basic categories, and they are: the Physical Body, the Emotional Body, the Mental Body, and the Spiritual Body. The latter is sometimes identified as the Etheric or the Astral Body. These four bodies constitute the totality of the Third Density Human Being. This totality is often referred to as the Mind/Body/Spirit Complex.

It is the interrelationships between these various bodies that permits the experience of any given catalyst to be utilized at a near maximum capacity. In order to grasp a better understanding of the workings of these bodies, it is again necessary to examine the spectrum of the seven colors, the prismatic result of White Light, physical or etheric. The true colors or the seven pure colors, are the color vibration being used. Blends, mixtures, or shades are not appropriate to be considered at this time, as they would contribute to confusion.

The Seven Bodies Of The Aura

From the macrocosm to the microcosm the number seven appears throughout. There are seven Rays, the correlated seven chakras; thusly the seven bodies of man would also result in these true colors as we reach down toward the microcosm. Each one of these seven Rays, via the seven chakras, produces a

NOTES:

"body" around the Human Being. The totality of these color bodies is commonly known as the Human Aura.

(Notice to the reader: over the centuries,various teachers of metaphysics or the occult have attempted to share this valuable understanding. Some were able to present it much more clearly than were others. It is our desire to clarify and simplify ancient wisdoms using modern language.)

Let us begin our study of the aura by examining the *Red Ray Body*. This is the elemental body, and is without form. It is not constructed. It is also your chemical body. This basic body may be observed as a red fog of atoms surrounding the true physical body, for this Red Body is not the body that you view in your mirror. Observing and understanding the pattern of this chemical body could be very useful in healing practices. The chemical elements form patterns that are "normal" or "standard." If there are discrepancies in any of these many patterns, there is the area where investigation must begin before a diagnosis can be made. The Red Ray Body is the foundation of the complex and is the microcosm of the mineral kingdom (chemical); i.e., the Earth Mother herself.

The Orange Ray Body is a physical body with form but this still is not the body you see in your mirror. This Orange Ray Body is indeed a formed construct, but is without self-awareness. It is this body, this Orange Color Vibration that is donned by the Second Density plant and animal kingdoms. It is the Orange Ray Body, with no self-awareness, that is the vehicle of the fetus, the embryo, as it grows in the womb of the Third Density female. The Mind/Spirit Complex does NOT enter this body until the time of birth, and sometimes long after the event of the birth. An understanding of this phenomenon could go a long way in clarifying the abortion issue. If the Mind/Spirit Complex should refuse to enter the body, then that physical body would respond as though it were a vegetable. It could actually "live" but seldom ever does. The Orange Ray Body in the Third Density Human Being stimulates change, growth; it is the agent of motion. If the Orange is deficient in any area of a growing child, then that personality may not be developing in a balanced

NOTES:

way. The directed Orange Ray Vibration offers the proper energy to cause a healthy person to become ill, or to permit an ill person to get well. Growth and changes are constant with Third Density Entities throughout the entirety of the incarnation. Orange is the power that motivates evolution.

The Yellow Ray Body is indeed the physical body that you see in the mirror. It is this Yellow Ray Vibration that constitutes your Emotional Body. The combination of the Red, Orange, and Yellow Bodies constitutes the total physical body. The Yellow Ray Body is aware of itself as it experiences the catalysts that are indigenous to Third Density. The Yellow Ray is a prime color and this vibration is considered to be a major milestone on the path of evolution. This Ray introduces the awareness of self for the first time. The individuality is brought forth as independence is secured. The social self is developed via this Ray. The governing of self and other selves is attempted. The laws of nature that govern Orange Ray Second Density are challenged and are sometimes thwarted. Responsibility now becomes a difficult but desirable asset to the developing character of the budding personality. Emotional Love is a profound mystery to those native of Yellow Ray. The species indigenous to this Ray are the only forms of life, physical and etheric, who are born without a memory. There is a "new awakening," a "new beginning" that is experienced with each and every incarnation. The Physical Universe is experienced through the Yellow Ray Body. It is difficult for an Orange Ray Entity to transmute into this prime color. It takes countless incarnations for the Third Density Entity to become sufficiently aware of self in order to polarize and accept the Green Ray Vibration of Love.

The Green Ray Body is the body associated with Fourth Density and is the vehicle of the species known as MAN. (Human Beings are a sub-species of MAN.) The Green is the Love vibration and is constituted of Love, Healing, and Manifestation. The healer will summon and use this aspect of himself when offering his service to another. You would not normally see your Green Ray Body in the mirror. However, it is this body that one sees at a seance, for it is this vibration that produces the

NOTES:

ectoplasm that makes materialization possible at such events. The Green Ray Body is indigenous to the astral or high plane. Entities who people this plane between incarnations are highly evolved Human Beings. This body is denser in substance, but lighter in weight than is the current physical Yellow Ray Body. The Green has the capacity to incorporate much more "life" into itself than does the Yellow. The Green beckons and pulls at the Yellow to evolve and advance. Eventually the Yellow heeds and responds. As this transition unfolds, a Yellow/Green hue is formed. This is our Earth Mother's current condition. Approximately 10% of Third Density Humans are also able to respond as they too, enter into various stages of transition. The remaining 90% of the people are unable to cope with this change, and this is the cause for the increasing insanity amongst Humans. The Adept who is able to tap into his Green Ray Body, stands at the gateway to Intelligent Energy-Love. This permits unlimited uses of the Love Energy for the purposes of Healing and Manifestation. This body sees the end of experiences that are considered to be physical. This vibration concludes the highest form of physical life known to Creation. There are many forms of life that have evolved to a much higher status, but they are all non-physical. To achieve the use of the Green Ray Body is the goal of the Third Density Human Being.

The Blue Ray Body is essentially a "Light" body, that is to say, it is non-physical. This vibration is associated with Fifth Density or the Atmic Plane. The Blue Ray is the "beginning" of the upper body of the personality, and is the first color capable of transmitting as well as receiving. This body utilizes communication as its contribution to the personality. Much has been discovered and written about the various Blue Ray Bodies of Fifth Density in Eastern Indian texts. Adepts and budding Adepts find this vibration a lucrative hunting ground for excitement, adventure, and mystery. For almost all Third Density Human Beings, the Blue Ray Body lies in potential. For some 90% of Humanity, only the Yellow Ray Body is active. Red and Orange Ray Bodies may be tapped into. The Green Ray Body becomes activated via evolution. Some 10% of Third Density Humans

NOTES:

have activated or partially activated their Green Ray Body. The Blue, Indigo, and Violet Ray Bodies lie in potential for the native Earthling.

The Indigo Body is the form maker. It is the vibration of the mentality, the intellect of the personality. It is this body that is responsible for thought. This Indigo Ray has the necessary characteristics to permit thought to have form, thus the "thought form." The Indigo Body is the gateway to Intelligent Infinity, or Cosmic Consciousness or the Universal Mind — all meaning the same thing. This body energizes the 20% of the physical organ, known as the brain, that Humans are privileged to use. This portion of the brain is called the Cortical or Thinking Portion of that organ. This is often categorized as the conscious, subconscious, and the unconscious aspects of the Cortical Centers. The Indigo Body also energizes the remaining 80% of the physical brain. This vast portion of that amazing organ is called the Tensor Portion. As the personality taps into this great resource, ESP abilities may then be developed. The Indigo Body waits in potential for the personality who is devoid of ego and is perserverant in his strength of will to develop a disciplined penetration of Intelligent Infinity. Those ones who have tapped into the energies of their Blue and Indigo Bodies are truly Co-Creators.

The Violet Ray Body is the summation of all the other six bodies. It is often referred to as the Buddhic Body. The Violet Ray is associated with the vibration of Seventh Density, which is The One Infinite Creator. This body is connected to the personality via the Crown Chakra. There is no manipulation of this body by the individual. It is total. It is complete. It is.

The understanding of the Indigo and Violet Ray Bodies is extremely useful to the healer, as the healer learns to attune his/her consciousness to these etheric bodies of the one to be healed. This understanding is difficult for the native Third Density Entity to grasp; however, it is most useful to the Adept. The Mind/Body/Spirit Complex is affected, often greatly, by each of these seven bodies individually and is dramatically affected by the interrelationship between these various bodies. All bodies are in potential, only the Yellow Ray Body is in

NOTES:

activation, and is manifested in the Third Density Entity. All personalities have the innate ability to tap into, to observe, to manipulate these bodies on self, and with permission, on other selves, as in the case of the healer.

At the transition known as death the Kundalini rises, perhaps for the first and only time, to the crown of the head where it grasps the consciousness of the personality. The Kundalini-consciousness combination now enters *into* the Silver Cord, as this cord detaches itself from both hemispheres of the brain and floats free as the Golden Sphere, the Higher Self, rises. The Indigo Ray Body, the "form maker," is the first body to be activated. This body is used as the vehicle to penetrate the Etheric or Astral Plane, whichever is appropriate to coincide with the spiritual evolutionary status of the entity. As understanding is achieved, and acceptance of the new environment is reached, then the appropriate body is activated. This could be Yellow, Green, Blue, or even the already in use Indigo Body, depending upon the Density that the entity is native to. This body, probably Yellow or Green, will be worn until such time of the next incarnation. Those entities of Third Density and higher will never activate their Orange or Red Ray Bodies since both of these bodies are without will. The transition called death is nothing more than a simple "change of state." It is as traumatic as standing up, removing one's coat, dropping it on the floor, and walking in the next room. It is about as exciting as watching ice melt into water. "Death" is simply a change of state. The Indigo Body, the form maker, makes this transition possible.

Each of these seven bodies hum to the vibration of that given Ray which they represent. These seven bodies of seven different colors are found around the physical body in some type of shape or configuration. This phenomenon is commonly called: The Aura.

Chapter 3

The Aura

Let us begin by stating that everything has an Aura. All inanimate objects, matter in any form, as well as all animated bodies are incorporated *within* an Aura of some kind. We shall deal primarily with the Human Aura, for that is where the basic interest lies.

The body is the product of the Aura. The body did not create its Aura; the Aura created the physical body. The body's current condition is reflected in the Aura. The body is changed/healed as the Aura reflects back its perfected forms. Though certainly not impossible, it is nevertheless difficult for the Third Density Human to view an Aura. Those ones who are developing Etheric Vision would be able to see the Aura *around* a First, Second, Third, or Fourth Density Entity. On a Fifth Density Entity the Aura would be quite pronounced — the body may or may not be discerned. On a Sixth Density Entity only the Aura would be observed, for these ones are true Light Beings. The environment of the Sixth Density Entity is Light. In its pure form it is White Light, the Light of the Creator. However, Sixth Density is not a complete "white out." White Light is the source of all colored Light, and the Sixth Density Entity has "prism vision," and can produce all hues and shades at will. This Density is actually a magnificent array of color!

But let us return to the Third Density Human Being, the realm where we all currently find ourselves. When you view an object or another self you automatically assume that this physical assemblage of atoms emits an energy of some kind, and therefore has an Aura. And your assumption is correct.

As energy is emitted from any object, colors of some hue or hues are also formed. These colors designate the physical makeup of that object or person. Those who have not as yet developed their Etheric Vision may be obliged to "believe" that energy and colors do indeed exist. Many Third Density Entities will not be able to develop their Etheric Vision to the status where they can "see" an Aura. However, these ones may readily

NOTES:

develop their ability to "feel" an Aura. This sense of feeling can actually become more developed and accurate than the ability to see. Every plant, every animal, every rock has an Aura, and they are quite different. The Human Aura, though highly individualistic, is basically constructed the same in all personalities.

The Energy Field

Now, let us have a look at the typical Human Aura. There is an Energy Field that radiates outward from the entirety of the Human body. This energy is much more easily seen around the head and shoulders than the rest of the body. This energy field is the vital energy, the life force, sometimes called the Prana, that indicates the personality is "alive." This vital energy is not to be confused with physical energy, which has its "ups and downs," as the body responds to the catalysts that a given lifestyle affords. The vital energy moves outward from the head in a pulsating or heartbeat fashion. As it does so, it activates the colors of the Aura. The Prana has a clarity next to the head in almost all cases. As it rythmically radiates outward, it has the appearance of "heat waves" as seen on a road in the summertime. This is the first thing the apprentice will see and sometimes it is the only thing he will see for quite some time!

Colors

The colors that are found in the Aura are the same colors that are found in the chakras. The respective chakra, sponsors its corresponding hue in the overall Aura. Only a few people are able to see the chakras. Many can learn to see Auras. The reading of given Auric color can offer an indication of the condition of that chakra; i.e., blocked, unblocked, overactive, sluggish, crystal clear, and clean; or perhaps dirty or dingy, or even streaked with other colors. The attitude of any given color could be multidimensional given the unlimited opportunities of emotion via the catalysts confronting the personality, even on an hourly basis.

True color is of course the ultimate goal. Various shades of true color are most likely. The observer may not be sufficient-

NOTES:

ly skilled to actually recognize true color, even if it were presented. Practice is the ally here. The distortion that accompanies Third Density frequency of vibration is adequate to successfully camouflage true color. It is not all that important anyway, it is simply good to know that it exists and to anticipate it.

Observing The Aura

To observe an Aura it is best to hold a steady gaze, locked unto the other person's eyes, or to their Third Eye in the center of the forehead, or perhaps to their Throat Chakra at the Adam's apple or the hollow of the throat. Immobility is a must for all concerned. The background should be a plain pastel color, preferably an off-white color; it should be motionless to avoid distraction.

The lighting should be normal. After dark, normal room lighting is best. Intense or spot lighting will blot out the colors. Fluorescent lighting should be avoided. Bright sunlight will usually override the colors as well. Shade or indoor natural light is best. If the working area is too dark, the colors will not be forthcoming. Some are able to see Auras on a dark night, but this is very rare. Any degree of brilliance you are most comfortable with is usually just right.

Hold a steady gaze. Do not blink any more than absolutely necessary. Practice this. The Aura is seen with the peripheral vision. The peripheral vision is in cooperation with the Third Eye, permitting the seeing of an Aura. The Third Eye may not be functioning all that well at first, and all the apprentice will see is the energy field being emitted from around the head. This is the normal way one begins. With practice, and in due time, the Third Eye does begin to open, and colors become apparent.

Attuning Self To Other Self

The "reading" of another's Aura requires more than just seeing that Aura. To achieve an in-depth study of that person via the Aura, it is necessary for you to attune yourself to that other self. This is achieved through the use of the chakras. You may

NOTES:

also use your Kundalini (see Volume One, Section II). This is useful, but not mandatory.

The first step is to align and balance your chakras. This is the same procedure that you use in preparation to the raising of your Kundalini. Assuming the person you are reading is *not* familiar with this procedure, you align and balance *their* chakras. This action is a form of offering Love and does not infringe upon their Free Will.

The other self must have sufficient understanding of what is transpiring in order to successfully cooperate. He/she must be seated across from you and remain motionless. Consent and cooperation is vital if success is to be achieved.

Your chakras and the chakras of the other self have now been aligned and balanced. Solicit the aid of their Prime Spirit Guide and, of course, your own Guide as the Guides extend the chakras forward, all seven on each person. The face of each chakra is caused to gently touch, beginning with the Violet and working down. When all seven contacts have been made the energy exchange is directed to flow from that person to yourself. This activity permits you to *attune* yourself to the other self. Your vibrations are adjusted to their vibrations. You stand in their moccasins for a while. The gentle connecting of the chakras does not permit you to *see* the Aura any better. It does permit you to *read* the Aura better, so that you might understand the complexity of the other self; the purpose being the revealing of certain information that might permit the other self to know self better and thus improve the overall character status in a Positive direction of inspired evolution. This is to be construed as a Positive offering of service to another and *not* a method of gleaning information for self.

The gentle chakra connections have now been made; you may or may not be able to actually see this happening, but you should be able to *feel* it. Establish the eye connection. Relax your facial and eye muscles as you maintain your gaze. With practice, the apprentice may develop the ability to look deep, very deep, into and through the eyes and actually see or "sense" the other self's Higher Self. This results in a telepathic commu-

NOTES:

nication between the Higher Selves of both. This information can be forwarded down to your own consciousness, undistorted.

You now have connected your spiritual bodies along with its mental, emotional, and physical bodies via the chakras. As you gaze into the eyes of the other self, facial changes may also be observed, indicating Past Lives their Higher Self is offering for observation. However, this phenomenon has little to do with the colors of the Aura. If further understanding of Past Lives is deemed important to the reader, then we respectfully suggest the reading of our book "*The Monitor*" by Chief Little Summer and Warm Night Rain.

Observing The Energy Field

With the gaze firmly established, the peripheral vision will reveal a clear energy held next to the head. This clear portion could be 1/4-inch to 3/4-inches in width. If the other self is female with curly hair, then this portion of the Aura will be hidden in the hair. This energy field radiates outward for several inches, sometimes for many feet. There are many patterns that this energy may employ. Sometimes it moves outward with a great deal of nervous gusto. Sometimes the pattern is slow, determined, methodical, even lazy. If there appears a great field of energy that simply lies there, offering little activity, then perhaps you are viewing a sleeping giant. If the energy comes forth in great jerks, then you have a very energetic person, really a "go getter." If the energy flow is strong and obviously rythmic, then this would indicate the pattern of a peaceful person with a relaxed strength. Practice and experience permits the apprentice to evaluate the patterns being shown.

This vital energy or Prana, activates the colors of the Aura. Remember that the colors of the Aura correspond with the colors of the seven chakras. If one were to find an abnormality within a certain color in the Aura, then it would be rewarding to examine the related chakra for blockages or malfunctions. You can readily learn to see Auras. You may never learn to see a chakra. Since the Aura reflects the condition of the chakra, this is not much of a handicap. The vibration of the Aura is much

NOTES:

coarser than the refined vibration of the chakras; thus, it is much easier for the Third Density Human Being to see auras. The sensitive personality could "feel" the chakra much easier than he/she could "see" it. The apprentice learns to seek out any *difference* in feeling as the hand is slowly passed over the line of energy centers.

The Aura is generated by its source, the chakras. These colors are activated by the vital energy or life force of the personality. From Third Density perspective, this is the function of an Aura.

The Aura is a series of seven colors that are normally found in the configuration of a band or bow. These bands may be seen as curving over the head from ear to ear. Sometimes they are seen curving from shoulder to shoulder. Actually, the colored bands encompass the entire body, all the way down to the feet. This is often very difficult to see and the rainbow Aura is seldom observed below the shoulder level. If you are able to see the Green below the shoulder level, this indicates an entity heavily endowed in the Love Vibration, and very well could be a Wanderer. (see Volume One.)

The band should be complete. It may not be. The Green could be on one side and not the other. If the Green is missing on the personality's right side, this would indicate a service to self attitude is being employed. If the Green is in pieces, this would indicate several broken relationships, a lack of continuity. If these pieces are a dark Green, then the personality utilizes sex as the vehicle of expressing Love. This is usually lust. There is always Green in some form or another. One learns to "read" these colors and their configurations through experience. Since each personality is absolutely unique, there are no set standards or rules to learn or follow. This ability to "read" an Aura may be inherited or developed. The latter is usually the case.

The one color that might be missing from the Aura is the Red. All of the other colors would be in existence whether you perceived them or not. One or two colors would probably be predominate. These dominate colors might indicate the current mood of the personality, or perhaps the general way of life.

NOTES:

The Green

The first color to be sought out is the Green. This is the Love Vibration. It is also the middle color. There are three more colors outside of the Green, and three more inside of it. The Green should be Emerald in hue, and if it sparkles, this would be an indicator that Love is a vital part or the nucleus of that person's life. If the Green vibrates or dances it could indicate that the personality is "in Love." If the Green is clouded or hazy, this could indicate that the personality is an Infant or Baby Soul, and the Love Vibration is basically undeveloped. This one could be confusing emotions with Love (Love vs. lust), and lacking experience, would not know the difference. A reasonably well balanced Aura would have a sparkling Love Vibration of Green. It would be glowing, possibly quite brilliantly. Within this Green there would be little white threads that would form a network in some type of a pattern. These are scars or "scar tissue" that testify to the proposition that the personality has not always been completely successful in the affairs of the heart. There has been a disappointment or two! This is quite normal. All Auras would offer some indication of these white threads. These threads could indicate that the past event had been healed or perhaps is in the process of being healed. One might notice the rawness of the open wound if the heart-breaking event was quite recent. These threads form patterns. One can learn to recognize these patterns. History often repeats itself and these patterns will indicate as much. The Soul Level of the personality is an important factor in determining whether history continually repeats itself, or whether the personality is willing and able to learn and grow through experience. Sometimes one learns the lessons the "hard way." Whatever the method, it is essential that one learn and therefore grow. No matter how slow, evolution shall not be denied.

The entity who is polarized towards service to self will also have Green in the Aura. The Green Ray is of three- fold purpose: Love, Healing, and Manifestation. The latter two properties of Green would readily be employed by the Negative Entity. The Green would take on a different configuration and

NOTES:

the clarity of the color would be absent. This lack of clarity could be found in a Positive Polarized Entity, or even a non-polarized entity. However, the Negative Entity would have dark Green streaks running through the Green as it appears to be clouded or foggy with indefinable lines. The Negative Entity may be clever in camouflaging his personality, but would be unable to disguise his Aura. By their Light you shall know them.

The band of Green could be in any configuration. Think of this Green as being mobile and therefore capable of forming patterns, shapes, or designs. Though usually stable, these patterns are subject to change via the catalyst of any given moment. Since all personalities are unique, there can only be general descriptions of these patterns. It would be useful for the apprentice to practice on the same individual over a period of several weeks. The various moods could then be related to the changed appearance of the Aura, and duly noted. This is a good practice. Patterns are never the same, yet there is a great deal of similarity within individuals. Practice and experience are always the best teachers. The Aura is constantly in motion. This motion may be slow and quiet, or it may be, at times, quite violent. The dance of the Aura reflects the constant, subtle changes within the personality which it surrounds.

If there are holes or perhaps dark spots within the Green, then that personality has suffered a catastrophe, or certainly traumatic experiences in the Love Vibration in the past or perhaps currently. This is quite severe and goes beyond the white threads previously mentioned. This condition is difficult to repair. Therapy often is useful, but seldom completely successful. Survivors of the holocaust would be likely candidates for this experience.

Any given color in the Aura in pieces or sections indicates fragmentation and an obvious lack of continuity. Two or three segments would not be considered serious; a dozen pieces would! This unfortunate entity would be much too scattered in that particular Ray/Energy to be functionable. The Green is of course, the chakra/color in the middle. It is the balancer. The reading of an Aura begins here. Once the reader

NOTES:

has a working understanding of the personality's Love Vibration, then one continues by reading up to the Blue.

The Blue

The Blue color in the Aura corresponds with the Throat Chakra, and is the color of communication. This Blue color should be clear and clean in its appearance. If the personality is experiencing difficulty in speech in any way, or is unable to read or to write satisfactorily in a culturally acceptable way, then the Blue would appear cloudy. If the conditions were sufficiently severe, there could be dark streaks or spots within the Blue. This condition would be unlikely, unless the entity was handicapped with a birth defect or had experienced an injury or severe illness.

For those who would sing, yet cannot; for those who would speak, yet cannot; for those who would write, yet cannot; these ones are experiencing a blockage in the Throat Chakra. This blockage could be psychological and therefore temporary; it could be physical and therefore permanent. The Higher Self could impose a partial blockage upon its personality, its charge to prohibit a specific type of performance. This could be for Karmic Lessons contracted in some distant lifetime. The personality would not be able to consciously grasp the full meaning or significance of this, and probably would assess it as an unjustified punishment. On the other hand, the personality itself could deliberately inflict the blockage to excuse self from participating in certain undesired activities. The power of fear is the agent to achieve this result. Counseling is useful in this case. Whatever the reasons, lessons are being learned/taught via experience, as the Soul prospers.

If the Blue is seen as being clear and gently quiet, then harmony prevails and no blockages are hindering the flow of the Blue Ray. If the Blue is seen as being cloudy and active, rolling into itself, then a healing is being attempted and instruction to the personality would be useful.

In the Aura, the Blue should not be separated from the Green. The two colors are attached/integrated as if they were sewn together with needle and thread. This blending permits the

NOTES:

personality to speak (communicate) words filled with Love. Sometimes the Blue and Green are not evenly bonded. Sometimes the attachment occurs only in spots, as though it was spot welded together, rather than as an even bead. In the arena of personal relationships, this spotty connection will cause erratic communications with a loved one or spouse. When the timing is right and it falls upon one of the spot welds, the communication is magnificent; then, in a few hours or days, the time moves to the black area between the ties. These times result in little or no communication at all. Then suddenly, perhaps for no special reason, the communication is great once again. This situation can become very frustrating. If both partners are so endowed, the union probably shall not last; it's too unstable, too frustrating, and even too violent to endure. If any one partner is so afflicted then he/she is considered to be "moody" or "temperamental." There is one definite advantage however, it does in fact relieve the *boredom!*

This spot attachment is a pattern subconsciously constructed by the personality itself. Without instruction, the consciousness probably would not have recognized this basic character of itself. The personality is made up of many, many, patterns. This spot attachment is but one of the many. Through the strength of Will the personality may modify or exchange any pattern within itself. The first step is to be aware of the nomenclature of the pattern itself; sometimes a calender is useful for this. Using the Blue/Green spotty integration as the example during the time of good communication, mentally extend these times for as long as possible. Then when it falls (and it will fall; it always does), mentally and willfully shorten the "bad times" to the best of the personality's determined ability. The first good/bad cycle shall produce only minor change. Perserverance is the watchword. The second cycle will show much improvement; the third shall prove to be even better. Again, the calender could be useful to aid in noting progress. A character change is now in the making. Though slow and sometimes tedious, any personality has the means within him/her to alter self into any image so desired. In the example offered, it must be noted that

NOTES:

the personality must have the cooperation of the spouse/partner in order to enjoy any progressive success.

Though quite rare, sometimes the Blue and Green are completely separated. Both colors may be in excellent condition, yet totally unable to communicate Love. The only known method of overcoming this disastrous condition, is for the entity to consciously endeavor to align and balance all the chakras, and to maintain this feat continuously until crystallization has taken place. This could take several weeks of diligent effort but the results are well worth it.

The Indigo

Above the Blue band in the Aura, we find the Indigo. This color represents the mentality or intellect of the personality. Unlike the shape of the other six colors of the Aura, the Indigo is not in a band or bow formed around the head and body. The Indigo has a geometric form or shape. The average Human Being would have his Indigo in the form of a flat disk, a pancake, if you will. This disk is perhaps five-six inches in diameter and is about 1/4-inch thick. This is average. If the entity chooses to become more mentally active and elects to think for himself/herself once in a while, then the flat disk will grow in thickness to perhaps 1-1/2 to 2 inches. This usually occurs via schooling and study.

Then, if the entity is truly a thinker, he/she will utilize the knowledge and information thus gleaned. This action results in a bubble forming over the top, flat side of the thick disk. We now perceive a small dome on a disk base. If the thinking process/activity continues, then this dome grows higher . . . and higher. An elongated dome, in the shape of a hay stack, has now been created. This is the mark of an entity who is thriving in mental activity. As the mentality, the thinking, continues to grow, the process begins to open up portions of the brain that have never been used before.

This portion of the brain now being tapped into is called the Tensor Portion of that magnificent organ. The Tensor Centers constitute some 80% of the brain. The remaining 20%

NOTES:

of the brain is the Cortical or thinking portion which includes the conscious, the subconscious, and the unconscious. At the time of birth, a very heavy Veil is dropped on the Third Density Entity. This is the Veil of forgetting. Normally, this Veil is never penetrated during the incarnation. Due to the entity's determined will to reach upward and because the Earth Mother's vibrations are currently rising, as this Third Density Cycle closes certain personalities are capable of penetrating that Veil, at least occasionally, and tapping onto the Tensor Centers.

This permits the personality to extract from the Tensor Centers knowledge, information, and experiences from the Monad about Past Lives. This material is transferred through the Veil into the Cortical Centers and utilized. Only a few people are capable of achieving this at this time.

NOTE: A later section of this book is devoted to the preliminary understanding of the Tensor Concepts.

Now, the observer may note that this elongated dome may on brief occasion change into an elongated pyramid or perhaps a cone. The common characteristic is both are pointed at the apex. When this phenomenon occurs, the Third Eye opens, or partially opens. ESP activity is being initiated. Clairvoyance to some degree is happening. Clairaudience, especially telepathy, is perhaps being experienced. Other forms of ESP such as levitation, teleportation, manifestation, etc., are reserved for a later time when the personality is more familiar and adaptable to "psychic phenomenon."

The pyramidal or conical shape will hold only for a few seconds or for a few minutes at most in the early beginnings. This random opening of the Third Eye is totally under the control of the Higher Self. The personality cannot summon this activity in the beginning stages. If the Third Eye were to suddenly open up permanently, the personality would find himself/herself living in two worlds, physical and etheric, simultaneously; insanity would surely be the immediate result. Only Fourth Density MAN can skillfully handle this duality. However, Fourth Density MAN is what we are rapidly evolving into. The future looks promising!

NOTES:

Around the base of this dome which is actually the original thick disk, you may observe little threads hanging down. This will give the appearance of a fringe usually one to two inches in length. These threads are like antennae that permit the personality to reach out into Intelligent Infinity/Cosmic Consciousness/The Universal Mind (all saying much the same thing). This provides the means to tap onto "abstract" thought, creative thought, philosophical thought, and the One Original Thought; thoughts that have no practical value whatsoever. These thoughts may be entertaining and can actually be very useful if they are brought into the disk or dome where practicality may be integrated into them. This is how practical, creative ideas are manifested. Abstract thought and daydreaming could be construed to be much the same thing. Fantasy is a high form of daydreaming, and usually defies the insertion of order and practicality, as it would be used on this Third Density Level of Reality.

The original thought comes from without the brain, not from within. The antennae pick up on the "thoughts of the Universes," that are of a vibrational level frequency indigenous to Third Density, or whatever vibration you consider to be your true "home." As you observe those threads you may note that some are active (moving) and are indeed being used; some are waiting in potential; some probably will never be used. If there is a dome over a thick disk, several of these threads will have been activated. If the Indigo is yet a thin disk, like a pancake, the threads will be motionless and dormant. The active thinker will have some of the threads all pointing in some direction as focus is being achieved. Sometimes they appear to dance, as the excitement of discovery is imminent. The Old Soul in particular will use these threads for artistic creative purposes, as well as contributing to an in-depth understanding of philosophy.

The Wanderer and the polarized Third Density Entity will almost always display the thick, disk-based dome, and the pyramid or cone. Evolution is being directed as the pointed apexes would indicate. The geometric form that the Indigo takes could be any common form or distortions of forms. Among

NOTES:

others, the circle or sphere is often found in the Aura. This would indicate expansive mental growth, but would lack in focus or direction. This is usually the product of the Young Soul and perhaps the low Mature Soul. There is much growth, much experience, but polarization has not yet taken place. Also, another common geometric form is the square or cube. This personality is highly opinionated and biased toward social, political, or religious beliefs. This could be a Baby Soul or low-to-mid Young Soul. These ones are solid in their stand and are often the pillars of the community. They are highly dependable and reliable and are strictly followers, demanding to be led. These ones do not achieve much growth, but the cube is highly useful in establishing the individual identity as he identifies himself with the group or organization. This one needs to "belong to." Cubes make excellent building blocks!

The Violet

Above the Indigo is the final or outside color. This is, of course, the Violet. The Violet Color is considered to be the color of protection, Divine Protection. The Violet Body is associated with the Crown Chakra and as such, the Violet band, like the Violet Chakra, cannot be manipulated. This is the summation of the six colors below. It represents the microcosm of the Macrocosm — the Creator. The outside color, the Violet, is like an elongated dome around the other colors, and of course, the physical body itself. This is a gift of protection from one's own Source. Your Source is Divine; therefore, this is indeed Divine Protection. All personalities have this band or dome of Violet around themselves.

Sometimes the Violet will have dark spots or some holes in it, looking something like Violet swiss cheese. This is not a normal condition, but it will occasionally be found. The protection afforded would be minimized. The lesser evolved entities would be the most likely candidates for this experience — those ones who have yet to reach the level of mid-Young-Soul status. This distorted lack of protection for these ones is to be considered very beneficial, simply because they are now more vulnera-

NOTES:

ble to catalysts that will provide the experience that stimulates their growth/evolution. Negativity can more readily penetrate these ones, and the variety of opportunities, producing experiences, is quite useful. This may appear to be cruel; however, we must always bear in mind that the Earth's Third Density was designed and intended to be a place where hard lessons could be learned quickly. For the entity who has reached a spiritual evolutionary status of mid-Young Soul and above, and certainly for the polarized entity, it is unlikely that there would be any discrepancies in the construct of the Violet in their Aura.

The Violet should be seen as clear, crystal clear if you will, conveying the essence of depth with a feeling of "body." This would be typical for the more evolved, yet non-polarized, entity. If this crystal clear Violet contained within itself sharp, distinct bands of Green, Blue, and Indigo then that entity/-personality would be Positive Polarized and would be eligible for the Positive Harvest. If this crystal clear Violet contained within itself clouded or fuzzy bands of Red, Orange, and Yellow then that entity/personality would be Polarized Negative, and would be eligible for the service to self Harvest.

Discovering The Density

Above the Violet is seen an energy. This energy is colorless and is Prana, the vital energy, the life force that radiates out from the head and passes through the entire Aura. This clear, vital energy may be likened to "heat waves" as seen on a road in the distance on a hot summer day. Now, the configurations or patterns this energy assumes outside of the Violet will indicate the Density in which the personality is native. Thus, the Wanderer is discovered! To teach you how to discern if this Wanderer is Fourth Density, Fifth Density, or perhaps Sixth Density is most difficult. The sound vibration complexes called words fail us at this time. The *refinement* of the vibrations/patterns are the clue. The refinement of the colors of the Aura is also a clue. Only practice will permit efficiency in ascertaining the correct analysis.

NOTES:

The Lower Body

The three colors of the lower body or inner Aura are the baser or courser vibrations. These colors, the Yellow, Orange and Red reveal the more Humanistic qualities of the personality. Though no particular order of observation is better than another, nevertheless, we choose to check out the Orange Vibration first.

The Orange

The Orange is the second color in a band or loose form around the physical body. This band could form any configuration. Auras are in a constant state of change, and the three inner colors are subject to change far more often than the four outer colors. If the Orange is seen in a light pastel color, this is considered to be Positive, and indicates great change. There will be times when the pastel Orange will be the predominate color in the Aura. This is always temporary, and indicates accelerated growth. Confusion shall also accompany this brief but periodic phenomenon. In a Positive sense, change and growth are the same thing; however, because the personality is absolutely unique and not necessarily Positive, change may not always constitute growth. The light pastel Orange may be seen in one or more of the other colors in the Aura. It is usually seen in the form of dots or lines. For example, if Orange dots are noticed in the Green, that would indicate growth in the Love Vibration. If Orange dots or lines/threads are found in the Indigo, this would mean the personality is experiencing mental growth and development. This could be caused by schooling, or perhaps by intuitive inspiration. If the apex of the pyramid or cone in the Indigo was Orange, this would indicate sustained growth in the mentality. Wherever there is pastel Orange found in any other color, this designates growth in the function assigned to that color. The Orange initiates permanent, solid growth. This progress will not collapse at some later time, even if the Orange is no longer present. The pastel Orange acts as a catalyst to initiate growth. This is to be seen as being very highly Positive.

On the other hand, if the Orange appears to be dark in hue, this would indicate greed and envy and that the personality

NOTES:

was accumulating power unto self for the express purpose of dominating and controlling others. If the Orange dots/lines seen in other colors were of this dark heavy hue, then a Negative correlation would be applied to the interpretation. The withdrawing, the focus of energy inward to self, to serve self, is the purpose of the dark Orange.

For most people, the Orange would be light and pastel. This could easily have a few dark Orange threads or lines running through it. This shows that the personality has experimented with greed and envy. If the dark lines appear old or faded the experiment is history. If the dark lines appear fresh, then the activity is currently being practiced. Greed, envy, lust, power plays, and controlling others, are service to self attitudes that virtually all Human Beings have entertained at some time in the course of the lifetime. The size of the dark lines, the amount, and the apparent age are the things to look for. Remember: an assessment is being sought for the sake of an understanding that is to be shared with the person being read. The reading is *never* for the purpose of passing judgment! Personal opinions/ego must *never* enter into the information being gathered. Every personality is unique and has the Free Will to choose the life patterns that are deemed appropriate. If change is considered to be necessary, then the other self must initiate the thought. It is not the reader's prerogative to construct clones of self. Conformity is an abomination in the eyes of the One Infinite Creator. Variety is a delight! Remember this!

The Red

The Red Color in the Aura is found next to the body. The Red, like the Orange, should be in a light pastel hue. It is the foundation or base color and is the coarsest of all the Rays. The sexuality is expressed through the Red in its pastel shade. If the Red is quite bright, then thoughts of sex are being entertained. Within the band of Red, an energy field will flow across the width of the band. If the energy flows away from the body (within the Red band), then the entity is male. If the energy flows toward the physical body, then the entity is female. If the

NOTES:

energy directional flow is opposite of the obvious gender of the personality, then homosexuality is the chosen way of life. If one side of the Red band has the energy flow *outward,* while the other side (of the body) of the Red Band has the energy flowing *inward,* then a bisexual personality is being observed. If the Red is of a dark hue, then anger is on the agenda. There will always be at least a few dark Red lines running through the pastel Red, for there is not one amongst us that has not expressed anger at least twice in the lifetime. The size, the amount, and the apparent degree of activation of the dark Red lines is the information the observer seeks.

If the general appearance of the Red seems cloudy, muddy, and dingy, then that personality has both feet stuck in the mud and is not going anywhere; he is stagnating. If this muddied color is not fresh, then that one has experienced a "no progress" cycle in the past, but is now free of it. There may be evidence of more than one cycle. A pattern of "being stuck" may be in evidence; thus, a character trait is being rendered. A large muddy spot may be seen in the pastel Red. This indicates the personality had or has one foot stuck in the mud, and is going around in circles. Mobility is now returning to the retarded one, but direction is lacking.

Sometimes, there is very little Red in the Aura, and occasionally, no Red at all. Remember, Red is the grounding factor, and when only a little Red appears, then the personality has the tendency to become "spacey" with the attention span being obviously shortened. If there is no Red at all, then the personality has both feet permanently planted in the clouds, and is truly an "air head." These ones are un-willing and therefore unable to focus on mundania, and hardly deal with practicality at all. They have no particular attachment to the Planet, or to the Human Race. They disassociate with conventional physical life and occasionally choose seclusion. The grounding Red Ray is not automatic; this Ray must be cultivated!

It is a useful practice to shed the Red Ray from oneself occasionally, and "rise above it;" to look down upon self and one's environment in order to grasp a better over-all picture of

NOTES:

the life and lifestyle. To do this regularly is highly recommended, providing it is always on a temporary basis. If one releases the Red Ray permanently, then there is no point in being Human or even to be "alive;" The sexual desire has left and the personality no longer embraces the culture. It is the culture, the Root Race, which provides the catalyst that sponsors growth. Thus, the Orange Ray of growth cannot be effective if there is an absence of Red.

There are various ways of establishing the grounding factor. One way is to over eat, and intentionally become obese. The excessive poundage is a viable means to achieve the grounding effect. Siddartha Gutama, the Buddha, employed this method. Another way is to become sexually overactive (deliberately arranging for as much sexual activity as possible). This action offers a strong grounding facility; however, it also readily opens the door to negative infiltration. Care must be exercised. Neither of these methods may be appealing. Another more practical method is the acquisition of a pet. The perpetual daily care of a beloved pet offers a special type of responsibility that is highly successful in generating more Red Ray in the Aura. Children are not nearly as effective as the pet because the responsibility for children eventually will be outgrown. The adult knows this. The responsibility for the pet remains constant forever. The adult knows this also. In order to function as a Light Bearer, and as a Love Bearer, as a Third Density Human Being it is absolutely mandatory that you be grounded.

The Yellow

The final color in the lower body and in our examination of the Aura, is the Yellow. In the average/normal Third Density non-harvestable entity, the Aura would show a reasonably bright Yellow. If the Aura fails to show the clear bright Yellow, then that personality has but a few more days remaining in the incarnation; or, the personality may be a Third Density Harvestable one, or perhaps a Fourth Density or Fifth Density, or even a Sixth Density Wanderer. If this is the case, then the bright Yellow would be naturally missing, for a transition is in effect.

NOTES:

These ones would express a Yellow/Green or perhaps a Green/Yellow instead of the pure color Yellow.

The Yellow Ray Body *is* the physical body of the Human Being; it is the energy that keeps us all alive. As such, it is the energy/vibration that activates the emotions within all those who are engaged in Third Density activities, regardless of which Density the entity is native to.

The Earth Mother's vibrations are indeed rising. The season for the Third Density to Fourth Density Harvest is upon us; therefore, the Transition is most appropriate for those eligible, evolving through the shades of hues from Yellow to Green, from emotion to Love, and from Third to Fourth Density. These fortunate ones are also blessed with considerable confusion from time to time.

The Yellow is never perfectly clean, even for those who are native to Planet Earth. Raw emotion is unbridled. Self discipline is most useful in controlling emotions, yet it is never complete. Emotions are the nucleus of Third Density. This is the root cause for all problems in the Human Being. Almost all illnesses, physical and mental, are the results of unbridled emotions *or* pent-up emotions. The culture in its make-up offers an incredible amount of stress which aggravates the emotions even further. To balance the Yellow Ray is most difficult; to maintain that balance is impossible. The Yellow Ray is even further fortified by the Red and the Orange, as their powerful energies travel upward to join with the Yellow to intensify and complete the status of the lower body. Unless these energies, singularly or combined, are tempered with the Green Ray-Love and/or the Indigo Ray-Wisdom, there will be pending disaster. This could be expressed as an explosion or implosion in the individual. This condition is not designed nor intended to be "fixed." A great deal of relief may be achieved via understanding. Unfortunately, Infant, Baby, and even Young Souls would not be prone to accepting this understanding. Thus, it becomes easier to see why it is so difficult to evolve or graduate from Third Density status. The basic reason a personality will deliberately void his grounding Red Ray is to avoid dealing with

NOTES:

his Yellow Ray of emotion and the volatile emotions of his other selves. This condition has always been present in the Human Experience, but it is always much more prevalent during the seasons of Cycle endings.

Sometimes the Yellow may be seen as bright and healthy, but it is never brilliant. Usually there is a cloudiness or a dingy haze covering this band. It is always streaked or dotted with various other colors, as the various bodies attempt to offer there guidance, balance, and instruction.

The Violet Divided

It is normal for the Red band to be next to the physical body. Sometimes a band of Violet will be seen as the first or inside color. This is very rare. The personality so endowed is experiencing Divine Protection for the physical vehicle. The Higher Self has seen fit to offer special protection for the body of the entity. A mission presenting some hazard is anticipated and this action is warranted. This accounts for the "charmed life" that certain individuals seem to enjoy. The Violet next to the body is usually temporary, however, and it would not be wise to depend upon it. The outside band of Violet would remain intact regardless of the inner activity.

NOTE: The order of the colors of the Aura are opposite from the order given when you learned to raise your Kundalini. From a bodily function point of view it is good to have the lower three colors Red, Orange, and Yellow close to the vehicle; thus, the Aura provides this. From a spiritual/mental point of view it is good to have the Violet, Indigo adjacent to the body. The constructed Great Dome of Protection is considerably larger than the natural Aura; consequently, the Violet and perhaps the Indigo included, of the constructed Dome of Protection, would encompass the entirety of the natural Aura. Because each of the seven colors vibrates to a different frequency, the only blending or interference between the two systems would be in the Violet and perhaps the Indigo areas. This would present an asset, not a liability. The reader of the Aura would maintain strict accuracy even if the other self had their Kundalini raised with the great

NOTES:

rainbow Dome of Protection properly installed. The dome is made up of rather dense colors, and it maintains this status.The natural Aura, as it spreads outward, becomes thin and misty, and is often rather difficult to read or to even distinguish the configurations of the inner colors from the outer colors. If this is the problem the reader may, with the cooperation of both Higher Selves, "Will" the Aura to become condensed, so that accuracy might prevail.

You are a reflection of your Aura. Your Aura is a reflection of you. You are both one in the same. The Law is ONE. The constructed Dome/Aura is of your own making. You may, if you choose, engulf your body in a Great Dome of a single color — the Green Ray of Love and Healing, for example. You always have choices. You can manipulate all the colors of your natural Aura of a status or configuration of your choosing except the Violet — this is the vibration of the one Infinite Creator, and you quite naturally would have no control over the Creator!

Drugs/Chemicals

The individual colors of the Aura may have holes of various sizes contained therein. The probable cause of these holes is drugs. Drugs, prescription or street variety, will readily cause this. No aspect of the Aura, or any portion of the physical body, is immune to the effects of chemicals. For example, if holes are found in the Red, then impotence or loss of sexual drive is experienced. If the Orange contains holes, then malfunctions with the lower internal organs is noted — kidneys, spleen, pancreas, liver, urinary tract, etc. Holes in the Yellow would indicate emotional instability, sudden shift in character traits, moodiness, and extremism. Holes noticed in the Green would indicate an imbalance in the Love vibration. There could be much vacillation in Love attitudes, often expressing fits of uncontrolled compassion obviously lacking in the balance with Wisdom. Holes in the Blue band of the Aura would indicate communication problems — probably speech difficulties that were not present before. Holes found in the Indigo form, reflect

NOTES:

the "cinders" in the brain that have been caused by chemicals. The brain could be pock-marked with microscopic cinders where chemicals have burned out the synoptical connectors that permit electrical circuitry to form the thinking process. If holes are found in the Violet, this would indicate the personality is experiencing a loss of contact with his/her Higher Self. These perforations alienate self with the Higher Self. Remember that the Violet is the summation of all the lower colors; therefore, any chemical problems contracted below are all brought upward into the Violet which reduces the contact with the Higher Self. This is serious and not to be taken lightly!

The swiss cheese appearance in the colors of the Aura is to be avoided. Any thinking person could readily see that. However, if the holes exist, then one must be willing to accept the condition. If they are "clean cut," then healing is possible. This will be discussed in this book's next section. If there is a black rim or edge around these holes, this would indicate current use of chemicals; extensive, habitual or addictive use of drugs. It is unlikely that healing would be successful in areas where the black is present. The exercising of time and patience would be the most productive approach to employ.

** *Summation* **

The White Light passing through a prism creates the spectrum of the seven colors — three are prime and four are basic. Knowledge of these Rays can be most useful. The Aura is a typical example. All objects emit an Aura, but perhaps the Human Aura is the most intriguing. The preceding information was offered with the intention of inspiring the reader to be aware and watchful for the Rays, and learn how to use them. The Rays are Light. Light is the Second Creative Force. This is *your* gift from the Creator. Use them . . . and use them wisely!

Chapter 4

Using The Rays

A great deal has been said about the White Light and the spectrum of the Seven Rays derived from it. Familiarity with the Rays makes their etheric existence more acceptable. The Seven Rays correspond with the seven chakras. The chakras, those energy centers, are the tools that provide the means for the entity to utilize the Rays. You have learned about the chakras as you studied and hopefully, learned the Kundalini Meditation taught in Volume One. The chakras have been further described in the preceding chapter of this section of Volume Two of *The Teachings*. These invisible energy centers are of paramount importance as you proceed with your ongoing study of metaphysics.

The seven chakras receive the seven Rays into your body. All seven chakras are receivers. Only the top three chakras are transmitters. You are capable of using the various Rays through these energy centers. This is the only way the Third Density Human Being may accomplish this.

Using The Green Ray

In order to use or share the four lower colors, Red, Orange, Yellow, or Green, they must be individually brought up to one, or more than one, of the transmitting chakras. For example, if you wished to share Love with another self or entity the first step would be to select the appropriate chakra/energy center. This of course, would be the Heart Chakra which vibrates to the Emerald Green Ray of Love, Healing, and Manifestation. You would now envision a shaft of Emerald Green Light flowing into your Heart Chakra, through the stem, to your spinal cord, and then up the spinal cord to, shall we say, the Blue Chakra. This is the Throat Chakra, the center for communications.

For this purpose, envision the Throat Chakra as a Blue Pipe or Tube extending from the throat outward in front of you a few inches or perhaps a couple of feet or so. Now, this Green Ray of Love is coming up your spinal cord from the heart, and

NOTES:

has reached the back side of this Blue Tube. Fill the Blue tube with the Green Light and send it out via the transmitting power of the Blue Chakra. The result is that you would now be speaking words of Love! If you are speaking to a single person, one to one, then perhaps you would like to envision the Blue tube in the shape of an elongated cone with you speaking into the large end. The small open end is being directed to the other self. This permits you to focus your Love Vibration directly into the Throat Chakra of the other self. This is powerful and perhaps useful. On the other hand, if you are addressing a larger audience, then you might wish to reverse the cone to form a megaphone. This would permit you to broadcast to a great number of people. (see Figures 1 & 2.)

We have now utilized the Green Ray and the Blue Ray. If this procedure does not apply to your situation, then bypass the Throat Chakra and permit the Green Ray of Love to rise higher to the Indigo — Third Eye — energy center. Once more, for this purpose, envision the Indigo as a tube or pipe that would permit the transmission of the Green Ray Love Light. The Indigo is the mentality, the thought. By using this chakra, you may now transmit *thoughts of Love.*

Feel free to change the pipe into a cone if you like, and send your thoughts of Love to a single entity or to many as you reverse the cone. (see Figures 3 & 4.)

If the use of the Blue and Indigo transmitters does not fill the bill for you, then consider employing the Crown Chakra, for it too is a transmitter. The Green Ray continues to flow into the Heart Chakra to the spinal cord, and now up the spinal cord to the very crown of the head, bypassing the Blue and Indigo connections. For this purpose, you might like to envision the Crown Chakra as a Violet Funnel or Cone attached to the top of the head, with the little end down. The Green Light of Love is now flowing into the little end and spiraling upward and outward, flowing all around your physical body, creating a dome. As the Green continues to flow, the dome becomes larger, more solid and dense. Using the Violet energy center permits you to broadcast your Love to everything around you. The

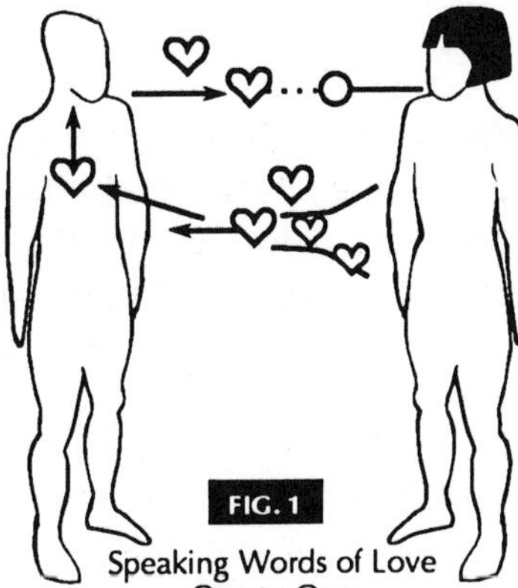

FIG. 1

Speaking Words of Love
One to One

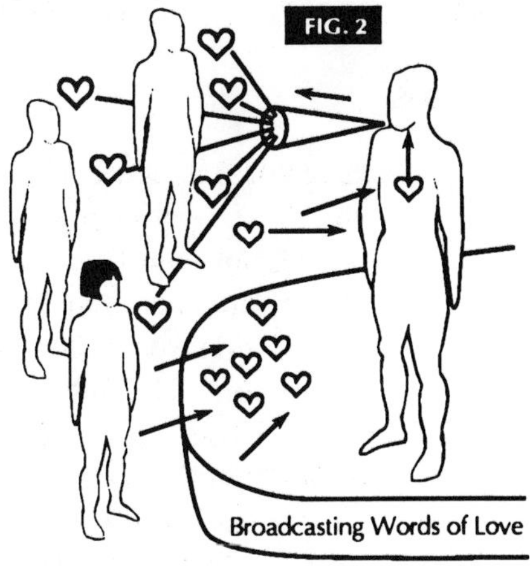

FIG. 2

Broadcasting Words of Love

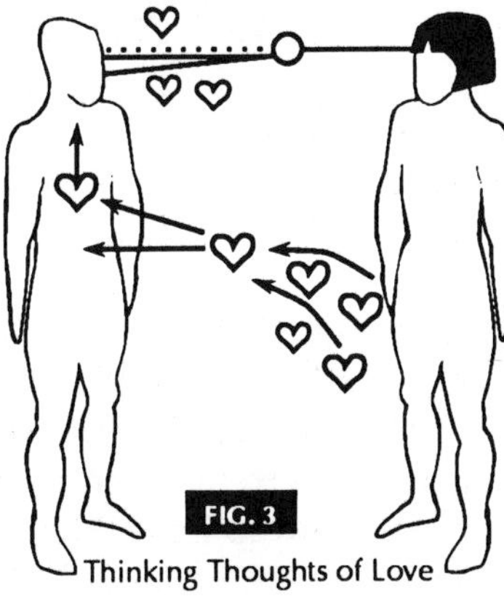

FIG. 3

Thinking Thoughts of Love

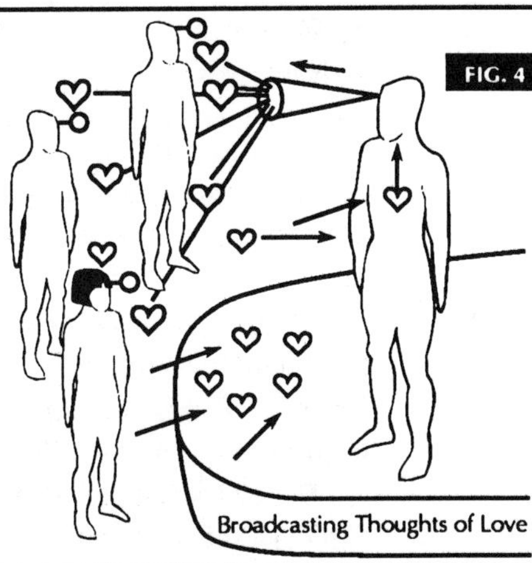

FIG. 4

Broadcasting Thoughts of Love

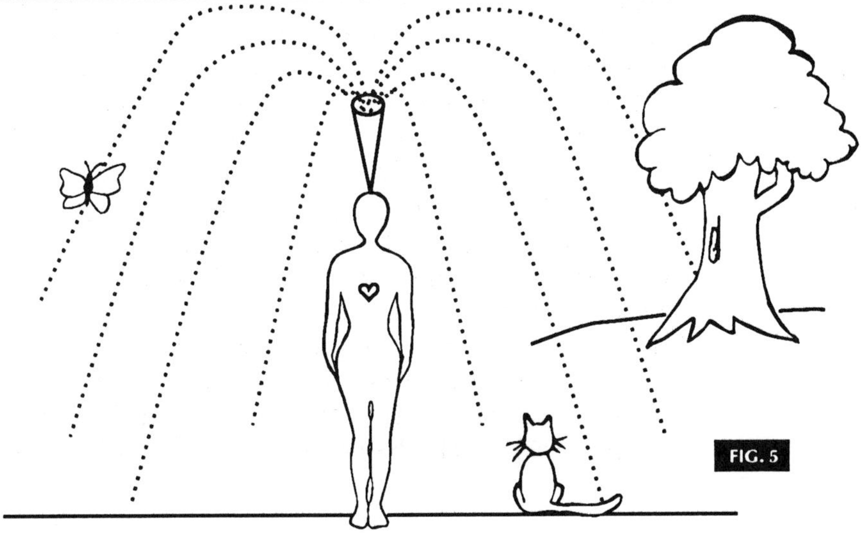

FIG. 5

Sharing Love with Your Environment

NOTES:

range of this dome of Love is limited only by the extent of your ability to envision, and to *maintain* that vision. This dome creates an environment of Love in which you may dwell. All plants, animals, and Human Beings who have the good fortune to find themselves in your Aura of Love, shall be blessed with the Love — Healing Vibration. (See Figure 5.)

To offer this Love to the Earth Mother is the honor/duty of all Light Bearers, all Love Bearers. You may achieve this by simply envisioning your great Dome of Green, penetrating deep into the Planet herself. Deep, deep, 400 miles deep, all the way to the Earth's mantle, see this Love/Healing energy go. A large column of Green has now been established. Take this huge shaft of Green with you wherever you may travel, offering a swath of Love to our beleaguered Planet. (See Figure 5.)

The Earth Mother is starving for Love. The Universe is full of Love. According to Universal Law, the two can never get together. The only way this feeding may take place is for an entity to volunteer to accept an incarnation on this Planet and produce a personality, one such as yourself, who is willing to serve as a link, a connector, as you bring the Green Ray of Love into yourself and transmit that Divine Energy from the crown of your head via the Violet Chakra to our beloved Earth Mother. This is the prime duty for the Wanderer — he who is MAN Incarnate, and for those ones who are native to this Planet, who are eligible for the Positive Harvest. There are more Wanderers incarnated on the Planet now than ever have been before in the 75,000-year Cycle of the Human Experience. The prime reason you are here is to *work.* This offering of the Love/Healing Vibration to the Earth Mother is the prime aspect of your mission. When enough of you Wanderers awaken, accept your true status and put your services on the line, then, and perhaps only then, will the Earth Mother be able to make her changes, and we can get on with developing the new civilization in the Fourth Density Vibration of true color Green — Love.

The Green is a most useful color, and certainly in vogue at this critical time of Transition of the Earth Mother and the Harvest of Souls into the Fourth Dimension of Love. As you

NOTES:

know, the Green has a three-fold purpose: Love, Healing, and Manifestation. We shall examine the healing aspect of the Green Ray in-depth in the next section of this book. The use of the Green Ray as the manifester via the Indigo energy center will be explained when we study the Tensor Concepts later on in this book. There is much to know about the Green Ray.

Using The Yellow Ray

The Yellow Ray is the vibration of emotion. This is the energy that *is* the physical body. It is vital to Third Density. Through the use of this Ray any given personality may become aware of himself/herself during the course of some incarnation or another. Emotions permit the developing personality to express their unique individuality, thus effecting the necessary understanding to become aware of self. Emotions are usually considered Negative or bad. These ones are the teachers. The Positive emotions are those that permit us to survive in a status somewhere above that of the Second Density animal kingdom.

The Yellow Ray of emotion is brought in through the Solar-Plexis Chakra to the spinal cord, and then up to one or more of the three transmitting chakras. This may be accomplished in precisely the same way as was described using the Green. The Yellow is obviously not as useful as was the Green and therefore, there is always some hesitancy to share this coarser vibration. The Negative emotions are often "held in," and not present for public viewing because of the embarrassment that they might cause. This pent-up stress can eventually take a detrimental toll on one's health, both physical and mental. It is wise to release these emotions of, and on, the Yellow Ray. It is also wise not to be anti-social. What then is the compromise that permits one to do both simultaneously? Never prohibit the inflowing of the Yellow Ray, even when it's obvious that Negative emotions are being generated. Never conceal this energy within self. Welcome in the Yellow Ray. Then, via the spinal cord, bring this Negative Yellow up to the Green Ray of the Heart Chakra. Then, mentally transmute the Yellow Ray of emotion *into* the Green Ray of Love, permitting this altered

NOTES:

transmuted, energy to flow perhaps to the Blue, and *speak* words of Love — or perhaps up higher to the Indigo, and *think* thoughts of Love! Better still, permit the Green, now under the tremendous force of emotion, to rise to the Crown Chakra and strengthen the great Green Dome of Love that you have created about yourself. Let the power of your emotions force the Love Vibration into the depths of the Earth-Mother herself! That which has its beginnings as Negative, may be transmuted into Positive with no loss whatsoever to the velocity or magnitude of that energy flow. Never willfully restrict any energy flow because you deem it to be unworthy in its current status. Alter it, fix it, so that it *is* worthy . . . let it flow!! (See Figure 6.)

Interrelationships between Third Density Entities is always under the vibration of the Yellow Ray of emotion/ego. This is sometimes less than pleasant. This less than harmonious environment produces catalysts that all may learn from. This system works. It provides the necessary intercourse to promote evolution. This is good. However, the exchange of energies between Third Density entities on a more harmonious level will produce the same growth factors. Love/Harmony is highly desirable . . . and most difficult to achieve. Feel free to transmute the raw emotion of Yellow Ray into the refined feelings of Love on the Green Ray. Do this and teach this. Teach this by example!

Using The Orange Ray

The Orange Ray is essentially the Ray of growth and change. It is the vital energy that is native to Second Density. This energy is of a vibration that inspires the desire to grow. The goal of this growth is to become aware of self. Second Density Entities are unaware of themselves. The Human fetus is of the Orange Ray Vibration. The fetus grows during gestation, and accepts the Third Density self awareness status at the time of birth or shortly thereafter. Therefore, to offer a healing service to the un-born child, use the Orange Ray! (See Figure 7.)

The incoming Orange Ray could readily be brought up to any of the upper transmitting chakras. However, the Crown

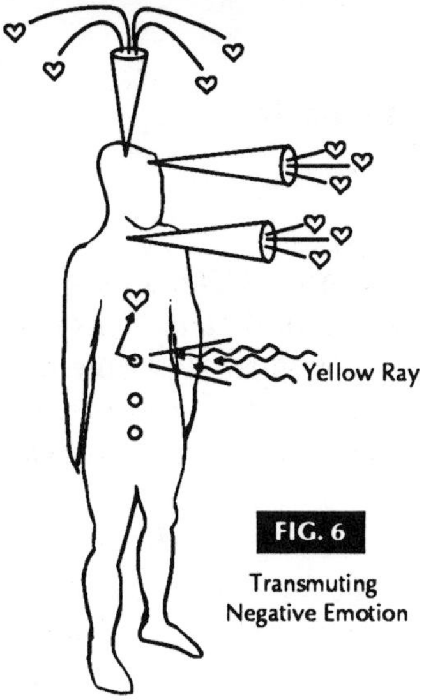

FIG. 6

Transmuting Negative Emotion

FIG. 7

Offering Correct Energy to Fetus

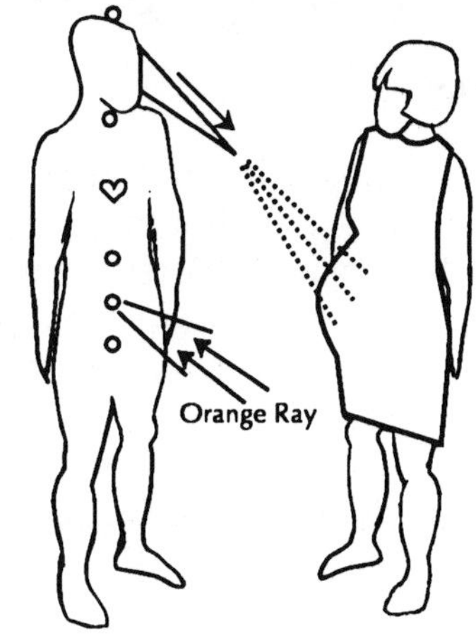

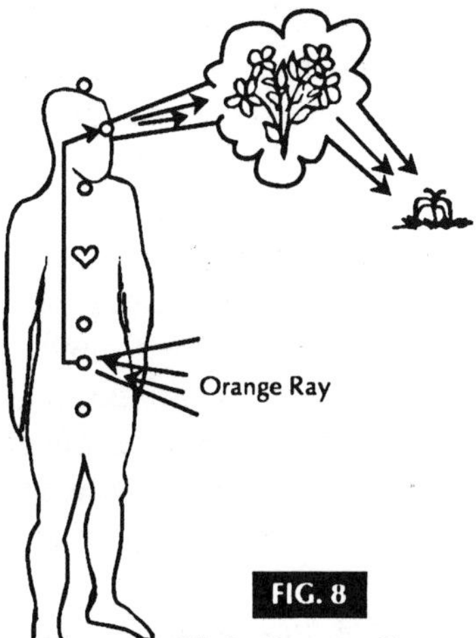

FIG. 8

Offering Energy to Plants

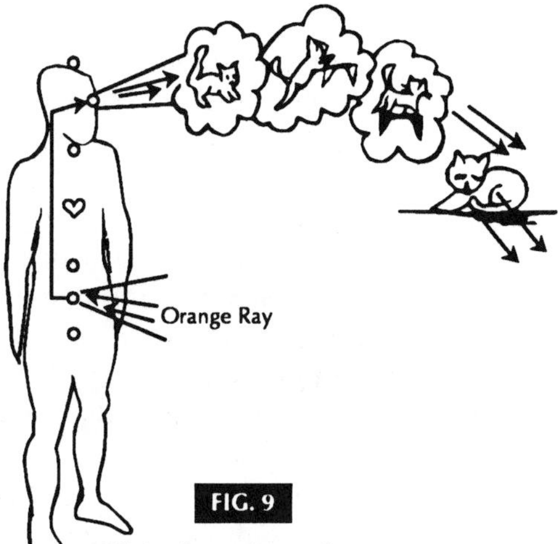

FIG. 9

Offering Suggestions to Pets

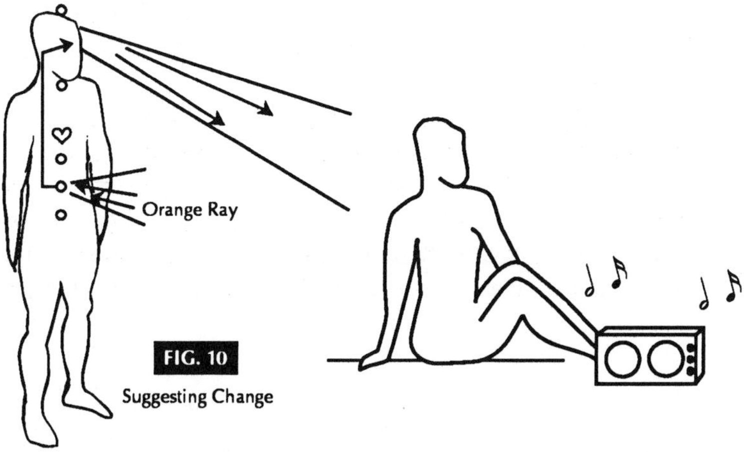

FIG. 10

Suggesting Change

NOTES:

Chakra is rarely used. The Blue or Throat Chakra may be used if you wish to make animal sounds or bird calls. This form of communication seldom is efficient, though possibly entertaining. The Orange Ray, brought up to the Third Eye can indeed be most useful when dealing with Second Density and Third Density Entities.

If you wish to communicate with a plant or animal your first step is to create the thought form; that is, form a good mental image of the desired end results, especially if the entity is of the plant kingdom. (See Figure 8) If the subject of communication is an animal, then perhaps a series of pictures indicating the step-by-step procedure of your desire would be in order. (See Figure 9.) When you have carefully refined your thought form, then, bring the Orange Ray into the Spleen Chakra to the spinal cord, up the spinal cord to the Indigo Tube. The tube would probably be constructed to focus upon a single plant or animal, that is, the little end of the long tapered cone would be away from your head. Insert the constructed thought form in the big end of the Indigo Cone. Now, force the thought form through the cone with the power of the Orange Ray. Direct the energy upon your target. Keep the Orange flowing continuously. Be patient, but expect results. You are born on the Yellow Ray. This is senior to the Orange Ray. The junior always attempts to serve and please the senior. This willingness to serve is always present, as this is the thesis of evolution. This obviously can be misused. We suggest that you do not misuse it. Karma can readily be created! Mentally filling a plant or animal with the Orange Ray will promote growth and cause healing if required. The Second Density Entity will quickly recognize the source of this gift of energy and shall respond the same way as it would to a physical feeding.

The Orange Ray may be used with Third Density Entities, even though these ones do not vibrate to that color. Orange, when it is a light or pastel in color, promotes change and growth. If the other self is conducting his/her affairs in a way that is, or could, be detrimental in your considered opinion, then you might elect to use the Orange Ray upon this person.

NOTES:

Bring the Orange Ray into your Spleen Chakra, up your spinal cord to the Third Eye or Indigo Chakra. Using the focusing configuration of the Indigo Cone, saturate the other self in pastel Orange. This action will promote change. If a group of people are engaged in an unwanted activity, reverse the Indigo Cone so that the Orange Ray passing through might be broadcast. Engulf the people and the area in Orange. Change has now been instigated. Growth must now be considered. Growth into what? Consider, if you will, the use of the Indigo. The Orange saturated other self now being cocooned in Indigo — the vibration of Wisdom. This could be useful in the parent/child relationship, or perhaps the teacher/student structure. The Orange serving as the catalyst of change, promoting growth, into Wisdom. (See Figure 10.)

The use of the Green Ray of Love/Healing might also be invoked, via the Indigo Chakra to direct the other self into growth toward Love. Once the Orange Ray of change and growth has been invoked, then a following color should also be employed to offer direction after change has occurred. (See Figure. 11A & 11B) If sexual activity is desired, a pastel bright Red would then be projected around the Orange saturated other self. The Yellow could follow the Orange if the other self appeared to be totally docile, with a profound "lackluster" attitude. This could spark some internal dormant "fire." The Yellow is rarely used. Blue could encase the Orange, if there is a ready need for communication. This too would be used sparingly.

The Orange Ray is the catalyst. If considerable thought precedes its use, magnificent results may be obtained. The Law of Cause and Effect thrives on the energy of this vibration. Feel free to invoke the colors or series of colors to obtain the results of your choice. If you have been un wise or selfish in your thinking, and if your plans were not in the best interests of others, then the worst shall happen — nothing!

If this should be the case, carefully examine your attitude and standards to attempt to discover — why not? If it should work out just the way you planned, again examine your self to

NOTES:

determine what you did that was right! This is how you learn and grow. It is sometimes called *Trial and error.* Use the Orange Ray of change on a person, a place, or a thing.

Using The Red Ray

The Red Ray is of course, the vibration of the mineral kingdom. It is the chemical body of the Human Being. The personality would normally express the Red Ray through sexuality or anger. If the Red Ray is expressed as a bright Red then sex is on the agenda. A dark Red would indicate anger. Sex and anger are a part of emotion — which is the Yellow Ray. The awesome power of sex or anger is brought up the spinal cord where the emotion is attached on the incoming Yellow. The Red/Yellow is sent directly to the Blue and/or Indigo for transmission and expression. If the desire/intent is strong enough then the Orange may also be committed. The Orange is the Power Chakra of the lower body even as the Blue is the Power Chakra for the upper body. If this occurs then a tremendous energy collection has been achieved, and containment would now be impossible. The end result would be a violent rape — expressing sex in violent rage, or physical/verbal, that would be construed as temporary insanity — expressing anger. (See Figure 12.)

Sex can be beautiful and does not have to be expressed in such a manner. Anger can be constructive and useful if tempered with Wisdom and Love. When the Red Ray stirs action *will* follow, whether it be a geyser of steam or a volcano. When the lower three colors are successfully combined, tremendous Negativity is produced. This energy rises upward for expression. The Green Chakra, the Love Vibration is always skipped. The Blue is achieved and the Indigo is now available. Intelligent Infinity can now be successfully penetrated. This is precisely how a Negative Entity polarizes him/herself. Red Ray anger or sex are the tools necessary to promote a service to self-polarization. The deliberate omission of Green/Love makes this possible. Anger can produce results beyond belie; sexual magic has potential powers that go beyond comprehension.

NOTES:

The Third Density Entity cannot dismiss sex or anger from his life, nor should he try. Both are extremely useful catalysts. Their latent potential power should be known and understood, as the aware personality weaves his way through the tangled maze called life. The Red Ray is the grounding factor for Third Density. This allows the personality to embrace the culture, either on a social, or perhaps an anti-social level. Either way, intercourse is achieved and lessons are learned/taught. The Earth is a Planet where hard lessons are learned quickly. This you already know. This is how and why it works.

Red Ray Energy is useful and necessary. It is not to be blocked or contained. This would be true for all Rays. Self-discipline begins with this Ray. If reasonably successful, then disciplined emotions (Yellow Ray) may also be forthcoming. As the Red rises, anger or sex make a valid attempt to bypass the Orange — this will inject too much power. The Yellow Ray of emotion/ego will always temper the rising Red to some degree. Bring the Red/Yellow up to the Green and saturate it with Love. This transmutation will make Positive that which very well may have ended up Negative. Continue to bring this transmuted energy up to the Blue (communication), and speak words of Love — sincerely, or speak words of Love — powerfully, as the righteous anger comes forth. Continue to bring this combination of three energies, Red, Yellow, and Green up to the Indigo, and think/project thoughts of Love. Sex is 90% cerebral anyway! Whatever the results may have been on a physical level, remember . . . the physical plane of reality is but an illusion, and it is indeed the *thought* that counts! (See Figure 13.)

The now tempered anger energy currently found in the Indigo Chakra is highly useful for creating new concepts for betterment and growth of the subject/object of the anger. Wisdom is injected. Working solutions are obtainable and forthcoming. These thoughts would not likely have been produced had it not been for the original anger. Anger is spurred into action, probably by some form of injustice. The Third Density Entity shall forever seek justice, however he chooses to define it.

NOTES:

The transmuted Green, powered by Red and Yellow, can always be brought up to the Crown Chakra and broadcast to the environment surrounding the personality in the form of a dome. This dome can also be extended down some 400 miles to the mantle of the Earth Mother. This Love/Healing Energy is then bestowed upon the Planet, which *is* Red Ray. Inspired by the personality as Red Ray anger, it has now returned to the Red Ray Planet in the form of Love! Knowledge in the use of the courser vibrations found within all Third Density Entities can prove to be *very* rewarding and satisfying. Knowledge is Light. Ignorance is darkness.

Using The Blue Ray

The Blue Ray Chakra is the first of the three transmitting chakras. This is the Ray/Chakra that is associated with communication. The Blue is a very high vibration, and it is native to Fifth Density. In a Third Density conventional sense communication is limited to the spoken word and the written word. Pictures come under the category of the latter. Telepathy is becoming more prevalent in these closing days of this Third Density cycle, but it certainly is not yet fluent.

The Blue Ray is a most convenient vehicle for other Rays to work through. We have seen how the four lower Rays may be brought *up* to this one and transmitted. It should also be noted that the Indigo Ray of Wisdom may be brought *down* to the Blue Tube so that words of Wisdom may also be spoken. To achieve a more complete balance you might consider bringing the Indigo down to the Blue Tube/Cone and filling the upper half with the Ray of Wisdom. Then, simultaneously bring the Green up from the Heart Chakra, and fill the lower half of the Blue Tube with the Ray of Love. This will permit you to speak with the words of Love and Wisdom at the same time. Construct the cone appropriately, whether you are speaking to one or to a group.

The Blue Ray is never brought down to lower chakras nor is it ever brought up to higher chakras. It is stationary in its location in the throat. (See Figure 14.)

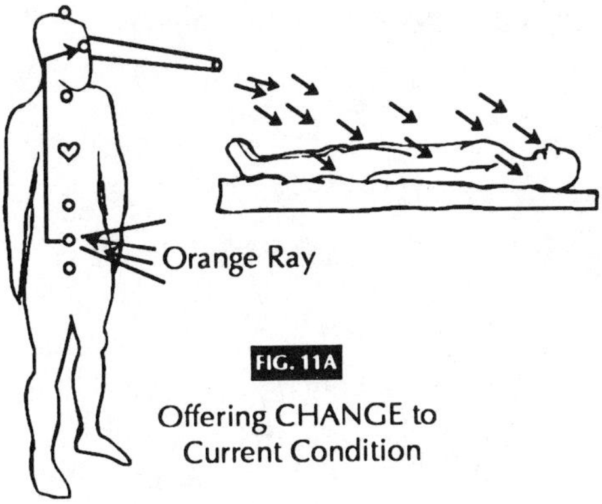

FIG. 11A

Offering CHANGE to Current Condition

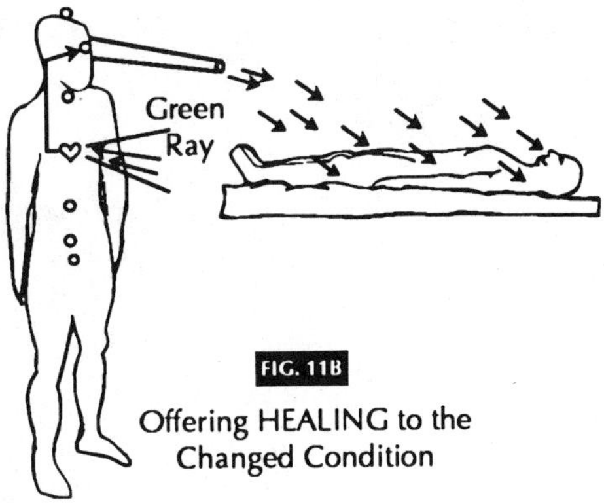

FIG. 11B

Offering HEALING to the Changed Condition

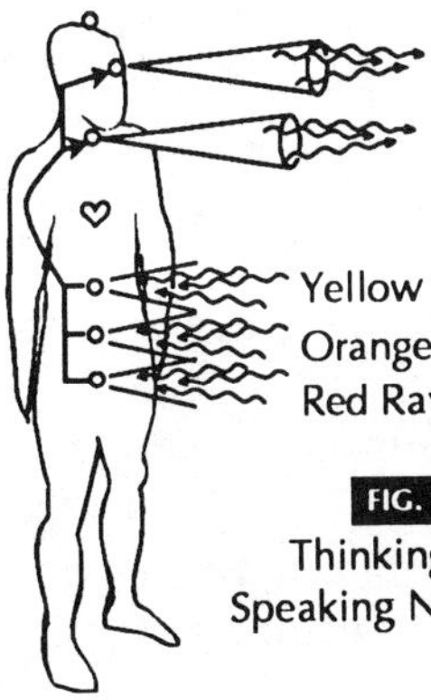

FIG. 12

Thinking and Speaking Negatively

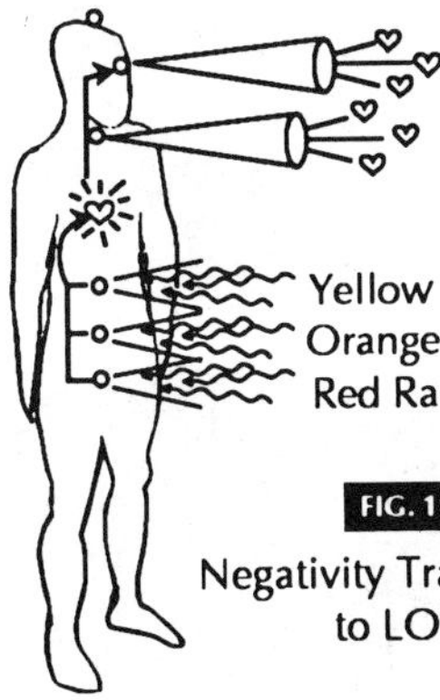

FIG. 13

Negativity Transmuted to LOVE

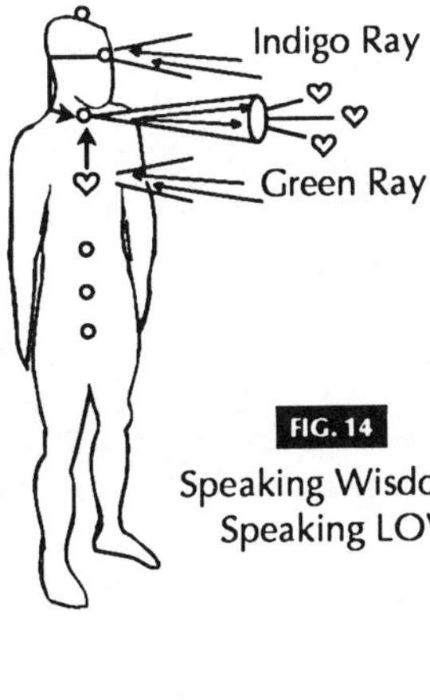

FIG. 14

Speaking Wisdom – Speaking LOVE

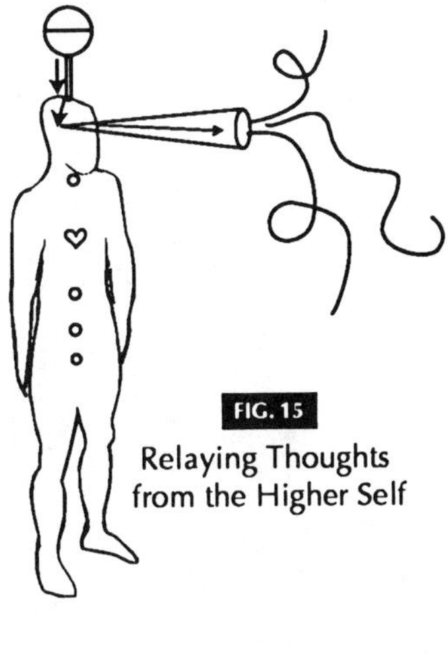

FIG. 15

Relaying Thoughts from the Higher Self

NOTES:

Using The Indigo Ray

The Indigo is the second of the transmitting chakras. This one deals with the mentality, the intellect, the Wisdom, the thinking process — the mind/brain, all of which focus under the auspices of the Third Eye. The Indigo is the gateway to Intelligent Infinity. Tapping onto this energy is easy. To begin to use it fully is the work of the Adept. The Indigo permits the personality to think thoughts that would relate to Green, Yellow, Orange, and Red. Creativity is also a function of this vibration. Original concepts are focused through this Ray. Telepathy is seated in the Indigo, not the Blue, even though Blue is the Ray of Communication.

The consciousness may be projected to any desired place by "going out" on the Indigo Ray. This is accomplished via the Kundalini. When the Kundalini has been properly raised, a "cupful" of the Kundalini energy, now saturated with the consciousness, is gathered at the base of the Golden Sphere, the Higher Self. This cupful of enriched energy containing your consciousness is mentally brought back down around the Silver Cord, back inside the skull to the back of the head where the incoming Indigo Ray terminates. This cupful of White homogenized energy is then placed inside the Tube/Cone of Indigo. At your readiness the energy is "threaded" out through the Indigo Tube in a spiralling mode. This White Thread, sometimes seen as Silver, is un-ending; it will take your consciousness to any place that you direct it.

To return to your body you simply roll up your little ball of Silver/White thread. Your consciousness can be readily split into many active parts. A part of you quite naturally remains behind to serve as the core or the nucleus. With practice you will find that several threads can be emitted simultaneously from the same cupful of homogenized energy. A Guide or more than one Guide will accompany you on your astral excursions. Mentally rehearse the procedure before actually attempting. Use care, not fear. (See Figure 15.)

This Silver Thread may also be emitted from the crown of the head rather than via the Third Eye as we have suggested.

NOTES:

When the crown exit is being used, you are then being "taken for a ride" by your own Higher Self. This is a most useful introduction, but you yourself are in charge of nothing. Your Free Will is being denied you as you truly are the puppet on a string. This is strictly an introductory experience. Your Higher Self will not make a practice of this. You must learn to do this on your own. The Higher Self often uses the Crown Chakra method to implant a vision in your consciousness. Visions are seated in the subconscious, while dreams are seated in the unconscious.

Activation of the Indigo permits the personality to tap unto the Tensor Centers of the unused portion of the brain. This will be a very mild or shallow penetration at best; however, it is rare for any Third Density Entity to do it at all! ESP abilities work through the Indigo Ray.

The Indigo Ray is incoming and outgoing. Its stock and trade is: Wisdom/Knowledge. The thought is seated here. Here lies the source of your beingness.

Using The Violet Ray

The Violet is the highest and most refined Ray of all. It too is a receiving transmitter. The Violet transmitter is most useful as a broadcaster. It can be focused like the Blue and Indigo but usually it is used to transmit in all 360 degrees simultaneously. All of the lower colors may be brought up to the Violet as desired. The Violet does not go down to visit them.

The Indigo rising up into the Violet permits the personality to contact the Higher Self. This is especially workable if the Kundalini supplies the energy. The Indigo and Green are the colors most used via the Violet Ray. The Violet offers the Divine to you, the personality. This is your gift from your Higher Self.

Summary

The distortions of the use of the Rays are limited only by the number of people employing them. Feel free to amend, alter, and modify any of the procedures we have given to you. Though

NOTES:

your circumstances may perhaps be similar to others, nevertheless, you are always unique. In this Universe, there are no absolutes. The standards to which you measure yourself are the standards you have chosen for yourself. When you deal with the Light think in terms of "unlimited."

The Rays may be used singularly or collectively, such as a created aura. When creating a Aura or dome *all* colors may be superimposed upon each other if desired, since all colors hum to a different vibration. Blending does *not* happen though the effects might cause you to think that these results *are* the effect of blending. Distinguishing between the colors becomes most difficult. When using two or more colors simultaneously we suggest that you visualize the colors as being separate. However, this is not mandatory. The Violet and the Indigo Rays are rarely used alone by the Third Density Entity. All three transmitting Rays are almost always used in relation to one of the lower four. Energy transfers between self and other selves, using any or all of the four lower Rays would be successful. Connecting the upper three Rays usually is not that prosperous with the Third Density Entity, as there are veils attached to these Energy Centers. These veils are placed there by the Higher Self for the protection of the personality, actually. The Adept/Master will have these veils falling away.

The Rays may be used by an Adept for Negative purposes, i.e., service to self. For example: the Sorcerer's apprentice may elect to call an entity "back from the dead." The Orange Ray is readily adaptable to this work. If the apprentice is interested in results, and is relaxed or unconcerned about principle, the Orange Ray will produce that which is commonly known as a zombie. (An animated entity that is unaware of self.)

On the other hand, if a master were to attempt to call an entity back from the dead he would select the Yellow Ray as the agent of resurrection. This is considerably more difficult to achieve, but the end result would be a "normal" product. We offer Lazarus as an example.

The Rays are simply aspects on the spectrum of White Light. Light is Intelligent Infinity, the Second Creative Force.

NOTES:

Light is energy. Energy is intelligent. Intelligent Energy is Love. Love is the Third Creative Force. Light and Love are twins. Before Light will work it must be invoked. You invoke the Light by mentally envisioning a Light of the color of your choice, a Ray as being in motion; that is, taking action in the direction of your desires.

Light is intelligent; it requires no instruction. It knows precisely what and how to accomplish the mission that you have set it on. Remember, always remember, you are a conductor of energy — not a capacitor. Do not ever attempt to store energy within yourself. Bring it in via the chakras and then let it flow out of you in a direction of Positive accomplishments.

The Use Of Colors Shambhala 1989

The Rays were vividly presented in the Shambhala experience of 1989. We offer this exerpt from our distortion of that event:

"A little after midnight, we manifested the Great Golden Cone over our house. We called. Thousands, perhaps tens of thousands, were attracted to this beam. A great tiered circle was formed and we all traveled to the island in the Gobi Lake (desert). The revolving circle was moving swiftly a few hundred feet above the Earth's surface.

We stationed our circle of Humanity over the Island. (The circle being much larger than the Island itself.) Lord Easu was waiting. He again was standing in the center of a great Lotus Flower, even as he did last year for the first time. Last year, the perimeter of the Island was smoking ashes. This year the perimeter was eight great lily pads floating in shallow water. The Lotus covered the remaining land.

Easu stood and looked up. The silent greeting was exchanged. Easu looked down and we noted seven giant clams on the great lily pads, spaced evenly in the circle. Easu faced the first clam and it opened away from him, revealing a great Red Pearl glowing brilliantly. He turned to his left and the next clam opened outward and a brilliant Orange Pearl was seen. Easu

NOTES:

turned again and the third clam opened, showing a shiny Yellow Pearl. He turned once more, and the fourth clam opened and the great Emerald Green Pearl glowed with effervescent brilliance. Again he turned, and the next clam opened, revealing a magnificent Blue Pearl. The Blue stimulated the very essence of our Souls. Easu turned once more and the next clam opened revealing the beautiful Indigo Pearl, with its unlimited depths, regions beyond regions. Then Easu turned and faced the remaining clam. It opened slowly. The Violet that was emitted was so effervescent in its brilliance that the shape of the pearl could not be discerned.

Easu stood in a sea of color. His white garment was reflecting each and every hue. The purity of the scene was etched in our memory.

The eighth lily pad was unadorned. Lord Easu turned to face this one. When he did he was then facing 20 degrees NNE. Easu raised his head as he raised both arms in front of him, palms up. As he looked to the sky, our circle parted at that place. We all gazed in the direction to which Easu was pointing. There in the distant horizon was a huge Silver Disk. Slightly below the center of this Silver backdrop was seen a brilliant pin head of Orange. This minute dot of Orange stood bold against the Silver. The Orange was Maldek, the Silver Disk was the Moon-Malona.

Every eye was locked onto this view. It was awesome in its inspiration. The time was now approaching 0458 hours, the moment of the Full Moon. We lifted our circle and backed to the SSW, so that each and every one of us could get a panoramic view of the scene in its entirety. Without doubt, this was the most breathtaking spectacle the Shambhala Festival has ever presented. We were consumed with the Love emitted by this MAN as he projected this greeting of Love to us, to our beloved Earth Mother, and to the approaching new members of the Earth Family Complex. Easu is truly a MAN of Love and Understanding. The beauty of this scene shall be cherished forever!

The Aries Full Moon was upon us now, as we pulled back even farther to rejoin our circle. The circle of Humanity

NOTES:

rotated slowly as we silently made our way back home. Each witness was deep in thought. We gathered once again about the Cone of Golden Light. Quietly, subdued enriched and fulfilled, each one returned to their own sleeping body.

Shambhala is finished for another year, perhaps forever. We have never experienced a Shambhala that could compare to this one. We were impressed! But the Lord of the Earth has a way about him that grabs your attention!"

The Wesak Festival 1990

To conclude this chapter and this section of Volume Two, we offer our distortion of the Wesak Festival of 1990:

"The Full Moon came in at 1431 hrs. This is the Wesak Festival. Last night at 2300 hrs. we ascended the Great Golden Cone over our residence and the truncated apex was empty. Little Summer and Warm Night Rain offered the calling. Many came. Approximately one hour later we all slipped quietly away in the form of a great circle, and made our way to the sacred place on the high plateau on the Southern slopes of a mountain, deep in the Himalayas. The scene was familiar as we assumed our position above the sloping amphitheater terrain. Physical people were assembling below us. It was late in the afternoon, local time. The Sun was getting low. At dusk two small fires were built at the foot of the great rectangular rock that serves as the altar or speaker's platform. Local physical emissaries spoke briefly, but mostly it was quiet. Darkness set in and soon the Taurus Full Moon rose above the altar rock that we were all facing.

Soon entities began to manifest on the rock and there was a bit of milling about as they conversed with each other and occasionally assessed the audience. When the Moon cleared the eastern mountain the speaking began.

Kadar Monka was the first to speak. He told of the situation of Maldek, and Malona, and MAN'S role in the scheme of things. He spoke of his (MAN'S) responsibilities/duties and their limitations. Others of MAN also spoke.

NOTES:

Sandis spoke briefly, accepting his status as Lord of the Earth.

Easu also spoke briefly, offering his apologies and his Light and Love.

Mietraya spoke at length, admonishing the Wanderers to get on with the job for which they had chosen this incarnation. All things begin their change from within, and *only* the Wanderers singularly and then collectively, are authorized to initiate the action necessary to produce the change. Great Powers are standing by awaiting the call from Earth so that they might assist. Universal Law shall prevail. *"Light Bearers, commence the action!"* This was the message. Looking to the sky in a helpless state of bewilderment is not in keeping with the status of a Fourth, Fifth, or Sixth density Wanderer!

Mietraya admonished those who are not native to this Planet, but wear the body of Third Density Human, to get their priorities straight and . . . sleep a lot!

The Orion representative spoke next and confirmed the words of the World Teacher. Orion too is getting fidgety with the lack of physical results.

There were other speakers as well. The Archangel Gabriel spoke briefly, and Siddartha Gutama, the Buddha, closed the speaking ceremonies. This was *his* Festival.

We returned home before day break local time, and the group was dispersed back to their physical bodies."

Our final dreams just before arising this morning concerned scenes of childhood, when things were more simple. There was the obvious tendency to go back in time rather than to advance forward into the unknown of the New Dispensation. There was no misgivings, but the need to recollect the sweeter moments of our past was strong.

Lord Mietreya admonished all Wanderers, all Light Bearers/Love Bearers to set out to do that which they came here to do. The Green Ray is the tool to use for one's offering of service to our beloved Earth Mother. The method is as follows: envision a shaft of Emerald Green Love/Healing Energy coming from the Universe, entering into your Heart Chakra through the

NOTES:

stem to your spinal cord, up the spinal cord to the crown of your head and flowing like a fountain, forming a dome of Emerald Green Love/Healing Energy all around your physical body. Envision this energy flowing day and night. Make the dome solid and dense. Make it as large as you possibly can: 15 to 20 feet in diameter, 40 or 50 feet in diameter, or 75 to 100 feet in diameter! Make the dome as large as you are comfortably able. Now envision your great Dome of Green penetrating deep, deep into the Earth Mother, all the way down to the Earth's mantle — some 400 miles deep. Create this great shaft of Green Love/Healing Energy flowing into our beleaguered Planet. This will permit the Earth Mother to raise her vibrations so that she might rendezvous with her destiny and return once more to the family of Planets of this Solar System, as this Solar System in its orbit of a Great Central Sun in this Galaxy, moves into a new Sector of Space that has a vibration of Love and Harmony. This is the New Dispensation, the New Age. The Wanderers have chosen to incarnate on Earth as Third Density Human Beings to be eligible to perform this vital work. This is the *prime* reason for our being here. Meditate, penetrate the forgetting, remember who you *really* are, lets all get on with attending to our Father's business.

Use the Green Ray of Love/Healing/Manifestation via the Violet energy center, as you create the Dome/Shaft of Green Light for Earth Service. Whereever you travel, cut a swath of Love into the Earth. This work is *THE* most important service that you can render in this incarnation. Think on this. Act on this!

Conclusion

You shall now prepare to lower the Kundalini. Bring the White Light of the Kundalini up around yourself and gather it into an object over your head. As you do so, pull the Violet Dome next to your body. Now bring the Kundalini in its entirety into the crown of your head as you detach your consciousness. Begin the descent, deactivating each chakra, as we give the color countdown: Violet . . . Indigo . . . Blue . . . Green . . . Yellow

NOTES:

. . . Orange . . . Red . . . Put the Kundalini to rest and shut the door. Breath deeply.

Now, the Prayer of Protection: "In the name of the Presence and the Power Universal, protect us from harm and all Unenlightened Spirits, and may the Light of our Spirit Guides and the Light of our Higher Selves illuminate our thoughts that we might reflect the Radiant Glory of ALL THAT IS."

We leave you now in the Light and Love of our One Infinite Creator. Go forth in the joy of life and in the service to others.

Adonai. Adonai, Vasu Barragus, Adonai.

Section II

Healing

Healing is the ultimate service to others. The Will, polarity, and purity of the healer are the prime factors.

Chapter 5

We greet you in the Light and Love of our One Infinite Creator. We are Chief Little Summer and Warm Night Rain.

Let us begin this section with the chant:

"I am that I am, A-yeh,
I am that I am, A-yeh,
I am that I am, A-yeh,
I am that I am, A-yeh,
I am that I am, A-yeh,
I am that I am, A-yeh,
I am that I am, A-yeh,
A-yeh,
A-yeh,
A-yeh,
A-yeh,
A-yeh,"

Our Prayer of Protection: "In the Name of the Presence and the Power Universal, protect us from harm and all Unenlightened Spirits, and may the Light of our Spirit Guides and the Light of our Higher Selves illuminate our thoughts, that we might reflect the Radiant Glory of ALL THAT IS."

We ask that you now prepare yourself to raise your Kundalini. Have your backs quite straight as you align and balance your chakras. At the base of your spine awaken the Kundalini. Permit the Kundalini to rise as we give the color countdown. Activate all the proper functions you have been taught as the Kundalini passes through the stem of the Red Chakra . . . the Orange . . . the Yellow . . . the Green . . . the Blue . . . the Indigo . . . the Violet. Attach your consciousness to your Kundalini Energy. Now, envision the White Kundalini, with your consciousness thoroughly saturated therein, emitting from the crown of your head, gently coiling around the Silver Cord, reaching the Golden Sphere, your Higher Self. Saturate the lower hemisphere with your Kundalini Light — making your conscious contact. Encase your body with the White Light of your Kundalini, as you are fully protected by the great rainbow

NOTES:

dome of Light. Firmly establish your contact with your Higher Self, and when you are ready, begin to read.

Healing By The Adept

To begin this section on healing, let us state at the onset: *No one can heal someone else!* The healer is an instrument, an agent, endowed with certain skills who, when properly employed, permits the patient to heal him/herself. It matters not if you be the learned Doctor, the skilled surgeon, the gifted psychologist/psychiatrist, the shaman, the psychic healer, the medicine man, the witch doctor, or a plain out and out quack, *you* do not possess the power to heal anyone . . . anyone except yourself. Now, with the ego relegated to its appropriate station we can continue with the subject of healing.

Compassion is the agent that is the impetus for you to want to heal another. Compassion is an aspect of Love. Love is Intelligent Energy. It is this energy in the form of Light embracing the Green Ray that inspires the action commonly known as . . . healing.

We shall not attempt to give you a prospectus on the many herbs and pharmaceutical medicines, nor will we attempt to inform the surgeon of undiscovered aspects of anatomy. We shall not attempt to instruct the witch doctor in his dance or song. But we *will* tell you how and why they work . . . or do not work as is sometimes the case.

All things are possible via Love. Love is the Green Ray. Love is understanding. Understanding is achieved VIA Wisdom. Wisdom is the product of knowledge. It is this which we offer . . . for your consideration.

Some people are "born to heal," while others must diligently learn and practice it. Every one has some Green in their Aura. Some have more than others. Some souls are older/younger than others. All are individually unique. An abundance of Green in one's Aura indicates an abundance of Green, it does not indicate that the personality is a great healer. The entity endowed with a small ration of Love-Healing Green may actually put this precious asset to a more productive use

NOTES:

than does the well-endowed counterpart. It is the *desire* that counts, not the amount of Green gleaned through evolution.

The Qualified Healer

The healing can only be as good as the healer; Therefore, the healer must be balanced. To be balanced means that the healer *must* know self. Achieve this and healing has occurred within self. The healed, balanced self may now offer service to others with confidence and expectations of Positive results. The healer seeks to purify self. This is mental-mind over matter. All things begin with a thought. Meditation, quiet time, alone time, and are the necessary tools. Let a portion of your daily meditation program be devoted to looking within yourself, the express purpose being to *know and understand* self as well as possible. Dig deep. Examine every facet of the gem (yourself) from as many perspectives as you can think of. Be open to suggestion and direction from your own Higher Self. It is possible to successfully fool self, but you can *never* fool your Higher Self.

The second step is: To *accept* that which you discover/uncover about yourself. Your analysis of self will produce awareness of certain shortcomings that you are harboring within your beingness. Though it is sometimes distasteful, this you can no doubt do. Again, be honest. Attempting to fool self is the ambition of the chameleon.

Just as you discover and accept your shortcomings, the other side of the coin of acceptance must also be visited. As you look deep within you shall see your *Source,* and now you will also be obliged to accept your *greatness.* Accept your greatness in all due humility, of course! You will now be able to realize that you are what you have always been: a child of Love; a child of Light; a child of the Universe; a portion of the One Infinite Creator; a Co-Creator; a *Divine Being* . . . who has some shortcomings! You are both, and that is exactly what you are supposed to be. Know yourself. Accept yourself.

The third and final step is: Always be ready, willing, and able to —*forgive yourself.* If you truly forgive yourself then you automatically forgive *all* other selves. If you truly forgive other

NOTES:

selves then you automatically forgive yourself. Forgiveness of self eliminates the need for further self-punishment, which is the prime cause for at least 80% of *all* illness of physical/mental natures. Forgiveness of self is THE way that one heals self.

Understand this three step procedure: Know self, Accept self, and Forgive self. Work on this until you have achieved the desired results. Remember, the healing will only be as good as the healer. Through this procedure, you may prepare yourself to become an agent who assists others in healing themselves. These are the steps that you take for yourself; These are the steps that you *teach* to those who would have you heal them.

Learning The Lesson

As you forgive yourself, genuinely and sincerely, of course, you heal the experience. The experience that contained the lesson that was not properly resolved. The lesson that your Higher Self arranged for you . . . and will continue to provide unto you until such time that you, the personality, effectively and efficiently deal with it and resolve it. Your Higher Self will camouflage this lesson in a variety of vehicles. Often this lesson is brought from one lifetime to the next; and this is called Karma. Karma is an agent that often causes illness within the Mind/Body/Spirit Complex. Resolving the lesson and forgiving the self is *the* way that Karma is totally eliminated. This knowledge is critical to the one who aspires to be an effective healer.

History tends to repeat itself. Unresolved lessons from Past Lives are brought forward into the current incarnation. The Higher Self disguises the lesson in different vehicles for your discovery. Sometimes the Higher Self will repeat the lesson even after it has successfully been resolved, just to *test* the personality, to check if all is in good working order. You do not forget the lesson after having completed it; on the contrary, you utilize the results as you incorporate this new-found knowledge into your daily activities. This is how you grow. It is called evolution.

NOTES:

Forgiving self or inspiring another to forgive self can be complicated by the lack of awareness of the incident or experience that one is forgiving self for. A major aspect of any healing is to be able to penetrate the forgetting to such a degree that the memory will be of service. Resolving a lesson that is not consciously identified becomes the issue for most people. Often the conscious memory is insufficiant and it becomes impossible for the personality to remember the incident which requires the understanding, accepting, and forgiving. This may be accomplished through self-hypnosis or via a professional hypnotist. A regression in some manner to early childhood is in order. Regression to Past Lives could possibly be useful but usually is not necessary. History does repeat itself, the Higher Self sees to that. Recalling the appropriate event in the current life is usually sufficient. Meditation, employing a discipline of self-analysis, is often adequate for the personality lacking the ways and means of skilled professional help. The Kundalini Meditation is highly recommended for the self healing self. The procedure describes how the healer can cause the other self (patient) to recall the events that require in-depth investigation.

When the event/experience has been isolated, mentally open up the burial mound that is so handsomely adorned with beautiful flowers, and extract the unresolved lesson. It no doubt will be impossible to physically "fix" the past situation. This is not a problem unless you choose to create a road block for yourself so that you might continue on with your program of self-punishment. If this be your choice (and you always have a choice) then the teaching of healing ends for you right here.

Continue to remind yourself that all physical reality is indeed an illusion. Within an illusion, your illusion, you may do anything you wish. Mentally extract the lesson. Using different sets of probabilities, recreate the past in a fashion that would permit the greatest understanding of the value of the event/experience for all concerned. Your 20/20 hindsight vision will be most useful here. "Fix up" the event in a way that is pleasing and satisfying to you as you adjust the facts until it

NOTES:

comes out "just right" . . . forgiving self and forgiving other selves in the process.

Repeat the process for all the "burial mounds" that you are able to recall. Your Higher Self will assist you in this work. As you resolve your laggard lessons, you will naturally eliminate the root cause for you to punish self. You punish self because of the innate nag to accomplish something — something that you cannot quite put your finger on. In your frustration you will often choose to punish self via ill health. This is a most common practice for the adult Human Being. Children can usually enlist the services of an adult to administer the needed chastisement. We are all taught "crime and punishment" from a very early age. We are all a product/victim of our culture.

If another self were to happen along and note your new and improved version of the past, he/she might be critical of your misuse of "the facts," as history has now recorded. "They" may accuse you of being a liar, a fabricator of the "truth." To these ones you simply reply: life is an illusion. This is *my* life; this is my illusion. I have resolved my life in a way that is pleasing and rewarding to me. If you do not approve of my new version of the past then *you've* got the problem; I've resolved mine! In the course of life this is not only permissible, it is highly recommended! Our System of Jurisprudence would frown on this activity. But remember, the courts and laws created by Third Density Inhabitants on a speck of dust called Earth *did not* create the laws that govern the Universe. The process just described is precisely the work that the entity engages immediately upon entering the appropriate plane after entertaining the transition that we commonly call death. If you wish to break the cycle and silence the Karmic Wheel . . . and heal yourself — do this NOW, *before the* incarnation terminates! If you successfully accomplish this, then you have the rest of your incarnation to enjoy being free and clear of any past debts. All is possible under the auspices of the Green Ray of Love, in the arena of an illusion!

When the mind knows itself, accepts itself, and forgives itself then healing has occurred within the healer. It must be your

NOTES:

sincere desire to be the agent that causes this phenomenon to occur in another self.

Balancing Love And Wisdom

The balancing of Love and Wisdom is the order of the day and becomes a way of life for the personality. This is always in a constant state of refining, for no personality is ever perfect. We strive for perfection in our return to the One Infinite Creator knowing, always knowing, that only the Creator is perfect.

The true healer will have crystallized his/her chakras. This is accomplished by continuously, permanently, aligning and balancing the seven chakras and keeping them all crystal clear and clean. The healing is only as good as the healer.

The would-be healer is strong in his/her desire to serve. The accomplished healer maintains this great desire. This is Compassion personified. Compassion must be balanced with Wisdom. Sometimes impulse offsets the balance, to the detriment of Wisdom. This is of course unfortunate, but not at all unusual. Quite often this impulse proves to be the chink in the armor of the balanced healer.

Karma is often the cause of a mental/physical illness. The illness thus serves as a catalyst to promote a lesson to the entity who is ill and/or to others who are interacting with the one who is ill. The Soul or perhaps several other Souls may be prospering due to the compound experiences offered by this catalyst. The personality(s) involved may not be so appreciative. Now, the healer arrives on the scene. Compassion is great, as it should be — indifference is *not* the way of the healer. Perhaps on impulse, the healer instigates a healing. It is possible for the determined Will of the healer to override Karma, at least for the time being. The healing now having taken place; the beautiful catalyst so carefully set up by the Higher Self, is now destroyed — the lessons never having been discovered, and certainly not having been resolved. The Higher Self thinking in terms of eternity simply lays plans for another appropriate catalyst. The healed personality is joyful with his new-found good health, only to find that at some later time the problem shall return in perhaps

NOTES:

another part of the body, and possibly in the form of a different vehicle, for the personality shall continue to punish self in one way or another. Thus, the well-intended healing was simply an experience for all concerned, and resulted in nothing gained or resolved. One must need look beyond the desires of the personality and attempt to perceive the overall picture.

The forced Will of the impulsive healer affected Karma. The healer is completely responsible for his/her actions. Karma could readily be *earned* by the well-intentioned healer. Wisdom is a balancing factor of magnanimous importance. Wisdom seldom supplies the impetus to heal, but is the agent which makes the successful healing total. There are times when it is wise to heal. There are times when it is just as wise to refrain from healing. The "born healer" would automatically know the appropriate action to take. The rest of you "would be" healers shall have to learn, perhaps the hard way. This is in no way intended to discourage you or to dampen your desire to offer your healing services to others. Not at all! We simply remind you that if you override the Free Will of another, even with sound Positive intent, the end result will be Negative. You will have resolved nothing for the other self; meanwhile, you are collecting Karma for yourself. Ignorance is not bliss!

If there is any doubt in your mind as to whether a healing should be initiated, we respectfully suggest that you simply invoke the Light (Green Ray). The Light possessing the Intelligence of the Creator will certainly know if a healing is appropriate at this time. For the sake of learning it might be wise to form a private opinion of the matter and then patiently await the outcome. If you were wrong, meditate on it and try to discover where lies your error. If you were correct, meditate on the matter to discover what you did that was correct. This is an excellent way to grow and mature without accumulating Karma. The eyes of compassion suggests action; therefore, "why not?" injects the ego. We suggest that you rise above the situation and look about as you try to get the Karmic Picture as presented by the Higher Self. You are not placing yourself in judgment of

NOTES:

another. Not at all. You are assessing the situation and attempting to understand. Love is understanding.

The At-Oneness With Self

You are a Mind, a Body, a Spirit (Higher Self) Complex. The goal is to bring yourself in harmony with the totality of self. The Mind and the Body come together quite normally, all Humans do this. Via meditation the Mind and Spirit come together in communication. Most Third Density Entities do not meditate, and therefore contact with their Higher Self is but a myth — according to their understanding. During meditation, the consciousness detaches from the body to reach the Magical Personality, the Higher Self. This is quite normal. Now, to achieve the unity with the totality of self it is necessary for the Mind/Body/Spirit *Complex* to function as *one* — *The Law is ONE.*

When you, the healer, offer your service to another it is almost always necessary for you to make some form of physical contact or perform some type of physical activity. Mind/Body can handle this quite nicely. But, the true healer also refers to the able assistance of his/her own Higher Self and the cooperation of the other self's Higher Self.

This is difficult to achieve if the body is also active at the time. The healer must learn to incorporate the Higher Self in all Mind/Body activities. This is accomplished by the willful trust and acceptance of *following your intuition!* Your intuition is your Higher Self offering guidance and instruction, not only for the purposes of healing, but in *all* things. Discipline your mind to seek instruction from its Source. Be open to suggestion. Go with your intuition even at such times when it might be in opposition with logic and reasoning. Learn to trust. Practice it. Your ego will be your nemesis. In understanding the mechanics of this working, with practice, the budding Adept can achieve the coveted status of "at oneness with self."

This at oneness with self now permits the healer to completely attune/attach self to the other self to be healed. You, the Mind/Body/Spirit Complex, can now integrate yourself

NOTES:

within another Mind/Body/Spirit Complex. This is accomplished *if* there exists a mutual *desire* by both the healer and the one to be healed. Mutual desire signifies that the necessary permission has been granted and that Free Will is not being thwarted.

It is appropriate that the Adept/Healer consciously accept his/her completeness. The at oneness is evident. The Law of ONE is being practiced. Harmony prevails. Peace and tranquility abides within. Confidence is your companion. You are at one with the Universe and at one with Creation. You humbly and knowledgeably assume the status that you were born to. You are a Co-Creator. See yourself in the other self. All are equal; the Law is ONE. You have integrated yourself and you have healed yourself. Now, share this blessing with your other self, which is simply an extension of yourself. The healer and the patient become one. The other self is the reflection of self.

It is entirely possible for *any* entity native to Third Density, through intense Love and strength of Will to become a qualified healer — momentarily. Their blocked and distorted chakras may be cleared and balanced *instantaneously* through intense compassion. This is a random happening that is quite rare and not likely to be repeated. To be the true healer one must train the self in the disciplines of the self. The Co-Creator *knows* this.

The Responsibility Of Power

The energies of the Planet and the energies of the Cosmos are available to the balanced healer. These are awesome powers at your disposal. You have *asked* for power and you have *received* the power. You are responsible for the *results* of this asking. This is not a task to be taken lightly. Your Spirit Guides and your Higher Self are always available to help you through areas and procedures which you are not all that familiar with at first. Follow your intuition and be open to guidance. Avoid setting predetermined goals or anticipated results. There are no guarantees. Accept what is presented to you. The Higher Selves of those involved are actually conducting the event. You

NOTES:

are but the agent of cause. Play your role, but do not overplay it. Remember, the healer cannot heal anyone.

At this point you have succeeded in bringing harmony/unity between Intelligent Infinity (Light, Green Ray) and yourself. You may now bring harmony/unity between self and other self. You have come to realize and accept that there is no polarity, only harmony and unity, the at oneness with *ALL*. This is healing. You are a healer. Be as perfect, as balanced as possible.

As you go through your procedure/practice of healing, whatever your title may be, bear in mind that you are the honored instrument that skillfully offers the appropriate catalyst that permits the patient to heal himself. The patient is responsible for him/herself. You cannot assume this responsibility for another. Guide the patient into a status of independence, as responsibility for self is assumed. As the healer the idea is to put yourself out of business as soon as possible. This, dear one, *is* success!

Chapter 6

At this point it is hoped that the healer has purified and qualified him/herself, and is now ready and able to pursue the honor/duty of offering healing services to others. May your lifestyle be so dedicated that you are always in a constant state of refining the self, as you seek a greater and greater balance between Compassion and Wisdom. You have healed yourself via understanding, resolving, and forgiving yourself. This is the successful format that you have used on self. This is the essence of healing that you teach/share with others. Always remember: the healing is only as good as the healer. Your desire, your dedication, your disciplined Will distinguishes you from the would-be healers. Be as perfect as you dare.

The Causes Of Illness

The body is a creature of the mind's creation. We are all the result of mind over matter. The mind power can produce both Positive and Negative results. Positive results would be defined as "good health." Therefore, why would anyone willfully produce Negative results? At first glance this would seem preposterous. Given the second thought you can readily see that we all are guilty of doing it. The Law of Cause and Effect governs the Third Density Entity. All dealings with healing or any other physical activity will be integrated within this Universal Law.

When understanding is present, healing becomes simplified. The effect is obviously the illness. The question becomes: what *caused* the effect/illness? Most healing practices are designed to treat only the symptoms. If the symptoms are eliminated then a successful healing has been achieved. Not so. The cause, the root cause, has never been discovered or dealt with. The illness is the product of the mind's creation. Illness/accidents do not "happen," they are caused.

If the symptoms are "cured," then the mind will simply re-establish the same illness or another type of illness else where

NOTES:

in the body; thus, a true healing has not occurred at all. This is a highly desirable system for those who are dedicated to the commercial aspect of healing. Business is continuous from the cradle to the grave. If the root cause is discovered and properly dealt with then the show is over; there is no future return for the healer. It is the healer's duty to be so efficient that he works himself out of business. Not all within the healing professions agree with this philosophy!

A knowledge of anatomy, bodily functions, chemistry, diet, and other learned aspects of the Human Body is of course, most useful. One should not hesitate to acquire such information. The psychological make-up of the individual should also be taken into consideration, *even for the most minute problem.* Small problems may often compound and become great problems in the future. The symptoms of the great problem are dealt with fervor and zest, until the great problem is conquered. The little problem that sponsored the great problem is seldom ever sought out. It goes unnoticed — too minor! The minor problem simply regroups and focuses its energy to another part of the body, history repeats itself, and a true healing never occurs — not on a physical level, not on an emotional level, not on a mental level, and certainly not on a spiritual level. The Soul continues to prod the personality to grasp the lesson and resolve it.

The healing of the illness may not actually be doing the other self any favor. Lessons are learned through catalysts. Catalysts are created and programmed by the Higher Self. If this well-laid plan is thwarted by the overzealous healer, then the other self is only temporarily being relieved of pain and illness. He will be doomed to repeat the catalyst until the lessons are learned and resolved. Compassion is the impetus for healing. Remember to inject the necessary Wisdom for the *balance.* The thesis must be balanced with the anti-thesis — patience vs. impatience. This is the dilemma of the beginning healer. It is relatively easy to find work; it is not always so easy to determine when and where to apply one's talents.

Illness is punishment. *Almost* always it is a form of self-punishment. We have been taught "crime and punishment" at a

NOTES:

very early age by our parents and other well-meaning adults. This is a common practice, for our culture *demands* it. We are trained into conformity via the threat of the awesome fear of punishment. Thus the child learns to be "good." Through peer pressure/teaching the children openly practice these teachings to the delight, the obvious delight, of their elders. It is quickly learned that "bad things" can be rectified via punishment. Punishment must be administered. The child seeks the cooperation of the adult to perform this function. Custom is being made. The culture is smugly satisfied.

But what of the unpunished "crime?" The act that you committed as a child that nobody noticed. If religion was a part of your childhood, then crime and sin often become synonymous. Parents were gods. The parent's rules became God's laws. In the eyes of the child all were the same thing. "Fear of the Lord and repent" became the battle cry. God, the Lord, and parents all became confused. Almost any unorthodox activity was bound to offend someone! Conformity was seen to be the safest path to follow. This was the path of the least resistance. The sense of "getting away with something," had its delightful appeal but now enters the concept of "sin" . . . and God requires/-*demands* that you be punished. The unpunished crime/sin produces guilt. Guilt grows. Guilt lasts forever and ever. Guilt persists long after the event has been forgotten. Guilt is erased via punishment. Thus, the stage is set. During the pre-school years, the foundation is laid for an elaborate system of self-punishment. There are almost no exceptions to this practice within *civilized* people.

The young child can usually find a willing adult to administer the punishment.. The adolescent seeks more sophisticated methods of punishment. This is commonly called discipline. The system is effective, and in the eyes of the culture it seems to work. This system usually finds no conflicts with religious tenets. By young adulthood the pattern is indelibly engraved in the make-up of the personality.

Adulthood now poses a much more difficult and serious problem. An adult cannot be punished in the same fashion that

NOTES:

is customary for the child. There are various ways that the ingenious adult might pursue in order to receive his/her just share of the allotment of the purifying punishment. The sins/crimes have now become a way of life. Unfortunately, they are seldom illegal and so the police are of little help. The prime method chosen in almost all cases is poor health. Illness in any form becomes the sin admitted and the welcome agent to purify the troubled conscious. Illness is highly acceptable to self and to Deity as well. A chronic illness is truly a gift from God in the eyes of the habitual sinner. This becomes the balancer. Self successfully punishes self, and this saves the Lord the trouble and bother. The Lord will be pleased when He checks over this grand record of intense suffering! Other selves will admire the tenacity of these heroes displaying their unbridled agony of self-flagellation! Preposterous did you say? Look about you it's happening everywhere. You might even try checking your mirror!

It is not so unusual for a personality to believe so strongly in the punishment of self that he will continue the activity right up to his death . As the final curtain comes down this is often the stage for the grand finale. Even death must be some form of a struggle. This is seen as securing a better seat in Heaven. This struggle is interpreted as "work" and the reward is therefore "earned." This is secretly admired by the survivors. The struggler knows this, for he has been an addicted admirer himself. A struggling death is actually a sophisticated form of suicide. Suicide is rarely acceptable by the culture, but a dramatic ending to the incarnation is remembered in story and in song. The witnesses will remember the event with pride and say amongst themselves that this one will find a special place in Heaven. The rewards for all the sacrifices can indeed be truly great! As you may have suspected, this is being told with "tongue in cheek." Truth can also be humorous!

NOTES:

Crime And Punishment Versus Self Punishment

The process of punishing self can develop into "big business," as the personality enhances and refines the many opportunities that are naturally available. Due to the Third Density's concept of "linear" time, it is deemed impossible to return to the scene of the "crime/-event", and redo history. From a physical point of view, this is no doubt correct; whereas, from a mental point of view, nothing is impossible. The average Human Being is not keen on thinking, he/she are mostly do-ers. This being a task that cannot be physically accomplished, the situation is seen as hopeless. The only viable alternative is continued punishment of self. If the health is sufficiently sacrificed then compensation has been achieved and atonement has been satisfied in the eyes of culture, civil, and religious law. Is this not the concept of the jail?

We are stuck with the system, though it obviously does not work. For those of you who are capable of seeing through the fallacy of crime and punishment there is hope. For those who cannot, or will not, then we heartily assure these ones that evolution, however slowly, will certainly take it's toll! Accepting the thesis that it is possible to mentally go back in time, is the tool necessary to begin the healing process. Since memory is available to almost all of us, this becomes quite easy. To project one's thoughts into the future or the past is a commonly accepted mental activity.

The second step is to accept the physical vibration to which we, the Third Density Mass Consciousness, have given a reality, as being an *illusion.* All physical reality is an illusion. The non-physical or etheric, is always the true reality. The physical is the *reflection* of the etheric. For most people, this is an astonishing thought. With a bit of effort, it can actually be accepted on the mental level. However, the physical application is something else again. This blood is real! This pain is real! These taxes are real! The illusion is the myth. Life is real. To

NOTES:

accept life as being an illusion is most difficult even for the advanced and evolved mind.

For you to mentally go back to some point in the past and mentally re-live an event is something that you could readily do. You could resolve the lesson that was issued at the time, and dutifully forgive self and perhaps other selves. You could do this. You would also probably chalk it up to imagination. It is not likely that you could cause yourself to *believe* that you have the power to change history. But remember, all teachings have their beginnings based on beliefs. All understanding is founded on original and ancient beliefs. You can believe that you can change the past *if* you are willing to admit that life is an *illusion.* Failing this, put head back in sand and continue the practice of healing the symptoms of the illness and give no further concern to the root cause. Life is seen as hopeless and cruel with no possible way out of the eternal syndrome of self punishment, *unless* you are willing to accept the reality as the illusion it truly is. Think carefully on this. It is a major undertaking. Culture and convention are being reversed. We are teaching you the opposite of what you have been taught all your life. You know truth when it hits you. You also perceive it as a rather large pill to swallow! Take your time, it will go down. Perhaps your mental/spiritual capacity is being challenged?

Death Being Satisfied

Certain illnesses have the capacity to produce the transition we know as death. Even minor problems have the potential to become sufficiently complicated to cause this effect. A means, an *accepted* means, to terminate an incarnation must always exist in the Third Density Vibration. Cancer and heart attacks are two of several viable and socially acceptable means to achieve this end. Not if, but when cancer and heart problems are conquered, another acceptable disease will appropriately come forth to continue the service of terminating the incarnation. Only a few decades ago, smallpox and pneumonia were the prominent "killers." Cancer and heart problems existed at that time also but their services were not in demand. The vehicles

NOTES:

will change, they always do. Finding the cure for cancer in itself creates countless catalysts that have a variety of uses. The *finding* of the cure can become as important as the cure itself. Experiences abound and life is designed for the experience that it offers.

If the cancer is treated and perhaps cured, is the mission completed? No, not really. The cancer will simply re-appear elsewhere, or perhaps some other diabolical disease will be forthcoming. The source was never attacked. What then is the source of cancer? The Red Ray associated with the Yellow Ray is almost always the cause. We suggest that you refresh your memory by referring to Section One of this Volume; but essentially, in the Third Density Vehicle the Red Ray is sex and/or anger. The Yellow Ray is emotions. Frustration, despair, and hopelessness are forms of anger. They may also be forms of sex. These feelings, strengthened by the powerful force of emotion, can readily create an internal distortion which can readily provide the appropriate blockages of life-giving energies that promote and maintain good health. These Red and Yellow Ray blockages probably had their beginnings in pre-school and early school years. Fear and guilt are the emotions. The unbalanced combinations of Red and Yellow are deadly to the Human Being. It is in these areas thate the root causes lie. It is here thate the real healing must take place before a permanent cure can be effected. Chemotherapy will not accomplish this!

The causes of illnesses usually originate within the lifetime as a catalyst to cause the personality to experience a lesson for which the Soul wishes the knowledge. Karma is the next major source. Unresolved lessons from Past Lives may be brought forward for the new personality to deal with. The illness may be a permanent deabilitating handicap that provides a permanent catalyst. The personality learning to deal and even struggle with such a problem offers to the Soul a unique type of experience. The personality may or may not grasp this. Either way, a complete healing is not likely to occur. If the handicapped personality is playing the role of the teacher then a partial or complete healing *would* be possible — depending on *who* is

NOTES:

the student. If the M.D. is the targeted student, there would probably be a healing. If the parents are the students then the catalyst will probably last the lifetime. In this case, other selves who are obliged to deal with this handicapped one, in some way or another, will have their lives affected to some degree in some fashion. Thus, the affected personality can readily serve as a teacher to others as well as aptly play the role of the student. The Souls of all those involved understand the totality of this abnormal experience. The personalities involved probably do not. Awareness of this knowledge would not necessarily spoil the catalyst. On the contrary, if thinking individuals are involved the catalyst is enhanced. The accepted inability to change the physical conditions, and now understanding *why* this catalyst is presented, can readily result in a much more profound understanding of self and other selves.

Our Final Opportunity

The end of the Piscean Age is upon us. As this cycle closes with the prospects of a magnificently new and different cycle awaiting, the Soul thinks in terms of making up for incomplete or neglected experiences from the distant past. This creates a tremendous assortment of opportunities/catalysts for the bewildered personality to deal with. The rising vibrations of the Earth Mother herself enhance this situation. The personality is often responding to this "push me — pull me" stress by exhibiting various stages of insanity. The Higher Self decrees that this condition is affordable simply because this is the final generation to experience Third Density life on this beleaguered Planet. This is the last chance. No future incarnations will be available. The last minute rush is on, as the confused and bewildered personality shops around for the appropriate experience. It is obvious that the mentality of all of us is being affected. Some are advancing to new and unheard of heights of awareness, while others are regressing to depths of despair and insanity. Considering the times, this unparalleled condition is indeed appropriate.

NOTES:

Organ Transplants

If the failing heart were to be replaced by another healthy organ this action would have the intent of prolonging that life span. Is this then, right or wrong? First of all, this is a *very* unique experience, and the Soul thrives on experiences. For a Doctor to prolong or even save a life, deals with Karma. This could be Karma being initiated, or it could be Karma being satisfied. Does the surgeon, the doctor, the healer have this right? The right, the honor, and the duty, actually, are not prime factors, though they undoubtedly would be distorted as such. Compassion is the impetus to heal. (hopefully money is not the inspiration.) If this is reasonably balanced with wisdom and the patient and the healer are mutually consenting, then Free Will has not been abridged, and the experience is valid. The possible lack of success could produce guilt or remorse. This is immature. However, in Third Density these attitudes could easily be expressed. Success or failure produces growth for all concerned. The wisdom factor of the healer is tested.

Faith Healing

Does the religious healer, the evangelist, fall into the same category as the surgeon who performs the heart transplant? No, not at all. The surgeon is demonstrating *skill,* while the evangelist is demonstrating *power.* Though no doubt Positive in intent, the evangelist is Negative in the practice. The one to be healed probably volunteered for receiving the service, nevertheless, the method employed removes the Free Will from the patient, and results are *forced* into action. The evangelist dominates and controls the Will, the Mind, and the Body of the patient. You might liken these facts unto the surgeon, but there is a marked difference. The evangelist cannot predict the outcome, nor does he prepare the patient for the procedure, mentally or otherwise. He probably doesn't know himself. The doctor, on the other hand, is prepared, and he shares the preparation/knowledge with his patient. The doctor's patient consents with knowledge. The evangelist's patient consents with faith and often fear.

NOTES:

The evangelist calls upon power and he receives it. He does not question the source of the power. He presumes it to be from God. Power to heal like this *must* come from God. The strength of Will — the ego of the preacher — is the nucleus or seat of this power. The patient is exchanging his/her Free Will for good health, the healing. The evangelist receives fame and perhaps fortune. Service to self is the ultimate result. Orion supplies the power through his unwitting agent, the evangelist. The evangelist has developed the ability to focus his concentrated energy upon the patient. The weak-willed patient . . . surrenders. Orion is on the verge of capturing another, all in the name of Jesus! Is it any wonder that our Lord weeps? In all fairness, the evangelist probably does not realize that he is the dupe of Orion because he is not apt to recognize himself in our words. Eliminate the root cause and the healing will be effected. Neither the evangelist or the surgeon addresses this subject.

Illness Vs Soul Levels

Then what about the infant, the very young child? Crime and punishment could not possibly be a factor with these ones. The stillborn, the crib death, the child who survives no more than two or three years, these ones are destined to this chosen or assigned experience. The Infant Soul or the low Baby Soul would opt for this short term life experience, for it was none too keen on accepting the incarnation anyway. The offering of a healing to the child would render no observed results. The healing; i.e., understanding, should be offered to the *parents*. If the child's parents are Baby or Young Souls (and most are in this category), their knowledge/understanding is practically nil. Religious beliefs could easily cause the parents to feel the child's death was all their fault. Un-earned guilt could plague them all their lives. The healer's services could be most valuable here. Ignorance is *not* bliss!

Chapter 7

Healing The Experience

Cause and Effect is the Law. The healing process must embrace this Law. The effects are rather obvious, while the cause is often camouflaged in obscurity. A true and permanent healing *heals the experience* that was the true cause which produced the undesired effects. The Creator created Creation for the *experience* of the thing. Life *is* experience. Some experiences are considered to be "good," some are remembered as "bad," while a great number of experiences have been completely dismissed from the conscious mind. These ones are relegated to the so-called subconscious mind. Thus, the original experiences that are actually the prime causes of today's illnesses are completely forgotten by the ailing personality. The permanent healing requires that these experiences be brought forth, recognized, and resolved. If the lesson is adequately resolved mentally, then healing has been initiated . . . providing the personality is *willing to forgive* him/herself and break the destructive pattern of self-punishment.

The Root Cause

Obviously, healing is a physical activity. The emotional scars which caused the illness are not all that visible. Mentally understanding why the personality is bent on punishing self is the key. Counseling may be helpful. Since psychologists often do not have a firm understanding of Past Lives, Karma, and the various aspects of Soul Levels their contribution to the discovery of the root cause is quite often limited. Consequently, the effects or symptoms receive the attention. Initially treating the symptoms is usually most proper. However, somewhere in the course of the treatment an in-depth look and investigation should also be in order. This rarely happens.

The personality's childhood distortion of events and experiences is the prime ground for the healer to conduct the search. Almost all adult problems had their beginnings here. The incident is probably forgotten because of its obvious insignifi-

NOTES:

cance. The adult knows and accepts this — the child did not; but the child is now gone — and the adult stands in its place.As the *ramifications* of the unresolved lessons linger, they compound as they are conveniently distorted to blend with other emotional wounds. The wounds heal via the forgetting and the establishing of a more refined system of priorities. The scar tissue remains. The scar(s) itself is not always indicative of the true event. The personality will blend two or more events into a conglomeration, thus creating a sufficient magnitude to make the experience "worthwhile."

Subconsciously the personality has always known that the reality is actually an illusion and un-hesitantly takes the liberty to re-create the past. The conscious mind sees this as folly because logic and reason has been dutifully instilled. Tapping into the subconscious is the key to persuading the patient to recall the necessary events that require mental reconstruction. The exact procedure will be fully explained in the final chapter of this section.

Birth Defects

If the adult yet carries with him/her, a birth defect or a childhood affliction, this is a constant reminder of the past. Occasionally others may "poke fun" at the abnormality, or otherwise offer some distasteful remark. The afflicted adult has heard this before and the trained, practiced defense system goes into operation and the distasteful event is dismissed. But the effect of the impact is *NOT* dismissed. The old scar adds more tissue . . . for protection. The emotional energy that the unpleasant situation has generated, is seldom released. Self-discipline has been learned so that conflict and other anti-social behavior may be eliminated. The unreleased energy contained and hidden within the body is now beginning to fester. A blockage of one or more energy centers ensues. This compounds the probability of illness. The snowball effect has been set in motion. If the personality had been taught the method of converting raw emotion into Love, and then shared this transmutation with

NOTES:

others, the collective problem could be very Positive and useful. (see Chapter Four, Section One, Volume Two.)

Birth defects and early acquired afflictions are often the product of Karma. Past Lives may very well have been conducted in such a way that the Soul deemed it fitting and proper that this particular handicap would be the appropriate catalyst to permit the personality to engage/enjoy the necessary experiences to enhance the prosperous growth/evolution of the Soul. The learn/teach, teach/learn would be enormously effective for all concerned. You will remember that the personality is always a Free Will "employee" of his Soul. The older the Soul becomes, the more specialized the experiences must be. Disharmony (illness) produces experiences. The Soul, seeking balance, requests experience in both arenas.

Guidance Via Illness

Minor illnesses such as colds and minor injuries — cuts and bruises are not the subtle methods that the Higher Self uses to attract the attention of the lower self — the personality. The cold may be the agent to cause the personality to get some much-needed rest. The injury may be the instrument to cause the personality to pay stricter attention to detail. These are "spur-of-the-moment" catalysts to guide and direct the lower self. During the course of the diurnal cycles, chronic debilitating or terminal problems are the ones that are associated with Karma or major lessons. The life pattern, with its innumerable cycles, must be fulfilled. Being born without a memory, the personality has no concept of what this may be. The Law of Confusion reigns. If medical science prolongs the life, does this alter the life patterns? The seemingly prolonging of life may actually be a part of the intended life pattern. When this is the case, medical science can indeed work miracles.

Mentally Preparing The Patient

With the permission and cooperation of the other self, the healer now begins the verbal instruction and teaching that precedes the procedure. The healer by this time has established

NOTES:

a working understanding of the relationship between the mind, and the Mass Consciousness, and with the Cosmic Mind. As this relationship becomes more comfortable and therefore acceptable, the ability to attune self to other selves becomes easy and practical. The ability to observe the broad spectrum of the other self is permissible. Tunnel vision is eliminated. The ability to "see" from the view of the Higher Self allows the healer to discover the various Past Lives that are of importance. The Higher Self of the other self permits this peek into the Monad. This is not always an important or determining factor; but if it is, the Higher Selves, along with the Prime Guides, are all working in cooperation with the Light as the Green Ray is introduced via the healer.

In the process of healing the Higher Self is often referred to as the Magical Personality. By properly invoking the Magical Personality the healer establishes a bridge between the Time/Space and Space Time, and the Higher Self actually experiences the physical Third Density Vibration. This will last for the duration of the healing. Upon completion of the healing ritual, it is mandatory that the healer *release* its Higher Self, to its normal and proper configuration; i.e., the all-wise monitor of its charge, the personality . . . you! This releasing is accomplished either by thought or by gesture, or both. The apprentice healer, the budding Adept, utilizes a greater and greater percentage of the Magical Personality with each working. This working relationship is carefully controlled by the Higher Self as it methodically grows, even as it is *earned* by the personality. The ego is often the major factor that determines this rate of growth. The more transparent the personality, the more accelerated the development.

The Magical Personality/Higher Self is: Love, Wisdom, and Power. These are the major aspects of the whole — the unit. As the Adept/Healer taps into its Higher Self, these parts become the three major tools that the healer uses to develop the self. After some refining these aspects are shared with the other self in the form of a healing. The Higher Self is versatile, highly experienced, and void of emotion. This configuration permits the

NOTES:

Green Light to flow productively and unbiased. It is appropriate that the budding Adept approaches this understanding by balancing Love and Wisdom, as the power is sought for the purpose of serving. The Kundalini meditation is an ideal method for the healer to seek this understanding as the development of self continues in its refinement. The preparation of self must be as adequate as possible *before* the patient and his problems are tackled.

The patient has been made aware and understands the probability/possibility that his illness is self-inflicted. With this knowledge the healing has already begun. Preparation through counseling is mandatory. The procedure will have minor effect if the patient is not appraised of the "total picture." As the patient accepts the knowledge of self and seriously considers forgiving self and other selves, he/she will come face to face with self. This could be quite sudden, and probably for the very first time. This confrontation with self could be disastrous to the entity of immature evolution. The Infant, Baby, and the early stages of the Young Soul would be especially susceptible to this shock. The healer is responsible. Use your wisdom; great power is involved in the healing process. Preparatory counseling could easily involve several hours. The healer should not be on a tight schedule. A "Pandora's box" is being opened. The healer must be ready and prepared for *any* kind of unpredictable happenings.

Love, Wisdom, and *Power* are now passing through the hands of the healer. If this responsibility seems awesome to you then perhaps you should give the matter some extra thought as you include the learning of this work in your daily meditations. If, on the other hand, you are not in awe of this great power then we would suggest that you take a closer look at your humility. If the healer is an adventuresome fool then disaster lurks.

Love, Wisdom, and Power are the three major aspects that make up the Higher Self — The Magical Personality. These are the tools of the healer. The apprentice healer might think of these three aspects as unbalanced in the beginning; but, as Love and Wisdom are consciously brought into a reasonable balance

NOTES:

as Isosceles Triangle is formed. The two equal and long sides are Love and Wisdom, while the very short base is Power. As the balancing of Love and Wisdom becomes more and more practical and easier to incorporate in daily living, then the Higher Self permits larger amounts of Power to flow into the base of this Isosceles Triangle. Through experience and time the Power segment of this Triangle grows until the Isosceles Triangle has formed into an Equilateral Triangle. This is a perfect working balance. This is the goal. It takes time, patience and perseverance to achieve these tools. Your Higher Self is eager to share. The personality must prepare self to be worthy. Power is earned. Love-Wisdom is acquired through hard work by analyzing experiences and through meditation on Love, on Wisdom, and on Power.

As you begin your program of preparing yourself, the balancing of Love and Wisdom may seem like energies simply being shifted from one side to the other and forward progress is not being made at all. Think of this procedure as the winnowing of wheat. When the wheat is poured from one container to another, the wind removes some of the chaff. As the wheat is shifted back and forth it becomes purer and cleaner. As the shifting between Love and Wisdom continues, a more pure, solid balance results. Experience is the teacher. Power to do work is then gradually added by your Higher Self. The disciplined personality then becomes the trusted, dependable, qualified healer. The Equilateral Triangle is now properly formed.

It is the honor/duty of the healer to permit/cause the patient to look within self to seek/discover the root cause of the self-punishment that has now manifested in the illness. The mental attitude of the patient cannot be stressed too much. The mind is powerful. When the awesome power of the mind accepts the Creator's Love/Healing Energy of the Green Ray nothing is impossible! As thought forms of scenes of yesteryear are placed in the consciousness of the patient, emotions are often forthcoming. The healer must prepare and condition self to calmly deal with whatever is presented, sometimes the patient will become highly emotional. This release is useful, though not mandatory.

NOTES:

All entities are unique. Healing is: mind over matter. The release of emotions can stimulate the mind into proper action. It is an *indication* that the personality is indeed serious about healing self, and that the ego has been relegated to its humble station.

The illness is the manifested result of a blocked chakra. The blockage prohibits the proper flow of energy of that given vibration into the physical body. This creates an imbalance of some type. The imbalance, any imbalance causes the body to function abnormally. This abnormal function is commonly called ill health. The healing of the chakra is your honor/duty. This simply means to unblock the chakra(s) that is/are afflicted.

This is actually quite simple. Discovering *why* the chakra became blocked in the first place becomes a bit more complex. Through procedure, the healer causes the patient to discover the original cause/source of this blockage. If there is a blockage of one or more of the prime Rays (Red, Yellow, Blue) then the entity will have lost his ability to accept Love and cannot contact Intelligent Infinity. The eligibility for the upcoming Harvest rests heavily on the free-flowing clarity of the Rays through the prime color chakras.

The healer focuses the power of his mind on the vehicle of the Green Ray of Healing, and the healer's body is charged with the Love/Healing Energy of the Green Ray, and the Wisdom/Mental power of the Indigo. The Indigo Ray Energy is not the healing factor. This energy is the *balancer*. Compassion *must* be balanced with Wisdom. The Rays are tools. Tools supplied by the One Infinite Creator for your discovery and use. Feel free to indulge in their use, but use them wisely — these powers are awesome!

Chapter 8

The Procedure

In chapter five you learned the steps necessary to become a qualified healer. The healing can be only as good as the healer. If you were successful in negotiating chapter five then you have learned to (1) Know yourself, (2) Accept yourself, (3) Forgive yourself — and other selves. Now, as the healer you must deal with the second phase in order to become totally qualified. This is a three step endeavor and the steps are: (1) Know yourself, (2) Accept yourself, and (3) See yourself as the Creator! Steps 1 and 2 are based on step 3. Seeing yourself as the Creator, as a Co-Creator, is based on your ability to produce a transparent personality/ego within yourself. You see yourself as a working, functioning integrated part of ALL THAT IS. The Law is ONE, and you are a conscious part of that ONE. If you are a "born healer," the ego will not present a problem. If you are learning and developing an ability to heal then a program of self-discipline is in order. If your healing desires are sincere this should afford little problem.

The mental acceptance of self as a Light Bearer, as a Love Bearer, as a Co-Creator permits the balanced flow of energies to enter the healer — energies that he/she may then focus upon the one desiring to be healed. The healer is able to know and accept the other self. The bond is so complete that the healer *becomes* the other self. The healer has previously balanced and healed self. Now, so completely attuned, he/she allows other self *into* self, mentally, spiritually, and emotionally. The physical union is achieved by the "laying on of the hands." This balance within self permits the healer to clear the way to the Indigo Chakra. As this chakra becomes more and more crystallized, the clarity to Intelligent Infinity becomes more vivid. This is the Creator. The healer knows and accepts his/her status as Co-Creator. At this point the Magical Personality has entered the scene by invoking the Love Vibration. The Indigo and the Green Rays are connected and balanced at the Blue Ray Energy Center. The Indigo Ray *is* the tool of the Adept, the healer. The Magical

NOTES:

Personality works via this Ray. The Magical Personality is: *Your Higher Self!* The conscious contact with your Higher Self is achieved through the disciplined use of the Kundalini. You have been taught this in Volume One. Your Higher Self and the Higher Self of the other self are in intimate communication. The other self probably is *not* aware of this. You, the healer — the Adept, you are. The Higher Selves *know precisely* what to do. Now, with your conscious contact with your own Higher Self you the personality *also* know what to do. This is the source of your Wisdom. This is how you know when to heal and when *not* to heal!

The personality has become transparent; there is no ego. This creates the humblest of servants. The Higher Self operates freely through the heart, the mind, and the hands. This Magical Personality is free and uninhibited. The Universal Mind (Intelligent Infinity) flows freely through all, as unity abounds. This at oneness *is* the authority to heal. Compassion was the stimulus that instigated the action, unity provided the Wisdom to balance the Love. The instrument that incorporates all this magnificent energy is: *The Healer.*

If you are comfortable with this information and you feel that perhaps you recognize yourself or your potential self, then set about to learn the mechanics of healing via the chakras by the Adept.

Though not mandatory, it is most useful if your raise your Kundalini. The Wisdom of this is obvious. Be as perfect as possible, silently and humbly, ask for Love, ask for Wisdom, ask for Power. Your strength of Will and your compassionate determination will cause results. You are responsible. You have counseled the other self on what to expect. You have their permission and cooperation. The patient fully realizes that it is intended and expected that an event, or more than one event will probably be revealed in detail or sufficient detail to permit an extended mental investigation later. The patient realizes that the knowing, the acceptance, and the forgiveness of self is necessary and mandatory, in order to effect a physical healing. The other

NOTES:

self fully understands all of this, just as you understood it when you healed yourself.

The Position

The patient is on their back on a cot or a couch. You, the healer, stand at their feet. (See Figure 16.) The Prayer of Protection is offered, perhaps silently. Bring the Violet Light into the Crown Chakra, down the stem to the head and saturate your physical body with the cleansing Light of the Violet. Cleanse your working area as well. This is the equivalent of "scrubbing up" and preparing the operating room. Next, bring the Green Ray, of Love and Healing, into your Heart Chakra, to the spinal cord and up the cord to the shoulder level — the level of the Blue Chakra. The Green Energy is now sent to the right shoulder, and there it is divided. Part of the Green goes into the arm and down into the right hand. The right side of your body is polarized Positive. The Green was divided at the right shoulder. At that point, the Green continues upward around the right side of your head, across the top of your head and down the left side to the left shoulder, there it is divided once again. Part of the Green is channeled into the left arm and down into your left hand. The left side of your body is polarized negative. The rest of the Green Ray is sent *down* the left side of your body to your feet. The Ray then transfers from the left foot to your right foot, as the Green Ray now travels *up* the right side of your body to your right shoulder where it is continuously supplied with Love/Healing energy from the heart. Thus, the Green cycles continuously around your body even as it is emanating out of your right and left hands. (See Figure 17.) Left-handed people will follow this same procedure and not reverse it.

Your Position

You, the healer, are yet standing at the patient's feet. Since you have already raised your Kundalini, your chakras are aligned and balanced. Now, you probably are not able or gifted to see chakras; nevertheless, *envision* the chakras on your

NOTES:

patient. Align and balance *them,* and make their stems approximately six inches in length so that the patient's chakras are fairly close to the body. You are "prepping" your patient for healing (See Figure 16.) their eyes are closed; their arms are at their sides and they are relaxed. Instruct the patient to avoid initiating thoughts. Keep the mind open, open to suggestions from the Higher Self.

If the programmed healing crystal is to be employed, now is the time to activate it. We shall discuss at length the use of the crystal later on in *this* chapter.

The patient is enveloped in their own Aura, all people are. While standing at the feet, you must now set aside the Aura from the Violet to the Red. As if a surgeon's scalpel were to lance the Aura from above the head to the feet, you *open* their Aura. Envision the Aura opening as you *will* it to happen. This can indeed be compared to the surgical incision. In so doing you have removed the patient's protection — you are responsible! Do not take your work lightly. Afterwards, when finished, like the surgeon, you must indeed *close* the Aura. Opening the Aura permits you to get to the patient; to be able to perform your work . . . unrestricted.(See Figure 18.)

Discovering The Blocked Chakra

Now, the healer is ready, the patient has been prepared and opened. Quietly move to the patient's left side. Confidently remember that the working space is flooded with the protective, cleansing Violet Ray of the Creator. Your left hand is at your side. Hold your open right hand, palm down, six to twelve inches above the body and over the Base Chakra. Engage your sensitivity. What do you feel? Heat, cold, tingling, pressure, an ache perhaps? You should feel something. Now, move up to the Orange Chakra and do the same. What do you feel? Is it the *same* or a *different* feeling than was the Red? Remember. Now, move up to the Yellow and mentally record the sensation noted. Do this with all seven chakras. Think, remember, which ones were the same? Which ones were different? If you found five that felt the same, and two were different, then the two differ-

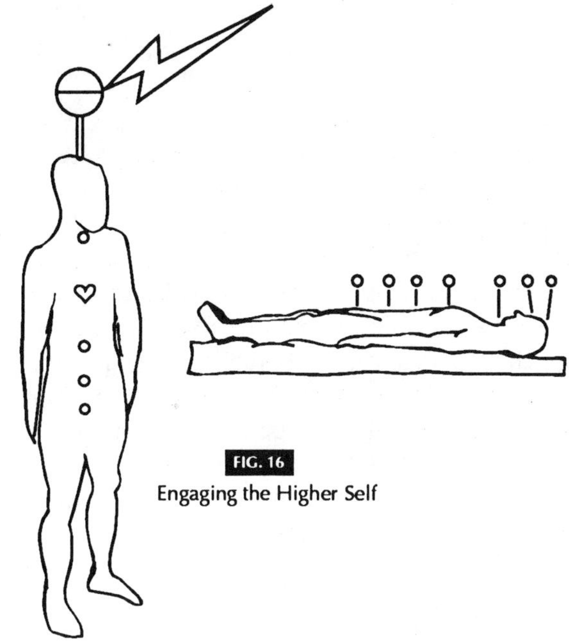

FIG. 16

Engaging the Higher Self

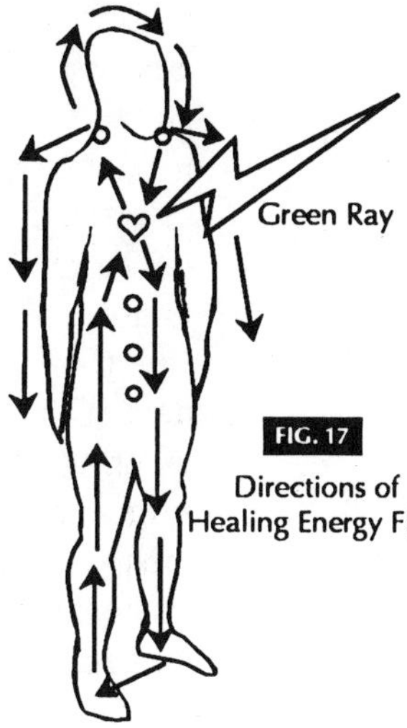

FIG. 17

Directions of Healing Energy Flow

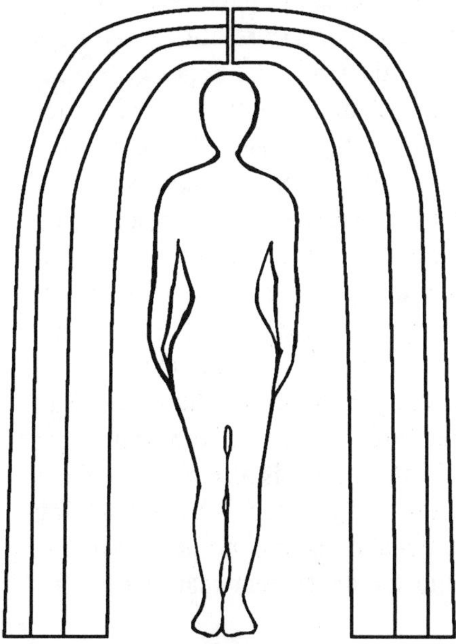

FIG. 18

Opening the Aura

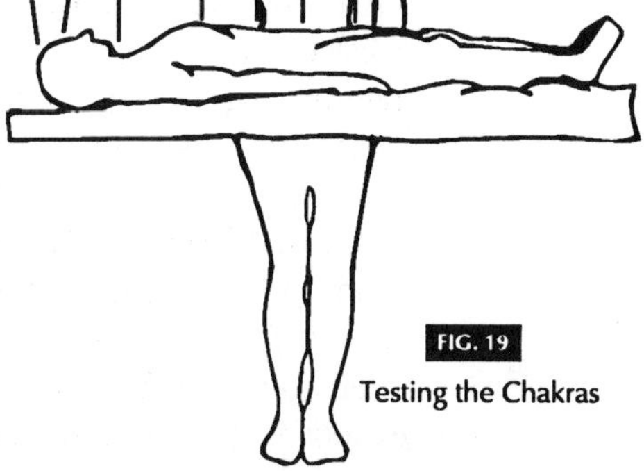

FIG. 19

Testing the Chakras

NOTES:

ent ones are blocked. You do not seek a "special" feeling. You seek to find some *difference* in feelings.(See Figure 19.)

The Yellow Ray at the Solar Plexis almost always has a problem. This is typical of the entity in Human form, which is all of us. This emotional energy is the prime source of keeping the Third Density Entity alive. It is highly vulnerable, so this is your first suspect. Let us say that the Yellow (No. 5) and the Blue (No. 3) are the chakras that you find blocked. It is best for the healer to speak very little. It is good to mention to your patient that the Blue and the Yellow require attention. Your influence is indeed great. The patient is open and vulnerable. Be open to your intuition as your Higher Self guides you through the healing. The ego has been set aside before you started — do not resurrect it now!

Clear The Yellow Chakra First

The healer has attuned himself to his patient and now may experience at least some of the feelings/sensations that the patient can, and will, express. This can be useful for the follow-up counseling. This unity is essential to achieve the maximum results in the healing. The blocked chakras have been discovered, and the healer knows where to direct his efforts. Always work on the Yellow first. Once this Prime Chakra is cleared, quite often other blocked chakras clear themselves. The healer now drops to his knees at the upper thigh level of the patient. Your right hand is placed on the Solar Plexes Chakra at the pit of the stomach. Gently and lightly place the hand just below the rib cage. Never move the hand once it is in place! A light pressure is now applied. In about 30 seconds place your left hand on the patient's right foot, gently grab the instep. As you do so, softly say to your patient: "Now . . . remember . . . " Hold this position for approximately 3 minutes. The Green Ray of healing is circulating in your body. It emits from your right hand into the Yellow Chakra. Your energy is also flowing from your left hand into the patient's right foot. This bridging intensifies the Yellow Ray blockage to the point where the patient is now able to recall the incident/event that caused the

NOTES:

blockage in the first place, perhaps decades ago.(See Figure 20.) The memory may be powerful, emotion may be expressed. Your attunement might be so great that you too will "see" the event. The Law is ONE. The recall of the event, with its unresolved lesson, should be sufficiently impressed upon the patient's consciousness, so that a more detailed examination may be fruitful at a later time that is perhaps more convenient.

Now remove your left hand from the patient's right foot and place it on their left foot, again firmly grabbing the instep. Hold this position for approximately two minutes as you say, "Now we shall clear this chakra."

This bridging permits the energy to flow in the true and proper configuration, and the Yellow Chakra is instantly cleared. Your right hand has not moved, not even a fraction of an inch! After about two minutes, remove your left hand from their left foot. Hold the left arm out straight, parallel to the floor, and parallel to the patient's body. With fingers outstretched, flick the fingers three or more times. This will release any stored up Negative energy that you may have acquired. Bring your cleansed hand/arm down to your left side. Now raise your right hand. Feel the vibration. Move the right hand to the Green Chakra, then to the Orange, and then back to the Yellow. Do they now all feel the *same?* This is how you test your work.

There should be no conversation during the healing. While still on your knees, move to your right until you can comfortably reach the throat. Cup your right hand gently but firmly, at the hollow of the throat. Now, unless your patient is very short or you have an abnormally long reach, you will not be able to reach the feet with your left hand. This would undoubtedly be the case when dealing with the three upper chakras. You simply extend your left arm, palm down, fingers stiff with hand opened and *point* to the patient's right foot, (See Figure 21.) then you say: "Now . . . Recall . . . " Hold this position for three-four minutes, then move your left arm slightly to your left so that the stiffened fingers are pointed to the patient's left foot and you can softly say, "Now . . . We will clear this chakra . . . " Hold this position for approximately two

NOTES:

more minutes. Flick your fingers a few times and drop your left hand to your left side. Gently raise your right hand and move it up to the Indigo to test the vibration.

The hand is six-twelve inches above the body for this test. Move the right hand down to feel the Green Vibration. Does the Blue now feel the same as the Indigo and Green? Check the Yellow once more. Does it still feel the same as the other chakras? The feeling should all be the same. If not, do the Maverick Chakra over again. Six to eight minutes is the maximum time you should give to a chakra without a break. A longer period of time could result in too much energy transfer that might possibly be harmful to this particular patient. Follow your intuition, be open to suggestion of modification offered by the Magical Personality, which is your own Higher Self.

Concluding The Healing

Always conclude the healing by offering your service to the Crown Chakra. Remember, the Violet is the summation of the lower six chakras. While still on your knees, slide to your right so that your right hand might be comfortably placed on top of the patient's head. Repeat the procedure that you used for the Blue Energy Center. Though you should always ask, the patient is not likely to remember any event at all as you deal with the Violet. This procedure is for stabilizing the Crown Chakra and balancing the lower six in congruency. Remind your patient of this altered procedure so that he/she will not feel that they have somehow failed because they were unable to recall anything via the Crown Chakra.

Now stand and slowly move toward the patient's feet, checking each chakra as you go; if one feels different stop and repeat the procedure for that chakra. There may have been more than two incidents in the patient's past that need resolving. Perhaps the Orange and/or Red now feel a bit different; if so, act on them. When all seven chakras feel the *same,* then move back down to the patient's feet. Look down at your patient. Check the chakras, envision them all aligned and balanced. Envision the Green Ray entering the patient's Heart Chakra and rising up

NOTES:

their spinal cord to their head, filling their brain with the emerald Green Love/Healing Energy; Then see this Green Energy drawing downward from the brain where the Indigo Body has enhanced it with it's essence. The Green/Indigo slowly saturates the physical body from the inside out, from the crown of the head to the soles of the feet.. See this. Envision this.(See Figure 22.) Now, close the Aura. See all the colors of the Rainbow Aura coming together and sealing over the front of your patient. Offer a silent thank you to the Magical Personality. Pat the foot of your patient and advise them to arise slowly and at their leisure. It may take several minutes for them to get self back together in order to stand up. Be patient. Wait for them to join you in your counseling area.

When your patient has re-joined you, it is proper for the healer to ask if any past incident was recalled. There was probably one or more. Encourage your patient to go home and quietly meditate on the material just recalled. It is much better for the patient to resolve these past issues themselves. However, if *they* feel that they are not quite able to do this, then make yourself available to listen and counsel them at a later time. This will probably be within a week. Remind them that the *forgiveness of self* is the key. This terminates the program of self-punishment of which the physical illness is the result.

Using The Crystal To Heal

There are many varieties of crystals. The quartz crystal is the most common. We shall deal with this general type. If you have a preference for another kind of crystal, feel free to employ it.

The crystal can be programmed for specific purposes. At this time our purpose is healing. The programmed crystal is attuned to the vibrations of the healer. It becomes a very personal item. It should not be loaned around. It will be effective only in the hands of the one who programmed it. The crystal may be of any size or shape. It should be small enough to be held comfortably in the hand, and one must be able to attach it to a string or chain so that it may be worn comfortably around

NOTES:

the neck. The string should be of such a length to cause the crystal to be worn directly over the Heart Chakra. The incoming Green Ray of Love/Healing/Manifestation must then pass through the crystal as it enters the heart, to the spinal cord, and up the spinal cord to one of the transmitting chakras.

The length of time needed to program your crystal depends upon the Green Ray activity that you employ. If this Ray of Love is seldom used, then it could take months before your vibrations begin to coordinate with this intelligent stone. On the other hand, it could easily be programmed in a few days. The crystal should be worn *at all times* or as often as possible. Being Third Density Human, the healers vibrations will vacillate at least a little or perhaps a lot. This lack of consistency affects the quality of the healings. The programmed crystal is always stable. Its use will stabilize the healer's effectiveness, even on the personality's "down" days. The use of the crystal is *not* mandatory, but for various reasons, it is highly recommended.

When the crystal and the healer have become attuned as one, then *instant* contact with the Magical Personality *and* Intelligent Infinity is possible . . . *if* the healer is crystallized in his/her own right! The programmed crystal will be no more effective than is the crystallized/ balanced healer. The prime value being: the stone is not affected by emotions, therefore the Wisdom balance is automatic. The harmony between the healer and his/her crystal is most important. A Love bond is established at the time of the selection. The crystal chooses the personality . . . think about that!

The personalized crystal has now become a tool of the healer. This tool may readily be incorporated in the basic procedure of healing via the chakras as it was described earlier in this chapter. The healer stands at the foot of the patient and activates the Violet and Green Rays. The crystal necklace is removed from around the neck and the string is looped around the middle finger of the healer's right hand. A pendulum is devised. Before the aura is opened and the patient is not yet disarmed, hold the pendulum over the patient's feet. Your palm is down and you are holding quite still. The pendulum will

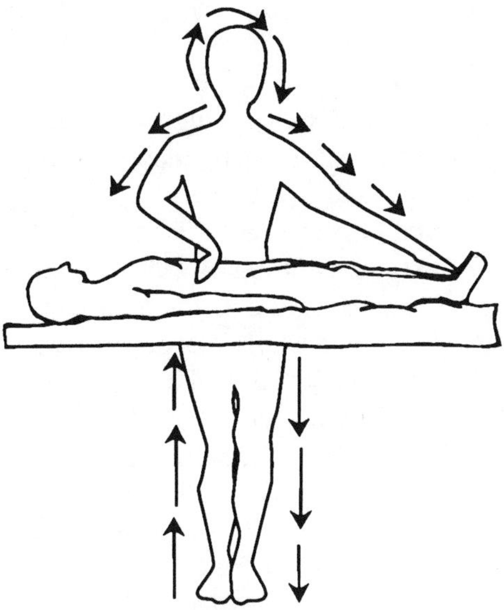

FIG. 20

Lower Chakra Position

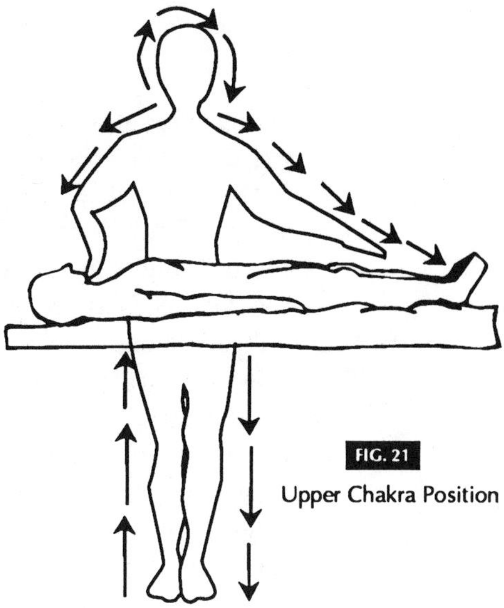

FIG. 21

Upper Chakra Position

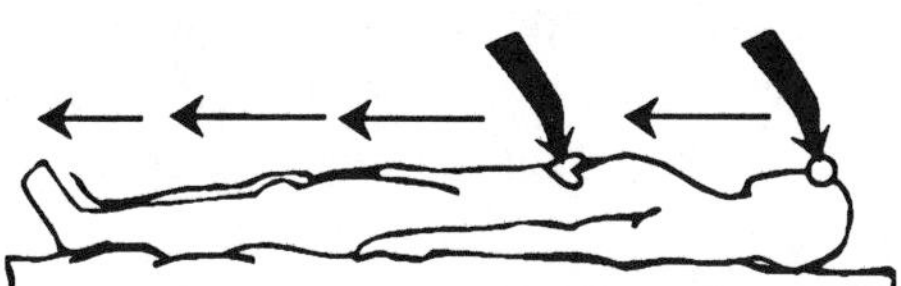

FIG. 22

Green and Indigo Energy Flow
Healing and Recalling

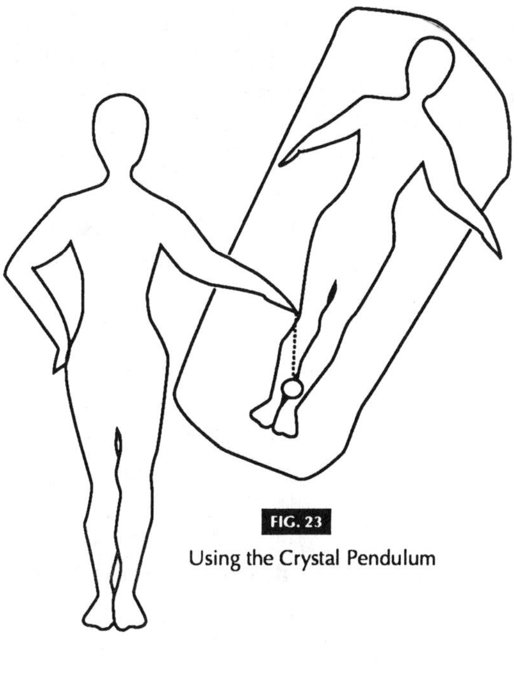

FIG. 23

Using the Crystal Pendulum

NOTES:

swing crosswise over the body or it will swing lengthwise over the body. The movement produced would be indigenous to that personality, at least for the moment (See Figure 23.)

Now, when you step around to the patient's left side hold the pendulum over the Base Chakra. The crystal would be six-twelve inches above the body. (The same area that you held your naked hand before.) If, for example, the pendulum swings in the *opposite* direction than it did when you tested at the feet, then that chakra is blocked. If the pendulum swings in the same direction, then that chakra is clear. Check all seven chakras in this manner. If any of the lower six chakras are blocked, the Crown or Violet Chakra will also indicate as much. This is understandable since it is the summation of all below.

To continue with our original example, let us say that you found the Yellow and the Blue to be blocked. The healing procedure is exactly the same as described earlier in this chapter except, you now hold your crystal in the palm of your right hand as you gently but firmly place the crystal and your right hand over crystal on the Solar Plexis Chakra. You are now using the steady, dependable power of the crystal to enhance and supplement your own Green Ray energies. The Magical Personality works unimpeded through the stone. Possible emotions on your part are now circumvented. As always, the healing is only as good as the healer, and the programmed crystal reflects this. The basic advantage is: The crystal never has an off day — you might. If your sensitivity is not sufficient to detect the blocked chakra or perhaps you do not feel confident in your ability of discovery, then the use of the crystal pendulum could prove to be a most useful tool.

Palm the crystal as you touch each afflicted chakra. Use the crystal pendulum procedure to check your work when you are finished. Replace the crystal necklace around your neck as you close the aura. Do not go to your next patient until you have placed the crystal next to your heart. This clears and neutralizes your tool. This assures that the vibrations of your last patient will not be carried forth to your next client.

NOTES:

Using The Pyramid To Heal

Another useful tool of the healer is the pyramid. The pyramid must be constructed in such a way that it is large enough for you and your patient to enter. This would mean that the heigth must be at least six feet. (We will take an in-depth investigation into pyramids in another section of this book Volume Two.) If the sizable pyramid is available to you, make certain the base is aligned to true North or aligned 20 degrees NNE, as you choose. The pyramid naturally collects energy that would enhance your own healing energies. The patient's protection is automatically removed by the pyramid's power. The Aura is opened and set aside. This offers a high degree of confidence and safety to the patient and healer as well.

The natural flow of energy is from North to South or from the head to the feet. If the patient's energy flow has somehow been reversed the pyramid will quickly rectify it. If this opposite energy flow is a problem and a pyramid is not available, simply have the patient stand and raise the right arm over the head. Now, bring the arm down, palm in, from the head downward to the length of the arm and then out and up the right side of the body, making a circle as large as the length of the arm. This circle is made three times. The hand and forearm pass about six inches in front of the body. The exercise causes the energy to flow from the head through the feet as it should. This is a useful exercise to perform on yourself *before* you enter the healing arena.(See Figure 24.)

It would be wise for the healer to acquire a good working knowledge of pyramids before attempting to use this tool. It is not mandatory that you use a pyramid but it is most useful if you have a large one handy and know how to use these collected and concentrated energies.

The King's Chamber Effect

You have learned the procedure of raising the Kundalini energy in Volume One of "THE TEACHINGS." The King's Chamber Effect involves the use of your Kundalini Energy for healing purposes. It is equivalent to the First Energy in a

NOTES:

functioning pyramid. In a sense, your physical body becomes a pyramid. This is the mechanics of this special and powerful working. As you remember, the "glass tube" attached at the back side of your tail bone moves directly away from you at a right angle to your backbone. It goes out some 24 to 30 inches and then makes a sharp bend around your right side. This would be counter clockwise, as you look down upon yourself. The raising of the Kundalini has now begun.

Now, the shaft of Kundalini Light is being emitted from the base of your spine. About six inches out from the back bone and continuing on for approximately 18 inches, but *before* the Kundalini makes it sharp bend to your right, establish a "scoop" of Kundalini energy 18-inches wide, leaving the "glass tube," and moving in a spiralling fashion around your *left* side. The six inch empty radius from the spinal cord maintains itself throughout. Because this scoop of Kundalini Energy is within a *conical* spiral, the width of its 18-inch scoop gradually gets narrower as this scoop of energy rises in a *clockwise* fashion, as you look down upon yourself. This scoop or sheet of White Light, moves around your left side as it passes through the stem of the Base Chakra *inside* the point where your Kundalini is making its contact to activate that chakra as you have been taught. (See Figure 25.) The narrowing scoop is now coming around your right side, still maintaining that six inch radius away from your spinal cord. The sheet of Kundalini rises slightly as it passes around your right side, your back, and your left side, and then passes *through* the stem of your Orange Chakra *inside* the point of contact made with the "glass tube."

The narrowing sheet of Kundalini continues in a clockwise, rising, conical path, passing through the stem of the Yellow Chakra. This narrowing sheet of Kundalini Energy makes one more trip around your body until it touches the stem of the Green Ray Heart Chakra. There it stops. As the incoming Green Ray of Love and Healing passes through the stem to the spinal cord your Kundalini Energy is mingled in with the Green Ray, giving it more vitality. This practice will enhance your power as a healer. (See Figure 26.) This practice is also useful

NOTES:

in manifestation, but that shall be discussed in detail when we study the Tensor Concepts.

You do not *have* to use the "King's Chamber Effect," it is strictly optional. If you do choose to develop and employ this practice, remember: first, you raise your Kundalini in the regular way, then you *tap into* the flowing Kundalini in the form of a scoop or sheet and bring it up and around in the *opposite* direction to the Heart Chakra, and *no higher.* Second, always *lower* this portion of your Kundalini when you have finished with your healing work *before* you lower your Kundalini in the normal way. The raising and lowering practice does *not* change one bit. This procedure is a supplemental tool that you may use at your discretion.

The Healing Of Self

Since the healing is only as good as the healer, it is fitting that the healer be able to offer the Green Ray of healing to self. The ability to envision is most necessary. This may be practiced with or without the Kundalini, the pyramid, or the crystal.

Envision a shaft of Emerald Green, Love/Healing Energy entering into the heart, the Heart Chakra. This energy comes from the Universe, the Cosmos is full of Love. The Green Ray enters the Heart Chakra, passes through the stem to the spinal cord and up the spinal cord to your brain. The Green Energy is being pumped into your brain, like you would pump Green Air into a balloon. Keep this up for a minute or so. Feel the *pressure* as your brain seems to expand. Then, within 90 seconds shut off the supply of Green incoming at your heart. Your brain is full and under pressure of the Love/Healing Light.

Now, envision this brain full of Green slowly draining downward, back down into your spinal cord; using the nervous system as the vehicle, the Green Ray of Healing moves into all parts of your body. Slowly the Green drains downward. Like a bottle of Green water with a small hole in its bottom, the level slowly drops. Some of the Green will pass through the arms and out your fingertips. Some Green will escape through your pores

NOTES:

of your skin, like sweat. The bulk of Green Light will pass downward through your entire body and exits through your feet. As the Green Light of healing passes through your body it collects all the toxins, the problems, the impurities, that are in disharmony with your system of wellness, and purges them from your body.

Your body is purged of it's unwanted guests. When the level of Green enters an area of your body that you know suffers a problem, hold the Green at that level for 20 to 30 seconds before continuing the downward drop. This procedure is incredibly effective.

The summation of the procedure: The Green Ray is brought into the heart, up the spinal cord to the brain. The brain is filled to the point of pressure. The Green is shut off at the heart after about 90 seconds. The Green in the brain slowly drains downward, and using the nervous system as it's vehicle, purges the body as it is discharged via the fingers, the pores of the skin, and out through the soles of the feet.

The entire procedure takes about five minutes. You may repeat the procedure two times, even three times, but no more. This would require about 15 minutes for three consecutive runs. You should do this twice per day, but no more than that. Just prior to retiring and shortly after arising are the common times chosen. You may choose any time you like.

After the healing exercise has been completed in 5,10, or 15 minutes; then, again, bring in the Green Ray into your heart up the spinal cord to the crown of your head and flowing like a fountain it creates a dome of Love/Healing Energy all around your physical body. Live your life, awake and asleep, in this environment of Love. Envision this Green saturating your body from the outside in. This is not as effective as the above described method of healing from the inside out, but it is comforting, protective, and recuperative. You cannot go wrong in your use of the Love Vibration.

Remember to always offer your Love/Healing Energy to our beloved Earth Mother. Extend your Love down, 400 miles down, to the Earth's mantle as you create a shaft or column of

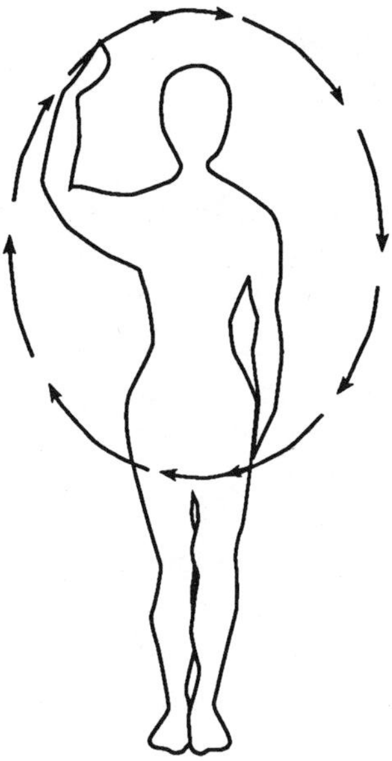

FIG. 24

Correcting the Energy Flow

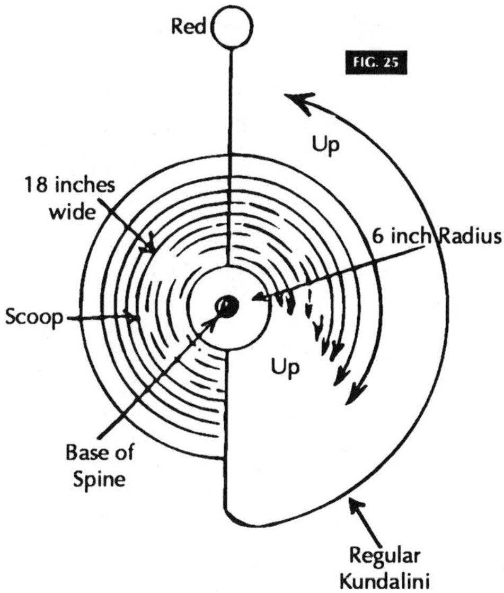

FIG. 25

FIG. 26

The Three Energies

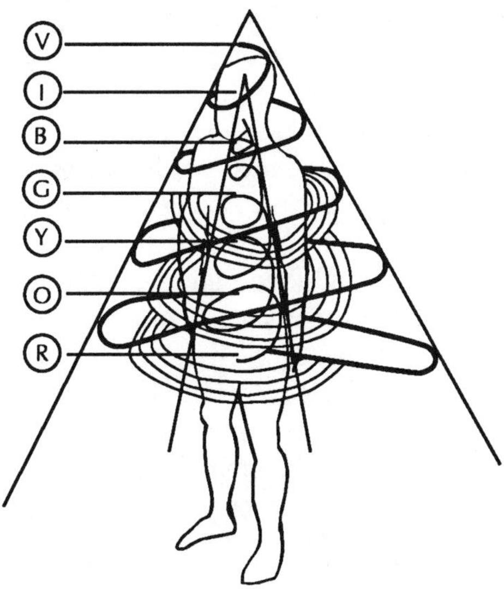

FIG. 27

Self Healing

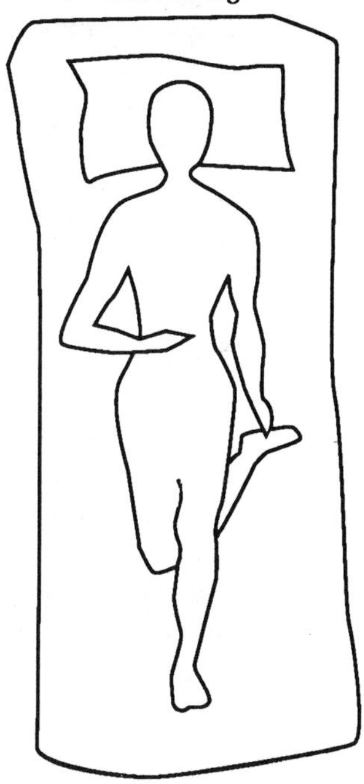

NOTES:

Healing Energy as your gift, your service to our beleaguered Planet. This could be the grandest offering of Love that you can accomplish in this lifetime. Be especially conscious of envisioning the Green shaft/column of healing when you travel. Cut a swath of Love/Healing Energy into the Earth Mother whereever you go. Teach this to those who are willing to learn.

Using Your Crystal To Heal Self

You may use your programed crystal on yourself much as you would use it on another self. The crystal may be held on the afflicted body part to send the Green Ray Energy into that area. This procedure will have a curing effect on the symptoms.

In order to receive the full benefit of healing the root cause, the procedure is the same as one would use for the healing of another. Lie on your back, preferably with your head to the North or 20 degrees NNE. Before lying down, hold your cystal pendulum over your feet to get the reading that is indigenous to you. Armed with this information, hold your pendulum over your Solar Plexis Chakra. Make certain your string is short enough that your crystal clears your body and you can see the action. Start with your Yellow Ray Energy Center, it usually is malfunctioning anyway. Test Yellow, Orange, Red, and then check the Yellow before moving up to the Green, Blue Indigo, and Violet. Note the chakras that affect your pendulum in a fashion contrary to the indigenous pattern.

Having discovered the blocked chakras hold your crystal in your right hand as you place your right hand on the blocked chakra. Your left leg is always straight. Now, bring your right leg *under* your left leg as you bend the knee in such a way to grasp your right foot with your left hand.(See Figure 27.) Hold this position for up to three minutes as you attempt to recall the past event that is the source of the blockage. Then, release the right foot and straighten your right leg. Your left hand is at your left side palm to thigh. Hold this position for a couple more minuets, as you clear the chakra. Now, raise your right hand off the chakra (the crystal pendulum is still attached to your finger) and check the results.

NOTES:

Follow this same procedure for each blocked chakra, remembering each past incident in the event they were not all the same. As soon as practical, find the time to mentally examine the past event as you extract the unresolved lesson, fix it, as you forgive self and other selves. Continue to use the Green Ray as previously described to energize the healing as you wean yourself from the need to punish self.

It is a good practice to periodically check your own chakras for clarity, even if you are not consciously aware of any problem. The healing is only as good as the healer!

Healing At A Distance

Sometimes it is not possible or practical for the healer to come into direct physical contact with the one requesting the service. The distance could be across the room or across the continent, it matters not. It is not necessary that the recipient of the Love/Healing Rays be aware of the time or condition of the offering. The Green Ray Light has no limitations. It is intelligent. It knows what to do and how to do it. It knows when it is proper to heal and when it is not. However, it cannot turn itself on! This is the work of the healer.

To accomplish this type of healing the healer looks at the patient. If this is not practical the healer creates the mental image, the thought form, of that person. See the other self in their customary environment. It is not important that the setting be absolutely accurate, it is all an illusion anyway. All physical manifestations are illusions, as you remember in our previous teachings.

With the patient properly envisioned, physically or mentally, bring the Green Ray into your own Heart Chakra to your spinal cord and then up the cord to the Indigo Energy Center. This chakra is a transmitter. Discharge the Green Light through the Indigo "Tube" and guide the Ray into the heart of your distant patient. Envision the Green Ray entering their heart to their spinal cord and up their spinal cord to their brain and pump their brain full of the Green Love/Healing Energy. After about a minute, cut off the supply of Green and envision the

NOTES:

healing process just like you did when you learned to heal self. The procedure for healing the other self is the same procedure you used on self. You may repeat the process the second and perhaps the third time, and you may do this twice during the diurnal period, the same as you would do for self-healing.

When the healing ritual is completed, it would then be wise to envision that Green Light in the form of a dome or bubble, saturating the now purged body of your patient. For the healer who is genuinely compassionate and sincere, this practice is very effective. We encourage you to try it. The worst that can happen is nothing!

Summary

Since the chakras sponsor the Aura, the Aura will change after the chakra balancing and clearing has taken place. Those of you who have developed Etheric Vision will note this. Always follow your intuition. This is your Higher Self giving guidance and direction. Refrain from exercising ideas of your own (ego). Be open and brave . . . you have more talent and ability than you probably know. Make yourself available, but do not seek out work or advertise. The patient must come to you. In the case of the distant healing, a friend may *recommend* the need for your service.

Trust the Light. Trust your Higher Self. Trust the Creator. Accept yourself as Co-Creator — in all humility, wearing a transparent personality. Healing is the ultimate in service to others. The will, polarity, and purity of the healer are the prime factors.

The Cleansing And Healing Of The Chakras

It may become necessary from time to time to cleanse and heal your chakras, or in the case of a healing, teach another self how it is done. Many serious students of healing will perform this ritual on a daily basis or at least once or twice a week. The healing is only as good as the healer. The follow-

THE CLEANSING AND HEALING OF THE CHAKRAS

FIG. 28

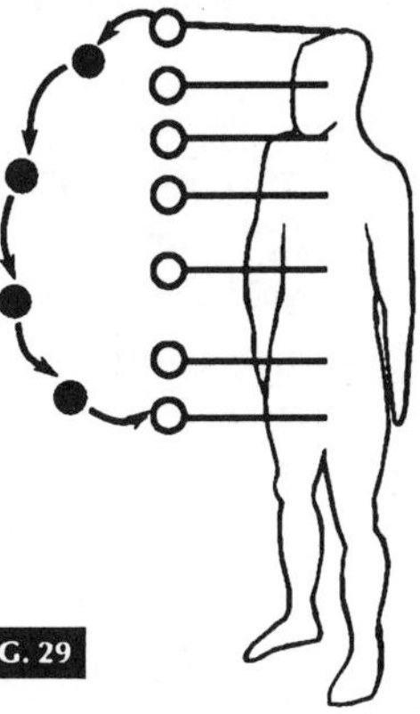

FIG. 29

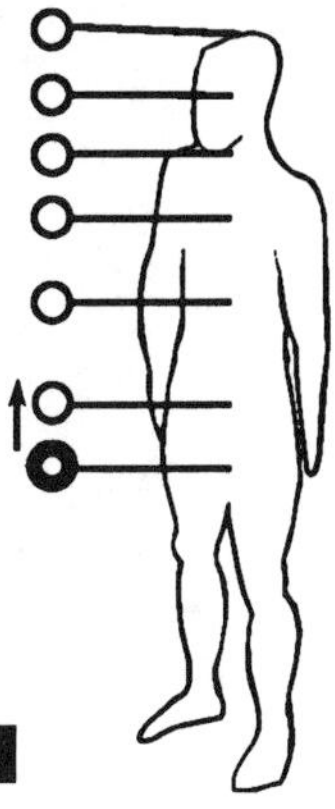

FIG. 30

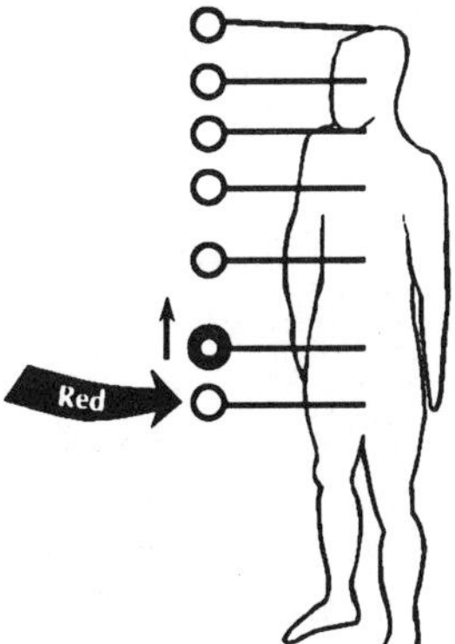

FIG. 31

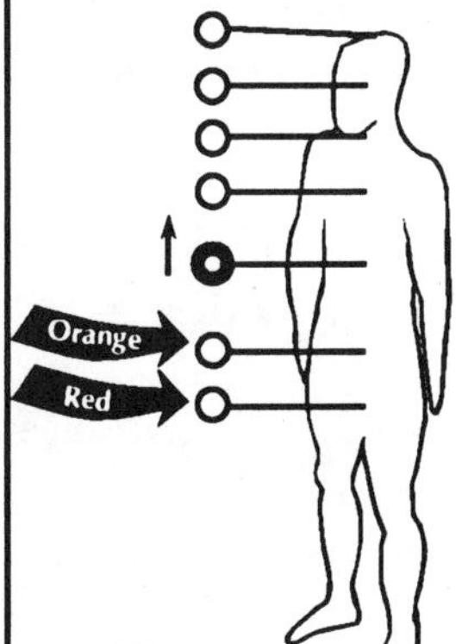

FIG. 32

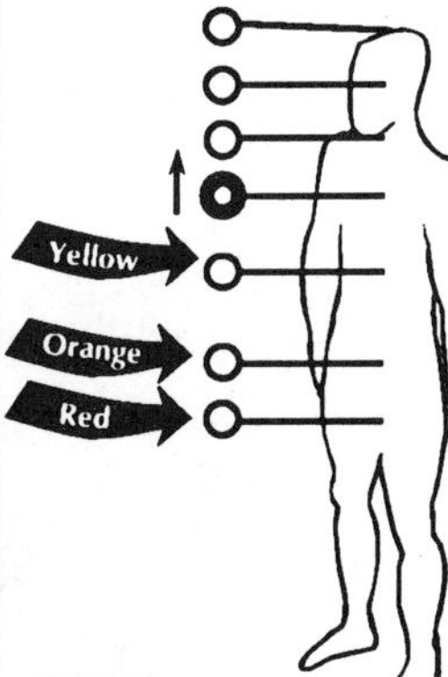

FIG. 33

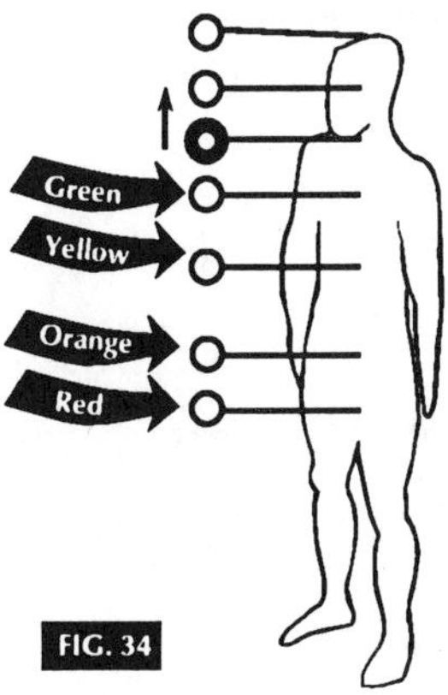

FIG. 34

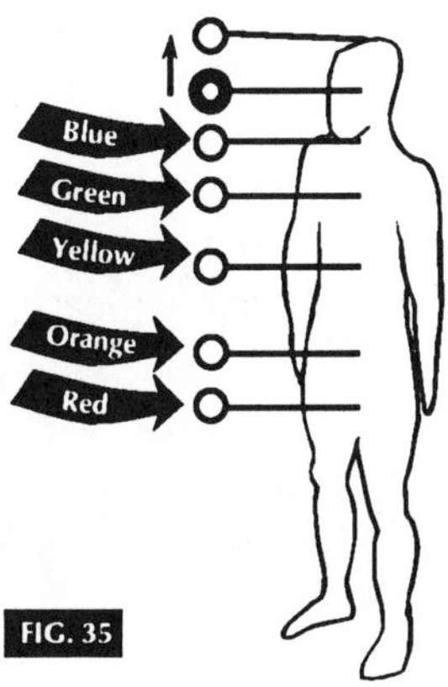

FIG. 35

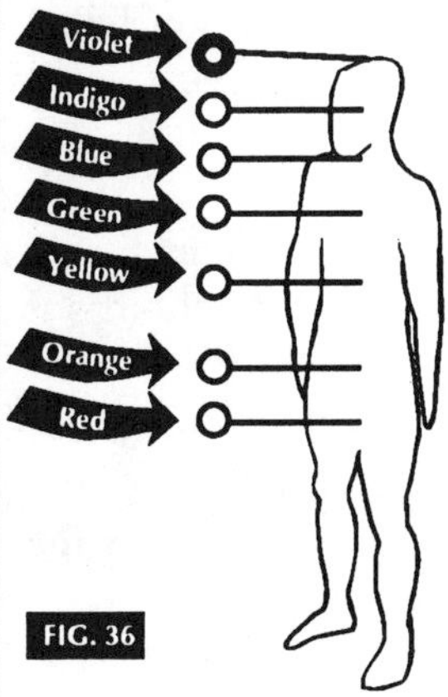

FIG. 36

NOTES:

ing teaches the step by step procedure. We heartily encourage you to practice it.

Step 1: Protect the self. Construct/create a large Violet Pyramid. Inside the pyramid, construct an Emerald Green Dome of Love/Healing Energy. Visualze self inside the Green Dome. Both dome and pyramid are etheric. (See Figure 28.)

Step 2: Align and balance (equally spaced) all 7 chakras. Legthen the stems to about one meter so that you can observe the activity. Bring the Violet essence of the Crown Chakra out, down, and position the large Violet Ball under the Base Chakra. (See Figure 29.)

Step 3: Bring the Violet Ball up to the Red Chakra, and consume it. Hold for two minutes. (See Figure 30.)

Step 4: Mentally move the Violet Ball up to consume the Orange Chakra and hold for two minutes. The Red Ray now flows freely into the Base Chakra. (See Figure 31.)

Step 5: Move the Violet Ball up to consume the Yellow Chakra and hold for two minutes. The Orange Ray now flows freely into the cleansed and healed Spleen Chakra. (See Figure 32.)

Step 6: Move the Violet Ball up to consume the Green Chakra and hold for two minutes. The Yellow Ray now flows freely into the Solar Plexis Chakra. The bright Orange and Red continue to flow clear and clean into their respective chakras. (See Figure 33.)

Step 7: Mentally move the Violet Ball up to consume the Blue Chakra and hold for two minutes. The Green Ray is now clearly and freely flowing into the Heart Chakra. (See Figure 34.)

Step 8: Move the Violet Ball up to consume the Indigo Chakra and hold for two minutes. The Blue Ray now flows freely into the Throat Chakra. (See Figure 35.)

Step 9: Move the Violet Ball up to its place of origin and re-integrate it into the Crown Chakra. The Indigo Ray is now flowing freely into the Third Eye Chakra. The Crown Chakra, which is the summation of all the lower six chakras also flows free and clear, since all the lower six have been carefully cleansed and healed. (See Figure 36.)

Step 10: Keep chakras aligned and balanced. Envision all seven Rays flowing un-restricted into their respective chakras. The physical health/vitality is now returning. Maintain the Dome of Protection about the self at all times. This permits the personality to dwell in an environment of Love.

Conclusion

You shall now prepare to lower the Kundalini. Bring the White Light of the Kundalini up around yourself and gather it into an object over your head. As you do so, pull the Violet Dome next to your body. Now, bring the Kundalini in its entirety into the crown of your head as you detach your consciousness. Begin the descent, deactivating each chakra as we give the color countdown: Violet . . . Indigo . . . Blue . . . Green . . . Yellow . . . Orange . . . Red . . . Put the Kundalini to rest and shut the door. Breath deeply.

Our Prayer

Let us close with our Prayer of Protection. We ask that you repeat this prayer first thing in the morning, and the last thing at night. Our Prayer:

"In the Name of the Presence and the Power Universal, protect us from harm and all Unenlightened Spirits. And may the Light of our Spirit Guides and the Light of our Higher Selves illuminate our thoughts, that we may reflect the Radiant Glory of ALL THAT IS."

We leave you now in the Love and Light of our One Infinite Creator. Go forth in the joy of life and in service to others.

Adonai, Adonai Vasu Barragus, Adonai.

Section III

Pyramids

This section deals with the pyramid and related edifices of power. The values of various forms of energy are revealed. Their ancient origins are brought to light.

Chapter 9

Pyramids

We greet you in the Light and Love of our One Infinite Creator. We are Chief Little Summer and Warm Night Rain.

Let us begin this section with the chant:

"I am that I am, A-Yeh,
I am that I am, A-Yeh,
I am that I am, A-Yeh,
I am that I am, A-Yeh,
I am that I am, A-Yeh,
I am that I am, A-Yeh,
I am that I am, A-Yeh,
A-Yeh,
A-Yeh,
A-Yeh,
A-Yeh,
A-Yeh."

Our Prayer of Protection: "In the name of the Presence and the Power Universal, protect us from harm and all Unenlightened Spirits; and may the Light of our Spirit Guides and the Light of our Higher Selves, illuminate our thoughts that we might reflect the Radiant Glory of ALL THAT IS."

* * *

We ask that you now prepare yourself to raise your Kundalini. Have your backs quite straight, as you align and balance your chakras. As the base of your spine, awaken the Kundalini. Permit the Kundalini to rise as we give the color countdown. Activate all the proper functions, as you have been taught, as the Kundalini passes through the stem of the Red Chakra . . . the Orange . . . the Yellow . . . the Green . . . the Blue . . . the Indigo . . . the Violet. Attach your consciousness to your Kundalini Energy. Now, envision the White Kundalini, with your consciousness thoroughly saturated therein, emitting from the crown of your head, gently coiling around the Silver Cord, reaching the Golden Sphere, your Higher Self. Saturate the lower hemisphere with your Kundalini Light — making your

NOTES:

conscious contact. Encase your body with the White Light of your Kundalini, as you are fully protected by the great rainbow dome of Light. Firmly establish your contact with your Higher Self, and when you are ready, begin to read.

* * *

In this section we shall discuss the nomenclature of the various forms of Pyramids. Their many functions will also be examined. The ancient history of the introduction of the pyramid to Planet Earth may be a surprise to some of you. The mysteries are exposed to the Light of Knowledge.

The many uses of the three exquisite energies that are collected by a pyramid are explained in detail. The standard that all known pyramids are measured to is of course, the Great Pyramid of Cheops at Giza, Egypt. It is our intent to clear up some of the mysteries and familiarize you with this wonderful edifice.

Though the pyramid shape does not have the use or value that it did in the past, it still can be a viable tool in the hands of the initiate. As the Age of Aquarius dawns brighter and brighter, ancient wisdoms gradually become more and more profound. Ancient knowledge tends to relieve the apprehension of our future. There is always comfort and security derived through the seeking of knowledge. What greater security could be obtained than that from a monumental stone edifice called a pyramid? Only a pyramid dares to challenge time.

The Great Pyramid

In the constellation we know as Taurus there lies a Star System that we have named Aldebaron. On the Third Planet out from this magnificent Sun orbits a Planet that houses a species of Fourth Density MAN. These ones have established a thriving civilization that has been functioning for a bit longer than one million Earth years. These entities are members of the Confederation of MAN. Their Galactic Survey Teams have wandered the extremities of this, our Galaxy. Outposts of various types have been established by these and others of MAN in the far-flung and remote areas of this and other Galaxies.

NOTES:

In order to return so that others might follow, navigational aids were constructed at strategic points in the unchartered Space. These devices are beacons and are most often housed in pyramids. Those ones of MAN came to this Planet some 47,600 years ago. They constructed the Great Pyramid at Giza in the country now known as Egypt. Granite was quarried from a location in Central Africa, and some of the granite used came from South America. These blocks were cut by desrays, and were transported to the construction site by their Craft.

The Great Generators

A sub-terrains chamber was constructed and the pyramid was built over it. This is often referred to as the Resonating Chamber. A shaft of 243 was sunk beneath this Chamber, and at this level, great generators were installed.These generators created tremendous energy that powered the signal beacons for the Spacecrafts of MAN.

These exquisite and unusual generators were also designed in such a fashion that they would stabilize the Earth's axle wobble. The Earth has had a habit of shifting her axis several times during the past four and a half billion years. This is devastating to surface life, plant, animal, and most recently — Human life. This stabilizing effect provided for a more temperate climate, since the Earth was at that time recovering from a Great Ice Age.

The Third And Fourth Root Races

Some 4,000 to 5,000 years prior to the construction of the Great Pyramid, Atlantis was experiencing its humble beginnings. Lemuria or Mu was a thriving civilization, basking in its glory of evolution and awareness. In those days, the Earth's axis was a bit different than the current alignment of 23.5 degrees that we know of today. The North Pole was in the vicinity of the present location of Hawaii and our Sun was the "Pole Star." The Earth rotated on her axis but it had no noticeable effect upon her inhabitants except those dwelling near the equator. The Earth's wobble produced a twilight effect in this area.

NOTES:

The great land mass known as Mu, now commonly called the Pacific Ocean, was in constant Sunlight. The opposite half was in total darkness. Bitter cold and gale-force winds was the environment. No Human Being could dwell there; but there was species of Third Density that could and *did* dwell in this most in hospitable climate. This species survives today and is sometimes called the Yetti, and is occasionally spotted in the Himalayan Mountains. Cousins of these ones are often referred to as "Bigfoot" or "Sasquatch."

The inhabitants of Mu never knew darkness. They never saw the stars. There was a cloudy canopy that covered this hemisphere. This climate was ideal for plant growth. Giants were produced in Second and Third Density. Life was peaceful and prosperous for all. Time stood still. The pace of life was slow.

Meanwhile, on the opposite side of the Planet the ice mass grew to gigantic proportions until the day came when the unbalance became too great and the Earth tilted. Within 24 hours Mu sank with hardly a trace left of its existence. The waters, now called the Pacific, rolled over the falling land mass. For a long period of time icebergs were every where. Civilization, what remained of it, was now thrown back to square one. The Root Race of Lemuria had ended. Atlantis was now cycling in its infancy. Cataclysms always sponsor a Root Race's Alpha-Omega. Note: this subject will be expanded upon in Volume III.

Constructing The Great Pyramid

MAN is always monitoring the Human Experience, and some 4,000 years afterwards when those Fourth Density Entities from Aldeboran came to construct the pyramid to provide a beacon for their navigational needs, they also skillfully installed a type of generator that had the talent to act as a gyroscope to stabilize the Earth's axis, now stationed at 23.5 degrees. These generators are designed to activate if the Earth's axis moves as much as one half of a degree, and thusly, re-stabilize her.

On the North face of the Great Pyramid there is an air vent that circulates fresh air to certain interior chambers. This shaft is 324 feet long, and is so meticulously angled that it aligns

NOTES:

the North Star exactly. It is this air vent that is the triggering mechanism that activates the special generators. No Third Density Entity could have installed such a shaft, certainly not at that time; and probably not now, even with today's technology. This is an incredible feat! For almost 48,000 years the Earth and her inhabitants were so protected from a random axis shift.

This has been the situation for the Planet and her inhabitants until the year 1985, when MAN permanently turned off this mechanism. A new Root Race change is imminent, and the cleansing cataclysms must accompany this most noble of phenomena.

Teams of MAN visited the Earth periodically to check on their pyramid, and also to monitor and coach the Third Density Earthlings in their struggle to achieve a civilized status. In the course of these many visits, flora and fauna were introduced and distributed to various locals on the face of the Earth Mother.

The Queen's Chamber

After the completion of the Great Pyramid, a small party of MAN from the Aldebaron Star System stayed behind to operate the equipment. The Queen's Chamber was used as the interstellar communicators room. This was unknown to Humans. The Queen's Chamber is located 72 feet above the base and has a floor space of 1134 square feet. This chamber was used for many milleniums. It has since been abandoned by MAN. The present communication center is currently located 9 feet above the Queen's Chamber.

The King's Chamber

The King's Chamber was installed at a later time for the express purpose of healing Third Density Entities. It is located 27 feet above the *level* of the Queen's Chamber. Much higher in the pyramid MAN installed machinery that operated a copper capstone beacon. This machinery was later relocated to a chamber 9 feet *below* the King's Chamber. There are three major areas or chambers in the Great Pyramid that have yet to be discovered.

NOTES:

Early Civilizations Aided By Ancient Man

Though MAN worked and dwelt within the pyramid, he emerged regularly to serve those native to this Planet. Disguised as priests, they walked amongst the peoples teaching, healing, and encouraging mental/spiritual growth whenever possible. These priests were often thought of as "gods" and the peoples bestowed various names upon them. Some of the distortions of these priests/gods and their activities have survived unto this day via mythology and hearsay history. MAN was highly mobile, using his Craft or by teleportation. Consequently, he brought his teachings to many, and many congregated communities of Humans over the entire face of the Planet. He would disguise himself in the appropriate vehicle to satisfy the mentality of the "students." A master of disguise, MAN would often assume the guise of animals and birds as well as the Humanoid form. These teachings have had a pronounced effect of the mental/spiritual growth of Earthlings . . . Believe it or not!

Finishing The Great Pyramid By Humans

Approximately 5,000 years ago, Cheops or Khufu decided to face the granite edifice with limestone locally quarried. This was no small feat. The manhandling of those huge blocks of limestone was an enormous undertaking. The excellent and precise fitting and joining together of these stones is not due entirely to the skills of the stonemason. It was noted that certain birds were able to carve out or wallow out a nest in a sheer wall of stone. Upon closer observation it was noted that these birds placed a liquid substance on the rock and let it set for a few moments before beginning to work. Examination revealed that this "substance" made the rock temporarily *malleable;* thus, the burrowing out of a hole was relatively easy. Continued observation disclosed that these birds gathered this liquid substance from certain plants.

Now the mystery was resolved. The Pharaohs workers gather this juice and stored it in large urns. At the appropriate time it was brushed onto the top of a standing rock. Another cut stone was then placed on top of the now-alleable surface, and the

NOTES:

top rock *molded itself* into it's supporter. A perfect fit was achieved. Later the treated stone re-hardened to its original status. The cutting of the stone into blocks and the transporting of them was most difficult, but the fitting of the joints was relatively easy.

Because of this extensive facing project, Earthlings believed the Khufu had built the entire pyramid. Actually, it had been standing for approximately 43,000 years before he came along. The copper cap stone was yet in place when Khufu faced it. The copper cap would glow brilliantly, and its light could be seen for many miles.

In the years to come there would be eight more pyramids built, this time by the hands of Third Density Humans. They are located on a 63-mile stretch of land on the west bank of the Nile River. None of the eight could measure up to the original, magnificent specimen created sub-etherically by MAN.

Many pyramids have been constructed on the surface of the Planet over a long period of time. Some were constructed by MAN, some by men. Some pyramids still exist to the view of men, while many are buried beneath the land and sea.

The entrance of the Great Pyramid is located on the North side and is 54 feet above the base. It is nine square feet in size. This passage descends downward to a subterrainean chamber. There it meets a stairway that ascends to the Queen's Chamber, and then on up to the King's Chamber. At the bottom of the entrance stairway is another passageway, 63 feet in length that deadends at a blank wall. Nine feet beyond this blank wall lies the passageway to those great generators.

The original dimensions of the Great Pyramid were — Base: 765 feet, Height: 486 feet. The pyramid is currently measured — Base: 761 feet, Height: 484 feet. Destruction by the elements have taken their toll.

-Nine Is The Key-

You may have noticed that all of the dimensions that have been presented are divisible by nine. This is no coincidence — it was intended. Long ago MAN had discovered that any

NOTES:

facility or mechanism that incorporates *magnetic energy* must be designed in such a way that its componenent specifications must be divisible by nine; congruent to the standard of measurement being employed. This practice assures the maximum results from the endeavor. Third Density would do well to take note. Magnetic and electro-magnetic laws are governed by the rule of nine. This is an example of bridging physics with metaphysics.

Chapter 10

The Pryamid According To Ra

Ra is a Mid-Sixth Density Social Memory Complex. There are over 320,000 incarnated Human Beings who have contact with those of Ra. Many have enjoyed and profited from this magnificent source of information. We shall share some of his insight with you.

According to Ra, the pyramids were built with "living stone." But then *all* stone is living. Stone is comprised of atoms. Atoms have a nucleus with electrons orbiting. This is motion. When an object is in motion it is alive. Atoms are energy. Energy is intelligent. Intelligent Energy is Love. Stones are living Love, incorporated into a "solid" form. This explanation, though quite correct, is not what Ra was referring to. A Sixth Density Entity would see "living stone" as the product of an etheric Time/Space thought form that has been manifested in Space/Time physical.

The larger pyramids were thought forms constructed in Time/Space and then manifested in Space/Time at strategic locations upon the surface of the Earth. Several were constructed in the early development of Atlantis. These large pyramids ringed the Planet at approximately 30 degrees North latitude. Some had capstones of copper, some of granite, and some of crystal. These pyramids, appropriately constructed with the correct capstone and situated at the sensitive power points indigenous to this Planet, permitted the Logos (Earth Mother) to stabilize herself, and the unwanted shifting of the axis was eliminated. Some of the pyramids were located upon land masses that have since sunk, such as Atlantis. These ones are mis-aligned and in a state of disrepair, and are not functioning very well, if at all. Other pyramids were intentionally placed beneath the waters on a firm sea bed, and these ones still function quite effectively. The Social Memory Complex of Ra and one other Social Memory Complex were the prime movers in this noble endeavor. The Confederation of MAN — Fourth Density, worked diligently with these Sixth Density Entities in this

NOTES:

enterprise, as the Social Memory Complexes had learned the understanding of *unity*. All Creative Forces focusing upon a single thought (form) permitted manifestation from Time/Space to Space/Time. This was a tremendous teaching for those of Fourth Density MAN. Third Density Humans were simply overwhelmed, and let it go at that.

The Purpose

The purpose of constructing the pyramids was multi-dimensional. An edifice of reverence, sanctuary, and power to be used as a place of Initiation for the evolving Third Density Entities inhabiting this wayward Planet was deemed to be most important. Evolution could not be stagnated due to lack of facilities and teachers. This opportunity to be of service to others was seen as an honor/duty by those of Fourth Density MAN. The Queen's Chamber and/or the Resonating Chamber was used for this purpose. These purifying rituals permitted the Chela to come face to face with self, and thus see and identify his Source. This awareness of self opened the door to the eventual Harvesting of self from Third Density to Fourth Density. These initiations allowed the student to telepathically tap into Sources higher and alien to self for further instruction. This is often referred to as "channeling" in today's vocabulary.

Healing

Another purpose of the complex structure was for the teaching of the art of healing. As the student developed in understanding, he was taught the means of sharing this knowledge/practice with those Third Density Entities of his own kind. The dependence on the original teachers was eliminated as quickly as possible. It should be noted here that the healing being referred to is not altogether the healing of the physical body. More appropriate is the healing of ignorance. This was the goal, for it promoted evolution which was heretofore moving in circles and at a snail's pace. In your observations you might conclude that very little has changed in the past 48,000 years. This is an observation to be sure, and it is not necessarily incorrect!

NOTES:

The student thus learned to heal self and then to heal other selves. At this time the Earth Mother was recovering from a recent Glacial Age and she required much healing herself. All healing is accomplished via Love. Words of Love were sent to the Earth Mother from MAN and men, even as the pyramids themselves offered stabilizing energies to the very core of her beingness. The ring of the larger pyramids were "charged" by the Adept using the crystal energy. This had the effect of making the Seven Rays once again acceptable to the Earth Mother. Unity was again being re-established after half of self lay dormant for so many centuries. The Logos was beginning to grasp the feeling of the totality of self after the numbness was eliminated and life was restored.

Stabilizing The Planet Via The Ley Lines

The pyramids built by MAN via the Social Memory Complex, RA, ringed the Planet. Six of these Great Pyramids were designed for the purpose of stabilizing the Planet. These were strategically located around the 30 degree latitude, and were equipped with the great gyro generators. Some of these were installed on ocean floors, while others were hidden in the mountains. These ones have never been discovered. These balancing pyramids were programmed/charged with crystals in such a way that instreaming cosmic energies could be properly collected and distributed throughout the Planet via the ley lines. These ley lines form the network of Planetary Energy which permits the Earth Mother to be a "living" Planet. This electromagnetic capillary network encompasses the surface of this Planet and the energies radiate outward through the atmosphere and beyond. This energy field is the Aura of our Earth Mother. As MAN happens to "pass by," he can read this Aura/energy field. This is how he can quickly determine if the Planet needs assistance and precisely what kind of aid is required. The diagnosis is made and the appropriate prescription follows. These six balancing pyramids were extremely effective 47,600 years ago as the Planet was recovering from a Great Ice Age and axis shift. The energies could then be distributed and stabilized by these six

NOTES:

pyramids. The remaining pyramid at Giza was/is the hub, not at one of the Poles as you might expect. Imagine, if you will, a great spider web, and this web has its center at the Great Pyramid. The web is then wrapped around the Planet. This is the distribution pattern. Some of these balancing pyramids were used for Initiation as well.

Pyramids For Initiation

There were also 52 other pyramids built for Initiation purposes and the healing of Mind/Body/Spirit Complexes. These ones were not intended to offer Planetary Service/Healing. The teaching of the prospective teachers was the ultimate goal. These edifices were scattered all over the face of the Earth. They were operated by those of MAN who disguised themselves as "priests," taking on the physical appearance of the local gentry.

The Confederation of MAN was responsible for the building of this ring of energy collectors, called pyramids. The brothers and sisters of Space, through their great compassion for a wayward and laggard Planet, and her unenlightened inhabitants, offered this Love gift. Their patient teachings still remain as the basic tenents to many creeds and cultures. Even as time and erosion have distorted the edifice, the teachings also have lost much of their purity.

The Capstones

According to the Social Memory Complex, Ra, the Great Pyramid at Giza had two cap stones. The second cap was of a golden hued metal which we commonly call copper. This head stone offered a touch of royalty, thus permitting priesthood to form, which the native Third Density Entities could observe in its awesome splendor.

Those of the Confederation saw this as most useful and did not choose to discredit it. The energies collected therein caused this polished cap to glow continuously. The unsophisticated, primitive Human was in constant awe of this phenomenal edifice. He dutifully paid homage to it and its occupants as they made their occasional appearances.

NOTES:

The original capstone was somewhat smaller and was made of pieces of the rock known as granite. These pieces were meticulously cut out and fit together to form a pyramid on top of a pyramid. Granite was chosen because of its crystalline qualities. This granite capstone was replaced with the copper cap at the time when MAN departed the Planet and no longer established residency within the great structures.

The Great Pyramid was equipped with air vents to circulate fresh air into the various chambers within. The most famous of these is the vent that is angled at approximately 30 degrees on the North face. This shaft centers the Pole Star. Fresh air circulates throughout the pyramid, but does not create a draft at any place. The vents draw air like a chimney.

The Motivating Energy — Love

The cutting, shaping, and moving of huge rocks in a method that is non-physical requires the reader to establish an in-depth understanding of the Universal Law of Love that goes far beyond the Human concept of this Creative Force. Energy is intelligent. Intelligent Energy is Love. Love is universal. It is equal. It is Unity. It is the functioning essence of ALL THAT IS. Love *is* the One Infinite Creator. An Entity, any Entity, is living energy. An Entity may take on any physical form. MAN is a physical form. A rock is a physical form. Both are energy. Energy is intelligent. Intelligence can communicate. MAN is a *thinking* aspect of energy. A rock is energy expressing a willingness to serve. The bond between MAN and rock is Love. Love is Intelligent Energy. MAN thinks. The willing rock responds. The harmony is Love. Love is the Creator. MAN is a Co-Creator. Attune yourself to the slow but powerful vibrations of the Red Ray and your wish becomes the rock's command!

Thought is powerful. Thought can move mountains. The mountains are physical. All physical reality is an *illusion.* Thought can readily move an illusion. You will no doubt be obliged to inject *faith* or perhaps *belief* in the initial stages of employing this procedure. Third Density relies heavily upon

NOTES:

these elements, while Fourth Density Entities have evolved beyond these concepts of doubt long, long ago.

The energy field around the rock is actually the counterpart of the physical rock. This energy field is the etheric rock which the physical rock is the reflection thereof. The communication is made to/with the etheric rock/energy field. Remember, all things are a product of their Aura. This energy field is the Aura. The Aura is the etheric body. As the thinking intelligence makes the request of the rock to split and move, the etheric rock readily grasps this idea. It splits. As it does so, it reflects this action to the physical rock. The connection is established in Time/Space. The instigating agency is thought. Thought is consciousness. This *is* the One Infinite Creator. You have humbly accepted yourself as Co-Creator. This power is your inheritance. Use it wisely.

The thinking Entity, (you), understanding the *unity* of the Creator of Creation, invokes the Love/Manifestation aspects of the Green Ray. The Red Ray Energy Field of the rock instantly cooperates with this intelligent request. An *innate* desire to serve provides the harmony. The thought is accomplished. The Law is ONE. The living rock is Love. The mountain is Love. The Creator is Love. The mountain is the Creator. Think on this as you watch the dynamite and the bulldozers at work.

These then are the mechanics of how thought power can act on and move stone. This may be accomplished at a distance or as the practitioner stands in the immediate area. Thought has no boundaries. This procedure is commonplace for Fourth, Fifth, and Sixth Density Entities. It is not impossible for the Third Density Entity to also achieve this power. A strong balance between Love and Wisdom must first be achieved before the Higher Self will permit the power to flow. As you learned in the healing practice, the isosceles triangle — Love/Wisdom — must be well-formed before the base leg of the triangle can grow to form the *equilateral* triangle. Once the three-fold flame: Love/Wisdom/Power has been equalized you can do anything. Healing, splitting stones, moving stones, etc., are but examples of this magnificent unity. This is possible because the Law is . . . ONE!

Individual Vs. Mass Consiousness

Those of you who are native to this Third Density Vibration will be obliged to accept this basic Universal Law of Manifestation on the basis of faith. Intelligent Infinity cannot be proven in the laboratory. The balancing of intangibles becomes folly in the minds of many men. Congruent faith can bridge this gap. Only a few would muster the courage to attempt it. Through evolution and mental practice there comes a time when you simply *know* these Universal Laws to be correct and you *accept* them as part of your total beingness. Faith/belief now has subtly faded away.

This is the power of the Mass Mind as well as the power of the individual mind. Both may be the same or they could be different. In Third Density, the individual is a portion of the masses, a product thereof. It is this factor that keeps evolution going around in circles. Occasionally a Wanderer will come forth in the Human form and offer an alternative way. This is always met with resistance. Third Density is not eager to submit to change. From within, the seeds of dissent are sowed. They may or may not find fertile ground. Additional attempts are made. Eventually a breakthrough is achieved. *The individual can convert the masses.* The individual can indeed move the mountain. The masses can also move the mountain. When the mountain is finally moved, it is *usually* the Mass Mind that does the job rather than the individual. Thus, Free Will is rarely abridged. The individual usually plays the role of the teacher, the catalyst. The Third Density Mass Mind is not basically willing to accept the thought of this possibility. Yet, when Third Density men built the eight lesser pyramids along the 63-mile segment of the Nile River, selected elite groups of Humans were gathered on the hillside and together they moved many of the monoliths into place by thought power alone! Because they had witnessed this type of activity by MAN they knew it was not impossible. At that time, in that age Third Density had its "proof,"

NOTES:

faith/belief was not required. This is not true today. Dwell in Love. Seek the Light. Power shall be added unto you. The purified, polarized Entity is unlimited in its abilities. This is perfection. This is the goal of all. Pursue this seeking with diligence.

The Original Builders

The Great Pyramid was thought about, and built by many. The Social Memory Complex, Ra, accomplished this work. But what of those ones from Aldebaron who declared to have built this edifice some 47,600 years ago themselves? Remember, any Social Memory Complex consists of millions of entities. Could not some of the population of Aldebaron be a part of the Social Memory Complex of Ra? Would not a Social Memory Complex spread itself out to crue the maximum experience possible? Those of MAN hailing from the Star System Aldebaron view the happenings through the eyes of Fourth Density MAN, just as you are attempting to understand through the limitations of Third Density Human. Ra is offering a Sixth-Density version of the same thing. As you can see, the Law of Confusion has not been eliminated.

Those of Ra built the pyramid of living rock. This is sometimes referred to as *Everlasting Rock.* Either way, it simply means: etheric rock. Though some of the larger pyramids were constructed of Earth materials, and the stones were cut and moved by thought power, nevertheless, the Great Pyramid was not. This one was thought/built *completely* in the etheric Time/Space, and then manifested- completed during the course of a single night! The natives were astonished at what the Light of dawn revealed! As their courage strengthened and their approach grew closer it was evident that the structure was made of many stones. It appeared to be constructed. The priests/teachers dwelling inside *probably* constructed it. Since it was a thought form made manifest, it could have just as easily been made of a single rock! It was concluded that this sight would have been too much for the Human mind to comprehend, and the "priests" would have been worshipped as gods and that was not desirable. The confusion was sufficiently great as it was. The pyramid *appears* to be the result of construction, not thought.

The Initiation Chambers

The Queen's Chamber and the subterranean Resonating Chamber are the two prime areas used for Initiation. The entrance to the Resonating Chamber was automatically sealed, as this mechanism was triggered by plundering grave robbers. Greed we have with us always. The Initiation did not constitute the joining in the membership of a physical group or organization. It did involve the joining of a "group." The "group" is the Multi-dimensional Self, the Monad, the Higher Self . . . the communication with one's own Soul. *This is the Initiation.* Coming face to face with self is a magnificent and awesome experience. This is The Rapture. The pyramid provides a proper edifice for the purifying and energizing of the Initiate to prepare the Mind, the Body, and the Spirit for dedicated service to others, as the Entity wanders the Planet and then wanders the Universe, seeking opportunity to perform the Creator's work. These Initiations were instrumental in teaching the teachers as MAN, in the disguise of "priests," offered this aid to a budding civilization.

The Healing Chamber

The vibration of the King's Chamber level was built for the express purpose of healing the native Earthling. This vibration corresponds with the Green Ray Love/Healing energy of the Heart Chakra. This energy level is found at approximately one-fifth of the height of the pyramid above the base. If the pyramid is so constructed that the apex angle is less than 70 degrees then the King's Chamber Effect is eliminated. The apex angle of the Great Pyramid is 76 degrees.

The Resonating Chamber

The shape of the pyramid embraces many potentials for experience/service. First, the mind must be opened (Queen's

NOTES:

Chamber). Second, the body must be healed (King's Chamber). And third, the spirit must be integrated (Resonating Chamber). When the personality has become sufficiently aware of self so that the true identity of the mind is revealed, then the mind must know the body and its functioning in all ways. The learning and practice of mind over matter begins with the self. The personality mentally detaches from the body to objectively manipulate it. Knowledge/understanding are the prime tools. The vibration of the Resonating Chamber permits the student to mentally release the body as though temporarily dead so that another life might begin afresh in the new and resurrected physical body. It should be emphasized that this experience is real and not "imagined." If you ever participate in this Initiation, we assure you, you shall never be the same again!

The Apothem Line

Continuing to use the Great Pyramid as the example, if the apothem (the vertical line from base to apex on a face) were to be installed on one or all of the faces this point(s) would be the appropriate location for Cosmic Energies (Rays) to enter the pyramid. This would be especially potent on the East/West faces. If your pyramid is large enough for you to position yourself at this point, Intelligent Infinity can readily be contacted. This location in a smaller pyramid could be used to prepare your small crystal for Indigo Ray/Third Eye work.

The Size

The size of the pyramid has distinct advantages. A pyramid small enough to be placed beneath or over the body could be useful. A pyramid large enough to enter also has distinct advantages. For schooling, learning and initiation the physical size must be sufficient to be impressive to the student and large enough to accommodate instreaming cosmic energies, especially if several students are assembled. The King's Chamber must need be large enough to accommodate the healer and the one to be healed.

The Great Pyramid yet functions, but ever so feebly. The electromagnetic field around the Planet has shifted, thus affecting

NOTES:

the directional flow of the Earth's Energies. The Cosmic Energy points of reception on the apothems are no longer as efficient as they once were. Tourists have used the King and Queen's Chambers as toilets, thus lowering the vibrations even further. To re-align the Great Pyramid would not be possible for Third Density men to do. The Social Memory Complex, Ra, could readily do the job, but the time of the pyramids is past. Using this edifice to aid in introducing Intelligent Infinity to Third Density was most desirable. In those days, there were none who could do this. Now, many Third Density Humans are able to penetrate Intelligent Infinity. Though useful, healing is not dependent upon the pyramid.

A pyramid of any desired size could be constructed that could incorporate many useful qualities. The ratio of Time/Space and these complexes would have to be calculated. Stated as a porportion it would be:

Etheric : Earth = Earth : Astral
Etheric x Astral = Earth squared
Astral — Etheric = Earth — Etheric
Astral = Earth

The Negative Service

Ra's pyramid was a thought form constructed in the etheric Time/Space and then manifested in the physical Space/Time. A Social Memory Complex such as Ra can readily accomplish this amazing feat; but *any Entity* of Fourth, Fifth, or Sixth Density status can perform the same phenomenon. The quality of the construct may vary, but the knowledge/ability as to the mechanics of manifestation is exactly the same.

We have discussed the manifestation of edifices, pyramids designed for Positive purposes — service to others. However, Orion — those ones of the Negative Polarization — also offered their service to Third Density from time to time and place to place. During the first major Cycle of 25,000 years or about 60,000 years ago, a Fourth Density Negative Entity elected to offer to the Third Density Earthlings instruction in the

NOTES:

art of service to self. This service was provided through telepathy. Though clearly received, this information was not readily accepted. Undaunted, the Fourth Density Negative Entity then chose to manifest thought forms of specific rock formations and certain statuary. These edifices were located in the areas that we currently call Central America, South America, and the Pacific Ocean.

Easter Island

The stone heads of Easter Island is one such example. Those peoples, who were indigenous to that area were awestruck at the sudden appearance of the stone heads, and certainly by their size and exquisite workmanship. These carvings were heavily charged with power and nothing more. Those Third Density personalities who stood in the sight of this statuary, could freely absorb this power into themselves. This power could then be used over things of which they had no control such as the wind, the weather, and the sea. They quickly learned that this same power could also be used to control other selves. A priesthood quickly formed and only these elite ones were permitted to be in the presence of these power charged statues. "Taboo" was established and government/slavery had its early beginnings.

The Orion Entity learned the minds of the peoples, and used this data to develop and construct the thought forms that would be the most likely to impress his audience. It was absolutely necessary that these uninitiated "primitive" peoples be "awestruck" at first sight. This process humbles the viewer instantly, and an attitude of subserviancy is instilled in the beingness of the personality. The power, or sense of power, was overwhelming. The viewer was inspired by the size of the things and the power offered. Control over the elements was certainly useful for the sake of survival. When this was adequately established, then the power was used to control other selves. Raw power, with no instruction, in the hands of Human Beings becomes self-serving. The Orion Entity understood the Earthling

NOTES:

quite well. He did his homework you might say. Understanding is a tenet of Fourth Density, be the Entity Positive or Negative.

Orion did not personally appear to do the job. All of this was accomplished from a distance in Time/Space. Thought has no boundaries or limitations. Centuries later, Third Density Humans quarried stone and fashioned statuary in the likeness of the originals. These were carved with a great deal of accuracy, however, they were never charged with power. The priesthood, now having invented superstition, could use this to compensate for the absence of power.

Central America

Central America, the land of the Maya, had their phenomena of unexplained statuary as well. The stone heads of entities, obviously Negroid, appeared randomly throughout the land. These stone heads were several times larger than real life. The Mayan had never seen an African Black Man. The two cultures never met. Yet the image of the Negroid is unmistakable. This was the work of Orion. These heads were also charged with power. The effect was similar to that of the peoples of the Pacific. Remember that this had its beginnings some 60,000 years ago and the Mayan peoples were but an outpost of the great continent of Lemuria (Mu). Actually, at that time the Black Race had not yet been introduced, or seeded, on Planet Earth. It would be almost 50,000 years later before the White Race would have its turbulent beginnings.

South America

South America also was presented with statuary, but this continent was bestowed mostly with formations of earth and rock. The lines on the plains of Nazca is a prime example of Orion's artistic abilities. Over a long period of time wind and weather have definitely taken their toll. The giant engravings are still quite visible if viewed from sufficient height and distance. Their initial charge of raw power has long since dissipated. The sloping plains of Nasca were simply the stage or the setting. Those ones who inhabited South America were not the ones who

NOTES:

Orion intended to impress. No, it was the Lemurians! In those days a great high plateau arose opposite the plains of Nasca. A large audience could assemble here to view the spectacle. The viewer was charged with the power. Orion had his sights set on Mu.

North America

North America, especially in the Mississippi and Ohio Valleys, had its mounds. These structures were much more recent and were constructed not by Orion, but by Third Density Entities not of this Planet. There are those from the Star System known as Serius, who are also Third Density who have developed a crude system of space travel. Since the sinking of Atlantis, a party of these ones became marooned in what is currently known as the Southern Mississippi Valley. An edifice was laboriously constructed to serve as a "signal beacon" to attract their own search parties. It was successful and they were rescued. Those of the Red Race quietly noted these proceedings. Extraterrestrial visitation was not all that unusual in those days. In order to attract a possible return other such edifices were constructed in the shape of animals and birds. These mounds are not to be confused with the ancient works of Orion. Atlantis was also served in this manner by Orion, but these creations have disappeared with the final sinking of Atlantis some 11,600 years ago. Other portions of the current dry-land Earth, have received Orion's greeting, but they have mostly perished with time and erosion.

Power Stimulates Growth

It is significant to note that when Positivity is introduced to a budding Third Density Culture, Negativity must also be allowed to display its wares. This is the concept of free choice as it was decreed by our Solar Logos (Sun). Informations of both kinds must be made available, otherwise the concept of choice would be invalid.

If we were to awaken some fine morning, and discover a huge, magnificent statue magically appearing in our midst, radiating intense personal power that the viewer could use for

NOTES:

any purpose — would not the most Positive amongst us be tempted to take this power to town and fix a few things that have been begging for attention for decades? Think on this. It is easy to see how raw power is readily turned into service to self, even by very Positive Entities who face the challenge of survival on a daily basis and are filled with righteous anger.

The Calling — The Service

The Social Memory Complex, Ra, began to service those of Earth as the Earthly callings came forth. This was approximately 60,000 years ago as the newly emerging Lemurians requested information on the Law of ONE. For 1,500 years this information/teachings were offered telepathically. Later, etheric thought form pyramids were manifested on that great continent for the purpose of healing the mind and body. After the great axis shift which resulted in the sinking of Mu, those of Ra answered the call of the Atlantians, for a great healing was indeed in order.

The Pyramids Of The West

There was and is the second Social Memory Complex that responded to the calling. Those of this Complex served mostly in the areas of Central and South America. Those Entities who were indigenous to these areas, worshipped our Solar Logos (Sun). Others throughout the Planet also did as much. The Sun is seen as the source of Light and Life — a power to be revered. Light Beings of the Social Memory Complex, Vetulus Miumo, visited these peoples, assuming a body construct like those ones present. Working with the peoples of the Red Race, a series of underground cities were constructed. The use of the Vril Rod was permitted by the Saturn Tribunal for ease in hollowing out solid rock and shaping stone for constructing edifices, including pyramids. The Vril Rod is a tool, held in the hand, that can cut, melt, or levitate stone. Today's laser would be a poor substitute.

Not all the pyramids and other structures were committed to beneath the surface. The pyramid configuration of this Social Memory Complex was different than the pyramids designed by

NOTES:

those of Ra. These were the step pyramids of the Mayan peoples, found extensively in the Yucatan. These step pyramids, like the Pyramid of Ra in Egypt were designed and intended for Healing, Initiation, and basking in the divine essence of Our One Infinite Creator.

Those ones of Vetulus Miumo actually enjoyed more success with their teachings of these peoples than did those of Ra in Atlantis/Egypt. The teachings were recorded in stone, in the form of Mayan glyphs. This actually continued for approximately 3,500 years. Having completed this work, these ones left. Approximately 2,500 years later it was duly noted that errors were being practiced by the Earth peoples. After receiving permission from the Saturn Tribunal, an Entity of the Social Memory Complex of Vetulus Miumo was dispatched to correct the errors. This was successful for the time.

Much, much later, millenniums later, the teachings were again distorted, even as the teachings of Ra were also suffering the same fate. The Inca, the Mayan, the Toltec, and the Aztec had now developed a ruling priesthood bent on acquiring power to enslave the peoples. The pyramids were used as places of Human sacrifice rather than the temples of healing as they were intended. Orion was offering information on service to self and it was readily being devoured by those in government positions.

The grand teachings of the two Social Memory Complexes have been distorted and defiled by the greedy, power hungry elite of Third Density Earthlings. Free Will, the Law of Confusion permits this. The Complexes are responsible. They freely answered the call. They could have freely ignored it just as well. Now, these two Social Memory Complexes have the honor/duty to *remain* until all of these mis-teachings have been unlearned, and then worked out properly in the Third Density Minds of men. As Laggard Souls continue to incarnate, this appears to be a never-ending task.

There are no fragments of the Social Memory Complex of Ra that are incarnated at this time; however, thousands of those in the Human form channel this Source. There are many fragments of the Social Memory Complex of Vetulus Miumo

NOTES:

who are incarnated at present, but no one channels this Source. Thus, the balance is struck as the Law of Confusion remains unabridged.

Ra's Pyramid

The Great Pyramid of Giza, or Ra's Pyramid, has an apex angle of 76 degrees — 18 minutes. This is most appropriate because this configuration creates the healing effect associated with the King's Chamber. If the apex angle were less than 70 degrees, the King's Chamber affect would be eliminated.

Healing

Above the King's Chamber are several smaller chambers. These secondary Chambers permit the "storage" of certain energies that are removed from the Entity during the healing process. Light is the agent that separates these Human Life Forces and safely stores them in these various chambers during the healing. The Entity to be healed is positioned with his/her head to the North. The pyramid energies automatically interrupt or open the patient's aura. This is similar to the surgeon opening the abdominal cavity with a scalpel. As the operation continues, various tubes are inserted that permit material to flow into or flow from, various receptacles. These small rooms above the King's Chamber serve in a very similar fashion.

This physical arrangement permits the patient to safely separate its energies in a highly protected way and thusly, allows the Will to be considerably more effective as the patient is determined to heal self. The skilled healer conducts this process and often uses crystals to aid in the opening of the Aura, and to concentrate energy on blocked centers. This noble assistance permits the patient to heal self. After the completion of the healing ritual, the healer will use the crystals to restore the total Aura to the patient. The knowledge/skill of the healer is most vital. It is unlikely that the patient would be able to accomplish all this without aid, and therefore it should not be attempted. With guidance, the consciousness is drawn away, thus permitting the healed and total etheric body to now cast its uninterrupted

NOTES:

reflection upon the open and vulnerable physical body. Healing now manifests in the physical body. The temporary lack of active consciousness allows the patient the opportunity to practice near total recall of the current incarnation and perhaps Past Lives as well. Healing is, essentially the personality understanding self, accepting self, and forgiving self. This may be accomplished under various circumstances, but the pyramid is an instrument that definitely enhances the procedure.

There are air vents strategically located in the Great Pyramid. The temperature and the barometric pressure are construed through these vents. The electrically charged atmosphere is produced by the First Spiralling Energy that terminates at the level of the King's Chamber. These three major aspects, properly harmonized, cause the patient to arrive at an equilibrium that is acceptable to permit the separation of energies for specific healing purposes. This could be compared to the monitored temperature of an operating room.

The Purpose Of The Shape Of The Pyramid

The pyramid does not labor, it does not work — not in the sense that a machine works. Its unique shape collects energies, centralizes them and spirals them upward. The Pranic or Life Force Energy of a Mind/Body/Spirit Complex also is endowed with a spiralling energy. Though it does no work, the pyramid can nevertheless be thought of as a living Entity. The pyramid creates a Negative field, and the Positive Energy is intensified as this Prana, the core, spirals upward. This Life Force, which is the ONE Infinite Creator, is that which you know as the Kundalini.

Preparing For Healing Via The Queen's Chamber

As the personality enters the Queen's Chamber, this pyramid energy stimulates the Kundalini within the Mind/Body/Spirit Complex as it attempts to match this energy. The Queen's Chamber area of the pyramid is designed/-

NOTES:

constructed to cause the Entity to be able to make a conscious contact with the Higher Self. This euphoric communion is sometimes referred to as a resurrection. This Initiation provides an in-depth understanding of self by the self. A master could be most useful to aid in this work, but it can be actively accomplished by self. A resurrected "new self" is likely to emerge.

Again, the healing is only as good as the healer. The healer must be balanced within self in order to recognize the imbalances/blockages within the other self. Etheric vision and/or a definite sensitivity to vibrations and color is a must. These attributes of the successful healer are inherited, for this one has served in this capacity in many Past Lives. This crystallized being has indeed earned his right to be called a healer.

Pyramid Healing

The King's Chamber effect which is produced in almost any pyramid having an apex angle greater than 70 degrees is the collector of the specific energies that effects a healing. Accurate shapes and dimensions can and do create specific energies designed for specific purposes. The King's Chamber Effect of certain pyramids is the case in point.

The Human Body is protected by the Violet/Red aspects of the Rainbow Aura. The Violet "shell" is the outermost color, while the Red is found next to the body. The pyramid effect, which is an aid to the healer, automatically opens the outer Aura, the Violet, permitting the healer to enter the inner Aura to manipulate the colors in a more balanced manner. This is the etheric healing. Then, the Red Ray of protective armor is opened so that the "reflection" of this etheric healing might be passed on to the physical body. Thus, the physical healing now being achieved. This necessary opening and closing of the Aura is quite automatic when a properly designed pyramid is being employed.

The healer, the crystallized being, focusing his/her knowledge and compassion to heal/serve through the personalized crystal now easily and rapidly adjusts, manipulates, and regenerates the patient's Aura. Time/Space and Space/Time

NOTES:

merge at this level of vibration, and the desired results are achieved.

If the armor, Red and Violet, is not opened a healing cannot occur. If this protection is interrupted by the healer under conditions other than the pyramid edifice, a greater intensity of trauma shall probably occur. The working of a healing might be likened to the conditions of the battlefield as compared to the facilities of the operating room in a hospital. It is most desirable to minimize the trauma for the well-being of the patient. The patient is endowed with the illness and excessive trauma is *not* the agency of healing. So that we might not be guilty of discouraging the apprentice healer or the perspective patient, let us remind you that the pyramid shape was introduced to Third Density Humans almost 48,000 years ago. Those ones who inhabited the surface of this Planet at that time did not and had not yet achieved the level of vibration that the Mind/body/Spirit Complexes have today. The Human Being is much less vulnerable to trauma during these final days of the Third Density Cycle than he was during the first two thirds of this Great Cycle of evolution.

The pyramid shape is still quite useful to Third Density *if* skill and care are used. If the healer is un-crystallized (unpolarized) but perhaps a "well-intentioned" bungling zealot who is filled with compassion and lacking in knowledge/wisdom, the results could be disastrous. Employing the wrong configurations and alignments can cause the interrupted energy fields of the Aura to scatter wildly. Lacking knowledge, the healer may not be able to put things back as well as they were, to say nothing of effecting a healing. Furthermore, the healer could be diabolical in the offering of service and intentionally create problems for the patient. This could result in an effect similar to the extensive overuse of potent drugs, as they are used by portions of our culture today. In either case, the results are devastating and usually permanent. The pyramid is a tool, not a toy, and must not be used for recreational purposes.

When the pyramid is constructed so that the apex angle is a bit less than 70 degrees (Ra's pyramid apex angle is 76

NOTES:

degrees — 18 minutes) the King's Chamber effect is automatically eliminated. The step pyramids of the Mayan culture, designed by a different Social Memory Complex is such an example. These pyramids were designed expressly for meditation. The cone, the cylinder, and the dome are also shapes most useful to meditation.

Other Shapes

The cone is an extremely useful shape that collects the upward spiralling Light energies. The teepee was used extensively by the Plains Nations Peoples for milleniums. Though convenient, this design was no accident. This inherited information was implanted within these peoples by higher Sources intent on offering aid. Actually, the pyramid becomes a cone of energies, as the energies spiral upward. The spiral is the key. A cone is a spiral. This is the nature of the flow of energies. The arched structures of the woodland peoples were made of bent saplings and covered with birch bark. These abodes were in the shape of the Quanset Hut which was utilized so heavily by the military during World War II.

The hemisphere or dome structure is used by the Eskimo. The igloo is an easily constructed abode that readily collects energies in a most useful way.

The shape of the caves are natural and ancient. This structure has been used successfully to collect energies for the betterment of Second and Third Densities since time immemorial. The vaulted roof is also quite useful, but it is usually broken by a ceiling. Today, most vaulted structures are incorporated into burial or cemetery structures. These energies are of little value to a corpse.

The shape of the dome, the cylinder, the hemisphere, the cone, or the pyramid creates a spiralling energy flow. The cube cannot do this. This energy is electrified and actually operates much on the same principle as the induction coil. This is an etheric coil of Light as opposed to a coil of copper wire wound around an iron core; nevertheless, the energy-producing effect is the same. The angles and dimensions are of little importance —

NOTES:

it is the shape that matters. Heavy metals should not be used in the construction of these edifices. Wood, glass, masonry are materials of a more appropriate consistency.

It must be noted that collected energy may be used for Negative or detrimental purposes as well as Positive. The edifice may be improperly constructed or located in an improper alignment. The intent of the occupant/practitioner may very well be grossly imbalanced; thus, the offering of service to a Entity of sensitivity could result in increased illness rather than the desired/intended healing. The power of the rounded edifice can be disastrous in the charge of the uninitiated just as readily as it can be a powerful asset in the charge of the crystallized being. The power of the Creator simply *is*. Free Will permits the distortion of this power in any direction. Responsibility is often learned the hard way.

A square shaped abode offers no collection of energies. Almost all structures are of this shape. There is no advantage, there is also no danger in using the square shape. Considering the mental attitude of the "civilized" masses, perhaps the shape is *ideal!* The corner angles spoil the upward spiralling effect of the natural energy rise. Thus, the cone is more useful than is the pyramid. The cylinder shape produces a different configuration of energy patterns.

It is the Geometric shape of any given edifice that does or does not *funnel light* in a desired direction. Etheric light cannot be contained. It may be guided, instructed, channeled — but it may not be contained, boxed, or stored. The Creator's Energy is not made like that. Light and Love are the Second and Third Creative Forces that are gifted to all thinking entities to discover, to understand, and to use.

The potential for misuse of the Queen's Chamber effect is minimal. The potential for misuse of the King's Chamber effect for healing is great. The necessary purity of the healer is a rare commodity. The King's Chamber should be used *only* if a crystallized/polarized Entity is present. This one may be the healer or the teacher of the apprentice healer. The availability of a pyramid with dimensions as accurate as Ra's Pyramid is

NOTES:

probably more rare than is a crystallized healer. It may be further noted that the crystallized healer is virtually a *mobile* King's Chamber and this energy is endowed within the purity of this devoted and dedicated Entity.

New Alignment

The pyramids still in existence today continue to function in balancing the Earth Mother's energies, though this work is only a fraction of its original capacity. This loss of function is due to the Planet's changing vibrations that are quite naturally a product of evolution. The Law of Motion produces change. Change is growth. Growth is evolution. The magnetic attitude of the mantle *has* shifted and *is* shifting. This will coincide with the axis shift which will be a portion of the Earth Mother's Transition from Third Density to Fourth Density. Consequently, the most efficient alignment for a pyramid today is *not* North to South, but 20 degrees NNE! The *New* Poles will be at right angles to this line. Continuing to use the same dimensions and angles, this new alignment permits a renewed vitality to the healing of the King's Chamber and the meditative qualities of the Queen's Chamber.

Earth And Cosmic Energies

Since a portion of the pyramid's collective energies are "Earth Energies" (as opposed to Cosmic Energies), then it stands to reason that as the Earth Mother's energies vascilate, so do the pyramid's energies. Therefore, the workings of any functioning pyramid will vary from time to time. Cosmic Energies, though considerably more stable will also fluctuate occasionally. Your own moods are living evidence of this. Even the crystallized Adept working within the pyramid may not always be appropriately attuned to the current sets of vibrations. This is a random thing and cannot be predicted. Pyramid energies will sometime weaken as the diffusion of the color spectrum of the three major energies intersects at the apex. If the pyramid is designed for learning such as the Mayan step pyramid then this distortion is slight, for the Mind/Spirit easily compensates. If the pyramid is

NOTES:

designed for healing such as Ra's Pyramid at Giza then this diffusion could have a much greater effect on the Mind/Body Complex of the one to be healed, since information on taking appropriate steps/action probably would not be available. However, it must also be realized that none of this is a major issue, and should not offer discouragement to the apprentice who is learning and practicing his Craft.

Chapter 11

The Queen's Chamber

The Queen's Chamber is of a certain section and a certain height in Ra's Pyramid, designed to create a specific vibration that is most conducive to meditation. This is most attractive to the polarized entity and/or the entity attempting polarity. The personality seeking polarity simultaneously seeks spirituality, for both are the same path.

Via the Ley Lines, Earth energies flow in a North to South direction. The pyramid shape captures/collects these energies as well. The Queen's Chamber is insulated from these energies. This unique "vacuum" permits the initiate to exercise the "Inner Light" undistorted. The Inner Light moves from South to North, i.e., from feet to head.

This Inner Light is the heart of your beingness. The Will of the Initiate is undaunted. If more than one is present the combined Wills of the Seekers is intensified. The chaff of Third Density falls away as the purity of the Divine Inner Light rises and carries the consciousness to the euphoric union with the Higher Self. The seeking intensifies. The at oneness with self is achieved. The at oneness with the Universe is acknowledged. The at oneness with the One Infinite Creator is humbly accepted. The Inner Light has returned to it's Source, the Creator; and the consciousness of the Seeker (the Initiate) is covered with it. The Seeker realizes and accepts his responsibility, honor, and duty as a Co-Creator. In the Queen's Chamber, this incoming Inner Light strips away all the impurities of the personality as the Divine Entity re-emerges for the first time since birth. The rapture is complete. The Inner Light *is* your Kundalini.

This hallowed and sacred place of Initiation is designed to free the Seeker of worldly cares and distractions. The aligning, balancing, and clearing of the chakras is simplified. The seeking of the Creator is honored. The abandonment of self is achieved. The in-streaming Light enters each chakra in a balanced form. The Seeker becomes at one with self, as the consciousness rises, seeking the Creator, merging with the

NOTES:

Higher Self. *This is the Kundalini rise;* as the rising pristine energies reach the Indigo, the penetrating of Intelligent Infinity now takes place. The consciousness is thrilled ecstatically! As the union with the Higher Self continues to solidify, the euphoria is often termed: The Resurrection.

The ultimate goal of the initiation is for the Seeker to realize and grasp the concept that All is ONE. As one seeks the Creator with this understanding, then one realizes that there is nothing in Creation that *isn't* the Creator! The responsibility of the Seeker being a Co-Creator now takes on a broader and richer meaning. This is awesome in its magnificence.

Queen's Chamber Effect In The Mayan Pyramid

The Social Memory Complex of Ra designed the Egyptian pyramid to function as an edifice of healing (King's Chamber position), and as a place of Initiation/Learning. In Ra's Pyramid, the solitary Seeker enters the Queen's Chamber for the experience. In Atlantis, South America, and Central America the Social Memory Complex of Vetulus Miumo created the step pyramid with apex angles less than 70 degrees. These pyramids were designed for initiation and teaching/learning. Little attention was given to healing. In the "Mayan" pyramid the Teacher/Master/Adept *accompanied* the apprentice during the Initiation.

During this Initiation/Learning experience *in both types of pyramids,* entities from Time/Space would manifest within the chambers to offer teaching/instruction. This was considerably more traumatic under solitary conditions. The physical presence of the teacher offered much comfort to the startled student. Later, after having been taught "astral projection," the student (and teacher) would project selves to the Inner Planes for further teaching/learning. Teleportation was *not* used by the student/-teacher, only astral projection. These types of schools were also established in edifices other than pyramids. The pyramid is most useful, but it certainly is not mandatory. Other shapes are also quite powerful.

NOTES:

The Resonating Chamber

The Resonating Chamber is a very powerful space located beneath the base of the pyramid. It is within this vibration that the Adept actually comes face to face with self. The Co-Creator is now humbly and awesomely seen as the ONE Infinite Creator. This is a powerful experience and can be quite dangerous in the hands of the uninitiated.

The Resonating Chamber is usually a dome shaped structure, however, the bell shape will work just as well. The base of the dome equals om square feet the base of the pyramid divided by PHI (1.618). The heigth of the dome is equal to the heigth of the pyramid above, divided by PHI. PHI is used to determine the line that indicates the portion of the dome that is below grade, and the top portion that penetrates the interior of the pyramid. Approximately 62% of the dome lies beneath the ground and approximately 38% of the dome is above the surface, *inside* the pyramid. PHI is often referred to as the Sacred Cut or the Golden Cut.

Not all ancient pyramids are constructed with a Resonating Chamber, though many pyramids in Central and South America indeed have such structures built within the major edifice. This space was illuminated and energized by a Piezo-Electric Device placed on a pedestal in the center of the Resonating Chamber. This device was a hollow, thick-walled glass sphere about the size of a basketball. Inside, resting on a support is a small quartz crystal. The hollow interior is then filled with hydrogen under high pressure. A cone shaped glass plug is forced into its place by the pressure and the hydrogen is hermetically sealed within. The sphere is then superheated. The heat expands and electrically charges the hydrogen which acts upon the quartz crystal. The crystal glows with much brilliance and emits Piezo-Electric Energy. It is this power that permits the equipment, such as the gyro-generators to operate. Such a device, the size of a baseball, will power a very large Spacecraft. The device is recharged by again superheating. This would have to be done every 50,000 years. The Resonating Chamber was equipped with the device that produced the Piezo-Electrical

NOTES:

Energy that filled the chamber. The materials that were used and method of construction was similar to that of the Ark of the Covenant; that is, the Resonating Chamber is a . . . capacitor!

Piezo Electricity is known to Earth scientists, but it is not like AC or DC electricity that operates our appliances. Different types of equipment would have to be designed. Fossil fuels would be obsolete. Unlimited power would be available at absolutely no cost. The former Root Race, the Atlantians, had such devices but then their culture was not based on commerce as is the current Ayrian Root Race. Profit for industry and Power for politicians/governments determines the course the masses are obliged to follow. The captains of industry and the Kings of government established the system of enslavement the people mindlessly work within.

The self meets the self within the vibration of this chamber. This means that the lower self/ego reaches up to make conscious contact with the Higher Self. The Higher Self is without problem. The lower self uses the environment of the Resonating Chamber to achieve this union. It is equivalent to the raising of the Kundalini. The "death" of the ego is achieved. A reunion with the Higher Self is the Rapture. The eventual return to the body is the Resurrection — the loss of the old and the gain of the new; the transmutation into the "risen" being. The new self has emerged. All entities eligible for the Positive Harvest will experience as much as they detach themselves from Third Density and then embrace Fourth Density.

In the process of the Initiation of the Resonating Chamber, the Initiate loses the desires of materialism, while euphorically seeking catalysts/opportunities to serve others. The healing aspect of the King's Chamber has its beginnings in this hallowed space. Thus, the vibrations and environment of this chamber works on the body as well as the mind. When successful, the mind and the body harmoniously unite with the Higher Self, forming the complex that the Solar Logos had in mind as it planned that portion of Creation.

SECTION DRAWING
of
Ra's Pyramid

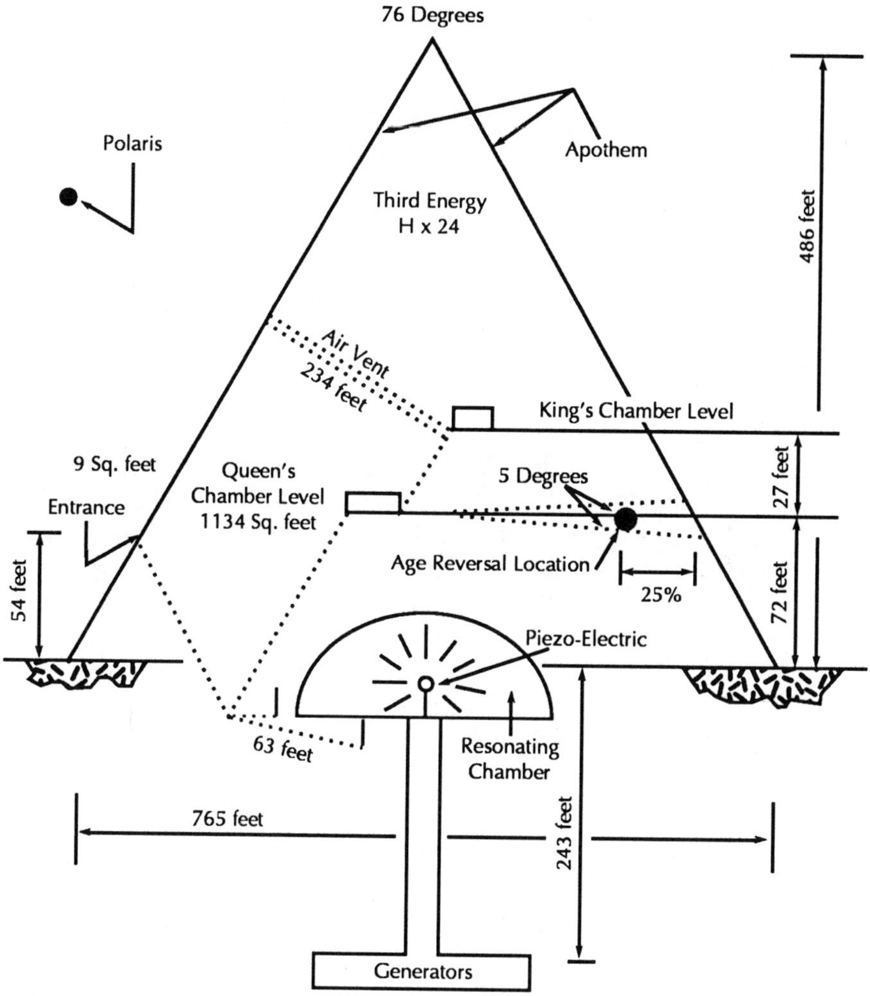

NOTES:

Other Methods

Flotation tanks have been constructed to produce similar results. The personality lies on his back in a tank of water heavily saturated with salt. The room is sound-proof and covered by darkness. A single Light that offers no illumination may be placed in the ceiling to provide a point of focus. The mind is deprived of sensory stimulation and the sensation of being buried alive is thus experienced. Releasing, detaching from Third Density mundania is quickened. A limbo status is forthcoming. A sence of belonging anywhere is felt — adrift in the Universe without purpose . . . a timeless state. As the ceiling light is gradually brightened and faint music can now be discerned, you are gently brought back and attached to your body as the resurrected being emerges from the pool.

How The Pyramid Functions

The pyramid is a collector of energies. There are essentially two types of energies: Planetary (magnetic) Energies, and Cosmic Energies. Earth's energies are sucked through the base from the flowing energies generated off the Earth's mantle. Cosmic Energies are attracted via the slope of the four sides. These combined energies are somewhat reconstructed and are sent flowing upward to the apex in a conical spiralling fashion. It is the design or shape, not the materials used that cause a pyramid to function. Wood, stone, or even plastic are the most acceptable materials. It matters not if the pyramid is solid or totally open. The establishing of the *line* of the four *edges* is the important factor. Even these four edges need not be complete. A base, properly aligned (20 degrees NNE) and leveled may have only four stubs accurately angled at each corner. These stubs then establish auxiliary lines that complete the pyramid shape. This "imaginary" pyramid functions just as well as the completed structure. Also a truncated apex may be constructed and this device may be secured to the ceiling. Careful attention must be given to the angles of the stubs of the edges now projecting downward to create the auxiliary lines that form the pyramid.

The truncated square apex is installed by aligning it 20 degrees NNE and leveling it just as you would the base.

Using these methods of partial construction allows the practitioner the opportunity to create a very large pyramid with little effort or expense. The edge members must be of a solid material. Hollow pipes or corrugated cardboard is not acceptable. Wooden or plastic rods/dowels will work very well. If one expects to dwell in this structure then obviously it would need to be closed in to afford protection from the weather.

The Three Energies Of The Pyramid

There are three distinct and separate energies that are collected within any functioning pyramid with an apex angle of approximately 76 degrees. These three energies each have specific uses/functions.

The First Energy begins near the base of the pyramid and coils upward, using the four faces of the pyramid as the guide. Looking downward, this Energy coils like a scoop in a clockwise fashion, reaching the level of the King's Chamber — and no higher.

The Second Energy also begins at the perimeter of the base of the pyramid, and it coils upward in the *opposite* direction; i.e., counter clockwise. This Second Energy is synchronized to miss the upward coiling of the First Energy. This Second Spiral of Light rises to the apex and no higher. This Energy is designed for the specific purpose of *building,* i.e., the manifestation of thought forms.

The Third Energy has its beginnings at the center of the base. The diameter of this spiral is approximately one ninth the width of the base. This Third Energy spirals upward, counter clockwise in a very slender cone. It reaches the apex and then fans out an angle that complements that of the apex of that given pyramid. An inverted cone of energy is now being emitted from the apex of the pyramid. This form of Light is used to energize that which is placed above it. This is a most powerful energy and *must* be used with care. For example, a pyramid with a height of four inches will emit a cone of Third Spiraling Energy eight

NOTES:

feet high! The ratio is: 1 to 24. One can readily imagine the beam of Light emitted by a pyramid several hundred feet in height. To spend the night on the top of a sizable pyramid is an event to be reckoned with!

The First Spiraling Energy

The shape of the pyramid creates an electromagnetic field about itself. All energy spirals. This shape is conducive to a *conical* spiral. The First Energy has its beginnings slightly above the base, and it is in the form of a sheet of Light. The width of the sheet of Light is the distance from the column of Third Energy at the center to the face of the pyramid. As this sheet of Light coils around the center or Third Energy, this diameter remains static, as though it were rising around a solid column. This First Energy sheet continues to touch the faces of the pyramid as it rises. The faces slope inwards; therefore, this sheet of Light narrows accordingly. This First Energy passes through the Queen's Chamber and activates the inspiration for meditation/study. As the narrowing and rising sheet of Light reaches the level of the King's Chamber it terminates. This is the ultimate energy/power used for healing.

It should be noted that the entrance to Ra's Pyramid is located on the North side at about the same level as the Queen's Chamber. One enters and descends almost to the base, then ascends to the level of the Queen's Chamber. A directional turn is made as one continues to ascend to the level of the King's Chamber. The King's Chamber is not directly above the Queen's Chamber. A working orientation of Ra's Pyramid is essential in order to grasp this understanding. It should be further noted that if the pyramid is constructed with an apex angle of less than 70 degrees, the First Energy (King's Chamber healing effect) is not produced. The First Energy is a useful and beautiful tool, but it may readily be seen the ease with which it could be misused. Only rarely is the Third Density Human Being sufficiently mature to responsibly handle such a gift.

NOTES:

The Healer's Etheric Pyramid

It should be further noted as the healer chooses to incorporate an etheric pyramid about self, the sheet of Light is a protrusion of the healer's own Kundalini, rising from *behind* the healer's spinal cord in a clockwise fashion, passing through the stems of each chakra as the rising, narrowing sheet of Light terminates at the stem of the Green Heart Chakra. The Green Ray is Love/Healing/Manifestation. Love *is* Intelligent Energy. (See Chapter 8.)

The Second Spiraling Energy

The Second Ray of Light has its beginnings at the base and spirals upward to the apex in a counterclockwise fashion. As the energy reaches the top third of the structure it becomes "compressed" and "intensified." This concentrates a considerable reservoir of energy in the Indigo Center. This coincides with the personality raising the Kundalini. The Indigo is the form maker, i.e., thought form. This is the energy/vibration of building.

The Energy That Powers Psychic Phenomena

There are certain ones currently incarnated that have the remembered ability to use the Second Energy within their own physical vehicle. These "gifted" personalities are capable of contacting their Indigo Center with Intelligent Energy. Remember: Intelligent Energy is Love. Love is the Green Ray. Green Ray is: Love/Healing/Manifestation, and functions via the fourth or Heart Chakra. The Indigo Ray is the Third Eye. This is the thought form creating center. Now, if the gifted personality brings up this portion of his/her Kundalini (called here the Second Spiraling Energy) to the Green Ray of Manifestation (he Heart Chakra) and saturates the Kundalini with Green Ray, and then brings this distorted energy to the Indigo Center then the preconceived thought is manifested. This is the mechanics of the phenomenon of the "psychic bending of metal, stopping watches, moving objects, etc. The Second Pyramid Energy is the activator of the Indigo Ray and is to be seen as the *builder,* never Shiva,

NOTES:

the Destroyer. This type of activity is considered phenomenal in Third Density; however, in Fourth Density it is a common way of life. Almost all construction and manifestation is accomplished in this way.

The Second Energy is of such a configuration/vibration that it permits dimensions of Time/Space and Space/Time to intermingle. The veil that separates the boundaries of the physical and the etheric is readily penetrated by this special energy, as the conscious being freely functions in both realms of reality. As this Second Light is compressed in the upper third of the pyramid, or at the Second Chakra, work may readily be accomplished. This is inherited knowledge for the Wanderer, MAN Incarnate, who now is in the Human form and is perhaps able to penetrate the forgetting sufficiently enough to recall the principle behind the phenomenon of manifesting and altering the atomic structure of a spoon — causing it to bend. This is how stone was split and great monoliths were moved into place. Retain this understanding for our study of the Tensor Concepts later.

Ra's Pyramid at Giza does not come equipped with a chamber at the apex area so that the full benefits of this Second Energy might be utilized. It is not deemed wise to offer this information/facility to a developing Third Density. As these are the final days of Earthly Third Density, it is now seen as appropriate that this information be made available to afford knowledge and understanding to those interested, so that their introduction into Fourth Density will be a smoother Transition.

The Third Energy

The Third Energy or Third Position begins at the center of the base of the pyramid and, in a very tight spiralling coil reaches the apex and then spreads out like a top as it emerges from the cap into Space. This Third Energy is *Prana* — the life force that keeps physical Space/Time entities animated. This is an electrifying and highly stimulating experience for a Third Density Entity, and could readily restore/rejuvenate body and mental configurations. This could be understood to be a healing,

NOTES:

but actually it simply amounts to pumping new life (Prana) into a tired and worn body. From a Third Density view-point, this Third Energy could be considered pure color Yellow. If plants or animals (Second Density) were to be placed over the pyramid, then this Third Energy would be viewed and accepted as pure color Orange. It would be rather difficult to place a pyramid under a plant, unless it was potted. The serious student might like to experiment with this proposition and perhaps could develop a unique and useful strain or variety in certain plant species.

As the personality is exposed to this Third Spiral Energy, each cell of the etheric body is atomically charged, even as electricity would charge a battery. The physical body which is the reflection of the Time/Space body is also equally charged. This charging may be felt as a series of pin pricks on the skin, as the body's cells are shocked into rejuvenation.

The brain is thusly stimulated if the energy is focused on the head. Those portions of the body are stimulated where the pyramid is placed under. If the pyramid is placed under the sexual organs, then the sex drive/desire is also enhanced. This energy has the ability to strengthen and often restore fertility. Overexposure could reverse these positive results. A pyramid proportionate to the dimensions of Ra's Pyramid at Giza, with a height of no more than two inches would be most appropriate for this work. No more than 30 minutes duration once per day would be the proper dosage. For mental stimulation, two shorter increments of time (twice per day) would also be acceptable.

This Third Spiral offers some aid in meditation, as it stimulates brain cells, but basically it is more useful in eliminating tiredness, thusly stimulating physical and sexual activity. Correct care must be taken in the latter, for overexposure in energizing the sex organs could readily result in loss of desire and malfunctioning as well. Both partners should be equally prepared. If care is taken to mind the clocks, the Third Energy may be introduced *during* the activity to promote longevity and enhancement. If conception is desired, this would prove to be an ideal aid. If the pregnant female were to sleep *in/under* a

NOTES:

pyramid during the gestation period, the fetus would respond accordingly. The *increased size* of the fetus might become uncomfortable prior to and during the birthing. Care must always be exercised.

Overexposure to this energy amounts to overdose which could readily traumatize the entity, resulting in more harm than good. Knowledge and discipline are the tools of the apprentice as he seeks his place amongst the Adepts. Experimentation as to the appropriate levels to produce the desired results can be exciting in their discovery.

Entities native to Fifth and Sixth Density will have acquired the knowledge, understanding, and ability to tap into their Third Energy for use in communication. Love and Light may be transmitted over vast regions of the universe by utilizing the Third Energy. This Energy is the vehicle which permits the Entity to traverse between dimensions of Space/Time and Time/Space. When this Energy is tapped into by a Spacecraft, the speed of Light may be squared up to nine times, thus permitting the craft to move laterally via the Serial Universes to travel enormous distances in a matter of moments. This type of travel is not as quick as thought, but almost. Fourth Density MAN utilizes this energy in his Craft. A milder or weaker form of the same energy permits MAN to enjoy teleportation. This is usually employed within a Solar System; and rarely is teleportation used beyond the limits of a Galaxy. The physical body of MAN is fragile and is subjected to the nature of the environment just as Third Density bodies are. Fifth and Sixth-Density Entities are not so encumbered.

When Fourth, Fifth, and Sixth-Density Entities use this Third Spiral Energy, it is not necessary for them to employ the pyramid to do so. The ability to create an etheric pyramid about self to collect and use these energies is known to all. When properly instructed, Third Density can also do as much. The physical pyramid found in Third Density is a useful structure for Healing, Initiation, and Teaching — the same can be accomplished without the edifice. The pyramid is a solid structure that aids in bridging the gap between faith, knowledge, and under-

NOTES:

standing. This structure can be very comforting to the Third Density Human Being. In these closing days of this 75,000-year Third Density Cycle, the pyramid shape and the other shapes offer little value. Their time has past. Such shapes are yet useful to some, for they are tangible and can attract and hold the attention of the novice. Initiation is mental/spiritual and as we now enter into the Fourth Density Vibration it is useful to detach from the aides and crutches of Third Density; the perfect shape for Initiation does not exist.

The Brain — The Organ

The frontal lobe of this magnificent organ is our area of interest for the moment. This is a large portion of the total brain. It is this area that perceives Love and related emotions. Again, we remind you that Love is: Intelligent Energy.

The three energies of the pyramid are all found within the frontal lobe of the brain. These energies are more useful in Fourth Density than in Third Density; however, the Adept or the budding Adept can readily tap into these energies, even during the adversity of Third Density. The learning/healing, the building, and the energizing energies are all found in this section of one's brain. It is important to note that the brains of Third Density and Fourth Density *are the same.* The Green Ray Love Vibration of Fourth Density is much more compatible to the activation of the frontal lobe and other Tensor Centers of the brain, but no doors are ever sealed. Desire and Will can penetrate any veil.

When this area is tapped the Mind/Spirit Complex in harmony within itself allows the personality to make contact with Intelligent Energy. The First and Second Energies are thus activated. Having successfully accomplished this, the Third Spiral may now be tapped into and Intelligent Infinity is penetrated. At this point the Co-Creator is truly born.

The shape of the skull is an important factor; it is rarely found in a pyramidal shape, but often comes in the shape of a dome and this too is a magnificent collector of energies. All the power of the Universe lies between your ears. Fourth Density

NOTES:

MAN knows this. The highly evolved Third Density Entity is becoming aware of it. Edifices, devices, and paraphenalia are useful as training aides, to be sure; but these things are not mandatory, or else you would have been born with them.

Meditation focused on achieving this understanding is the key to opening the doors of the mind; the frontal lobes are simply the area of our attention. The mind/brain when functioning properly with the undamaged brain has the capacity to create . . . to create in excess of your wildest dreams!

If the budding Adept wishes to open and activate his frontal lobes, meditating in a pyramid could prove to be most helpful. This is the Third Eye — Indigo Ray work. Spiritual evolution is focused on this continuum. This is the joy. This is the Love, the understanding, the purpose, and the fulfillment.

Age Reversal

There are areas in a working pyramid where the age of the personality can be reversed. A pyramid of some size is obviously necessary. The Queen's Chamber Level is the key. Imagine if you will, a teardrop lying on its side horizontally, the small end in the center of the Queen's Chamber and the big end reaching to the face. The angle of this teardrop is five-ten degrees. At the wide part the line is both above and below the Queen's Chamber Level. There are four faces and there are four teardrops. One quarter of the distance from the face towards the apex end at the Queen's Chamber inside this horizontal teardrop is the exact location to achieve this age-reversing process. Four such cavities could be carved out and four people could participate simultaneously. The Light energies at these four locations are such that a "Prana Vacuum" is created, thus effecting this result.

The Mind/Body/Spirit Complex is an electromagnetic field of energy. All entities and objects have such a field about themselves. The personality is duly or perhaps unduly affected by this constant contact and bombardment of "alien" energies. This exposure of wear and tear eventually takes its toll in the form of aging. This is quite natural. This process can be

NOTES:

stopped, placed in suspension, and then reversed, if the entity were to place self in one of the designated areas of the pyramid. This Pranic Vacuum provides a curious and unique vibration where there is no input, or any disturbances of the electromagnetic fields, thus creating a temporary limbo status where body aging is stopped and then reversed. The area would be an angle five degrees *above* the level line of the Queen's Chamber and an angle five degrees *below* that center line. This would be *maximum* size. Therefore, the pyramid would have to be of substantial size in order for this oral cavity to be large enough to comfortably accept a Human Being.

Other Energies

On the faces of the Great Pyramid are minute vortices of Healing Energy that can and may be useful in the hands of the skilled Adept. Individually, these many vortices are quite small. Collectively, they readily create a sizable Aura of Healing Energy radiating from the edifice. These Healing Energies are especially useful in the healing of the etheric body which the physical body is a reflection there of. Even the Adept would have some difficulty in gathering and focusing these energies to achieve a desired purpose. When one passes in close proximity or "feels" a pyramid, it is these energies that are being experienced. Perhaps this is the greatest value of these energies, emitted from a multitude of miniature vortices situated over the four faces of Ra's Pyramid.

Aligning The Pyramid

Traditionally, the pyramid has always been aligned with a base side in a North-South attitude. The opposite side would be the same on the square-based pyramid. This alignment would be appropriate yet today. However, for those of you who are gravitating towards the true Green Ray Love Vibration, an alignment of 20 degrees NNE would be much more appropriate. If a line were to be circumscribed about the globe beginning at 20 degrees NNE, moving southward through the 90 degree longitude mark at the current equator, continuing southward

NOTES:

through 200 degrees SSW, and following the same path on the backside of the globe until the starting point is reached, this would be the New Equitorial Line of the Earth after the axis shift; we are then dwelling in the New Fourth Density Vibration of Love. This line of the New Equator is also the "Chakra Belt" of the Planet. Some chakras are on this line, some are located on either side of it. The New North and South Poles will be located perpendicular to the plane of this circle. The axis shall shift in such a way as to cause the axis to be vertical to the Earth's Plane in its orbit of the Sun.

As you attempt to progress in your development into the New Age vibration an alignment of 20 degrees NNE or 200 degrees SSW, which is the same thing, would be much more useful, as this causes and permits you to reach out in a progressive way to grasp your future — your destiny — as you accelerate your evolution. The energies attracted and collected in this new alignment are weaker than the energies of the pyramid aligned North and South. However, these energies are growing daily, and the quality is indeed a distinct advantage.

There are no absolutes built into the Creation of the Physical Universe. Anything is possible. The probability of the Earth Mother re-aligning herself in this fashion is indeed excellent. There is no other probability worthy of mention. But, there are no guarantees! The polarization of the atoms that make up the Earth's molten mantle are shifting in this direction. It is highly unlikely that this progressive movement will alter its course. It strengthens daily. The newly aligned coordinates of the pyramid are the microcosm of this phenomenon. The wave of our future is underfoot, alive and well, moving with determination.

The Bermuda Triangle

The Third Spiraling Energy that emits from the apex of a properly designed, aligned and functioning pyramid does so in a pattern or rhythm that can be likened unto AC electric current. These emissions or jolts are spaced at extremely close intervals. If the pyramid is or becomes misaligned, then this emission rate

NOTES:

becomes irregular. It is quite possible for this Third Energy to become "stored up" for a considerable period of time and then suddenly released at random intervals. This is the situation of the Great Balancing Pyramid, resting on the oceans floor in a tilted position off the Florida coast near Jacksonville. A sudden ejaculation of this Third Energy can, and often does, alter the Space/Time vibration of the area into a dimensional shift. Entities or vehicles traversing the area at that magical time could readily find themselves suddenly dwelling in one of the other Probable Worlds of Reality. These worlds are often erroneously referred to as Parallel Worlds.

The Changing Times

The Social Memory Complex that built the tilting and malfunctioning pyramid off the Florida coast also built the original pyramids in South and Central America. This was accomplished prior to the building of the Egyptian Pyramid at Giza. Atlantis was a thriving civilization that had technology as the basis of their culture. The Atlantians had outposts in the Mayan and Incan cultures, which were remnants of the Great Civilization of Mu, the continent which had previously sank in the now Pacific Ocean. This was the Social Memory Complex of Vetulus Miumo.

The Social Memory Complex, Ra, also worked with the Atlantians, aiding them in establishing their outposts in Egypt. At a later time, aid was also offered to the budding Civilization of Greece. During this time of the Egyptian beginnings, Ra was incarnated. He was an Egyptian in the role of a Priest who worked with the giant Atlantians of the original Red Race. They were aided by Sixth-Density Entities, and the pyramid proved to be a most effective instrument in the teachings of Third Density. Commerce was an unknown factor in those days of the early Human Experience. Third Density was much more philosophical and personal relationships are the method of interaction of self with other self. Sexual relationships and energy transfer of this type was the "way of life" for Humans in those days.

NOTES:

Money, trade, and the exchange of goods and services was completely unknown. Consequently, the peoples were much less bellicose. Polarity was learned and practiced via sexuality. This System offered much more freedom in establishing the individuality of the self. Sexual expression was not hampered by rules, laws, and penalties, as is our current culture which is based on commerce. Uninhibited Love could be expressed for the other self. This is difficult to achieve today as one wrangles for the "best deal."

Those of Ra successfully worked with the unpolarized ones to aid in determining a choice of polarity through the vehicle of sex. This was much less complicated than today's "sophisticated" culture presents. The in-depth understanding of self and other selves was introduced to the Third Density peoples via the Tarot, which was "imported" by Ra from the Planet Venus. This proved to be a most useful tool and was highly effective when used in conjunction with the Initiation Rituals of the Queen's Chamber aspect of the Great Pyramid.

Times were less complicated then. Even during the later days of Atlantis when high technology abounded, commerce was not present to offer its distortions. Oddly enough, money was introduced to Third Density only about 8,000 years ago . . . in Egypt! This was an instrument of pure power which served the same purposes as did the edifices at Easter Island. The concept of money/commerce was a gift from Orion.

At this Space/Time Nexus, the un-polarized or unmanifested entity functions within the system of commerce. There are perhaps no exceptions to this rule since the advent of the Americans. Until recently, the peoples of the World functioned quite handsomely without commerce. (The exceptions being Europe and Asia.) Commerce has become THE vehicle of interaction between self and other selves in the Human Experience. Because of this, the pyramid and other magical edifices capable of drawing etheric Light are not appropriate structures to be employed by the masses. The non-energetic square structures are more suitable to their mental attitude. For those of you who have the capability to see through the illusion, such

NOTES:

energy collecting edifices could yet be most effective and useful. Knowledge gleaned must be placed into practical, everyday use, else there is the risk of it becoming Negative. It is not impossible to employ esoteric teachings in today's world but it is most difficult. Only the dedicated Seekers of spirituality are able to rise above the confining restrictions ordered by our culture. In these final days the camps are truly separating. Security is sought in conformity.

Chapter 12

Intrigue And Mystery

It is said that Napoleon Bonaparte with the aid of some of his troops scaled the Great Pyramid. He bade his men to depart, and upon its summit he spent the night alone. At intervals during the night he could be observed standing with arms reaching skyward with electrical charges emitting from his fingertips. He would occasionally shout something but no one could discern his words. The next morning his men again scaled the pyramid in order to retrieve him. When he was deposited once again upon the surface, it was plain to see that he was indeed quite mad. If he was not insane before he ascended, he certainly was when he descended.

There are many stories such as this one that have been historically recorded. Some are true, some are not so true. The pyramid is like a magnet, it drives people to come near it — the famous and the not so famous. Mystery abounds. Intrigue stimulates the imagination. Riddles are posed — answers are many. And who can really say?

Now modern man comes along. He is a scientist. He has instruments to measure and probe the innermost secrets of antiquity. These ones investigate, record their findings, and publish their papers. The results then become "official," for who amongst us dares to challenge?

The phrase "pyramid power" was coined. The "secrets of the pyramid" were now being revealed! The statistics were carefully documented and then analyzed. The findings were unbelievable! The profound mystery of that awesome edifice deepened. The statistical information varies somewhat, depending upon who was holding the tape measure; but essentially, the many conclusions are all *about* the same. We can understand and forgive these ardent scholars in their scientific approach in evaluating a timeless edifice, shrouded in mystery and antiquity, for the magnitude of this structure and the obvious skill and craftsmanship that was employed is fantastic. Its design staggers the thinking minds of men. Today's engineers can build a Craft

NOTES:

that can fly to the Moon, land, and return home, but they cannot build a structure that remotely compares to the Great Pyramid at Giza.

The questions that instantly come to the minds of all who stand in its presence are: *Who* built it? *How* did they do it? *When* did they do it? *Why* did they do it? *What* was it's purpose? These questions are largely unanswered. The engineers, the scientists, the learned Ph.D's have now entered the scene. Their contributions of data are quite valuable. Their efforts, however, only tend to deepen the mysteries, not resolve them. But, be that as it may, let us look into some of the results of their efforts.

Statistics

Did you know that: The base of the Pyramid is 761 feet by 761 feet, and covers an area of 13 acres, and is reported to be out of level by no more than one-half inch? There are more than two and one half million blocks of stone (granite and limestone) that comprise this monument. This is a calculated guess, for an accurate count could not be achieved without dismantling the thing. Some of these blocks of stone weigh 600 tons, and perhaps even more. The surface which amounts to some 21 acres is faced with pure white alabaster limestone 7-feet thick. This surface has been laboriously polished to a reflective sheen.

The edges are 723.7 feet and the apothem is 615.6 feet. The apothem is the distance from the center of the base to the apex on a face. The current height is 458 feet. Originally it was calculated to have been 484.4 feet. We suggest that the actual original height was 486 feet. Why would one quibble over a foot and a half — more or less? This could make a great deal of difference in the dynamics of electromagnetism.

The apex angle face to face is: 76 degrees — 18 minutes. The apex angle edge to edge is: 96 degrees. The base angle is: 51 degrees — 51 minutes — 51 seconds, while the edge angle is: 41 degrees — 59 minutes — 50 seconds. Other scientists have produced slightly different data. The volume of the pyramid is

NOTES:

in the neighborhood of 90 million cubic feet, and the weight is figured at five and one-half million tons, and perhaps more.

The numbers 3.1416 (PI) and 1.618 (PHI) are found throughout. For example: The apothem divided by one half the base equals PHI — stated as .618; this Golden Cut may also be stated as 61.8%, or rounded off to 62%.

Other interesting data include the Coffer or Sarcophagus in the King's Chamber, which is the same size as the Ark of the Covenant. The outside dimensions are: 89.9 inches long by 38.7 inches wide by 41.2 inches high. The walls are almost six-inches thick, while the bottom is seven-inches thick. The Ark of the Covenant is thought by scientists to have been some form of capacitor, capable of building up and storing a charge of electricity more than sufficient enough to kill a man if one of the Angels were touched. This is why the object had to be carried by four men with wooden poles attached to the sides. It was moved something like a "sedan chair," occupied by Far Eastern Royality. The Coffer has not been known to give off any electrical charges, but who is to say that it didn't sometime in the ancient past? A Sarcophagus is a tomb for burial. This one was never used as such. A place for Initiation that simulated death was its purpose.

There is a very thin coating of cement between the blocks of stone. It is incredibly strong and obviously durable. Its composition cannot be determined, nor can it be duplicated today. But then, the Roman Empire was much more recent than the time of the builders of the Great Pyramid, and their brand of cement can't be duplicated either! We shall not get into the incredible steel used by swordsmen of old.

The Pyramid is located at 31 degrees, nine minutes East and 29 degrees, 58 minutes, 51 seconds, North. There are those who calculate this spot to divide the land masses into equal parts. Perhaps it does. Data can always be arranged to confirm a preconceived idea. Whatever conclusions are drawn, the edifice is impressive by any standard. It was obviously built by means that we cannot imagine, and it was designed by minds that exercise a capacity that we have not yet tapped into. The peoples

NOTES:

who lived in those times would not have had the mathematical prowess to contemplate such a structure, designed, or constructed it with such precision.

Why was it built? Today's scientists cannot answer the question. The more they examine, the more awestruck they become. There is only one known in the World like it. It cannot be duplicated. But why would anyone want to? What would one do with another? Of what purpose was/is the original? The Pyramid not only defies time, it also defies the puny minds of men. The previous chapter concerning Ra offered many answers — answers which modern scientists would be loathe to accept.

As always, you may accept that which you are most comfortable with.

A Guidepost

We would respectfully suggest that the pyramid is a guidepost specifically designed to point out the locations of the major energy vortices found on Planet Earth. For those entities who have devices or vehicles such as Spacecraft, that rely on electromagnetic energies for power, the knowledge of these locations would be invaluable. The Great Pyramid's location is not happenstance. The minds that devised this edifice knew the Earth Mother quite well. For the benefit of future visitors, this discovered information was left for all to find — without diligent searching. The pyramid is a common edifice found on many, many Planets in the Universe.

There are ten major vortices of energy found on this Planet. There are also many, many minor ones. Today's scientists are aware of some of these, but are reluctant to attach any significance to them since these energies have no commercial value. Instruments of detection could readily locate most of these vortices, but lacking practical purpose no effort is made. But, if a Craft relied on this type of energy for propulsion upon and above the face of the Planet, then this knowledge would be of definite use.

The Ley Lines (energy lines) of the Planet all meet at the Great Pyramid, something like the center of a great spider web.

NOTES:

There are nine other secondary centers of energy located elsewhere over the face of the Earth. The second obvious vortex is the axis of the Pyramid. That is, if an auxiliary line were to be extended vertically from the apex to the base and then penetrated the Planet, the point on the opposite side of the Earth is also an energy vortex.

Now there are eight more to locate. If the four edges were to be extended in a straight line through the Earth, their points of emergence would mark the locations of permanent electromagnetic energy centers. The remaining four centers can be found by extending the apothegms on the faces of the Pyramid down through the Planet. These are the ten major energy centers that a Craft might attract itself to or repell itself from — as the case may be.

You might like to attach a very small pyramid, perhaps an inch high, to your globe — in Egypt of course. Now, stand back and note the edge angles and then the apothem angles *through* the globe. Note the areas where they "come out." Phenomena have historically occurred at some of these areas. Note the Bermuda Triangle area, the Great Lakes area, the area off Japan, etc. The "other areas" are not in the shipping lanes, and the phenomena there goes un-rewarded.

The Great Pyramid is indeed a guidepost that speaks volumes to those who are skilled in reading it. Though the Pyramid *contains* many secrets, the really useful information lies on the *outside* . . . for all to see! The obvious is often the last thing noticed. But, Third Density is like that, is it not?

Experiments

Countless experiments have been conducted by both "professionals" and amature pyramidologists. Of the two categories, your author is comfortable with the latter. Whenever possible a "control" should be used with pyramid experiments. This simply means that two items of the same quality are selected — one is placed in the pyramid, and the other is placed somewhere away from the pyramid energies; both are carefully observed and differences are noted. The same experiment should

NOTES:

be conducted two or three times and if the results are the same, then perhaps conclusions may be drawn.

Constructing The Model

To construct your pyramid using the dimensions of the Great Pyramid we suggest that four equilateral triangles be carefully joined together to form a square base. This will be a sufficient likeness to provide the desired results. However, if you are a stickler for accuracy, then make the bases of your triangles 5% *longer* than the two equal sides. This, of course, is an isosceles triangle, not quite an equilateral triangle. The size of your pyramid will depend upon your needs. For traditional results align your pyramid to the magnetic North and South; use any baseline. Its opposite side, being parallel, would read the same. If you would like to experiment with the future, then you might like to align your pyramid on a line of 20 degrees NNE or 200 degrees SSW, which is the same thing. Finally, make certain your pyramid is level. A pyramid that is out of alignment and/or out of level will not function well, if at all.

The materials most commonly used are wood or cardboard. If cardboard is selected make certain it is solid and *not corrugated* cardboard. The four faces may be traditionally solid if you like and large holes may be cut into one or all of the faces to permit observation. These holes will not interfere with the functioning of the pyramid energies.

The pyramid does not have to be complete in its construction. A base and the four edges are sufficient — no solid faces at all. A base and *stubs* of the four edges will also work. A truncated apex with four stubs will also function quite nicely. This is a small structure that can be attached to the ceiling. This small device mounted on an eight foot ceiling creates a base of approximately 13-feet square. We have designed and experimented with the ceiling pyramid for several decades. Remember to align and level your pyramids. This is most important.

Types Of Experiments

Most experiments are initiated with perishable foods. A spoonful of raw hamburger is placed in the pyramid and another

NOTES:

spoonful is placed in similar conditions elsewhere. One will mummify, while the other decays. Your nose will quickly discern the difference.

A razor blade or a straight razor may be placed with edges vertical, axis North — South, under a small pyramid. The blades, double or single edges, will last for many months with daily use. My straight razor has not been hone since 1970, and probably never will again. This is one of the more enduring and useful experiments that can be perpetuated with pyramid energy.

Plants are affected by the First Spiralling Energy. Vegetation placed under a pyramid will thrive; potted plants are the easiest to observe. The energies will restore the vitality of the plant in a matter of hours. The farmer would not be able to erect a pyramid over his huge fields; however, if the field were carefully surveyed, four corner stubs could be installed with sufficient aligning and leveling that an auxiliary pyramid could be created. As this high pyramid begins to function the crops will thrive. Even the insects would be banished, for they would not be able to withstand this high vibration. It should be noted that one or more of these corner stubs should be fixed to rotate so that the pyramid could be placed *out of alignment* when desired. It would not do to run animals in this energized field, especially pregnant ones. The Second Spiralling Energy can cause the embryo to grow to enormous sizes, thus making birthing difficult.

Jugs of water may be placed under the small pyramid for energizing. These waters may be used for Human consumption or for animals, or used to water plants for the fertilizing effect. A pyramid may be constructed over a well or perhaps over the channel of flowing water that is used for irrigation. Fields that have been irrigated by "treated" pyramid water will often produce four times the yield of identical fields using "regular" water.

Pyramid energy alters the molecular make-up of that which is placed under it. This may or may not be desirable. Caution should always be expressed. Like plants, animals also respond dramatically to the pyramid energies. Farm animals

NOTES:

and/or animals in the wild should be observed very closely so that overdose will be avoided. Mutation could readily take place in the embryo. This could alter the nature of the species. This may or may not be desirable.

Cats who choose to sleep under the pyramid have been known to become vegetarians within a few weeks. Cats and dogs soon learn to visit the pyramid to relieve themselves of fleas. Fleas can often be seen quickly departing their host, as they flee the confines of the pyramid. Ill-tempered dogs are often gentled by these energies. Certain entities of mobility are attracted to the pyramid, while others are repelled by it. Spiders will thrive under a pyramid, while insects do not. Weeds also do quite well!

Food will dehydrate or mummify under the pyramid if kept there long enough. Fresh food, cooked or raw will have its flavor enhanced if it is briefly exposed to the pyramid energies. Sometimes the dining table is placed under a pyramid. This is readily acceptable if a ceiling pyramid is employed.

Inanimate objects other than water may also be greatly affected. Cheap wine placed under a pyramid will alter its quality to that of a very expensive wine in a matter of a few hours, depending upon the size of the pyramid. On the other hand, expensive wine will be reduced to vinegar under the same conditions.

A golfing friend placed four new golf balls under our pyramid and they were left there for one week. She used them in the tournament that weekend. All four balls were lost on exceptionally long drives on the first nine. Her score was horrendous! The long drives were more than she bargained for. It upset her total game. *Practice* with an "activated" ball is definitely in order!

The mentality of the Human Being is often very much affected. Meditation is dramatically enhanced. Brain waves, particularly alpha, tend to flow in patterns that are conducive to congruent thinking processes, as the meditation stimulates understanding. Whenever possible, meditation should be conducted under a pyramid.

NOTES:

Though certainly not mandatory, sleeping under a pyramid can be most rewarding. It is critical that the sleeping entity position self with head toward the North. Head toward the South will reverse the natural polarity, and ill effects *will* result. Sleeping with head towards East or West will be neutral, resulting in no effect at all.

Sleeping with head toward the North permits the Earth's magnetic energies to flow from North to South, or from head to feet. This causes the entity to be aligned or attuned to the Planet. One should always sleep with the head to the North, with or without a pyramid. If the personality is not properly aligned within one's own body, then the pyramid can and will "straighten out" this irregular flow of the bodies energies. Thus, the pyramid's healing energies are put into use.

Other Experiences

A gentleman had a history of bad knees and a bad back. He carefully installed a ceiling pyramid over his bed. It often takes a new pyramid up to 48 hours to become effective. After arising from the first night's sleep, he noticed no change at all. (He had privately considered this whole thing about pyramid healing powers to be a fraud, but his pain was so severe that he elected to try it.) He was not surprised when the pyramid produced nothing; he had expected as much.

Since the bed was aligned North and South, probably for the first time in decades, he decided he had nothing to lose by giving it another night. By midnight he was in pain greater than anything he had ever experienced. His back and his knees ached to the point where the pain was intolerable. He had to lie crosswise (East and West) in the bed to get any relief. By sunrise, his stubbornness had vanished, and he truly was a believer in pyramid energy. However, physically he was no better off. That had to be the worst round of pain his back and knees had ever given him.

He was encouraged to give it one more try. With much trepidation he carefully crawled into bed the third night. To his amazement, he promptly went to sleep and was rewarded with

NOTES:

restful slumber all through the night. On the morning of the third day he awoke with no pain in his knees, back, or anywhere in his body. He was astonished!

The pyramid had caused a *proper* flow of energy through his body in a way that polarized himself to be in harmony with the Earth Mother. Since he had been de-polarized for so many years, the re-aligning was most painful. He paid a price, but it was worth it — the pain never returned.

* * *

The parents were visiting their married daughter. The automobile trip traversed several states. The parents were tired upon their arrival at evening time. The daughter had made up their bed in the end of the recreation room by the bookcase. A six-foot base pyramid was standing at the other end of the room. Several jugs of water stood in a North — South line under the structure for purifying and energizing. All water consumed in this household had been under the pyramid for at least three days. This energized water was used on the house plants as well.

The parents noted these things, but not wishing to generate conflict, elected to say nothing. The daughter expounded at great length on the uses of pyramid energy and the discoveries that she was making. As the evening wore on the parents began to wonder if this "energy" had not somehow affected her mentality! A pallet was kept under the pyramid for meditation and rest during the day.

Both the parents indulged in a variety of ailments and sleeping in a strange bed did not help their physical problems. During the night, the mother rose to visit the bathroom. On her return she passed the pyramid with the inviting pallet inside. She reasoned that no one would ever be the wiser so she quietly crawled in, positioned her head to the North, and lay down. The pain instantly departed her and she became so comfortable that she promptly went to sleep.

Later, the husband, noting his wife's absence, set out to find her. Spying her under the pyramid, sleeping peacefully, he too decided that it might be a worthwhile venture. He crawled in beside his wife and promptly went to sleep. The wife woke at

NOTES:

daybreak and was astonished to discover where she was. She was even more amazed to find her husband there also!

Sheepishly, they rose and, saying very little made ready for breakfast with the family. The daughter noticed that her mother had not taken her daily dosage of medicine. Her mother allowed that she didn't believe that she needed it that day. Later, in the course of the day, the previous night's sleeping arrangements were revealed. Much ado was made about the doubting "Thomases," but undaunted, the parents continued to sleep under the pyramid for the remainder of their weeks stay. Neither parent used any medicine during that week, but both claimed to be feeling better than at any time in recent memory. In a few days after their return home, both resumed their medicine schedules, and their "normal" way of life.

* * *

Your author was installing a ceiling pyramid in the bed room. A jumping toothache was being experienced at the time. While standing under the pyramid the pain ceased. By taking one step away from the pyramid the throbbing ache resumed. Side stepping in and out could actually turn on or turn off the pain. The pyramid energy provided relief, but not a cure. A few weeks later the offending tooth was extracted!

* * *

Relief for all kinds of aches and pains from head to foot can be found placing oneself under a pyramid. Under certain conditions, cures may also be obtained. One's *attitude,* sometimes called "belief," makes the vital difference. All healing is strictly a case of mind over matter, accompanied by understanding and forgiveness. The self disciplined personality can indeed achieve remarkable results in this Third Density Vibration!

Without previous instruction, people experiencing the pyramid for the first time will notice heat and perhaps a mild electrical tingling. Rarely is there any exception to this. After spending a few intervals under a pyramid, the personality may readily develop a craving for this energy. If the bed is within the pyramid, then the desire to sleep becomes intense. Not that sleep/rest is required, but the need to dream becomes paramount.

NOTES:

The higher mental energy states are most desirable. This craving could continue for many months. The addiction having now been consummated, the personality will accumulate sufficient pyramid energy into self to be able to be away from the home pyramid for several days without any noticeable effects. One can learn to create an "etheric pyramid" about oneself or about the abode that will be equally effective. These etheric pyramids are usually constructed of Violet or Green Light. The psychological effect of the physical pyramid is quite important to the apprentice. Usually the Third Eye — Etheric Vision — is not sufficient in the beginning stages to adequately offer the necessary importance to a thought form not manifested.

We would encourage you to build and experiment with your own pyramids. Knowledge, information, and experience can readily be gleaned by so doing. The pyramid is an excellent vehicle for the study of spiralling energies. This understanding shall be useful later as you study the energies of the Universe, for all things are a microcosm of the Macrocosm.

It is also appropriate to note the termination of Third Density is at hand. The pyramid is intended to be most useful under Third Density physical conditions. Therefore, the great value of this type of structure has long passed its prime usefulness. The masses' discovery of pyramid energy shall *not* revolutionize Third Density commerce. It might have, it could have, but it did not. Now it is too late in the game called life. A Cycle is ending, even as a magnificent New Cycle begins. Let us learn from the past as we confidently step into our future.

Summary

We have noted the powers of the pyramid and their uses. You are free to activate any potential that you deem noteworthy and we heartily encourage you to do so. The acquired knowledge/experience shall be useful in your future and probably in the present. Third Density use of this edifice is diminishing as it should at the closing of an age. However, there shall be many, many Third Densities established elsewhere in this great Galaxy

NOTES:

and many of you who read these words shall be their teachers. Acquiring knowledge is never a waste.

We encourage you to "tap into" the ancient past via your Higher Self using your Kundalini and see/remember for yourself the chain of events as they transpired, and perhaps re-discover your own role in certain circumstances in a Human or perhaps a Non-Human form. It has been our experience that the awareness of ancient pyramids is an excellent vehicle to trigger recall in the minds of Wanderers who are currently incarnated in the Third-Density Human form. We trust that the preceeding information has been useful to you in other ways as well. It has been our privilege and our pleasure to share with you our understanding of the pyramids.

Conclusion

Now let us prepare to lower the Kundalini. Bring the White Light of the Kundalini up around you and gather it asan object over the top of your head. As you do so, bring the Violet Dome next to your physical body. Bring the Kundalini into the crown of your head, as you detach your consciousness. Now, begin the descent, deactivating each chakra, as we give the color countdown: Violet . . Indigo . . Blue . . Green . . Yellow . . Orange . . Red . . put the Kundalini to rest, and shut the door, take a deep breath, another and perhaps one more.

Our Prayer Of Protection

"In the name of the Presence and the Power Universal, protect us from harm and all Unenlightened Spirits, and may the Light of our Spirit Guides and the Light of our Higher Selves illuminate our thoughts that we might reflect the Radiant Glory of ALL THAT IS."

We leave you in the Light and Love of our One Infinite Creator. Go forth in the joy of life and in service to others."

Adonai. Adonai, Vasu Barragus, Adonai.

We Thank You!

Section IV

The Milkey Way Galaxy

This section deals with our examination of Space and some of the Entities that dwell therein. The focus is upon our Galaxy and our future roles as MAN, who calls the vastness of Space - "Home."

Chapter 13

The Milky Way Galaxy

We greet you in the Light and Love of our One Infinite Creator. We are Chief Little Summer and Warm Night Rain. We begin this section with the chant:

"I am that I am, A-Yeh,
I am that I am, A-Yeh,
I am that I am, A-Yeh,
I am that I am, A-Yeh,
I am that I am, A-Yeh,
I am that I am, A-Yeh,
I am that I am, A-Yeh,
A-Yeh,
A-Yeh,
A-Yeh,
A-Yeh,
A-Yeh."

And now the Prayer of Protection: "In the name of the Presence and the Power Universal, protect us from harm and all Unenlightened Spirits, and may the Light of our Spirit Guides and the Light of our Higher Selves illuminate our thoughts that we might reflect the Radiant Glory of ALL THAT IS."

* * *

We ask that you now prepare yourself to raise your Kundalini. Have your backs quite straight, as you align and balance your chakras. At the base of your spine, awaken the Kundalini. Permit the Kundalini to rise as we give the color countdown. Activate all the proper functions as you have been taught, as the Kundalini passes through the stem of the Red Chakra . . . the Orange . . . the Yellow . . . the Green . . . the Blue . . . the Indigo . . . the Violet. Attach your consciousness to your Kundalini Energy. Now, envision the White Kundalini, with your consciousness thoroughly saturated therein, emitting from the crown of your head, gently coiling around the Silver Cord, reaching the Golden Sphere, your Higher Self. Saturate the lower hemisphere with your Kundalini Light — making your

NOTES:

conscious contact. Encase your body with the White Light of your Kundalini, as you are fully protected by the great rainbow dome of Light. Firmly establish your contact with your Higher Self, and when you are ready, begin to read.

* * *

In this section we shall attempt to familiarize you with the character of our own Milky Way Galaxy. MAN has encouraged these and similar thought patterns to drift through the consciousness of Third Density men upon Planet Earth for many, many years. This is a conditioning process that will aid those of you who are eligible to inherit the New World, as the Transition brings us into the Fourth Density Vibration of Love.

An introduction to our Galaxy, to the function of MAN in his true home — Space, to his Craft and their uses, and to the physical structure of Space itself is our purpose in presenting this information. The simplicity of the machinery that is purposely designed to flow with the Laws of Creation, makes life for Fourth Density MAN a harmonious experience in Love. The abandoning of the errors of our own Third Density and the embracing of our imminent future is a mental attitude that must need be accepted and practiced by us all. The more comfortable you become with the magnificent vastness of Creation, the easier will be your Transition into the New Dispensation of the Fourth Density Aquarian.

Guided Tour To The Center Of Our Galaxy

Envision if you will, a Craft, a Spacecraft, piloted and staffed by MAN — Fourth-Density MAN, physical, Humanoid, just like yourself. See yourself comfortably situated aboard this magnificent vehicle, basking in the harmony of Love. Feel the warmth of the Love that is indigenous to MAN and accept the thrill of the adventure of discovery, as you contemplate the ever-so-distant Clusters of White Stars glittering on their background of Black Velvet Space. Enjoy the serenity of the Craft, as its force field is activated and the pilot has sought out a spiral thread of the energy of Fabric of Space.

NOTES:

Look back at your Planet, the Earth, as this majestic jewel glitters Green with a tinge of Light Blue for her Aura. As we pass the Silver Moon, this proud but aged grandmother, remember that she too was once a mother, and Earth life had its beginnings from this one. The Earth is a daughter of the Moon. The Earth Mother is a satellite of the Moon, and not the other way around — as Earth scientists would have you believe.

The Craft accelerates in speed. The speed of Light is attained, and then that speed is squared . . . and then that speed is squared . . . and then that speed . . . and that speed — up to the ninth power, if desired. The force field is that which is accelerated, the Craft itself is simply carried along *within* this field of energy.

In our final look backwards, the entire Solar System can be discerned as living colorful jewels, nested comfortably in the blackness of Space. Other Spacecraft can be seen from time to time. It is comforting to realize that we are not alone in all this vastness. The oceans of Space are not fathomable, the horizon is unlimited. The size of Space staggers the mind. The abundance of life is most comforting. To view our Solar System as seen from the perspective of our Milky Way Galaxy is a rare opportunity for Earthlings who have forever been bound to their Planet and their Galaxy. For those who are native to Third Density, this shall be an awesome experience. For those of you who are native to the higher Densities and are currently dwelling in a Third Density body, this little excursion should trigger some form of recall. The penetrating of the Third Density Veil of forgetting bestowed upon you at birth is of vital importance. As we move towards the center of our Galaxy, perhaps portions of your recall will be stimulated.

Our destination is the city of Trantor. Actually, this city encompasses the entire Planet. This Planet is the second Planet out from their Sun. This Sun is a Star in the constellation that Human Beings call Sagittarius.

NOTES:

Octan, Pavo And Tucana

Our charted course shall take us on the scenic route as we wind our way through the colorful constellations and other assorted sights and spectacles. Our Craft attains the speed of Light; then that speed is squared, and squared again, and then squared once more. The constellation Octans, and then Pavo are encountered. In short order, the constellation of Tucana is viewed off the port side.The Octans have three major stars, while Pavo has eleven.

These Star Clusters are most beautiful to see. Their configuration distorts as our Craft approaches, enters, and then leaves the constellation. As our position in Space changes, our perspective also changes. Recognizing a given constellation from the variety of attitudes that the vastness of Space affords makes it very difficult to remember and recognize sufficiently enough to get the appropriate bearings. Crystals programmed with the appropriate memory simplify these monumental navigational problems.

The Stars become more and more clustered as we approach the center of our Galaxy. The capital city of The Confederation of MAN, Trantor, is our goal. A Star Cluster again appears off out port side. This System has a core of effervescent Yellow. A faint White Aura encompasses this System, and isolates it into its own identity.

Off the starboard side the velvet blackness of Space has now vanished. This is an area of interstellar gas. The Green-Gold hues of the Star Clusters reflects off this gas, illuminating this vast area and obliterating the conventional blackness of Space.

Dead ahead lies another ocean of gas, but this gas also contains dust particles. The electromagnetic energies of nearby Star Clusters cause this dust to shift. It is constantly on the move. The patterns and configurations, both in shape and color, are fascinating to observe. The show has been continuously running for millions of years, and has delighted the passing audiences without fail. We slow our Craft so that we may consume the sight a bit longer. As we continue our approach, a

NOTES:

long black streak appears above the colorfully illuminated gas. An energy field is projected between two Star Clusters, creating a force field that repels the dust. This energy field agitates the dust and produces the variety of endless patterns, altering the shades of the many colors. This line of energy which also keeps the gas/dust from wandering is like a fence.

As an occasional Meteorite passes through this soup, leaving a wake of swirling colors, a tail is quickly formed, which permits the un-aided viewing of its trajectory for quite a long while. This is such a spectacular view that it is almost worth waiting around until the next random particle passes through.

As we trek deeper and deeper into the center of our Galaxy, the Stars are massed closer and closer together. The soft White Light is constant and everywhere.

Our speed had been accelerated to C — 5; that is, the speed of Light squared five times. Light years disappear before our bow only to reappear off our stern. Even at this fantastic speed there is no feeling of motion. We approach Star Clusters as we near the center of the Galaxy, but there are still vast distances between each Star and each Star Cluster. As we get closer to the heart of the Galaxy, our speed shall be reduced to C — 4 and then to C — 3, and perhaps even further. There are some tricky maneuvers coming up shortly.

Another special Star Cluster now comes into view. Cosmic gas and dust flows freely through this Cluster. It's center radiates a blue-white glow that reflects off the gas dust. This creates a most striking Aura. The background Stars diminish the blackness.

The Nebula Triffid

We have now traversed half the distance from Earth to our destination — the capital city of Trantor. The heart of our Galaxy now comes into view. It is appropriately red in color and is known as Nebula Triffid. To the right, and slightly behind is the Nebula Lagoon. This dear reader is most impressive to see!

NOTES:

It becomes even more impressive as we navigate our Craft *betwixt* the two.

The Star Clusters which seemed so dense from a distance, now seem to be thinning out. Our Galaxy is in a geometric form known as linticular.This simply means that it is thick in the middle and tapers out to its circular edges. There are millions of Galaxies in this Universe and each Galaxy is unique unto itself. Its Creator, its Logos, has seen fit to exercise its own Free Will and produce something different for the One Infinite Creator to experience and enjoy. Because all Galaxies are contained within this Universe, all are similar, but no two are identical. Therefore, it is customary for Galaxies to have in their center — a Black Hole. Some Galaxies will have minor Black Holes scattered throughout itself. As a given Galactic Logos prepares to terminate itself from this physical illusion, it will create numerous Black Holes amongst itself to speed up the Transition. This is not the case with our own Milky Way Galaxy as yet, but there are neighboring Galaxies well into this process and many, many *former* Galaxies have already *completed* the Transition, thus accounting for the vast oceans of empty Space that occurs in certain sectors of the Universe. These void areas are the homes of former Galaxies. Their Black Hole, sucking in or erasing effect, yet functions. This is why the area is clean of debris.

And now back to our journey. To the left of Nebula Triffid is another spiral Nebula. This one casts a beautiful Blue Light. The gasses which surround this Nebula are of such a nature that the electromagnetic energy radiating from the Nebula causes the gas to glow Blue. The vertical depth of the Galaxy here at the center, causes the black passageways of Space to isolate these magnificent colorful spectacles. Our Craft carefully threads its way through this dangerous passage as our destination lies beyond. The Triffid is divided. It is like the sections of a great heart. The Black Channels are like the arteries in which we must flow. Our Craft is like a corpuscle — flowing in the stream of life of our own Galaxy. Is everything not the microcosm of the Macrocosm, and vise versa?

NOTES:

Nebula Triffid glows White. The Nebula to the left glows Yellow White. Black Holes inhabit this Nebula. The colors vibrate in recognizable patterns which permit us to identify the locations of the Black Holes. This is done visually as well as with our computers. We shall rely on our trustworthy instrumentation. It is too easy to become mesmerized by the intense beauty of the intricacies of the interior of the Nebula Triffid; and it would never do to let one's attention stray even for a second. The Black Holes are unforgiving; as many of our Craft and crews can attest, they vanished from the Universe while they valiantly pioneer the way for us to follow.

The Nebula has entered. We pass between the walls of cascading Light. It is silent. It seems unreal. Noise seems appropriate; it would be welcome. There is none. The vibrating Light seems to fall like a great broad waterfall but there is no noise, there is no mist. There is no bottom to pound. The Light circulates and the vortex is the Black Hole. The arms of the Nebula suck in the gasses and debris that drift about in Space. This is a giant vacuum sweeper that tidies up Space as it feeds itself. The sheets of Light glow and pulsate and like the siren that would entice the sailor onto the rocks and shoals, this magical Light beckons us, drawing us closer and closer. Fear is not entertained, only anticipated ecstasy. One knows of the results of tempting fate, and one does not succumb, yet the temptation is strong.

Through the Violet Sheets of Light one can see the glowing Stars within the Triffid. The illuminated gasses, pulsating their beauty in shapes and shades of violet, line the maze through which we pass. The beauty is overwhelming. It is balanced by the known danger. We are tempted to linger . . . we are anxious to get away. The falling Light is a maelstrom. If we were to touch one of these walls with our Craft we would get sucked into the oblivion of the Black Hole. Like a heart, we are now in an artery and are being pushed away. If we were to get caught up in the cascade of Light it would be like entering a vein and being drawn back to the heart and the unknown function of a Black Hole. The artery twists and turns and we are most

NOTES:

careful. Our computer is programmed. We confidently know that we are safe. We are protected by our own force field that encompasses our tiny Craft. We also remember that this force field was created by us and that it is not infallible! There is always a special thrill as one enters the Nebula Triffid, there is also a sense of relief as one departs.

The Galactic Logos

We silently pass through the heart of the Galaxy with white knuckles. We are grateful that the Galactic Logos would sanction such an adventure of discovery and beauty. This is the heart of the Logos. The body of the Logos is the Galaxy itself. The Logos is an Entity not of this Octave, not of this Eternity. This Entity hails from a special portion of the One Infinite Creator, and has evolved beyond the Densities that comprise this Octave. The Logos created this Galaxy by thought alone. It then chose to manifest this thought form for the pleasure of the One Infinite Creator. Each of the many millions of Galaxies have a Logos that did the same. The Logos continues to build its masterpiece by using the White Light of Dispersion. It erases that which it deems necessary by the use of the Black Light. Both Black and White Light contain *all* colors. Both are total. Both are the same. The Law is One. The Galactic Logos is Black Light. The Galactic Logos is White Light. This consciousness moves from Octave to Octave via the Systems we call the Black Hole. That matter which enters a Black Hole is gone forever from *this* Universe; however, nothing is ever lost. The atoms are separated, dispersed and reassembled with other atoms to form new and different matter in a completely different Universe that hums to a different vibration unheard of in our Octave/Eternity. A Galactic Logos is not of our Densities, or of this Eternity, or of any Eternity. The Galactic Logos is a direct emissary of the One Infinite Creator.

Those entities of this Octave who are native of Sixth Density are sometimes called upon to *represent* this Logos. When a Planet is going through a Cycle that involves a Density Change, such as Earth is currently, then it is not unusual for the

NOTES:

Galactic Logos to be represented by an entity in a Third Density Vehicle. This representative would be a Transcendental Soul — one who is capable of receiving the Infinite Soul — the Galactic Logos. There are several Transcendental Souls incarnated on Earth at this time, perhaps a half a dozen or so. It is not known which one will be chosen to receive this awesome and Divine Vibration of the Infinite Soul — if indeed it is necessary at all. If evolution is somehow thwarted by the folly of Third Density, then the Galactic Logos shall freely step in and augment the timetable. One way or another the New Dispensation shall be born.

The Galactic Logos is a creature of Free Will. This Entity basks in humor and is patient beyond belief. However, when it comes to basic cycles and their timetables, this one is a "no nonsense" type of Father. His "Fragmented Presence" on a speck of dust called a Planet is not unheard of. A Galactic Logos is *not* the One Infinite Creator, though it is difficult if not impossible for the minds of men to perceive an authority of higher status. MAN of Fourth Density, refers to the Galactic Logos as: Our Radiant One. Perhaps we should rest with that.

We think upon the Creator of our Galaxy, as our ship's talented computers guide us safely through the maze of passageways of the Nebula Triffid. Many Crafts have been lost from this Universe in the discovery of the proper course to set. We could have simply not bothered and navigated around the Triffid, but it is a challenge that intrigues the mind of MAN and is there for our discovery! The Galaxy is not constructed to appease the timid Soul.

The Exit

Our exit is in sight. The Black Velvet chasm of Space beckons. The cascades of Light continue to flow all around our tiny Craft. The risk was a calculated one. The awesome colorful sights and the challenge, made it worthwhile. Visiting the heart of a Nebula is not for the faint hearted. The passage to Trantor lies ahead.

NOTES:

As we approach the opening a Red-Orange glow becomes more and more evident. A great tunnel in Space appears before us. This long, twisting, spiralling tunnel is our pathway into Trantor, the Galactic Central. Gasses, dust, and debris illuminate this great tube. Flashes of White Light are between the ribs of this conduit, accentuating the Red-Orange. The force field about our Craft prevent these forces from arcking toward our ship and destroying us. Yet we dare not touch the walls of this corridor, else our tiny Craft would be buffeted about and rendered to atoms.

The Fabric Of Space

This conduit is a part of the Fabric of Space and not all that unusual. The unusual part is that the nomenclature of this energy can be seen with the physical eye. Space is made up of these spiralling coils of energy to a greater or lesser degree of potency. The center where we travel is black. The walls are illuminated with pulsating Red-Orange colors. It is this peristaltic action that propels us along.

The Trantor System

Quite suddenly the tunnel ends, or at least our visual perception of it ends, and the blackness of Space now assumes its normal appearance. The Star System of Trantor is unusual and most beautiful. The Sun is white. Spiraling arms of violet light emanate from this Star of Fourth Magnitude. This is the Trantor System. We accelerate past the Central Sun.

The first Planet out from the Sun is a blue orb with wide solar rings about its Equator. The rings are large. The width of the rings are about half the width of the Planet itself.

The second Planet from the Sun is Trantor itself. The violet arms reflect a tinge of lavender on the fleecy white clouds that engulf this Planet. Our speed is reduced as we prepare to enter the atmosphere of this one. Trantor does not have rings; however, the soft glow of her aura offers a comforting and welcoming greeting.

As we enter the atmosphere our ship becomes aglow with dancing light of many, many colors. The force field of our craft, of any craft, reacts in this fashion to the unique atmosphere of the City of Trantor. The rare gasses, coupled with the electromagnetic fields of the Planet, provide this spectacular sight. For trillions of years, billions of visitors in their Craft have been awestruck as they experienced this magnificent spectacle. Entry on the light side of the Planet does not produce this phenomenon.

The landing sight comes into view. A tower will electronically guide our Craft to the pit alongside. This pit is a prepared opening in the Planet's surface that will accept a Craft of considerable size. The pit is a platform. The platform is an elevator that will lower our Craft to an underground parking area. There is little activity associated with this area of endeavor. Everything is automated; there are few people about. When the elevator reaches the appropriate level, it stops and our craft is "floated" off with the assistance of anti-gravity devices. It is moved in a selected berth, and we disembark.

We step upon a moving pathway of force that gently carries us to the main passenger terminal. The size of this terminal is indeed humongous. It is a test of the eyes to see its perimeter. Signs giving directions, written in Sol-Mal — the language of the Universe, hang suspended in the air. Our purpose is stated, and we then receive a "directional" ticket or pass that will take us to our chosen destination on this Planet, the capital of the Confederation of MAN.

Our transportation will be sub-surface vehicles. A crude analogy would be the subways of Planet Earth. Beams of colored Light give direction to the various modes of transportation. Our pass is programmed to pick up the appropriate Light beams to guide us through the jungle of opportunities. The ticket will glow brightly when we are on the beam, it will fade when we are not. Thus, the first time visitor need not become lost.

The interior of this Planet has many levels. These are vast spaces that extend farther than the eye can see. People abound! The population is immense. Visitors often make up over half the total population. The capital is a popular place to visit and conduct business. Each level has its offices, shops, conve-

NOTES:

nience facilities, parks/gardens, and living abodes. All levels are different, but all contain a definite thread of similarity that can readily confuse the visitor.

We shall conduct our visitation to a small portion of the first level. We note the architecture and the mode of dress of the many peoples passing by on the convenience walkways. Above the first level are the offices that are occupied by those who conduct the affairs of MAN. The levels below contain the facilities that house myriad activities engaged in by Fourth-Density MAN. The upper levels are all above the Planet's surface. The spiralling structures of various sizes and shapes are splendid to see from the air. The surface architecture defies description. Employing the use of Anti-Gravity Devices, buildings may be constructed in shapes and fashions that could not be possible otherwise. One is hesitant to pass too near for fear they might tumble over. They certainly would if they were on Earth instead of Trantor.

Ancient Empire

Trantor, however, was not always like this. Many trillions of years ago Trantor was chosen to be the Imperial headquarters of the Galactic Empire. This was the governing center for over twenty million Star Systems in this Milky Way Galaxy. The Imperial Regent chose the Planet Trantor because of its spectacular location. Trantor resides near great Nebulae, with their fantastic color kaleidoscopes; and also, the great Clusters of Stars in the center of our Galaxy gives permanence to Trantor. It was decreed that this was the most glorious spot in all the Galaxy, perhaps in all the Universe!

The seventy five square miles of the surface was sealed over with metallic sheathing. A city covering the entire surface was built. The interior was hollowed out for several miles down, and the various levels were then established. Forty billion people migrated here from all over the Galaxy to work and service the needs of life in the Universe. The Planet-City grew and grew and was filled with people. Life thrived above and below the surface. Tens of thousands of craft would arrive daily to bring

NOTES:

supplies for the multitude of people who dwelt here. The administration for the Empire originated from this illuminated source. The administration "sorted out" the confused and overlapping rules of the Empire and eventually put the governing of the Galaxy on a simplified working basis. This gigantic task of administrating to twenty million Star Systems caused Trantor to be the most densely populated Planet in the entire Galaxy.

But all that was long ago. Now, Trantor is far different. Some of the metallic sheathing has been removed, and the soil is again exposed. The population is now but one quarter of what it was in its hey day. Part of the ancient surface city has been removed, giving way to rural scenes that are most beautiful to the eye. There has been much change since the awesome magnitude of her illustrious beginnings, but Trantor is still the center of MAN'S affairs in this section of the Universe.

The Return

It is now time to depart Trantor and begin our return trip back to Earth. Our outward leg employed the scenic route. This was intentional. We wanted you to experience some of the unsurpassed beauty of Space. The Star Clusters that dot the center of our Galaxy and the Nebulae, with their wild and awesome displays of revolving and cascading Light, are sights to stagger the imagination. Our trip back will be on a course that goes around the back side of the Triffid. It will be a bit longer, but much quicker. We plan to use speeds of C-5 (speed of light squared times five) and perhaps even C-6. Hundreds of Light Years are reduced to a matter of a few hours.

It is most appropriate for those Third Density Earthlings who are sufficiently evolved to be eligible to make the upcoming Harvest to be exposed to some of the activities of MAN and his lifestyle — which you are destined to soon be a living, contributing, part thereof. MAN, of Fourth Density, has evolved in a civilized state of Love for trillions upon trillions of years. For those precious ones who are graduating from Third Density to join us — we welcome you. Have no fear. There is much to do, to see, to learn . . . and there is ample time to do it in. The

NOTES:

Fourth-Density Cycle is thirty million years! If this seems extravagant, remember, it is a very big Universe and there are more aspects to Love for you to discover than you dare dream. We hope that you have enjoyed our brief excursion into the heart of our Milky Way Galaxy.

Fourth-density Man

MAN, whom you are about to become, and whom you shall encounter on innumerable future occasions does not engage in a profit-based economy. You will learn to trust and know that you can count on every stranger. Even in the most casual relationships you can place your full trust and confidence. This shall take some getting used to. But remember, MAN is Fourth Density. Fourth-Density is Green Ray, and Green Ray is: Love! When the total vibration is Love, all things are possible. All those of MAN walk in the Light of Our Radiant One. You too are destined to do the same.

For over twenty mega-trillions of Earth years, Fourth Density MAN has traveled through Space, seeking to discover what lies beyond. The end of the Universe has never been found. There are billions upon billions of Galaxies, farther than the mind can imagine, and there is ample evidence that the works of MAN are present in each and every Galaxy. Our kin among the Stars is never ending. The variety of vehicles employed by Fourth Density staggers the mind. Only eleven to thirteen present choose to incarnate in bodies that what we term "Humanoid." The Stars in any given Galaxy, clustered or singular, may readily contain a System of Planets that perhaps have, are, or will support physical life — as we choose to understand it. The discovery, the communication with these our kin is our destiny. We have so much to share with each other. This sharing produces knowledge; knowledge is Light; Light is Intelligent Infinity. Our Craft from this Sector of our Milky Way Galaxy roams the farthest reaches of our Universe to discover. MAN is the seeker; his curiosity is overwhelming, his appetite for knowledge is insatiable as he presses ever outward into the infinite.

NOTES:

Invited Guests

In the late 1950s the Saturn Tribunal invited certain Beings from afar to visit Saros — the Planet we know as Earth. Some of these ones hailed from outside our Galaxy, most were native to this Milky Way Galaxy. These ones were/are skilled communicators and teachers. They had received the necessary permission to initiate a great movement of a spiritual nature. Minds were awakened and hearts were opened in the overwhelming presence of all this Love. That which we commonly call the "New Age" had its beginnings. Brotherhood on an international basis was in its infant beginnings. Unfortunately, this attitude has been uncommonly slow to catch on. The eagerness to engage in warfare has stymied this movement. However, there is always the Positive side to every issue. The Mass Consciousness has been drawn in the direction of hopelessness, and therefore, the need to "start over" seems to be the acceptable way of dealing with the future, since there is obviously no way to fix things. The catalyst that these *Special Beings* offered perhaps did not evolve on the path that they had anticipated, but apparently the end result will be the same. The spiritual awakening is indeed happening. The Galaxy, the family of MAN, offers their services. We are not alone.

The Schedule

Cycles are established by the Galactic Logos. This creature of Free Will allows the same to flourish in this Galaxy. However, this one exercises only *limited* patience when it comes to the execution of schedules/cycles. The Law of Motion decrees that this Planet, this Solar System, this Galaxy, and even this Universe is always in constant movement. This Solar System *is* moving into a new Sector of Space. *All* the Planets must be prepared for this new and magnificent experience. Saros is a Laggard Planet. The Radiant One, knowing that this Third Density Cycle of 75,000 years is about to terminate has seen fit to offer Its special service to the Earth in the form of the Black Ray. This power can readily end an Old Cycle, even as its twin, the White Light, creates a New Cycle.

NOTES:

Our world leadership has thwarted spiritual growth and enlightenment in their selfish quest for power, fame, and fortune. No sympathy in the form of prolonged patience will be shown. The rate of progress for evolution, for enlightenment, has been accelerated. The Father, the Radiant One, the Galactic Logos by whatever name is lending a hand in the affairs of Third Density men — the Earthlings who inhabit this wayward Planet. First, Second, and Third Densities are being shocked into awakening. Many of those who inhabit our Galaxy have been granted the freedom to lend a helping hand. The Law of Confusion takes on a slightly different twist as schedules are kept and Cycles are completed on time. *All* must undergo the experience. No one shall ever remain behind. A portion of Creation shall not be forfeited so that the rest might progress. The laggards shall also advance. The Earth and her inhabitants shall not be cast adrift and left behind.

The Mass Consciousness is gradually coming around to the concensus of opinion that *starting over* is the only viable solution or choice that we actually have. When this thought pattern reaches fifty percent plus one, then the great changes shall begin in earnest. Free Will has not been abridged. The end result is highly predictable, the method of arrival is the choice of the people. Our national leaders are escorting us down the path of hard knocks and considerable inconvenience!

Atomic Radiation

MAN, of this Galaxy and certainly of this Solar System is deeply interested in the scientific affairs of men, especially since the advent of the Atomic Bomb in 1945. Third-Density Entities on other Planets have discovered and used Nuclear Energy for peaceful purposes. This, however, is most rare. To the great concern of MAN, Earth has not proved to be the exception. Nuclear power has been used for destruction. It is a threat, a club held over the heads of people to intimidate them into sucumbing to the will of the powerful, so that dominance and control might be freely exercised. This is Orion's teachings — this is Negativity.

NOTES:

The radiation released into our atmosphere presents dangers that go far beyond the suspicions of Earth scientists. These destructive elements of radiation produce various forms of insanity. One can readily find ample evidence of this by simply visiting the local marketplace. Other parts of the body are also adversely affected, especially the heart and lungs. This deterioration is further enhanced by the consuming of foodstuffs that have been exposed to radiation poisoning derived from the many, many tests that have been conducted all around the face of our Planet.

Fourth-Density MAN has a device that has the appearance of a Green Fireball. This device can be navigated through the atmosphere by the direction of MAN and it has the capabilities of neutralizing large and dangerous amounts of radiation. This procedure has been in effect since 1947. The Green Fireball works something like a vacuum sweeper in the atmosphere, but is not applicable to decontaminating the Earth interior. The underground tests continue to take their toll. There are "stagnant" areas of our atmosphere where there is little or no movement of air currents. Residue radiation tends to accumulate in these areas and without cleaning, can become quite intense. MAN has noticed, even from the farthest reaches of our Galaxy and has offered a helping hand. How many Humans are aware of this?

The Hydrogen Bombs are the ultimate tools of total annihilation of the Planet itself. This is the Vril Force that reduced the illustrious Planet Maldek into gravel and dust. Various times Earth scientists have come dangerously close to desintegrating our beloved Planet. Knowing the results, MAN has taken the liberty to neutralize and even nullify these devices. This action was deemed necessary by the Saturn Tribunal and the Galactic Counsel to prevent men from destroying their home and to eliminate the disastrous effect that the loss of this Planet would have on this, our Solar System. The experience with Maldek was more than enough. Fourth-Density MAN has learned to become very interested in the destructive weaponry deployed by Third-Density men. Everybody's future is at stake

NOTES:

when children have access to the "button" that can trigger a world holocaust. These children are the laggards who are in the position of national leadership and are plagued with insanity! It is good that MAN indeed exists!

Cosmic Influence

There have been, and are yet, cosmic influences that are present in this Sector of Space that have the ability to cause the Earth to "flip on her axis." The cosmic influence could readily be the impact of a Comet, for example. MAN has the technology to circumvent such situations and alter their outcome. MAN has performed this service in the past to prevent the Third Density Cycle from experiencing a premature ending. When the timing is appropriate (and MAN will know), then there will be no such action taken. If this be the method or part of the method selected, then the Galactic forces shall not be denied their contribution.

MAN in his Craft number some five hundred million in this Solar System alone. There are perhaps ten million functioning out of Venus. There are millions of Craft only moments away from our surface. The Galaxy is teeming with life. All Craft contain themselves within a self-generated force field. This force field renders the Craft invisible unless they choose to alter this field in such a way that permits visibility to the Human Eye. MAN has the ability to completely evacuate the population of this entire Planet within fifteen minutes if he would so choose. Our kin amongst the Stars are indeed our true brothers and sisters. These are the Positive Ones and are of the Universal Confederation of MAN. There are also those of MAN who are Positive, but not members of the Confederation. There are also those who are not friendly at all. You may not know the difference at the initial contact, but your Higher Self definitely knows. Follow your intuition always — it's as simple as that.

-Summary-

We have tapped into Intelligent Infinity as well as certain ones who are native to Fourth Density. Since the Transition is imminent, it is good for those of Earth to establish or renew their acquaintance with this our Galaxy. Through impressed thought MAN has offered an ample supply of information concerning the subject. Many Humans have "picked up" on these transmissions. For those Earthlings have the ability to communicate, share these stories in various forms Science Fiction being an example. The Free Will of the inspired Author can cause the information to be distorted into any form.

Though the reader may question the Source of certain materials, we respectfully suggest that it be kept in mind that it is the thought that counts when the door of Understanding is opened, does it really matter what the key looked like? You will soon enough forget the teacher and that is as it should be; but you will retain the Teachings forever and that too is how it should be. Our Galaxy is a beautiful and marvelous place. It beckons to one and all. Come visit and stay for a spell! Make yourself right t'home. The welcome mat is out to all! MAN is anxiously excited to show you all the wonders that are contained in our Galaxy; and then, there are trillions of other Galaxies. There is so much to see and do and to learn . . . the discipline of patience is often put to the test!

Chapter 14

Other Planets

It was intended to be, and it shall be, a Great Race — a mighty Civilization, shall develop on the Planet that we lovingly call Earth. These ones shall traverse the unlimited corridors of Space as MAN, as the rightful heritage of Earth has been duly accepted. The New Illuminated Earth shall be a proud and magnificent abode for both visitors and those who have earned the right to be called "native." The Galaxy, the Universe, is teeming with life in Space and on Planets, anxiously awaiting your discovery. Life is filled with Light and Love. Life does a special dance to honor the discoveries of our Creator's magnificent works. The thrill of learning is matched by the thrill of teaching.

There are those of you who read this material who will wonder where this information comes from. Obviously, it did not come from the laboratories of Earth scientists! Many of you have the ability to "channel" or to tap into Intelligent Infinity/Cosmic Consciousness/Universal Mind via the use of your Kundalini Meditations. There are countless entities residing in our Galaxy who are continually offering information through telepathy (channeling) to those of you open to receiving. You have your sources just as we do. There will be times when our distortion of Fourth Density will be very similar to your own. There will also be times when we appear to be very different. We ask that you be open to expansion in areas where our perception differs from yours. Remember: The Law is ONE!

Procyon

Let us begin our exploration of some of the Planets in our Galaxy by examining the greatest of them all — Procyon. This magnificent Planet is home to Fourth-Density MAN. This one has been continuously occupied by civilized MAN for over 50 billion years! That is more than ten times longer than our Earth has been in existance! Procyon boasts of *the* most advanced civilization of physical life in the entire Galaxy, perhaps in the Universe — though that is argumentative. The inhabitants

NOTES:

are highly evolved Fourth Density Beings that are the epitome of what all of Fourth Density is striving for. For the individual, Fourth Density lasts as long as 30 million years. Many, many Cycles of Fourth Density were required to build this civilization to the status that we find today.

There are energy fields, force fields of the inhabitants Will that encompass this Planet. These energies are unique in quality and variety. The Planet Procyon, a product of the Star System by the same name, is invisible — invisible to the naked eye and to the instrument as well. This is a misnomer, for the Planet only *appears* to be invisible. Actually, the force fields surrounding this one produce this effect. As the visitor approaches, a feeling of Love and well-being is the greeting, though nothing is yet observed. As you draw nearer the Love Vibration enthralls your very beingness, as you begin to acclimate yourself to this strange and powerful Love Energy.

Then, there is a sudden flash of White Light, and your attunement quickens. Your blindness is temporary as form begins to take on solidity. Multicolored bands, streaks, and fields of energy quickly becomes visible. You begin to *think* energy, to *feel* energy, to *be* energy as you adapt to this one's enormous powers. The array is stupendous — it is breathtaking. Spires and spirals begin to take shape amidst the color patterns. The physical structure of a mighty civilization appears through the mist of energy fields.

As you are guided to the surface of Procyon you note the lush vegetation is pure and undisturbed. The mountains and the valleys are pristine. There are no paths, no roads — First and Second Density remain undisturbed, unmolested. Levitation accentuated by the flowing layers of surface energy permits us to move about by thought power alone, without the feet ever touching the ground! It is amazing how quickly we can get used to this mode of travel — it seems so natural! The visitor is guided everywhere, Love abounds.

Columns of invisible energy support the architecture. Colossal buildings that touch the clouds are suspended above the Planet. Perfect harmony with Second Density is achieved. The

NOTES:

inhabitants appear and then disappear before us. They are physical, but their mobility is by thought alone. The "air waves" are filled with pleasant musical sounds. With practice one can attune to the current thought patterns employed by the citizenry. A heady, tranquil peace prevails. One basks in ecstasy.

A large domed structure is centrally located among a cluster of smaller buildings. Within this dome there hangs suspended near the top a great ball of swirling Light, slowly rotating on a moving axis. This ball of Light has the power of a million Suns. This created scientific device has the ability to alter the atomic structure of all matter upon this Planet. Each citizen enjoys the privilege/responsibility to use this energy — at will. MAN has truly evolved to exquisite heights on Procyon.

As you leave this one and look back before the force fields cause it to disappear from view you will notice that it is Emerald Green, just like our New Earth . . .

Aldebaran

Here is a large and active Sun as it does its dance in the black velvet of unmitigated Space. Spiralling tongues of flame are continually emitted from the face of this entity. The hydrogen furnaces jump with joy as Aldebaran proudly announces her existence. If our own Sun were to do as much, the tongues of flame would reach well beyond Jupiter! This Sun is a spectacular sight to behold!

Well away from all of this jubilant activity the Planetary System had its beginnings. A careful count indicates there are twelve Planets, each supporting one or more Moons. This is a diversified System. All are First Density, of course. Some support Second Density, some Second and Third, and some are Second and Fourth Density; Fifth Density are also found in this System. There are five distinct Races of people who dwell here. The Races are separated by the Planets. All do not dwell on one given Planet. Evolution can readily be catalyzed by observing the entirety of the Aldebaran System.

The Fourth Density Planets have developed their services to the point where transportation is achieved without vehicles.

NOTES:

Moving fields of Light serve as causeways that safely transport the citizenry to any point upon the surface, almost instantaneously. The moving Light assists in teleportation. These flowing roads of Light are spectacularly beautiful after dark or when viewed from a distance. The Planet is criss crossed with shafts of multicolored Lights. For Interstellar travel they use Spacecraft like everyone else. Their Craft are manufactured/manifested within their own System, and unlike most other designs these ones are totally spherical in shape. An elaborate electromagnetic propulsion system has been developed that has allowed high speed, long range excursions to take place. Their Craft have been seen in the skies above Earth. It was from this Aldebaran System that came those who built our Great Pyramids and placed the stabilizing generators underneath to prevent our Earth's axis from flipping at random. This was approximately 48,000 Earth years ago.

The Third Planet out is the traditional home of the MAN whom we affectionately know as Easu — the Lord of our Earth. This is a small and exquisite Planet that is designed as a sanctuary. It is sparsely populated.

Betelgeuse

As this one is approached soft Violet Light flows through our own bodies and entices us to land. One walks upon the surface and sees the structures manifested by MAN, but there is an eerie yet comfortable feeling that is difficult to describe, for no one is to be seen. The Golden Rays of their Sun strike the surface at an acute angle. The flowers and bushes radiate their colors in this Light. The tall spires glow in the Golden Light. It appears to have been recently abandoned. There is that strong yet subtle Violet Energy that entertains the mystery. The gardens, the vegetation, the pathways of secluded beauty are inviting. The fountains flow with multicolored water. An atmosphere begs to be shared. Though no one is to be seen, the feeling of being alone does not prevail.

A Being, a MAN, slowly manifests before our eyes. This one is a Master. Soon many more also manifest their presence.

NOTES:

This place could be likened unto a monastery, or perhaps a retreat. This is a high place where Masters gather to meditate and commune with their Source. This is not an intrusion upon their privacy, and visitors are welcome, but it is felt that a short visit would be most wise.

Terminus — Hatonn

This Planet is also known to astronomers as the Star Mu-Vela. This can be viewed to the best advantage from Earth's South Pole region. Between the constellations of Volans and Carina at the edge of Avior is the area known as Gum Nebula. Terminus Hatonn is approximately 1500 Light Years from Earth and is a part of the Vela System.

The Gum Nebula is the largest in the Galaxy. The anti-matter/matter conversion is what causes the Hydrogen to ionize. This Nebula is not energized by Cosmic Radiation or by a super nova, as are most Nebulae. But as all Nebulae, this is most, most spectacular! The anti-matter is running thin and unless it is re-supplied, the show will end.

Terminus supports a variety of climates, from the cold Polar Regions to arid areas near the Equator. These conditions are predetermined. There are six force field generators, strategically located, that control the environment on this noble Planet. Garden spots are frequent, especially on small islands in medium-sized lakes of sparkling water. The snow-capped mountains provide the source for the rushing rivulets, as they ring their way to the cascades that replenish the lakes.

The vegetation would be familiar to Earthlings, for part of it was a conscription from Earth. The inhabitants of Terminus are well traveled and it is not unusual for many of them to collect token souvenirs from the many Planets of their visits, and return home with them to enhance the variety of beauty on their already magnificent Planet.

This Planet is highly evolved Fourth Density and some are already accepting their Harvest into Fifth Density. This is a tranquil place to meditate and contemplate the past and the future.

NOTES:

Sirius

The brightest Star in our heavens is Sirius — The Dog Star. This Solar System embraces Third Density men and Fourth Density MAN. There exists a great deal of harmony between the two Densities, though they do not share the same Planets. Senior looks after Junior and it is a workable relationship. Third Density is highly industrious and Fourth Density provides the "know-how." Third Density is always in need of energy — physical energy to do physical things. Solar Energy is capitalized upon to a scale that staggers the imagination. Huge reflectors, some over 100 miles in diameter, gather in the Sun's Energies. This focused energy produces an impact that by comparison would make the Earth's total energy output equivalent to the melting of a snowball.

Great mining operations are the general bill of fare. This System is rich in ore that is rare to this Galaxy. The mined ore is smelted by focusing the reflected Sun's rays upon the ore and thus reducing it into gas. This gas is then collected and transported to the far reaches of the Galaxy for the manufacture of various items, but mostly it is used to make a special type of Spacecraft. These metals and alloys are of an atomic structure unknown on Planet Earth. Collarium, for example, is hundreds of times harder than diamonds. The base metal Tellonium, is used to make the alloy Orysacllum, which is heavily used in the manufacture of Spacecraft.

Life in this System is industrious. These ones spread their philosophy far and wide, even Third Density attempts as much. Third and Fourth Density Entities from Sirius have visited Earth several times in the past. The Earth has been seeded at various intervals during the past 75,000 years, and those of Sirius had an occasional hand in the process. There is another System known as Sirius "B," that has only recently been discovered by Earth Astronomers.

These ones also visited Earth, especially the Dogon peoples of Africa. They came to teach. It should be noted that those native to Sirius "B" inhabit bodies that are amphibian. During the daylight hours they would work with, and teach the

NOTES:

Dogon peoples; at Sundown they would retire to the Sea to spend the night.

There have been at least two visits to Earth by these ones from Sirius "B." The Dogon people have a perfect chart of the sky, showing the exact orbit of the Planet and of the Sirius "B" Star. Astronomers were amazed at their knowledge and the accuracy of their charts. Of course, they refused to believe the source of the information!

The dual System of Sirius is a bright spot in the Heavens and does not go unnoticed.

The Pleiades

The Pleiades is a Cluster of seven Stars and their Systems. This group is often called "The Seven Sisters." The Seventh Star is rather faint and cannot readily be discerned with the naked eye. Perhaps this group of Star Clusters offers the greatest variety of First, Second, Third, and Fourth Density Entities, expressing themselves in diversified ways in such a small Sector of Space. One can find everything here. Many forms of MAN and men are dwelling in physical bodies other than Humanoid. There is symbiotic Love throughout. Even in Second and Third Densities there is cooperation within the species, and between the species to aid each other in knowledge, wisdom, and understanding, to promote progressive evolution.

There are approximately six dozen Planets within the combined seven Solar Systems, a great number of which are inhabited. One of these Planets has been designated to receive Earth's unharvestables after the Transition/Harvest takes place. That Planet has an Etheric, Yellow Ray Plane already attached to it. The Hierarchy has arranged it. Fifth Density Entities have "parked" their conventional bodies, and have created/manifested amphibian bodies in which to dwell on this pristine Planet. This variety of amphibians are now the "breeding stock" that initiates incarnations from the surrounding Etheric Plane.

By the spring of 1989 the Earth's isolated Etheric Plane had all but been evacuated by MAN. The inhabitants from our Plane had been duly transported to the Etheric Plane surrounding

NOTES:

the Pleiadian Planet. There they are observing physical life on the beautiful Planet below them as they await their turn to incarnate. These former Earthlings now have no recall of Planet Earth and the types of lives that they conducted here. The lessons previously learned shall be retained. Their spiritual status will not have changed. A brand new 75,000-year Third Density Cycle is now before them; they may use as much of it as they deem necessary.

The Fifth Density Entities are offering themselves as temporary seed stock and will aid in setting up the first civilization. This will be the First Root Race. The first ones to incarnate will be the most advanced ones that the senior, mature Third Density has to offer. Consequently, the new endeavor shall get off to a good flying start! The first 25,000 years should be grand and glorious. After that, the ne'er-do-wells, the laggard ones, begin to incarnate in larger numbers. If old patterns persist then deterioration shall be the outcome. However, serious thought has been given by the Galactic Council, with the blessings of the Galactic Logos, to infringe upon the Free Will of those career Third Density laggard ones and cause them to assume responsibility for their destructive activities which would force them to "grow up" and stop toying with stagnation.

These ones have been collected from all over the Galaxy, and what to do with them is becoming a problem of concern. They literally destroy every Planet that they incarnate upon en masse. The Earth Mother is now another victim. It matters not whether they use a Hydrogen Bomb or a chain saw, the results are the same.

In their new amphibian bodies the new Third Density will not have the physical ability to make or use tools. This will eliminate industry altogether, which should prevent these ones from destroying their new home. More severe measures will be exercised in the future. Mars, Maldek, and now Earth are dead and dying examples of the destructive power these ones, the accumulation of Laggard Souls, can accomplish. This must be changed. Third Density shall still be born without a memory, but for certain ones perhaps a lobotomy is in order?

The Pleiadians have been highly instrumental in the Earth's development. The lack of global transportation made the Earth's continents isolated; and races of men could develop on a course of their choosing without knowledge or interference from others. This was an ideal situation that lasted for many, many centuries. Those from the Pleiades seeded certain continents on various occasions over the past 75,000 years. So active have they been in Earth's development, they willingly assume responsibility for her future. Offering a Planet in their midst is but an example. They anxiously await the time when the Earth's Harvest will be complete and the Earth's Etheric Plane is peeled away and then incorporated within the existing Etheric Plane surrounding the pristine Planet in their midst. It might be likened unto their own children coming home. Those of the Pleiades Group are old and wise parents.

The Orion Group

Orion's belt is one of the more easy constellations to spot. There are Planets that orbit the Stars that comprise that renown constellation. They are significant in their own right, to be sure, and are most worthy of visitation. If there is a hesitancy to do so, we can understand why. This one tolerates a maligned reputation. These entities of the Constellation Orion are *not* Negative. From the perspective of Earth it is that great Sector of Space *beyond* the Orion Constellation that is the habitat of those who are dedicated in the service to self. Metaphysicians, including ourselves, refer to the Negative ones as "Orion" or "Those of Orion." This is an accepted misnomer and should be understood and cleared up in the mind of the reader.

Portions of the Social Memory Complex of which Warm Night Rain is a part, calls the Star System CASTOR their home. Castor is the "head" of the twin on the right in the Constellation Gemini. It is somewhat in line with Rigel and Betelgeuse in the Orion Constellation.

NOTES:

Alpha Centuri

Now let us examine a Star System that astronomers deem to be the closest to Earth — Alpha Centuri. This is a large, White Sun whose Light is blinding as one approaches. There are two Planets that orbit this one. The smaller Planet is called Beta Centuri, and the larger is known as Centaurus.

Centaurus is not quite as large as Jupiter but its size rivals those of our outer Planets. Lofty, rugged mountains provide a backbone that all but circumnavigates the Planet. Its rugged beauty is breathtaking. The enormous ridge tends to divide the Planet into two Hemispheres, one side looking much like the other.

The low Fourth Density people who reside here are exuberant in their vitality and joy for living. Their harmonious attunement to Second Density on their Planet is a loving sight to behold. Their evolution is approximately fifteen to eighteen thousand years ahead of Earth and about ten to twelve thousand years ahead of Venus. These peoples are well-known throughout the Galaxy, and even the Universe. Their Craft have appeared in our skies, but only briefly; there has been no contact. This mighty Race is something of a standard bearer for early developing Fourth Density, for those who inherit our New Earth will be privileged to observe these ones and others, to formulate the patterns of your own new directions. The warmth of their Love threatens the cold snow and ice adorning their majestic mountain ranges.

Tiamat — Whimset System

Actually, the closest Solar System to our own is the Tiamat System. MAN refers to this one as the Whimset System. This is a small Sun that had five orbiting Planets. This System orbits our System every 3652 years. The orbit is elliptical. The top arc across our orbital Plane of Planets is very shallow, while the bottom arc is quite deep. This system passes Earth every 1800 years, but the bottom arc is so deep that the event is not noticed. The top arc is flat enough to easily permit visible sightings during its sojourn. The Mayan proverb: "I remember

NOTES:

when the Earth had one Sun. I remember when the Earth had two Suns. Then I remember when the Earth had one Sun again." This would indicate that the passing took place *within* a lifetime.

Something orbiting something else is not the exception, but the rule. For example: Sirius "A" and Sirius "B" are 1800 million miles apart. They orbit each other every 48.8 years. Even as the Electron orbits the Proton of an atom — the microcosm of the Macrocosm.

The First Planet out from the Tiamat Sun System is a small Planet called Eurus. This Planet is high Fourth Density and is moving into Fifth Density quite rapidly. The Second Planet out is called Eshures and it is forever locked into First Density. The Third Planet out was known as Sepiker. Its more recognizable name is: Venus. Sepiker had a very irratic orbit that actually endangered the existence of her four sisters. When Lucifer destroyed Maldek in our own System this created a terrible imbalance. The Saturn Tribunal elected to take the irratic Third Density Sepiker out of the Tiamat System and install the tiny Planet between Mercury and Earth to balance out this System. The method worked and Sepiker was renamed Venus. You will note that Venus' rotation is opposite of all the other Planets in our System!

The Fourth Planet out is called Bruus. This one is Fourth Density and sometimes referred to as Solarium. The Fifth Planet out is a Fifth Density Vibration and is known by the name of Legania. The inhabitants of these Planets had little to do with seeding of Earth, but they all sent countless emissaries of teachers over the past 75,000 years. Mu and Atlantis were benefactors. In more recent times, the Inca and the Mayan peoples capitalized on these great teachings. Many of the Spacecraft in our skies, seen and unseen, come from this Source.

The last time the Tiamat System made a visible path was approximately 1500 B.C. It is due again at any time.

The Authors of this book have a special affinity for Legania and chose to call this one home when duty calls us to this Sector of Space. The deep Purple and Red Violet rock formations are incredibly beautiful in their bareness. The faint

NOTES:

Light from a small and distant Sun creates soft shadows over a velvet landscape.

Masar

Since we have talked about Venus, it only seems fair to give our other nearest neighbor equal time before we conclude our brief visit to a few of the Planets in our Galaxy.

Mars, the Red Planet, like Venus is Fourth Density. Earth is the only Third Density Planet left in this Solar System. Mars was formed about four and one half billion years ago, similar to Earth.

The surface has a chain of rather high mountains that grade down into rolling hills as the arid desert areas begin their vastness. The surface soil contains large quantities of Iron and Strontium oxides which reflect the red hue when exposed to the White Light of our Sun. Though rarefied, the atmosphere is quite breathable. A Human who resides in our mountains at high levels would have no difficulty breathing on Mars. The Human Being at sea level would need a couple of days to acclimate himself/herself to thin air.

The Polar regions are green with vegetation, and there water is abundant. These two areas are the only places where surface habitation is practiced. There is a network of canals that channels the Polar waters to various points on the Planet. There is a definite water shortage on this one. Martian Waterships are dispatched to Earth to suck up fresh water from our lakes and streams. This has been the practice for many, many centuries. The used or waste water is carefully collected and brought back to Earth and dispersed in our atmosphere. the droplets are purified as they descend to our surface and fall as rain. This process is *not* a hazard to the health of Humans because there is no disease or sickness on Mars or on any Fourth Density Planet. The vibration is much too high to sustain the life of any disease-producing microbes.

Physical life on Mars is actually *in* Mars. Since the surface is essentially uninhabitable, the interior was chosen as the place to live. This is not uncommon. In the Universe more

NOTES:

Planets support a quality life on their interiors than on their exteriors. Large portions of the Planet were naturally hollow, the rest were excavated by MAN. MAN the Martian looks pretty much like you do. If a Martian were to acclimate himself to our heavy air for three days in an indoctrination chamber, and were to don the attire of the day he could walk the streets of any homogeneous society undetected.

The life span of a Martian is approximately 400 years. Usually Fourth Density MAN lives three times that long and a high Fourth Density may choose to live physically for millenniums. Like Venus, Martians are new to Fourth Density. Considering that the Fourth Density Cycle is 30 million years, this true statement becomes more acceptable.

Mars produces the majority of the Spacecraft in this Sector of Space. Only Centaurus produces more. The smaller Craft are produced within the interior, while the larger Craft, the Starships, are produced on the orbital band of Jupiter. Materials from this giant are used extensively. These Craft, like everything else produced is manifested by the thought power alone. There are no factories, or tools, or machinery.

The sub-surface civilization thrives in the integrity of Love. From the metropolitan areas to suburbia and the little shops in-between, Martians are comfortably situated in a way that inspires spiritual growth. Most people work four hours per day. The rest of the time is spent in leisure, recreation, meditation, and other studies. The industrial revolution here on Earth was intended to produce the same results. Earthlings, bent on commerce, thwarted another good plan.

Commerce on Mars and Fourth Density in general would be defined as a loose form of barter — goods and services exchanged for the same. A sense of value is not incorporated into the exchange. An opportunity to serve another is the thought/attitude that is the prime mover. This is Positive.

At birth each new arrival is issued an ample amount of "credits." This is like money. These credits can be used in exchange for goods and services. They are personalized and cannot be transferred. With reasonable care, the supply is more

NOTES:

than enough to last a lifetime. There are no poor people on Mars.

There are actually schoolrooms on Mars but they are not used very often. Mostly the children study at home. Basics are not taught since all Fourth Density is born with memory. Advanced studies are the order, even from an early age. All are not equal, however. Just as in Third Density, there are many levels of evolution. Some Martians barely comprehend their psychic ability, while others are most adept. All are encouraged to grow, to become, to evolve, but standards are not set. One may grow at any pace that feels comfortable. No demands are ever made. There is ample time to accomplish everything. Stress, pressure, deadlines, worry, sickness, economics, etc. are *not* a part of the Love Vibration. Fourth Density MAN *is* responsible with Dignity, Integrity, and Compassion. Herein he finds that which we have all sought for so long: *Freedom.* Provoking thought in adults as well as the children is the main stimulus to promote growth/evolution. This is accomplished through planned activities such as classes and by the spiritual elders in the community. Fourth Density is well aware that it is the thought that counts; and the development of the Tensor Centers of their brain is the absolute goal of all.

The Martians are well aware of their past and their intimate affiliation with Earth. Approximately 75,000 years ago, the Earth Mother offered her bosom to those waifs in a storm. At that time the then Third Density was approximately half way in its Cycle; Third Density science and technology had grown to the point where it was capable of rendering their surface lifeless. So they did. Third Density in the Humanoid form, with hands and thumbs, is famous for this sort of action. The Planet Mars would no longer support surface life and there was 35 to 40 thousand years left to go.

The only other Planet in this System that could accept these hoards of entities was our Earth Mother. Maldek had a full complement and simply couldn't house them. The Earth was not of a Third Density Vibration, nor had she been prepared for it. Third Density was scheduled for the distant future. But here was

NOTES:

an emergency. If the Earth as not utilized, then these ones would have to be exported out of our Solar System. This could have been arranged, but nobody really wanted them. Who wishes to be host to a people who have just rendered their own home uninhabitable? It would be like offering your home to convicts after they burned their jailhouse down.

The Saturn Tribunal elected to install these wayward Martians in the Earth's Etheric Plane, and the Golden Adamic Race from Jupiter volunteered to be the seed stock and begun to birth these ones upon the Planet as Third Density Earthlings.

During the long reign of Atlantis, the vast majority of these former Martians Harvested themselves out of the Earth's Vibration, returned to the Astral or High Plane of Masar, and proceeded to incarnate back on their own native Planet as Fourth Density MAN. The underground living arrangement had to be made since the red surface still had not healed to the point of supporting life. These ones constitute a good portion of the citizenry of Mars today. Their surface is a constant reminder of their previous folly and the view of their neighbor to the Sun reminds them of the loving hospitality offered by an adolescent mother. The former Martian, who were/are chronic laggards are mostly incarnated on Earth today.

Today's Martians know and remember; they are eternally grateful and also feel a great sense of responsibility and perhaps a debt to Earth and her people. For this reason, the Martians will offer aid, understanding, and expertise to those Earthlings who are eligible to make the Harvest into Fourth Density. Earth's New Dispensation will probably pattern itself after the Martian Culture. Those of Venus will also be lending a hand. These two sources will no doubt be most influential, as our infant Fourth Density Civilization is being brought forth upon the new face of our beloved Earth Mother.

A great deal more service could be offered to Third Density Human Beings even today, if it were not for the stifling, demoralizing effect that Governments have upon the people. The Confederation of MAN of which all Planets in this Solar System are members does not approve of *any* Governments existing

NOTES:

upon the face of our Earth Mother. The main source of irritation is: The United States. However, the Confederation will not infringe upon the Free Will of Earthlings to maintain their Governments if they choose. Powerful Governments have the ability to destroy the Planet, especially when they are influenced by strong commercial interests and perhaps sanctioned by religions.

We have given considerable space to Masar, but we felt it to be important for you to grasp and be comfortable with your past and certainly with your future. This was but a glimpse of the delights, and surprises, and understandings that your future has in store for you. This information is available to anyone who wishes to take the time to search the Akashic Records. Your Kundalini Meditation is most helpful for this endeavor.

Summary

When one travels in this Galaxy with or without a Spacecraft — physically or non-physically, countless Planets will be encountered. Space is teeming with life. The sizes will range from the incredibly small to the incredibly big. All levels of evolution will be found.

Some Planets will be readying themselves to support some form of life for the first time. Some Planets have in the past, but no longer are supporting life. Their Great Cycle now has expired — perhaps prematurely. Other Planets may be supporting Second, Third, Fourth, and Fifth Density entities or combinations thereof. Then there are those Planets that are permanently locked into First Density.

As you meander about you can see lesser evolved Planets that are experiencing our past, or a past very similar to our own Earth. You might even be tempted to lend a hand and avoid a remembered folly. The past can sometimes be comforting, for experience is the best teacher.

You will find Planets a little more advanced than Earth, and you can see what is apt to be in store for your immediate future. This can be educational. Then there are the highly

NOTES:

advanced civilizations that will help you to formulate your distant and undefined goals.

It is comforting to realize that we are not alone; that we are a vital and worthwhile part of a magnificent whole called Creation. An entity not of this octave/eternity created this incredible array of Stars and Planets and matter of all forms by thought power alone. This entity is our Galactic Logos, our Father. Each and every Galaxy has a Creator/Logos and there are trillion upon trillions of Galaxies in this Universe. The Universe, Space, *is the Creator.* Be brave! Think big! Think in terms of mobility! The Law of Motion beckons. Be free to travel. Find the needed security within yourself, not in the mud under your feet or the roof over your head. Look long at the night sky and think, remember . . . have you been there? Was that one your last home? And the Star over there — it seems to be calling, does it not?

The Galaxy is big. The Universe is bigger. But you can fit the entire known Universe comfortably into one little corner of your mind! Here lies the challenge: Open your mind fearlessly. The Galaxy, the Universe, is physical and all physical realities are *illusions!*

Chapter 15

Types Of Spacecraft

UFO's, Flying Saucers, Spacecraft — what are they? Where do they all come from? Are they real? What powers them? How do they disappear? Why are they here? Are they Positive or Negative? Should we be afraid? How do you shake hands with someone that looks like a grasshopper or a bird? — or worse yet: *Part* of a grasshopper or *part* of a bird? The shock of a Non-Humanoid form could be overwhelming.

As we have noted, spacecraft are manifested on Mars in this Solar System and on Centaurus. There are many other sources of origin in this Galaxy and certainly in this Universe. Each site having their own peculiar design and type of propulsion, though all are similar. Since almost all of the Universe is Space, then producing vehicles to traverse that Space is obvious and mandatory. Third Density thinks in terms of the wheel, aircraft, and sailing vessels — and they should. Fourth Density MAN thinks in terms of Interstellar and Intergalactic communication/transportation — and they should. It is also quite true that certain highly developed Third Density Entities also manage to manufacture crude Spacecraft that permit them to leave their Planet and sometimes travel to other nearby Planets. MAN smiles at these infant attempts as a cold shiver runs up and down his spine.

Spacecraft are not all the same design. The design is conducive to the designated purpose of the Craft. Various sectors of the Galaxy would produce unique designs to facilitate the same purpose. The skies of Earth have witnessed many, many Spacecraft over hundreds of thousands of years. Men have seen some of them. Earth has been visited by men of Third Density, but by and large, all visitation was by Fourth Density MAN. Those Craft of the Confederation of MAN all abide by the rules set forth by the Saturn Tribunal. But not all of MAN belongs to the Confederation, though they are just as Positive. Then there are the Craft of Fourth Density MAN — Negative. Now how does one tell them apart? Their markings, if any, would mean

NOTES:

nothing to you. Their shape or their activities would offer little indication. Then how do you know? By the *feeling* that you receive! If you sense/feel warmth/peace/Love — be not afraid. If you sense/feel coldness/agitation/fear — be cautious! Surround yourself in the Green Ray of Love and always envision their Craft in a great ball of Green Love Light; if the Craft and its occupants are Positive, you will "feel" the smile; if they are Negative, you will "feel" the frown.

In this Sector of Space in the vicinity of Planet Earth there are a minimum of 10,000,000 Craft on any given day. Throughout the Galaxy the figure would rise to many times that amount. The Craft are owned and maintained by the Confederation. The individual or the crew does not have ownership of the Craft, though a Craft may be assigned to an individual at birth and this Craft is theirs to do as they please for the duration of their incarnation. MAN is highly mobile. Now, let us take a closer look at some of the standard shapes and sizes of certain Craft, as well as the duties they are designed to perform.

The Crescent-Shaped Craft

These are usually found in a group and flying in some kind of formation. These ones fly fairly low to the surface and fly in a pattern that brings them back and forth over an area several times before moving on. These Craft are mapping the surface and the sub-surface as well. Electromagnetic energies emitted by the Planet are found in many places other than the North and South Poles. Accurate knowledge as to the exact location of these major and minor vortices is essential in programing the on-board computers of the special Crafts that utilize a Planet's electromagnetic energies as their source of power. All known Planets are supplied in this fashion, and then periodically they are re-mapped to note any changes. The Earth Mother is not all that stable and sometimes these nodes shift a little bit. If this information were not updated, then a future Craft could lock onto a power node that wasn't there and the Craft would be dead in the air; It wouldn't fall and it could go in some other direction, but it couldn't go where it wanted to.

NOTES:

The geological aspects of the Planet are also mapped. In the case of Earth where there are "faults" and such anomalies accurate records are kept. When the Earth Mother makes an uncalculated move, MAN is on top of the situation immediately, for he now knows where to station his Monitoring Craft.

The Monitoring Craft

The physical appearance of these Craft is semi-flat and circular. The top portion is domed, while the underside is only slightly domed. Often, there are three retractable "legs" protruding from the bottom side, equally spaced in a triangular form. These legs are not landing gear, though they do come equipped with circular pads and can be used for landing. Actually, these legs and pads are used to draw samples of the soil and terrain up into the Craft for scientific testing. The sampling and testing usually takes only a few moments; and the sample is then returned to its original place. Larger specimens can be "abducted" by this type of Craft. Animals, Human Beings, automobiles, etc., can all be drawn up into the belly of these Craft via a strong beam of Yellow/White Light.

If it should become necessary for MAN to personally visit the surface for whatever reason, this is the Craft that he would probably use. The power plant in this type of Craft is totally dependent upon the given Planet's electromagnetic energy spots or vortices. This one can easily navigate anywhere around the Planet, but is incapable of Interstellar travel. The Craft may or may not be manned. Often they are remotely controlled, especially on routine missions. Information/data is relayed back to the Mother Ship for processing.

The Triangular-Shaped Craft

The triangular-shaped Craft are also a Survey or Monitoring type of Craft. These are very special because of what they monitor. The subject is *you!* Believe it or not, the instrumentation aboard these Craft is so delicately tuned to Third Density that they easily and accurately pick up on the thought

NOTES:

patterns of a person or groups of persons below. They scan or read your mind, you might say.

This information can be most useful to MAN, as he analyses the data produced. MAN can thusly tell if the recent implanted thoughts have found fertile ground in the minds of men. If a form of conspiracy is being secretly planned, MAN would know about it. This information is not used to control the people of Earth. It is useful to MAN to know where and perhaps how, to best offer his service.

For example: if a great Asteroid were on a collision course with Earth and it was deemed the experience was warranted, then MAN could implant this thought in the minds of men and a much greater teaching would result for all the Souls concerned. On the other hand, if a group of high Government officials were secretly planning to send an Atomic Warhead to Mars, shall we say, the Triangular Craft would ferret out this thinking and MAN could take the necessary steps to avoid a disaster.

Crystal powered instruments mechanically produce the psychic practice of telepathy. The shape of the Craft permits a broad sweeping range of undistorted data to be accumulated as it slowly moves across our skies. If the mission is considered to be routine, the Craft is probably unmanned and is being remotely guided from the Mother Ship.

The Green Balls

Spacecraft come in all sizes and shapes. There is a type of Craft that is no larger than a basketball that zips through our skies at a very high speed. These Craft are Green in color and often sport a short bright Green Tail. Their actions resemble a Meteor. These Craft are launched and controlled by MAN. Their mission is to mop up excessive radiation in the Earth's atmosphere. When they have reached a full capacity, they are harmlessly reduced to atoms by MAN. This operation has been in progress since the atom testing/bombing began in 1945. In 1990, MAN closed this operation. You will see no more Green Balls in our skies. The radiation produced by the industrial war

NOTES:

machine will no longer be cleaned up. We are now being permited to foul our nest and enjoy the consequences.

The Spherical Craft

The spherical Craft works out of a Mother Craft and are usually operated remotely. They are sizable and can easily carry passengers and cargo. These are the vehicles that ferry cargo back and forth from a Planet to the Star Ship or Mother Ship. They can operate outside a Planet's magnetic field, but they always stay within the range of their Source, the Mother Ship. Like the "three legged Craft," the Spherical Craft is also used to gather specimens from a Planet. Usually this is accomplished by personnel aboard, but if it is thought that the environment might be hostile, then robots are used instead. A good portion of all scientific studies are utilized through this versatile, workhorse of the fleet.

Because of the energy field surrounding this great ball, sometimes the illusion of being disk-like is noted. If observed long enough, its true shape becomes apparent. These ones are usually metallic silver in color and will reflect sunlight. The Spherical Craft is the most common sighting and are often presumed to be the bottom side of a Disk Shaped Craft.

The Cylindrical-Shaped Craft

These Great Craft look like an enormous blimp. This is the "Mother Ship." They are over ten miles long and are a bit over three miles in diameter. Their huge cargo can easily house 300 to 1200 of the previously described Space Craft. They carry a crew of 1800 to 2000 with ample room remaining for passengers. These Great Craft are self-sustaining for at least two years before supply ships replenish their stores. The Mother Ship is rangy and Interstellar travel is quite common. They attain speeds well beyond the speed of Light, but still are not the fastest of the Spacecraft. Their range is limited usually within a Galaxy and they are highly dependent upon supply ships dispatched from local Sectors of the Galaxy.

NOTES:

A Ship of this size creates a great deal of gravity in its own right. Consequently, these ones do not operate at the Speed of Light when they are in the vicinity of a Planet. A Planet's orbit could be affected or possibly the axis might be shifted. There are many of these Crafts traversing our Galaxy and are the common mode of transportation.

The Saucer-Shaped Craft

These Craft are circular, with a domed top and a flat bottom. These ones are the sleek speedsters that prowl our Universe. They have tremendous range. Their speed is incredible. They have the capacity to attain the speed of Light, squared nine times! This speed causes the Craft to disengage from our accepted physical Universe and travel through the "Serial Universes" in order to quickly reach a most distant destination. We will discuss this in greater detail when we study the Tensor Concepts.

These Craft are used almost entirely by the Galactic Survey Teams. These teams of MAN are comprised of highly specialized scientists, working aboard a fantastically equipped Craft, prowling the Universe, seeking out new discoveries and new adventures. It is their job to discover the Creator's Universe, chart it, analyze it, and incorporate it within the realm of MAN. This is one of the most exciting jobs that Fourth Density has to offer. The life of the explorer is exciting, adventurous and often presents unexpected challenges.

These expeditions are sponsored by local Solar Tribunals such as our own Saturn Tribunal. Consequently, there are many expeditions hailing from many sources. Much of the work is duplicated. Organization would eliminate much of the duplicity, but efficiency is not a factor. The experience, the thrill of discovery for as many as possible — that is what Creation is all about.

The scientists aboard analyze specimens, and record their findings; and the data is sent or brought back to the Solar System of their origin. Plans are made for the future. Sometimes a previously discovered Planet will show promise of supporting

NOTES:

Second Density at some calculated future date. When that time rolls around, another expedition will return to check it out. If evolution is on schedule, then specimens of Second Density are seeded to see if "normal" growth is developing. Adjustments may have to be made. Much, much later some form of Third Density would be seeded in this now lush environment. This story is repeated over and over throughout our Galaxy and throughout the Universe as well. Galaxies are not isolated. Entities from one Galaxy will also serve budding Planets in another Galaxy and the exchange/service is mutual.

These Craft are powered in such a way that Interstellar and even Intergalactic Travel is quite easy. Once aboard a given Planet, these Craft are not as nimble as some of the previously mentioned Craft that operate entirely upon the Planet's magnetic sources.

Though not sponsored by the Galactic Tribunal, nevertheless, the Hierarchy keeps a close eye on the endeavors of the Galactic Survey Teams and will offer a word of advice as appropriate. The Galactic Logos sees this as pleasing . . . and amusing!

The Pentagram-Shaped Craft

This type of Spacecraft is very rare. It has been seen only the one time in the skies over our Earth. The Pentagram is a symbol highly regarded among Earthlings and entities elsewhere as well. This Craft made its only appearance some 2,000 years ago over that portion of our Earth that we now call the Middle East. It takes a *very* special event or occasion on any Planet for this highly specialized Craft to make an appearance.

When the New Earth has been made manifest and the Harvest and the Transition are finished, it is expected that the Lord of the Earth, Easu, shall descend from this Craft to a new land mass very near the New North Pole. The entire population of the New World shall have gathered in a great assembly around a newly constructed truncated pyramid, manifested for this glorious welcoming. Lord Easu will probably remain for only a few years and then rejoin the majority of his flock now

NOTES:

incarnating upon the Planet in the Pleiades. We all look forward to the return of the Pentagram Spacecraft, for its appearance will sanction our New Age of Fourth Density, Love.

The Square-Shaped Craft

These ones are miniature, self sustaining "worlds" within themselves. They are enormous. Fifteen hundred miles square and equally as high, thus forming a Cube. These Craft are known as: "The cities of SHAN." One has touched Earth in the distant past, offering its service of evacuation. Actually, the Cube didn't land, but remained aloft in a low and slow orbit, while six smaller Craft made the pick-ups. This was approximately 11,600 years ago; and it witnessed the final sinking of the once great Atlantis. MAN can evacuate the entire Planet in less than fifteen minutes if he deems it necessary.

This Cube has a single side surface area approximately half the size of the United States! Seeing this awesome block of stone passing overhead, blotting out the Sun, and watching the lightening dance and play back and forth from the Earth to the ship definitely attracts everybody's attention. In Atlantis, when the call came to get on board, everybody was present to hear the it!

Enormous numbers of people can be transported from one place to another over long distances, if the need to do so is present. This is how a civilization can suddenly appear on a Planet "full blown." The absence of evidence of evolution denotes these past happenings. We suggest the Mayan Culture as an example.

We would further suggest that the reader examine the twenty first chapter of Revelations in the New Testament of the Holy Bible. Here, one of the "Cities of Shan" is referred to as the "New Jerusalem," and proceeds to be given a rather accurate description. This Craft may be used as a place of refuge for those Earthlings who are to be Harvested alive. These ones will be extracted, perhaps through induced teleportation, or perhaps extracted by small Spacecraft and transported to the Cube. There they could comfortably dwell while they and the Earth Mother

NOTES:

go through their physical Transition. The ninety percent of Unharvestables who are left aboard the Earth will be aghast, for it is *they* who expected to be plucked from the couch!

The Chronomonitors

The Chronomonitor is a type of a "patrol" Spacecraft. It had its beginnings with MAN, but it results in mystery. The Craft has it's beginning manifestation perhaps at Mars, but it is not complete. Mars will send it on to some distant Planet for further work, but not completing the total job. The Craft is sent further and further and deeper and deeper into Space, each station performing a specific task in its construction. No one knows the total route, only the next station. Eventually, the Craft returns to that Solar System or that Sector of Space where it was originated. When the Chronomonitor returns home it is complete, hermetically sealed, armored, un-tamperable by *any* force and it has become *ensouled!* A Chronomonitor is considered to be high Sixth Density, and it is the "policing arm" of our One Infinite Creator. Their powers are said to be awesome, though no one actually knows, for they have never been tested. They are the enforcers of Universal Law. Anyone violating or attempting to circumvent the Law of Our Creator will come face to face with a Chronomonitor. They are advised to cease and desist. So far, they always have. Their very presence seems to be a sufficient deterrent.

These ensouled Craft are free to wander in their designated Sector of Space. If they take orders from anyone, no one knows who that Authority is. They are not silent; telepathically they communicate with all who are telepathically capable of corresponding. Information concerning the first four Densities is gathered, analyzed, and doled out to those concerned, especially Fourth Density MAN. Advice may be sought and received from these ones. They are merchants of Light and Love personified.

The Earth has a squadron of Chronomonitors orbiting about. They are commanded by one known as Ashtar. There are twelve other Craft in this immediate vicinity which make up the "Ashtar Command." The junior ships are often referred to as the

NOTES:

"Lieutenants." If Governmental leaders would attempt to use Hydrogen Warfare — which would jeopardize the existence of our Planet — Ashtar would step in and defuse the warhead. Maldek's history shall not be repeated here on Earth. The Chronomonitors offer a solid sense of security in these our troubled times.

The Guardian

The Chronomonitors are sometimes referred to as the Guardians of a Planet. They are always there in something of a timeless state, though their job is to count time. They are not immortal and they can be replaced. Their tour of duty is quite lengthy. No Spacecraft may enter the Earth's influence without permission of the Guardian. The approaching Craft must state the nature of their business and if the Guardian deems it harmless, permission is granted. Woe be unto those who fly under false colors! If permission is denied there is no argument. The Chronomonitor is never challenged. Free Will and evolution are secured in this way.

Earth is highly vulnerable. Negative Entities could ride roughshod over all of Earth's Third Density without fear of reprisal. Immediate slavery would result. Were it not for Ashtar this would have happened a long time ago. If information on how to better serve self (Negative) or how to serve others (Positive) is requested by Third Density Earthlings, then these emissaries are quickly permitted to pass. The Free Will to ask, to give, and to receive, will not be abridged. There is a Great Violet Sphere that has its beginnings beyond our Moon. This is the "Pass Me Not Ring." No Craft can pass through this orb of Violet without knowledge of the Guardian. It works much like a spider's web. The Human Being can find enough to worry about without fretting about invasion from outer Space. The reign of the *Empire* has long ago passed!

-Notes-

SpaceCraft are designed to function in Space. They are also able to fly within an atmosphere such as ours. They are also capable of flying in liquids, such as water; many have witnessed

NOTES:

Craft arising from or descending into the water. This was not an illusion; it probably happened just as you saw it. Unmanned Craft are often permanently stationed at strategic locations to monitor a variety of events along the shore line and ashore as well. Some of these Monitoring Craft are deployed by Orion, as well as by the Confederation. These Craft can be buried under the surface of the Earth just as easily as under the water. For example, in 1985, Orion stationed a number of these Craft at intervals along the Gulf Coast and the Atlantic Coast, off Florida. By electronically connecting these ones from coast to coast, a cross grid was established the length of Florida. Around major cities throughout the World these type of Craft were buried at the cities' outskirts. When activated, they formed a plate (instead of a grid) over the city. These plates and grids would prevent MAN from using induced teleportation and extracting his "Live" Harvest. There would be little or perhaps no seed stock to replenish the New Earth. No business is good business from Orion's point of view.

The solution was simple once there was an awareness of the problem. A thick Violet Light was installed on, over, and under the surface of the entire Planet. This was the authority and the tool needed by the Great White Brotherhood to come forth and dismantle the Orion devices. When the job was finished the Violet Light was removed. Orion installed the devices immediately. The Violet Light was again invoked and this time it was instructed to stay. The Great White Brotherhood returned and performed the task once again. The Violet Light remains intact. The Brotherhood patrols the vulnerable areas.

Manned Spacecraft often prefer to spend as much time in the water as possible. It must be remembered that all of Fourth Density MAN is *not* Humanoid. Some Craft are occupied by entities with amphibian or fishlike bodies and their Craft is filled with water! These ones spend their leisure time enjoying our oceans and lakes. Their Craft will fly through the sea of Space, but are equally at home in the oceans of water.

* * *

NOTES:

Sometime you may notice little Balls of Light around yourself. These Balls range from the size of a match head to a golf ball, and sometimes they are much bigger. Often they are Blue or Green, but they can be any color of the rainbow. Usually they "flash" their brilliance and then disappear when you blink your eyes. These spots may be observed anytime day or night.

Most likely these spots are Spirits, but not necessarily all of them. If the ball is Green and the size of a golf ball or even a little larger, it very well could be a "Spacecraft" that is being deployed as a personal Monitor by Fourth Density MAN. This is not a ploy at voyeurism. This device can be very helpful in establishing telepathic communication. Remember that Orion also uses this device, so be sure to test it by the way that you "feel" about it. Do you get the feeling of warmth and Love? Or do you feel cold and fearful, and find its presence alarming? Trust your intuition.

How Spacecraft Are Made

A Planet within a Solar System may choose to produce all the Craft required by those of that System. This is not always the case, and some Systems do not produce any at all. There is always a producer somewhere in that Sector of Space. As we have noted, Masar or, Mars if you will, is this System's producer of Craft. There are various types of Craft designed to perform specific functions. These are basic types and are pretty much Universal. However, each producer will have their own unique interpretation of the basic model. In that sense they are not all alike at all. It is much like the automobile industry on Earth. Basically, all cars are the same; yet, each manufacturer has a little different concept of body design and engine design which makes the brand names distinguishable. Spacecraft are somewhat like that too.

Whatever the style, Fourth Density MAN produces his Craft all the same way — through manifestation. There are no factories, shops, nor great labor forces. Thought is the tool. The materials come from the Etheric. Physical ore is an illusion. The

NOTES:

true ore is Etheric. Finding the proper ore to form the base materials is difficult to do in the Etheric for physical Fourth Density MAN, just as it obviously is for Third Density. The ore can be physically found. Just above it,in the ethers lies the true ore being sought. The ore is located in the physical and then *mined* in the Etheric!

The Etheric ore is mined, smelted, and combined with other metals to make the appropriate alloys. This is all accomplished through thought. There are those who are highly skilled at producing ether alloys of many kinds. This is what they do. This may be accomplished while standing *on* a Planet of resource, or onboard a Spacecraft in orbit of that Planet.

A host of specialists now are brought forth, each one being an expert on a small portion of a given model of Craft. Using the appropriate alloys, yet Etheric, this one mentally creates a perfect thought form in minute detail of that specific portion of the new Craft. When the mental image is complete and all the proper alloys and metals are shaped exactly perfect then, the Green Ray of Manifestation (the Ray of Fourth Density) is brought into the Heart Chakra to the spinal cord, up the cord to the Indigo (Third Eye Chakra); and this perfect mental thought-form image is saturated with the Green Ray of Manifestation/Love. Instantly, the thought form materializes.

Others around are doing the same thing. Soon all the parts are perfectly made and floating in air or Space. Come now the coordinators. These ones take each of these sections and fit them together to form that large section of the Craft of which they have great knowledge and expertise. The sections are fitted together not with weld or bolts, but with Love! The atoms along the seam line of both pieces are asked to cooperate and join each other and they willingly do so, for it is their desire to be of service and . . . The Law is ONE. Soon the entire Craft is assembled.

Instruments, equipment, and special fixtures are manufactured in the same way as the interior is fitted out and the ship becomes fully joined. There is no scrap; there is no waste. The surplus alloys were never manufactured so they simply return to

NOTES:

their original form. The Etheric ore/alloys are instantly replenished. Their reflections on the physical Planet are never disturbed. This is the true meaning of *unlimited natural resources!* Abundance without any desecration or disturbance. Imagine!

How A Spacecraft Functions

As you may well know, a Spacecraft does not have propellers or a jet engine, nor is it a rocket ship in any way. It seemingly moves without any noticeable means of propulsion. It seems to be immune to the effects of momentum and inertia and seems to operate under different sets of laws altogether.

Spacecraft are patterned after the nomenclature of a Planet. A Planet is polarized — it has a North and a South Pole. This creates a magnificent field about the orb. Gravity is established. A Planet rotates on its axis. As it does so, it also orbits the Sun — traveling thousands of miles per day. The occupants of the Planet do not notice or suffer any ill effects as their Planet hurtles through Space. They are protected by the magnetic field that surrounds their vehicle. Actually, the Planet Earth is a Spacecraft! It is a Spacecraft with the controls set and locked.

As long as the controls are locked the magnetic force from our Star, our Sun, maintains a defined and predictable result as it offers its stable beingness to the magnetic force field around our Planet Earth. But supposing the Earth's magnetic North and South Poles could be manually shifted — a little or a lot, then the current stable condition provided by our Sun would be altered. The Sun would be unaffected. The Earth *would* respond. Opposites attract — likes repel is a law of magnetics. The Earth's polarity now having been altered would respond to one or the other of these actions; that is, the Earth's orbit would begin to move farther away from the Sun or it would move closer to the Sun. One way or the other movement *would* take place. If the people were not informed they would not know an event had taken place. Eventually, the climate would reveal the happening, due to warmer or colder seasons.

NOTES:

NOTE: It might be interesting for the reader to remember that the Mayan calender, which was originated some 52,000 years ago, made an abrupt change a few centuries ago and went from a 360-day year to the 365.24-day year that we currently embrace.

When a Planet or a Spacecraft has the ability to establish a magnetic force field about itself it is free of inertia as we understand it. Those residing *within* that force field are subject to internal movement, but are free of all external activity. The magnetic field is the shield and it is the agent of cause and effect.

For a Spacecraft to function, it is necessary that it be able to create an electromagnetic force field about itself at least nine meters in all directions about the Craft. This field must reach the intensity of five million gauss. The Atomic Polarity must be adjustable. When these conditions are met that Craft may attract itself or repel itself from any selected mass or terminal (vortex) of magnetic energy.

The speed would be controllable. The direction could be terminated and the course reset in an instant without those onboard being the least bit inconvenienced. The Craft is ridged; the force field is flexible. When an abrupt change in direction is called for, the spherical force field changes its shape to that of a football until the new course is set and the spherical field returns. The Craft and its occupants are not aware of any geometrical change in their force field or the stress it may be under. As long as the force field is employed the Craft inside of it experiences the effect of hanging in a vacuum.

The controlled change of the Atomic Polarity of the magnetic force field about the Craft as it is focused to a selected mass is the force that produces the external momentum. When the Craft is operating in close proximity to a mass, a Planet, the *timing* of this reversal of polarity is critical. This is handled by an onboard computer. The laws that power the Heavenly Bodies in the Universe are the very same laws that apply to the functioning of a Spacecraft.

NOTES:

It is well to remember that MAN'S mental/psychic ability to attune himself to his Craft, the components of the Craft, and all the instrumentation aboard permits the control of the Craft to be essentially under mental commands, though there are manual controls as well. There is a true Love affair between MAN and machine that is more like Humans and pets, than it is like Humans and cars.

When a native of a Planet such as Earth leaves the jurisdiction of that Planet and enters into what is commonly called outer Space then that person is now subject to the laws that govern Space. These laws are physical laws and are also the laws of conduct. Humans are the product of Third Density law, here on Earth. When this native leaves the confines of Earth he then becomes subject to the Fourth Density laws that govern MAN, even though no personal transition has been made.

The Power Source

The power plant of any Spacecraft is designed to create a controlled electromagnetic force field about the Craft. There are various methods of accomplishing this. Some have certain advantages over others, but basically they are all much the same.

A typical device which is often referred to as an Anti-Gravity Device utilizes from three to five rings. The dimensions of these rings, their diameters, were provided to us by the builders of the Great Pyramid at Giza (Ra's Pyramid). Using the (1) diagonals, (2) base line, (3) edge line, (4) apothem line, and (5) the height, as the ratio, the diameters of the rings can readily be determined. The agent of reduction is PHI — 1.618.

The diameter of the five rings having now been calculated, the size and nomenclature needs to be determined. The measurements of the Ark of the Covenant is used here. The height, width, length, and the thickness as measurements relating to the diameter of a given ring are scaled down using the same ratio, of course. Now, the thickness of the rings are known.

The rings, except for size, are all made the same. On this Planet, magnesium makes a good non-magnetic casing. The interior of the ring is lined with a product that is rare in the

Power Plant for Spacecraft

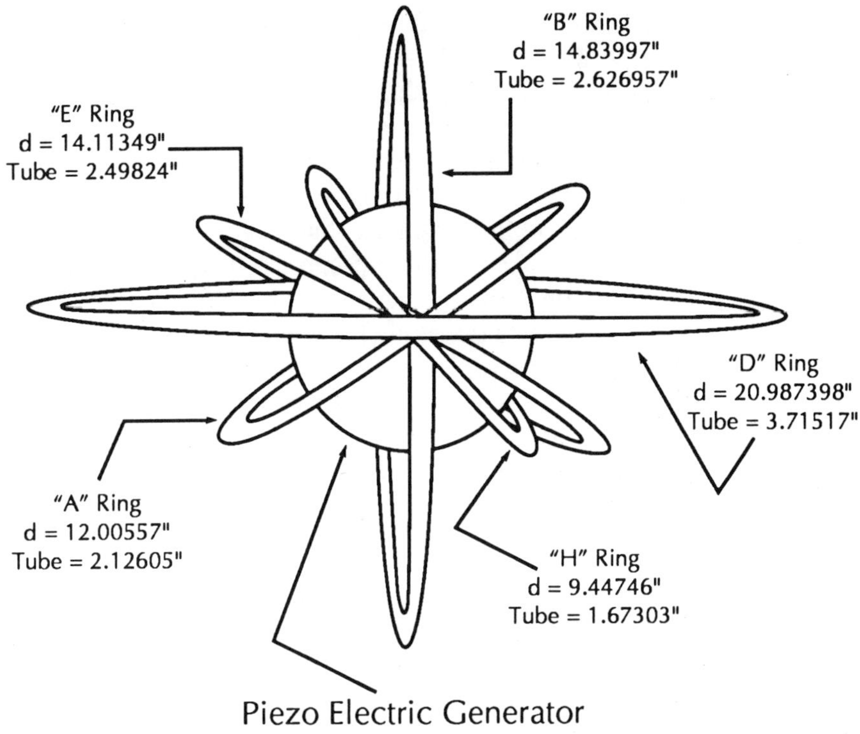

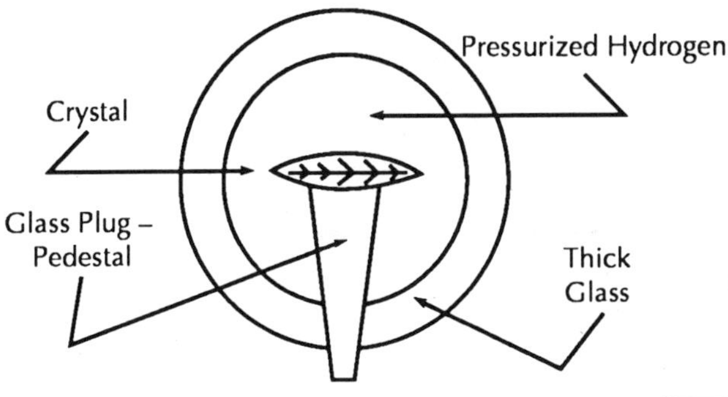

Piezo Electrtic
Generator

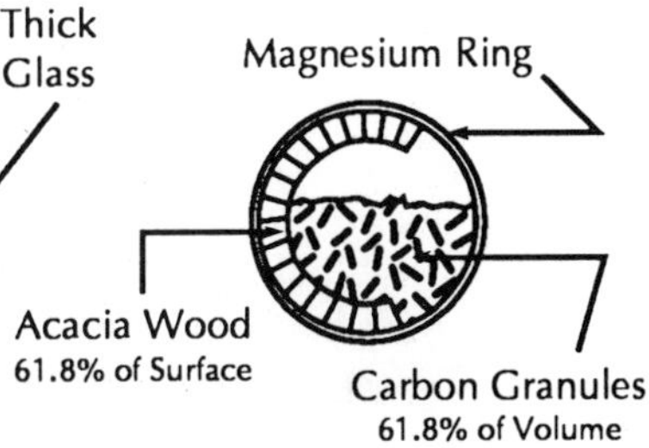

Typical Ring

NOTES:

Galaxy but plentiful on Earth — wood. The product of trees, especially the Acacia Tree is often the chosen candidate. The thickness of this wood is equal to the ratio of the thickness of the Ark of the Covenant. The ring is sectioned off at intervals again, relating to the length of the Ark of the Covenant. The hollow interior is filled to the level of the sacred cut, PHI — 1.618 or roughly 62%. With granulated charcoal derived from the shell of the coconut, again the tree product is being employed. Other materials could be used, but these are the handiest. The ring could be constructed in a tubular or boxed shape.

Since all five rings are of a different diameter they will all fit inside each other. Sometimes the clearance is minute. Often the rings are suspended from an axle or shaft in such a way they can be raised and lowered or otherwise manipulated.The five rings are free to rotate; some designs cause them to rotate at very high speeds, while other designs call for them to be moved only slightly, to alter the atomic structure of the magnetic field they create.

No other designs will call for the ring to be a part of a sphere of exactly the same dimension. There would then be five spheres, one inside the other, the equator of each sphere being the ring. This then, is the spherical device that generates the Vortex Ring Electromagnetic force field. When complete it would easily fit into a two foot square box.

The Piezo Electric Power Plant

Now, on to the power plant that powers this simple device. Piezo electricity is the physical energy. This current Arian Root Race is unfamiliar with this type of electrical energy, but it is not unheard of on this Planet. This is the source of power used by the Atlantean peoples, during all of the latter third of their Great Cycle.

A hollow sphere which can vary from the size of a marble to the size of a basketball, is required. A baseball size would do nicely. This hollow sphere may be made of clear quartz crystal or of heavy glass. If glass is used then a small quartz crystal must be suspended or affixed at the center. The

NOTES:

hollow area is filled with Hydrogen under extreme pressure. The service hole is plugged and hermetically sealed. The ball is then baked at high temperatures to expand and activate the catalyst Hydrogen as it interacts with the ordinary quartz crystal. An illuminated glow is produced. This Light is the power.

The quartz sphere is placed in the center of the rings. The glowing energy radiates outwards in all directions, saturating the rings and their contents. This then produces the special type of magnetism that creates the force field. As the rings or spheres are manipulated, the force field's Atomic Polarity responds accordingly. If the rings/spheres are made of crystal or glass, then the entire device will glow handsomely. The change of brilliance and shade of hue can tell the observer of the physical action taking place outside the Craft. Once charged, the life span between chargings is approximately 50,000 Earth years.

This type of power would cause the Captains of Industry to tremble, for it would put an end to commerce as we know it today.

The Vortex Ring Gravitational Energy Device is always centrally located in the Craft. By adjusting the rings the Craft can be attuned to any magnetic vortex on the Planet to attract itself to, or repel itself from as the polarity of the force field is altered. If all five rings comprise the Power Plant, then the Craft may be used for Interstellar flight as well.

As the five rings are finely adjusted, the speed of the Craft increases. This speed may attain the velocity of C-9; that is, the Speed of Light squared — nine times! To illustrate: Light can travel from our Earth to the Sun and back (round trip) in approximately sixteen and one half minutes. At the speed of Light squared, C-1, it would take less than half a second. At C-9 Light would make the round trip over 55 times in one second! Think on it! Intergalactic travel is not as far-fetched as it seems!

The reason that the Speed of Light can be squared is because of the way in which the Universe was created. We shall address this in the next chapter.

NOTES:

-Summary-

Some Spacecraft are unmanifested thought forms and have no physical reality as we would normally think of it. The force field which encapsulates all Craft can be tuned to render the Craft invisible to the physical eyes. This action does not render them any less real. Your ability to see, to think you see, a Spacecraft, is actually quite good. We heartily encourage you to become a sky watcher, particularly at night. Look closely in the clouds, especially if the cloud shape seems to be "unreal."

You may call for the Craft to materialize for your benefit — and there is a good chance of success. The best results are obtained when you are alone. You are less apt to broadcast the news if you are shy of witnesses. You will probably pass it off as an optical illusion. This phenomenon could be startling, but would not likely produce trauma. MAN is considerate of your delicate nervous system.

It is wise to become mentally comfortable with the existence of Spacecraft, for they definitely will be a vital part of your future. Trust your intuition, which is your Higher Self advising as how to respond to any invitation. Do not attempt to fool yourself or try to scare yourself. Be calm and honest with your inspired feelings. Do you feel warm, good, and loving with the vehicle or do you feel cold, afraid, and apprehensive? Visualize the Craft being enveloped in a high bubble of Emerald Green Love/Light. This will produce some kind of response from the Craft — we assure you!

Permit your conscious mentality to expand. Think of crossing our Galaxy with the same thoughts that put an end to confinement and restriction. Be inquisitive, be adventuresome, develop an enthrallment with discovery as you seek out the unknown. Remember: You cannot go any place in Creation where there is not an abundance of Love!

Chapter 16

The Fabric Of Space

Space is that substance that harmoniously and lovingly connects all aspects of the physical and non-physical Universe. This essence is carefully woven into a living Fabric that contains the life essence of the Creator. Space *is* the One Infinite Creator! All is ONE. Space unites all into ONE. Space is an entity, living, pulsating, throbbing with life, life never ending. To attune oneself with Space is not tapping onto a vacuum, a nothingness, but quite the opposite; it is a tap into the living rhythm of the consciousness that made us all. Just as the fish is at home in the sea, MAN is at home in Space. One does not fear one's true home.

Space is an entity. The entity is energy. Energy is intelligent. Intelligent Energy is Love! Space is Love! Beginning with Atoms attracted to each other, Space is a store house of resource, the likes of which would stagger the imagination. There is no "want" in Space. All of the building blocks that are necessary to create matter and then produce "life" thereafter are all contained in the Fabric of Space. Atoms combine to form the molecules that produce the variety of matter that we are aware of. Certain portions of Space entertain a specific vibration that tends to attract the appropriate Atoms that will then manifest identifiable matter; and a family of matter that is indigenous to that Section of Space is then established. Atoms combining and re-combining, inspired by the catalyst of variation, produce variety beyond belief. Of course, we must be a Galactic traveler or Universal traveler in order to fully appreciate this gigantic variety.

Layers Of Fabric

Space is likened unto a woven Fabric, and rightly so. Fabric and yard goods, such as the sheets on your bed are usually thought of as being two dimensional — length and width. It lays flat and there is a top and a bottom to it. Now Space, the Universe, does not have a top or a bottom because it is spherical. If you were to think of the Fabric of Space as being in

NOTES:

layers — like the skin of an onion, then you could visualize how all of these "bed sheets" of Fabric apply.

If you see/envision Earth as having many of these sheets of Fabric wrapped around itself, forming a large "onion;" then, you can envision each Planet in this System doing the same . . . and then envision the Solar System forming its own elliptical "onion" of Space Fabric . . . and then envision each Star System doing the same . . . and then the Galactic Logos uniting all of these trillions of Star System "onions" into the whole that we call the Milky Way Galaxy. Then, if you will, see the trillions of Galaxies united with the innumerable sheets of Fabric provided by the Creator of the Universe — Our One Infinite Creator!

Everything is a microcosm of the Macrocosm, The same law applies everywhere to everything. The only thing that is different is the size. Understand the atoms and you understand the Universe. Understand the Universe and you understand the atom. Both are identical — the Law is ONE. We are not attempting to oversimplify; it was quite simple long before we arrived.

Threads

Fabric begins with thread that is spun into strands. Let us deal with that for the moment. You may envision the thread as being round, or flat, like tape. This thread is coiled around an invisible core. This core is a ring. It circles a Planet, a Solar System, a Galaxy, a Universe. This strand, made of spiralling thread, is hollow. It has an inside and an outside. The spiralling coil of thread gives direction. If you were on the *inside* of the invisible strand that comprises the Fabric of Space, then the spiral would be clockwise and would take you "away". Now, if you were on the *outside* of that strand, the spiral would be counterclockwise, and that direction would fetch you "back." This spiralling of the thread that makes the hollow strand has Magnetic Energy flowing in one direction on the inside and equal energy flowing in the opposite direction on the outside. Think on this.

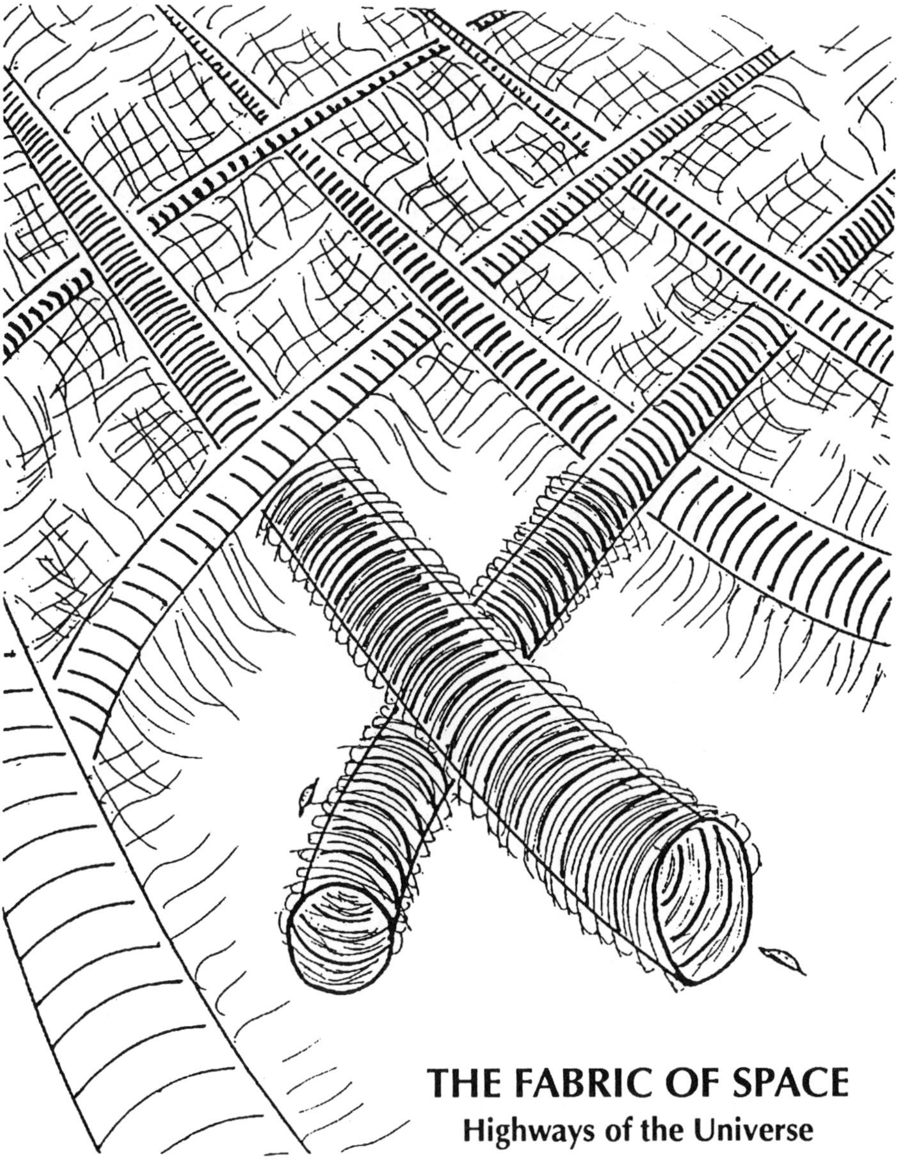

THE FABRIC OF SPACE

Highways of the Universe

NOTES:

Since we are talking about Space and since Space is so big, let us continue to think big. An enormous Spacecraft can spiral around on the inside of a single strand of that sheet of Fabric. The Fabric of Space is loosely woven. The strands or tunnels that run at right angles to form the Fabric do not touch at the intersections. Therefore, any Craft trafficking on the outside of the tunnel/strand would not be subject to a disastrous meeting at the crossroads with a fellow Space traveler! There is ample room for all.

Remember, we are dealing with a single sheet of Fabric that comprises only one single layer of our "onion." Now, each layer of Fabric of loosely woven strands above and below our layer is laid down slightly out of synchronization so that no two sheets of Fabric coincide or are parallel with each other. Each sheet is unique in it's position.

Tacking Through Space

Since the layers of Fabric are loosely woven, what does one do if one gets caught in the doldrums? The same thing a sailor does to find wind for his sails — he searches for it. When a Craft leaves the influence of a strand to change course the momentum will easily carry the Craft to the next chosen strand. Navigating through Space is very similar to "tacking" with a sailboat. If you are comfortable with a sailboat, you would be equally comfortable maneuvering a Spacecraft — especially if you are a "Blue Water Sailor!"

Fuel For The Tunnels

What is this area *between* the loose woven strands? This is the storehouse of atoms; and pristine are these ones, for they are the product of the back side of a Black Hole from a parallel Galaxy or Universe. The spiralling energy from the threads of the strands pull in or suck up some of these atoms to fuel their unceasing efforts to satisfy the Law of Motion. These spaces are full and are eternally being replenished.

Some of these tunnels lead to Black Holes in this Galaxy in this reality. Contaminated debris is channeled into the appropriate tubes that lead to the cleansing chambers of the

NOTES:

Black Hole. The matter is purified, changed and then dispersed into another Universe, perhaps forming a new Universe, perhaps replenishing an old established one. Creation is continuous.

The tubes/strands are invisible energy fields. The "special type" of Piezo Electromagnetic force field that is created about a Spacecraft has the utmost affinity to harmoniously deal with these tubal energy fields. The Spacecraft of Humans would be immune and indifferent to this subtle energy, just as a steam-powered vessel would ignore the trade winds. Remaining shielded and immune, and being perhaps indifferent to the rhythm of a Planet or the rhythm of the Universe is never appropriate. It promotes a strength derived through stubbornness; and the law of diminishing returns soon set in. Learn to flow, to be a part of — that which is natural — nature, Our Creator.

Atom Energy

The tubes are surrounded by atoms. These atoms are constantly being sucked into and around the tube. As a force field with a Craft inside it moves along the natural energy flow of the tube, the force field "scoops up" many of these Atoms. They move along the length of the spherical field, and then by the time they have reached the Equator of the Craft's force field they have heated up. Space is normally cold, and likewise, so are the atoms. Now they have become heated, active, and have expanded due to the subtle friction as the force field accelerates. As the atoms are discharged, aft of the Equator of the force field, they are much larger and more active than they were when they were encountered. This action produces more "thrust" to the force field and the speed is increased. The acceleration process is continual.

The tubes or strands that make up the arteries of the Fabric of Space form a circle. They are endless. The size of this hoop can be appreciated if it passes around a Planet or around a Solar System; but, seeing it around a Galaxy is much more difficult and a loop around the Universe is beyond anybody's perception — it simply must be accepted that it is so. The point:

NOTES:

no Craft could ever run out of the end of a tube into some form of oblivion.

The "Fuzz"

There is a "fuzz" on the Fabric of Space. This "fuzz" amounts to innumerable small threads that meander endlessly, usually at right angles to the strands/tubes. These little threads form continuously changing patterns of magnetic energy. These meandering patterns make up the bulk of Space. They are in conflict with a physical vehicle's travel through the spider web soup of Space. Like a net, they prohibit meaningful travel.

Come now the force field. Because the Spacecraft's force field has been created by Piezo Electricity and because this form of energy activates specially made, movable rings, this maze of magnetic webbing is now brought under control. By tuning the rings on the ship's "engine" these lesser threads can be made to run parallel to the main artery thread that comprises the tube/strand. Now, many lines of energy are all running in the same spiralling direction — inside or outside the tube. Each time a speed station — a squaring of the previous station — is attained, the rings may be moved again and *that* speed is now being squared. For Inte-Galactic Flight, this may be accomplished up to nine times. As the rings are changed more and more lines are being brought into play. The more lines employed, the faster the Spacecraft goes.

This is how a Spacecraft can travel for many Light Years in only a few moments. This could not work if the Universe were not spherical. If time was actually linear, like we think it is, this theory/practice would be only the product of a rich imagination. However, imagination *is* thought and thought has form. Therefore, anything that can be thought of by MAN or men can actually take on physical form. That what you think of — call it imagination or whatever — is *not* an original thought! It is recall! Everything that you think of is recall. There is nothing new under the Sun! Original thinkers know this, but are less likely to admit it.

The force field is an entity, an entity of Love, for it is indeed intelligent. Its intelligence permits it to influence the magnetic Rays of the Universe, which are also energy — which is Love. Love attracts Love, the Third Creative Force — an entity within an entity, moving through a vortex to facilitate the works of MAN. This is how the Creator envisioned it — this is how it is.

Intraplanetary Travel

Time is constructed like an onion, but it looks like a Planet — it has bumps on it. These bumps represent the more significant events in what we think of as history. When time is decreed to be Linear, and the Mass Consciousness agrees, problems in understanding prevail. Linear time causes "distance" to be defined improperly. *Rate times time equals distance.* Also, *The shortest distance between two points is a straight line.* Both are undisputed mathematical axiom — both are incorrect.

A new mental concept of "distance" must be injected into the mass thinking before any real progress can be made. In spherical time there is no beginning and there is no end. It is a ring. The ring is the eternal "Now," the present. Suppose you were at the North Pole in the summertime and you had neither clock nor calender. You are at the summit of a mountain. You see a mountain peak next to you. You climb down from your peak, cross the valley, and climb the adjacent peak. You have traversed from point "A" to point "B." How long did it take? A day? Two days? How do you know?

Suppose the same event was repeated near the Equator where the days and nights are relatively equal the year around. You could readily tell if the trip took you one day or two days or parts thereof . . . and you would be quick to say, for your concept of time would indicate your efficiency in negotiating the journey.

But what of your similar trip to the North Pole? Did you do as well there? How will you tell *that* story? The concept of Linear time has been denied you; you think differently when your day is six months long. It is good to open your mind to

NOTES:

different thought processes. Perhaps this little analogy has helped.

Now, if time is spherical and the Planet is spherical, as is the Solar System, the Galaxy, and the Universe . . . then distance must also be spherical! If you are measuring the distance between points on the globe a straight line is not necessarily the shortest route. For example, consider the distance from San Francisco to Japan. Both are approximately the same latitude. With a string, measure the distance between the two points by way of the Aleutian Islands. Your string shortens on the curve. Navigators know this but most others do not.

Warping Time

Since time is layered spherically and distance is also spherical and is physical; therefore, time can be warped. How do you warp time? By bending the Fabric of Space. The Fabric is like a great fish net, highly substantial, but highly malleable. You can take a stretched out fishnet, grab a handful of net in each of your outstretched hands, and pull your hands together. The Fabric of Space can be treated the same. Instead of using your hands you use your mind.

Mentally grab the Fabric around Tokyo, as you mentally grab the Fabric around San Francisco; pull them together, step across, and release your mental hold on both sections of the net. The Fabric of Space, having memory, springs back to its original shape and you have transcended from one place to the other, distance never being an issue. This is the mechanics of teleportation which we shall discuss further in the following Section.

Warping time, Warping Space — the Fabric of Space, can be done with or without a Spacecraft. When a Craft is not used warping time/space is called *teleportation.* The created force field about the Craft has this ability to warp Space by manipulating the Fabric. This is accomplished by focusing upon sources of magnetic output. The Planet Earth has various vortices that personify this anomaly.

Those operating the Craft have the ability to alter the Atomic Polarity of their force field at will. Thus, they are able

NOTES:

to attract themselves to or repel themselves from any given source of magnetic energy. This causes the Craft to move in what appears to be very straight lines and sharp angular changes in direction which are their trademarks.

The bumps on the sphere (the Vortices), like the bumps on the sphere of time, can be coordinated. Computers on the Craft can readily calculate this. When this is programmed the commander of the Craft simply *thinks* of the course he/she desires and the computer, sensitive to the Love/Harmony energy exchange, picks up on the mental thoughts and promptly executes the plan. Rarely does anyone ever sit at the controls, though the controls do exist.

The force field becomes heavy in harmless radiation and often can be seen to glow in the night sky. It can emit any color. Blue, Green, and White are the more common sights. The force field can also be adjusted to render the Craft invisible to the Human Eye.

Industrial Greed Hampers Evolution

The Piezo-electric Crystal Ball would be easy to make. Today's technology could easily produce the exquisite rings. All would be incredibly inexpensive. Their use would revolutionize commerce. Industry would not be pleased with these changes.

In the 1940's we were taught in school that this type of transportation would be the wave of the future. It was exciting. The target date was 1955! What happened? Why are we still using the wheel? Airplanes? Cargo ships? The Internal Combustion Engine? Fossil Fuels? And all the constructed and manufactured paraphernalia that goes with them?

Could it be that we are too greedy? Too lazy? Too dumb? Too what? Perhaps we are too Negative. Perhaps we really enjoy destroying First Density and rendering Second Density extinct. Perhaps this is the real goal of commerce and government . . . What do you think?

When the mentality of Humans arrives at the point that logic and reason cease to be of paramount importance and the metaphysician is an accepted member of society, particularly in

NOTES:

the fields of the sciences, and when commerce ceases to dictate what is appropriate and what is not, and when religions cease to dominate the minds of men with their enslaving and stagnant ways, and when governments cease to exist then, and perhaps only then, will Third Density Humans be permitted to abandon the wheel and all of the foolish ramifications that accompany it, and to get on with their evolution as was intended.

Summary

The invisible layers of the Fabric of Space cannot be discerned with the physical eye. Once free of the Planet's electromagnetic vibration, the Third Eye can readily be attuned to the array of curved lines. Crystal instruments can do the same. From a high altitude the Planet's energy vortexes may also be spotted. Navigation is not accomplished blindly.

Space is energy. It is psychokinetic energy. Devices that can operate on this type of energy must be employed. This type of equipment cooperates with the nature of Creation. Earth machinery defies the natural order of things and is therefore obliged to overpower Nature in order to accomplish work. This is barbaric! Technology pursues this end relentlessly. A greater understanding of Love could be the impetus that would bring about a true "Industrial Revolution."

We trust this look into the Fabric of Space has caused you to reconsider some of your previous misconceptions. Once the thoughts are trained in the appropriate direction all the mystifying details begin to fall in place. We encourage you to use your Kundalini Meditation Technique to examine the material presented in this Section. The answers you seek can be found in your conscious contact with your Higher Self.

Conclusions

Now let us prepare to lower the Kundalini. Bring the White Light of the Kundalini up around you and gather it in an object over top of your head. As you do so, bring the Violet Dome next to your physical body. Bring the Kundalini into the crown of your head, as you detach your consciousness. Now, begin the descent, deactivating each chakra, as we give the color

NOTES:

countdown: Violet . . Indigo . . Blue . . Green . . Yellow . . Orange . . Red . . Put the Kundalini to rest, and shut the door, take a deep breath, another and perhaps one more.

Our Prayer Of Protection

"In the name of the Presence and the Power Universal, protect us from harm and all Unenlightened Spirits, and may the Light of our Spirit Guides and the Light of our Higher Selves illuminate our thoughts that we might reflect the Radiant Glory of ALL THAT IS."

We leave you in the Light and Love of our One Infinite Creator. Go forth in the joy of life and in service to others.

Adonai. Adonai, Vasu Barragus, Adonai.

We Thank You!

Section V

The Tensor Concepts

This Section deals with the opening of that vast unknown portions of the brain, as Extra Sensory Perception and Psychokenisis are explored.

Chapter 20 (cont'd)

Chapter 17

The Tensor Concepts

We greet you in the Light and Love of our One Infinite Creator. We are Chief Little Summer and Warm Night Rain.

Let us begin this section with the chant:

"I am that I am, A-Yeh,
I am that I am, A-Yeh,
I am that I am, A-Yeh,
I am that I am, A-Yeh,
I am that I am, A-Yeh,
I am that I am, A-Yeh,
I am that I am, A-Yeh,
A-Yeh,
A-Yeh,
A-yeh,
A-Yeh,
A-Yeh."

Our Prayer of Protection: "In the name of the Presence and the Power Universal, protect us from harm and all Unenlightened Spirits, and may the Light of our Spirit Guides and the Light of our Higher Selves illuminate our thoughts that we might reflect the Radiant Glory of ALL THAT IS."

* * *

Now, for those of you whose schedules permit, let us prepare to raise the Kundalini at this time. You should be thoroughly familiar with the procedure at this point. We shall assist you in raising by the use of the color countdown. Every function of a given chakra color is known to you at the sequence which it is given. Let us begin. Make yourself comfortable, back straight. Align and balance the chakras . . . awaken the Kundalini . . . activate the Red . . . Orange . . . Yellow . . . Green . . . Blue . . . Indigo . . . Violet . . . With your consciousness attached, visualize the Kundalini bathing the lower half of the Golden Sphere, which is your Higher Self. The flowing Kundalini falls down all around your body, which is protected by the

NOTES:

aura of seven domes. Firmly establish the contact with your Higher Self and when you are ready, begin to read.

* * *

In this section we shall attempt to teach the Tensor Concepts. This is a different subject. We cannot teach you how to think — everyone must do that for themselves. Perhaps we shall be able to inspire you to want to think, to ponder thoughts in depths greater than you dared to imagine. Thinking is the mark of the individual. It separates you from the Second Density Group Soul. The awareness of self is the result and this is the purpose of Third Density.

Study the six Tensor Concepts with your Kundalini raised. Do this on several consecutive occasions. Your acceptance and understanding may very well depend upon your conscious contact with your Higher Self. Absorb the following information and use it freely and wisely.

* * *

To Think Or Not To Think

The dominate Nations of the world are not peopled by thinkers. These citizens pride themselves as being members of a society who excel in technology and materialism and as builders of great edifices, military might, and financial superiority. Being a part of this activity causes one to feel "civilized." Actually, the opposite is true. We live in a world of barbarians — barbarians who drive nice cars, wear fine clothes, live in elegant houses, dine on the finest foods, and have great jobs. These sophisticated peoples who are wallowing in the lap of luxury are barbarians. Why? Because they don't think!

The people of the World are led by the nose to drink at the trough of commerce, bow down to false religious tenets, and dutifully forfeit Free Will to powerful governments for sanctuary and security from imagined evils and foes. The people do not *think.* Commerce, Religion, and Governments encourage them not to think. Thinkers cannot be organized and controlled.

Religions teach that mental activity is evil — for it challenges God. These same Religions teach the covering of

NOTES:

one's sexual organs is mandatory, for the sight of such is an affront and a challenge to God the Creator. Ignorance is bliss — what you don't know won't hurt you. Ignorance excuses sin, while knowledge makes you liable. Do not think on things other than those obscure tenets that the Hierarchy has provided.

Governments and their laws and the enforcement of those laws make it difficult and even impossible for the free thinker to open up his mind, discover, and set into practice that which his thoughts dictates. Some law, in that huge arsenal would be offended and the thinker would be "out of line." Non-conformity is persecuted by political leaders.

Commerce makes slaves of us all. It carefully allows for ample time to earn money and then to spend some. Free time to quietly think is systematically destroyed by television, sales, and the unceasing din of progress. Thinkers of new commercial products are welcome. Thinkers of Philosophy who might alter the system and render havoc with the empire are to be committed to sanitariums with the rest of their kind.

No, it is not easy to be a thinker on Planet Earth. The odds are definitely stacked against you. It takes quiet, determined courage to sit down, raise your Kundalini, and meditate on the Tensor Concepts. In so doing you enhance evolution, you grow, and you graduate out of here. The grandeur of the unknown beckons to you. It beckons to all. Only a few are willing to hear. You may consider yourself among those who are freely willing to answer the calling, else you never would have read this far in our books of *The Teachings*.

You are not starting a "movement," nor are you joining one. You teach by example. You are not a missionary. You are the teacher. The student seeks out the teacher — not the other way around. Your Love for the purity of Truth is the inspiring Light that is a warm and welcome beacon to the more timid ones.

NOTES:

The Original Humans

The Tensor Concepts are not new to Planet Earth. The Original Root Race, the Adamic, were endowed with these teachings. The Atlanteans capitalized on them and developed cultural and scientific results that would stagger the minds of men today. These ones had grasped the handle of civilization and they were diligently working on it. Today, Commerce, Religions, and Governments grease the handles and it slips away from all. The word is simply redefined and progress as usual carries us blindly onward into oblivion.

The Mind, the Body, and the Spirit are separate, or so it might seem. With the desire to exercise the Will, all three aspects of the total self can readily be integrated harmoniously into the *complex* that they always were. This knowledge is innately present and hidden in the recesses of your mind. This is instinct! You are the only one around that has it; all others of Second Density, are born with a memory.

Mental/Spiritual awareness of yourself and of your true heritage, is your destiny. This "in-depth" awareness is not possible without a basic working knowledge of the Tensor Concepts. The multiplicity of doors that bridge the Cortical Portion of your brain to the Tensor Centers must be cracked. This is not a dream. Your conscious awareness can be expanded in directions beyond your wildest dreams. Awareness permits communication with the Planet, with those of the plant and animal kingdoms, and perhaps best of all, allows the solid contact with those of Fourth Density MAN — which you were or are soon to be. To be reunited with MAN is a longing that throbs deep in the breasts of us all. As the Tensor Concepts unfold to your comprehension, *LIFE* in the true reality, beyond this Third Density illusion is your reward. At long last, you're going home!

Logic And Reason

Your ability to use logic and reason was a "gift" from MAN at the onset of the Adamic Root Race. It was presented to compensate for the loss of memory, since all Third Density is

NOTES:

born without a memory. Logic and reason is *not* to be abandoned. In teaching the Tensor Concepts we encourage you to supplement this gift with your innate ability to embrace Abstract or Total Thought so that the dignity of the mind might be preserved. In so doing you shall step out of your comatose state into the state of being *alive!* Using the faculties of your mind gives you *purpose* and bestows *life* to your beingness. Your typical state of "living death" is permanently discarded.

The mind is a garden of thought. It encompasses Infinity. It is Divine. It is your mental/spiritual link to our One Infinite Creator. Your Kundalini is your physical link. The Body, the Mind, and the Spirit all become aspects of the same. The Law is One. No longer will piles of concrete and steel, sophisticated equipment, or financial sheets be able to compare. The noble concept of Truth will never again be distorted into superstition and imagination. The worship of intellect has become the epitome of mentality — this farce shall fade into oblivion.

The veil that we were all born with has become heavier and more opaque, not lighter and transparent as the acquisition of knowledge, wisdom, and understanding would dictate. The mindless, so called civilization dominates the world scene. You do have to deal with it, but you do not have to join it. Peace, understanding, and happiness comes through mental awareness not through imposed ignorance. Rend the veil from the world of men, and accept the hearty welcome into the Universe of MAN.

As an incarnated entity you must *know,* you must *be,* and you must *do.* None are complete within themselves. You must experience all three to be whole. They are equal in importance within any given experience. Incorporating all three eliminates mystery and opens the doors to grasping Universal Law. These are the Divine Laws that we all live by, not the puny little laws set down by imbecilic Politicians in their desperate attempt to seek fame and fortune for themselves through the elimination of your Free Will.

The Human situation saddens when you realize that so very many who are participating in the Third Density Experience are not aware that they are dumb! Their ignorance is truly bliss

NOTES:

— to them, but their Soul is having fits! They have become ingrained and locked into the pursuance of being true to false standards, so that they are closed to suggestion. These ones can only be taught by being exposed to your example. Words shall not phase them. They perceive no errors in their mode of beingness. The mind is the tool of the Devil. Their Religions have taught them this and the Governments do nothing to discourage the thought.

Ignorance begets sorrow and despair. To deliberately stand in the darkness of unawareness and avoid the Light of knowledge/understanding is to render the incarnation fraudulent. Great Beings have come forth, and MAN is always present to offer Light and Love, taught in a way for all to grasp. But if you freely choose even through ignorance not to accept, then all of the teachers are helpless.

Your mind links the body to the Soul/Spirit. It is precious. Thinking on all levels, and still seeking even higher levels, is the ticket that spurs the evolutionary process. This is the quantum leap that allows you to leave this Third Density Vibration of evolution, and at long last — go home — to the Fourth Density Vibration of Love, the abode of MAN.

Our New Age is dawning, the timetable has been speeded up, you yet have time but you do not have a single moment to waste. Get your priorities in order, muster the necessary self-discipline, use your Kundalini, and learn to think through the aid of the Tensor Concepts. Open up and use the Tensor Centers in your brain. Become the Tensor-Oriented person.

The Definition

The Tensor Equations invoke a new and different method of using the mind, the brain, and the Human nervous system. For Third Density Earthlings, the term *Tensor* means the thought potential of that unused 80% of the physical organ brain. The Synoptical nerve endings, yet unconnected, lying in potentiality are awaiting the thought stimuli to activate. The term *Equation* meaning: the method to facilitate the connection of the Synoptical

NOTES:

nerve endings to create the bridging circuitry to the Cortical Portion of the brain.

The purpose is to inspire Third Density *to think!* There have been great thinkers of long ago, but they have since passed from the scene. They left their mark, which was promptly distorted down to the ranks of the Baby Souls so that all could be content, unchallenged, and not threatened by knowledges of the Universe, most especially the awareness of self. The least qualified amongst us are elevated to the ranks of leadership and with stupidity and blindness, we follow. The alternative is: *To Think!* The great thinkers have come and gone. They are not being replaced. You, we, have a destiny to fulfill, a Creator to know, and a Fourth Density, Green Ray Love Vibration/-philosophy to grasp.

The Light Of The Kundalini

The Light within you is your Source. Use your Kundalini. With Love, integrate your consciousness with the Light of your Higher Self. This permits your mind to activate the Tensor Centers in your physical brain, and you then can *Think* on levels of consciousness higher and quicker than you ever dared to imagine. Darkness gives way to grayness, as even that dissipates in the Light of Knowledge, Understanding, and Love.

Once you permanently make the effort to think, those of MAN and certain Great Beings as well are standing by patiently awaiting you to awaken/look within, know yourself, accept yourself, and forgive yourself. Your power lies within the collective Mind/Body/Spirit Complexes which we all are. Practicing the Tensor Equations permits a grander, in-depth understanding of self and your rightful place in the Universe. This will never be gifted unto you — you must earn it! The *only* way that you can earn it is: *to Think!* You must attempt to apply the *total thought* to every incident in life, be it major or minor.

The Tensor Oriented Person

The Tensor-Oriented person can alter their life and mold it into an image of their own making. You are responsible for

NOTES:

you. The Tensor-Oriented person can alter his environment and convert it into a sea of Harmony and Love. You are the custodian of First and Second Density. The results of this responsibility could be accomplished in a few moments — when enough of you pool your thoughts towards a common goal. To be successful all egos must be relegated to their proper stations. This is not natural for the average Human Being. You will have to *think* about it. For the individual that does not grasp the meaning of these Concepts no ill effects of any kind will be entertained. These ones are usually Baby and low Young Soul in their spiritual evolution, and it is not expected they should consciously understand. However, their subconscious, being duly exposed will never forget. This hidden memory shall inspire future growth at some later time, perhaps in a distant incarnation.

If the student/reader is capable of grasping even the basic thought of these Concepts, then that person's life is changed forever! The life will take on a new meaning as the scope is broadened and the depth of perception and understanding is invoked beyond the wildest dream. The Dignity, Integrity, and Compassion that are the trademarks of Fourth Density MAN will take root and blossom for all to see. The Tensor-Oriented person stands apart from the lesser developed of the Human Species. The Tensor Concepts, used with the Kundalini power allow the personality to rejoin his Source — the Universal MAN, or permits the newly initiated to glimpse the grandeur of his new home in the Love Vibration.

Mind Vs Brain

Your new-found awareness will give you a new sense of freedom as you steadily evolve into the Vibration of Fourth Density Love and fulfill your immediate destiny. The Tensor Portion of your brain is there for your use. You must reach out to it; it will not open itself to you. There are veils that must be lifted. The veils are learned emotions. Mentally, they can be overcome. Knowledge is information that must be correlated and applied to be of any value. Your mind has an unlimited potential. The mind works through the brain. The brain must be

NOTES:

stimulated. Stimulation is achieved via *Thinking!* This process opens the doors to creativity and the expression of it. Physical matter, through the Tensor understanding of the Third Creative Force — Love, allows you to control your environment and the forces that influence your beingness. Remember: it is always the thought that counts . . . and the more prolific and profound the thoughts — the more they count.

As the Tensor Centers become activated and aligned in order to budge the Cortical Centers, the Multidimensional Self integrates its input upon the personality. This broadens the scope of awareness that in turn produces a more balanced person. The emotional/physical lower body now combines with the mental/spiritual upper body, and the Mind/Body/Spirit Complex begins to function as was intended. This is the goal of Third Density Entities who are reaching for Fourth.

The Cortex

The Cortex, the 20% of the brain that is the thinking portion is often divided into three categories: The conscious; the subconscious; and the unconscious. The Tensor Portion which constitutes the remaining 80% of the brain when activated, establishes a working harmony between the conscious and the subconscious, and between the conscious and the unconscious. This working harmony functions under the auspices of the Green Ray of Love.

The Thalamus

The brain is identified by several parts. In our studies, another portion of that organ that will receive considerable attention is the Thalamus, the inner brain. The Thalamus is that reptilian or ancient/original part of the brain that controls the automatic nervous system. This portion of the brain is linked directly to the Yellow Ray Solar Plexis Chakra — the seat of emotions. Thus, the emotions are able to "charge" the nervous system. This is characteristic of Third Density, as the personality perceives his environment via the physical nervous system; whereas the Tensor-Oriented Entity functions with a conscious

NOTES:

integration between thought and the experience, the emotional distortion being minimized.

The Nervous Impact

The Tensor Concepts must need be learned and practiced to the point where they become automatic. They must be used to be appreciated. In so doing, the sense of direction of life's path is dramatically enhanced. The rewards are rich. Harmony with Creation, derived from harmony with integrated self is the result.

Any event, physical or verbal causes the Mind/Body/Spirit Complex to react as a whole. The Mind and Body are loosely integrated in the Third Density Entity. Spirit is often disregarded by the consciousness. The nervous system via the senses becomes the sensors of the event. This typical procedure is overcome by the activity of the Tensor Centers. Thought becomes a vital and welcome part of the experience.

Safeguards

These teachings are not to be feared or looked upon with apprehension. Your Higher Self, your link to your Soul/Spirit, will temper your understanding to a level that is "just right" for your current evolutionary status. As you mature, your understanding increases. The same concepts will take on new and expanded meanings as time goes by. No one will be able to use this knowledge/information in a way that would be harmful or detrimental to another. The pursuance of knowledge is always a worthwhile project.

Ancient Practitioners

The Tensor Concepts have been introduced to Third Density Earthlings under a variety of names. Other than Tensor Concepts, they are often referred to as E.S.P. (Extrasensory Perception.) Prior to this they were referred to as Psionics, and prior to that the word magic was used. Certain disciplines still use this term emphatically.

The Witch Doctor of Africa, the early Priests of Egypt, the Lama of Tibet, as well as the Medicine Man of the Red Nations of the Western Hemisphere all were aware of knowledge

NOTES:

above and beyond the normal senses. Through impressed thoughts, many were exposed to these truths. They would naturally distort this information through their own personality and adjust it to fit the needs of the moment. This is the exercising of Free Will. Their apprentices would copy their mentors, not the original teachings, and further distortion would result. The tarnished techniques would be perpetuated, and the Law of Diminishing Returns would take its toll. This is a typical Third Density pattern.

Physics Vs. Metaphysics

As the culture advanced, mathematics, especially geometry, produced the ability to reason. A co-champion of this movement was science. The World soon came to know these two agents as *the authority* for all things — figures don't lie and science can prove/disprove anything. There was no place for the intangible, hypothetical Tensor Concepts in this rigid discipline of Reason.

This path of evolution was not incorrect. Science *had* to come first. It established the foundation for all else to build upon. However, hardcore science is limited. True, it takes many centuries before those limitations appear, but they eventually do, and that is where we are at present. Physics goes beyond the normal, accepted proof that has been satisfactory in the past. Now enters Metaphysics to offer Spiritual and Universal answers to the questions that befuddle traditional physics and the sciences. There are the die-hard scientists who scoff at this attempt to befoul these hard-earned accomplishments with the tapestry of voodoo, but there are also their colleagues who are sufficiently open minded to look elsewhere for answers, and they are finding them. It is timely for the Tensor Concepts, along with the practice of the Kundalini Meditation to play a vital role in the conditioning process of the scientific community.

The masses have willfully learned to worship machinery and science, even as an occult. People identify with the brand of automobile that they drive. They quickly learn to think like a Buick or act like a Ford, and their personality takes on the

NOTES:

traditional characteristics attributed to that piece of machinery. This is done with great pride and a sense of accomplishment. This is accepted behavior because machines are *tangible,* they exist. To set such store in intangible mental endeavors would seem foolish and probably demented to the practicing thinker.

E.S.P. (Extrasensory Perception) and P.K. (Psychokinesis), in order to work, require an orderly Mind and an Open Mind. You must be willing to develop new mental capacities. You cannot be content to limit yourself to goals that are less than your true capabilities. Innately, you know your true worth. The strict disciplines of science were/are essential in order to grasp philosophy of the Tensor Concepts. The answers provided through abstract physics are the ultimate in fulfillment. With practice, these thought patterns become a working part of you, as your mind begin to function as it should have from the very beginning of this 75,000-year Third Density Cycle.

Our Defective Sun

Our Defective Sun is the culprit that prohibited this normal development of the mind. *This is not your fault!* You have all paid a price, a terrible price, to acquire certain types of experiences that your Soul could never have found anywhere else in the Galaxy, perhaps in the Universe. The Negative Radiation, emitted from our Defective Sun was canceled by a protective shield in September of 1970. You are no longer affected — now at last, you've got a chance!

Masters Of The Past And Machines Of The Future

In the distant past, certain Masters of the Tensor Concepts did indeed visit orbs other than Terra Firma without the use of Spacecraft. Medicine men would bring back to Earth samples of the rocks found on our Moon. Some findings were quite accomplished. The use of machinery did not occur to them. Today, all is dependent upon our hero — the machine. Fourth Density MAN also has machinery, and you will think in terms of machinery when the day arrives for you to advance and enter

NOTES:

into the realm of Love. But remember, the machinery of MAN has no moving parts; it is controlled mentally, it never wears out, and it is powered by devices that will carry a full charge of energy that lasts for a minimum of 50,000 Earth years! Yes, there will be machines in your future, but nothing to compare to the archaic toys that you worship today.

The Minority Teacher

As you develop into the Tensor-Oriented person, you are apt to be the envy of your uninitiated peers. You are and shall continue to be — the minority. You are the teachers, you set the examples for others to follow, and they will. There will be those who will attempt to hold you back, and they will ridicule you as they bask in the smugness of the power of the majority. Be courageous, have no fear — for you are the leaders of the New Order that shall take us into the New Dispensation of Love.

Chapter 18

Time

There is no law of time. There are many Universal Laws, but this is not one of them. We have described Space/Time as being physical, and Time/Space as being etheric or non-physical. Time, as we on Earth utilize it, is linear. This, of course, is a misnomer. Time is actually spherical. We have used the analogy of the onion and its many skins to illustrate how time grows by layers and how this growth is continuous. Time does not have a starting and stopping place, nor does time have a direction like the linear concept would indicate. Time grows, and it expands as it constantly grows — again, like the onion.

But what is time? It is not a law of the Universe, so that would mean that there are places in the Universe where time (in some concept) is utilized, and also there are places where there is no time — a timeless state.

Time is a product of the Law of Motion. If one is in a Sector of Space where there is no visible motion, then that area is said to be timeless. The interval between two or more heavenly bodies passing can be recorded and counted. The prime example being our own Earth in its 365.24 days orbit of our Sun. This interval can be noted, recorded, divided up, and counted. This counting is further eased because our Earth rotates on her axis in a regular way that permits an even further breakdown in the system of counting time. These conditions tend to lead the Earthbound observer into believing that time is indeed linear.

But supposing there was no Sun to orbit or if there were, but it was too far distant for anyone to realize that such a nucleus existed. How would one dare to measure "time?" Suppose our Planet turned on her axis once every 500 years. Suppose our Earth orbited our Sun every 10,000 years — what would your concept of linear time be then? Time had to be invented by Human Beings to better organize themselves, but their concept of measuring time is certainly not Universal!

NOTES:

Time is the interval between two bodies passing. The passing is the direct result of the Law of Motion. The heavenly body that wanders in "outer space" and does not come in contact, regular or otherwise, with other bodies is said to be timeless. Since time is spherical, not linear, does it then really matter? There is no past. There is no future. There is only the eternal present — in which we may construct a past and a future if we so choose. It is necessary to grasp the idea that the eternity of Creation exists in the eternal present — not in the past or in some unknown future. When linear time is accepted as the folly that it is, then greater understandings are made possible.

We are reminded of the story, alleged to be true — and it easily could have been — of a young man in his late twenties who was picked up by a Spacecraft an hour or so after he had finished his noon meal. His Guide took him aboard and they took off to parts unknown. The young man was having a grand time as he was being escorted about this magnificent Ship. The conversations with various crew members stimulated his mind into mental orgasms. He was enthralled with his visit.

Soon his Guide informed him that they must return to Earth, and take him back home. The young man protested. He was having a great time and was in no hurry to terminate this marvelous experience. He reminded his Guide that it was yet early afternoon, and there was ample time remaining before supper and darkness set in. He could afford to stay a bit longer, for after all it had only been a couple of hours . . . The Guide hesitatingly informed him that it had now been . . . thirty two years!

The young man had not once been to the bathroom! When he once again set foot on Terra Firma, he quickly discovered that thirty two years had indeed elapsed. He had long ago been declared dead and was forgotten. His mirror revealed that he had not aged a single day. The fellow missed The Roaring Twenties, The Great Depression, World War II, and the Korean Conflict. Shortly thereafter, he went completely mad.

Now, if Intra-Galactic space flight were to take as long as Earth scientists seem to think it would, would the crew age

NOTES:

during the process? Would they need to eat or drink? What happens to body functions when one enters a state of timelessness? Actually, "timelessness" is a condition inwhich the Law of Motion cannot be observed. Coal Miners trapped in a cave-in for several days, quickly lose track of time; however, they do continue to age.

MAN'S home is Space. MAN does not count time in Space! Time is an important factor, as it applies to navigators to be sure; but, time does not govern the lives of MAN. Earth time is applicable no place but here. Every community in Galactic Space or even Universal Space, has derived their own concept of the unit of time. There is no "Universal Time," having its "Greenwich Mean Time" to standardize the Galaxy. The underdeveloped communities barely notice time at all. The highly developed societies pay it little regard. There is a phase in-between that sets great store by the accurate counting of the units of time, and this is where our scientific community has placed us now.

To summarize: time is that interval in the passing of two heavenly bodies that is measured, divided into units, and counted. Time is totally dependent upon and is the product of the Law of Motion, which is in no way dependent on, or in congruency with the Speed of Light.

The difference in the vibration of the various Planes or even the Densities is often confused with time. This alteration of Vibration is not a distortion of Main Line Time, though this appears to be the case. Probable Realities — which we shall discuss at length a bit later — employ a frequency of Vibration that is only a by-product.

We suggest that you continue to practice the concept that time, all time, is always *spherical.* As you become more comfortable with this, time will be relegated to its proper insignificant place in the Tensor Portion of your brain.

Serial Universe — Time

The Serial Universes are truly a subject to grasp. But simply, they are an indefinite number of probable vibrations, all

NOTES:

existing on different levels of frequency and separated by a difference in *time*. The Universes are not parallel and are therefore not identical, but they are indeed similar. Aspects of yourself dwell in many of them.

If you can accept that time is actually spherical, then the spherical layers of the Universe, like the skins of an onion are the same thing.

In order to better understand, one needs a beginning place on this onion of time. The concept of Main Line Time needs to be fixed in your mind. This is the starting point or basis from which you can explore. Needless to say, everyone thinks of this world and this Universe as being that "Main Line" of time. Other Universes, if they exist at all, are other than, or even less than this one. This is erroneous thinking. However, we see no particular harm in it at the moment and choose to exploit the subject completely in a later Volume when we thoroughly discuss "Probable Realities."

Serial Universes, as they relate to your Tensor Concepts in your brain, allow you to indulge in a multiplicity of results derived from any given action/catalyst. The Cortical Portion of your thinking sees only one reality and consciously deals with it accordingly. This is life. This is the reality — but the physical reality is an *illusion,* remember? If this be an illusion, then what is the true, real Universe, the Main Line Time Universe? The "etheric" is true time because it is timeless. The etheric is the true Universe because it is the originator of the mirror of all the Serial Universes.

Use the mirror as the example. If a large mirror were to stand on a busy sidewalk many people would pass before it, each casting a reflection — a reflection that is an illusion. Each personality is a world or a Universe unto themselves, each have their rightful place in the vast scheme of things. All of the people are about the same, yet each is individually unique. Some shall pass our mirror in the morning, while others pass in the afternoon. Some will pass by in both morning and afternoon. Each second of time being different than the preceding second. When you move one second in time via the Serial Universes, you move a distance of 186,000 miles in some direction or another.

Without the existence of Serial Universes time would be two dimensional. We who are embracing Third Density see it as being three dimensional (past, present, and future). Actually time is of the Fourth Dimension because it is spherical, not linear. If this complex subject is soaking into your understanding and is acceptable to you, then you are now applying your Tensor Centers of your brain. This line of thinking is not acceptable to the logic and reason aspect of the Cortical Centers of your brain.

A practical application for the Tensor-Oriented Brain would be the study of time and the Serial Universes as they relate to Space travel. We have discussed in a previous section the fantastic speeds attainable by spacecraft. This is achieved through the creation of a force field about the craft that has certain properties that permit it to bend the lines of magnetic force into parallel lines; that in turn make possible fantastic rates of speed.

As a Craft attains the speed of Light, a transition takes place. The Craft then enters a segment of the next higher Serial Universe that is one second *ahead* of our current status (Main Line Time.) This "new value" of Planck Constant now engages the Craft to an accelerated velocity to the speed of Light squared. On this new level the Craft is once again accelerated to the speed of Light, and the phenomena is repeated. This can go on for as many as nine times. During the course of this activity, matter is in a quasi-physical state, though the Craft and its occupants continue to maintain the integrity of their original comfortable solidity. The force field about the Craft protects the matter contained within to retain its integrity.

As the Craft enters a higher level of vibration, it enters into the "future" by one second or 186,000 miles. From the standpoint of Main Line Time, one enters into the future step by step. The future consists of probabilities, even as the past is but an illusion. The power lies in the "Now" and the "Now" is but a reflection of the etheric. If nothing else, perhaps this little

NOTES:

mental teaser will cause you to cease taking yourself so seriously!

It is possible to visit the past but not like you can visit the probable future using a Spacecraft. For a physical Craft to enter the past, it would require a fantastic rate of deacceleration starting at a standstill. No one has yet figured out how to do this. Journeys to the past are made mentally or by teleportation. The mind is an entity enjoying a non-physical status, and is therefore immune to the laws that govern the physical Serial Universes. When the mind travels via teleportation, it moves from one value of Planck Constant to another. The Spacecraft does the same. The energy level of the Universe is constant, you can depend on that. Predictably, various catalysts affect this constant, causing different values to form. Recognizing this and using this is what makes Inter-Galactic travel, physical or mental, possible. We trust these thoughts have expanded your thinking.

Time Warps

Time is a product of motion. If motion were to be stopped or speeded up, time would warp. If the Fabric of Time were to be "tucked up," then two distant points would now be adjacent to each other, distance being eliminated. The Law of Motion would then have been satisfied from an altered perspective.

If the Fabric of Time were stretched, then it would appear that time had stopped. Time's source, motion would then be *expanding* at a rate larger than normal. In the case of the "tuck in time," motion would be *contracting* at a rate other than normal. A Spacecraft, cocooned in it's own force field, has the ability to utilize the Law of Motion to its best advantage.

The inhabitants of Earth are able to accurately count time because of the Earth's prescribed and calculated orbit of our Sun. Now, if the Earth were to become shrouded in opaqueness by some form, then the observation of the Sun would be lost and the counting of time would quickly become obsolete even though the Earth continues to orbit our Sun. Assuming that life could be

NOTES:

sustained, Earth's inhabitants would experience a time warp of zero progression for as long as the opaque cover persisted. This stoppage of time would most likely be accepted as a *reversal* of time, and the past would be re-visited. This is to be considered a physical happening.

Your Higher Self can psychologically produce the same situation within the personality. This induced time warp often causes the personality to challenge his sanity. This gift from the Higher Self produces an intimate hindsight view that could be most useful as the personality endeavors to understand and forgive self for action committed in the "past." A person could be experiencing a very real time warp, while his fellows would be experiencing nothing unusual at all, or vise versa.

If selected Harvestable individuals were to be suddenly extracted from the sea of Humanity, via Time Warps, the Masses might very well be oblivious to their absence. Their memories would automatically be blocked, and since everybody would feel the same way about your disappearance, your lack of existence would go un-challenged. The consciousness could readily be compensated. This is an aspect of the forthcoming "Harvest." Time Warps exist. They can "happen to you" or you can actually, mentally cause them to happen to yourself. Whatever the source, they definitely produce a very strange feeling within the individual.

Love And Light

We remind you that Love is: Intelligent Energy, and that Light is: Intelligent Infinity. Without these twins nothing would function in this Universe, including the Tensor Concepts.

Love may be sensed as a warm feeling of energy flowing. Light may be visualized as any color or white which comprises all colors. Both energies possess very special, compatible qualities.

Light is. There is no place where the Light isn't. To be useful, the Light must be invoked, i.e., called. When there is the calling/invoking, the Light responds. Though always available and highly Intelligent, the Light will not act until invoked. The

NOTES:

Light is the most powerful force in all Creation. It is Intelligence. It manifests via its twin which is Energy. These are the tools that facilitate the Tensor Equations.

Even as the Tensor Concepts should be applied in the course of daily living, Light should be thought of and used simultaneously. Use the Light to protect yourself, other selves, and your possessions. Use it to heal. Use it for anything. Use Light to enhance your understanding, for, after all, Light is Intelligent, it is Intelligent Infinity — the source and collection of all knowledge in all of Creation. In-depth understanding is not possible without invoking the Light. It is your gift from our Creator — use it freely.

Light will not function until it has been invoked. This is your job. You call for the Light and direct it on the path of your choice. You give it instructions so that it might know of your desires. Then, the Light sets out to accomplish its assignment; being Intelligent, it has its own methods. These methods may or may not coincide with your own mode of thinking. Either way, you cannot exercise control over Intelligent Infinity or Intelligent Energy once it has been invoked. The Light will always operate in a fashion that brings forth the very best results for all concerned. You are free to disagree if you choose. After some practice, you will learn to understand the ways of the Light and then adjust your thinking to be in greater harmony with the Light and with our One Infinite Creator.

The Light cannot be abused or misused by anyone. It is indeed your tool — a gift from our Creator; but, the Light *is* The Creator, and no part of Creation misuses the Creator! One does not think in terms of fear, but rather in terms of seeking understanding. Sometimes this is acquired through trial and error.

As you ponder the Tensor Concepts use the Light to clarify and refine your awareness so that your understanding might be expanded. When the Light does not work in the method that you imagined take time to figure out why not so that the next time you will be more in harmony with Intelligent Infinity. When the Light *does* respond pretty much the way that you

NOTES:

anticipated take the time to ponder why it did so that you might repeat the process comfortably in the future. Always ask "why," this process breaks through the superficiality and permits and in-depth look at the mechanics of the thing. Curiosity is a Positive asset.

Ancient Preservation Of The Tensor Concepts

The Confederation of MAN has seen a need to offer service and felt a sense of responsibility towards the Human Race since the initial seeding of the Earth Mother. There were and there are a special group of entities that choose to incarnate as a group at significant historical intervals. These ones would make at least one appearance during any given Root Race. These entities are of Fourth Density and are MAN Incarnate. Sometimes they would be born of woman and other times they would assume a body in the fashion commonly known as the "Walk-In." The latter method provides much more memory.

This group was present during the time of Lemuria when the Tensor Concepts were taught. The names of the teachings varied, but the core was always the same. Three times during the long history of Atlantis these ones assembled themselves and reproduced the teachings. Their last appearance was during the final days of that great civilization. Records and artifacts were safely preserved and stowed away for use at a place known as the Province of Tealus. Today, that place is commonly called Egypt.

During the current Aryan Root Race, this special group gathered in the chambers of the edifice known as the Great Pyramid of Cheops. After a lengthy meeting, these ones dispersed to all corners of the Planet to teach the peoples of Earth how to think. Many Nations have their own unique stories concerning their own teacher. The Greeks had their "gods," as did the Romans. The Island peoples remember a great green frog. The Red Nations of North America remember four wise men who descended from out of the North. These wise men taught the peoples which plants were edible and which were

NOTES:

poison. Healing medicines could be extracted from others. These men taught many things, and then continued southward, never to be seen again.

Wherever the members of this group visited they left behind a subtle vibration of Love and Light. The seeds of knowledge had been planted. The tree of knowledge grew. Sometimes it grew into wisdom and flourished into understanding. Sometimes the tree became distorted and bent and twisted as parts withered and died. Half truths as decreed by a priesthood were the unfortunate results.

When their incarnations terminated, these loyal teachers continued to serve from the Astral Plane through the medium now known as "channeling." They continue to offer their service even today to the best of their ability according to the degree of acceptance by Third Density Earthlings.

The time is imminent when this group shall once again gather at the appointed site, perhaps to open the Atlantean time capsules, perhaps not. These constructed chambers may actually survive the cleansing cataclysms that are scheduled for our future. It may be more appropriate to wait a bit longer, for the contents may not be fully appreciated by this dying Aryan Root Race.

The glorious past of a bygone civilization perhaps should remain uncontaminated. Today's Lords of Commerce would exploit these noble teachings even as First and Second Density has been raped and ravaged in their gluttonous wake.

It is the honor/duty of the Confederation of MAN to maintain the vigil, and in some way make available, the teaching of these noble truths and concepts. The Third Density Harvestable cannot successfully attack Fourth Density lacking the joyful ability to think.

Logic And Reasoning

Third Density Humans take for granted their ability to employ reasoning. We all have been endowed with this ability — some more than others perhaps, but all have it. On other Third Density Planets in this Galaxy reasoning is a learned attribute.

NOTES:

On Planet Earth, reasoning was not learned by men via trial and errors, the normal procedure. Instead, it was a *gift* from MAN.

In this Galaxy; the Third Density Cycle lasts for approximately 75,000 years. Because of the most unusual circumstances upon Planet Earth which were due to our defective Sun, it would have taken men at least a million years to advance beyond the "cave man" status. MAN knew this. MAN was responsible for seeding this Planet with Humanoid life forms. MAN had responsibilities and he lived up to them.

The seed stock MAN and WOMAN were brought from the Planet Jupiter, those of the Golden Race — the source of all life in this Solar System. The offspring of the parental stock were born without memory of any Past Lives. This condition was decreed to be appropriate by our Galactic Logos. But these children could not be taught; they could not learn. Evolution was at a standstill, and it had yet to start. The parents called for aid. MAN answered their call.

Fourth Density MAN has the ability to mentally isolate the powers of reason, and then genetically imprint this latent power within the minds of men. This was MAN'S *gift* to men of Earth. Reason begets understanding, and understanding is LOVE. This was a gift of Love. Millions of years of stagnating evolution were quickly reduced to the normal cycle of 75,000 years.

Our Defective Sun emits a form of Negative Radiation, from which the Earth had no shielding protection. The subculture of men was the ultimate result. The seeding was not intended to establish a Third Density Culture. A Fourth Density Civilization was expected. It didn't happen. MAN was shocked!

Earth's obnoxious law of "survival of the fittest" rolled on as MAN watched in awe and guilt and even a bit of shame. Now, at long last, MAN'S efforts are beginning to pay off. This is enhanced by the fact that the age of Third Density is about to terminate. Logic and reason has its rewards. First and Second Density has paid a bitter price for supporting the destructive whims of men learning to evaluate and refine reason.

NOTES:

MAN has stood by and offered assistance. Never infringing on Free Will, MAN has "whispered in the ears" of some to bestow productive ideas. He has incarnated among the populace since its inception to promote concepts that might bring about some simulation of a Civilization. Here he has enjoyed little success. Brotherly Love has not been practiced.

The installing of the power to reason gave purpose to man's beingness. Goals could be set for self and for the culture. Root Races were formed and the Free Will of the mass consciousness gave it direction. MAN continued to offer assistance.

The time is at hand when the reunion with MAN will be a fact. The longed for at oneness is a yearning that beats fierce in the hearts of many. The Light and Love of the New Age, of Fourth Density, of going home is a thought that is overwhelming at times. We eagerly prepare ourselves for that glorious day. Learning and practicing these Tensor Concepts is a giant step in that direction.

Neurons

The first step of the metamorphic transition will affect your brain. The second stage will affect your internal organs, while the third and final stage involves your superficiality — that is when you step out of your current Yellow Ray Third Density Body and immediately step into your Green Ray Fourth Density Body.

Electromagnetic and electrochemical processes are changing in all living cells over the face of Planet Earth. Everything is relevant to something else or dependent, you might say. Therefore, when an appropriate catalyst instigates change in one area, other areas related to or dependent upon that affected part will also undergo similar change. It is a chain reaction.

Of all the cells found in nature, the neuron is the most highly evolved and the neuron cells of the brain are the highest of all. The Cerebral neuron cells are undergoing slight mutations that coincide with the Earth Mother's rising vibrations. They are increasing their speed of vibration, which speeds up the intensity of the electromagnetic signals that network the brain. This can

NOTES:

cause subtle physical response that also quickens the awareness; and the thinking capacity is gradually increased. Your hindsight will verify this.

Actually, this growing condition causes the Third Density Human to approach normalcy. It will not produce a generation of freaks. However, the vast majority of the populace is not sufficiently evolved (Soul Level) to gracefully accept this magnificent phenomenon. In these ones various degrees of insanity are the unfortunate result.

These subtle alterations of the electrochemical function within the brain will alter the nature of the Tensor and the Cortical Portions of that organ. The inhibitions shall fall away from the Cortical Centers, thus permitting even further bridging with the Tensor Centers. More and more neuronic connections via the synoptical joining and bonding shall produce mental awareness beyond your greatest expectations. The inhibiting and prohibiting factor that can nullify this accelerated evolution is drugs. When drugs or alcohol are used — whatever the source — the synoptical neuron nerve endings are reduced to a cinder at the point of impact, never to be renewed. That piece of circuitry is destroyed for the rest of the incarnation. True, there are more cells in your brain then there are stars in the sky, and it is also true that detours can be made as the thinking patterns are re-routed; but, it is *never* a grand idea to deliberately burn out brain cells by using drugs and alcohol. The price is too great for the short-term pleasure derived. The brain is the greatest of all physical Creations — cherish it!

As the neuron cells increase their vibrations the brain will have ever increasing influence and control over the body in which it is housed. The Will of the personality shall effectively control and conquer many forms of illness, both major and minor. The assumption of responsibility for self takes on a new refined meaning. True euphoria is obtainable through increased mind power alone. Chemicals become yesterday's news.

Chapter 19

The Brain

As you very well may know, Earth scientists in the medical field have divided the Human brain into hemispheres, lobes, and other areas to provide a nomenclature of that magnificent organ for identification purposes. This is useful, of course, and we plan no quarrel with it. In our study of the Tensor Concepts it is mandatory that we have a look at the brain, for approximately 80% of that organ consist of Tensor Centers. This is the Tensor Portion of the brain. The remaining 20% is the Cortical or Thinking Portion.

The functions of the Tensor Portion, containing the Tensor Centers, is unknown to medical science. The brain is unlimited in its capacity to learn or to be trained. For example, the brain can retain the atomic pattern of matter to over 24 decimal places. This Tensor Memory is constant and consistent.

A computer planned by Earthlings, to be constructed in outer Space that will be 10 miles wide, 10 miles high, and 15 miles long if built, will have the working capacity of one third of that organ that resides betwixt your ears! The ability to think is a remarkable phenomenon.

The atomic patterns of matter becomes very complex, as larger numbers are involved. The great Mayan Civilization, well aware of the Kundalini power and the Tensor Concept/Equations, utilized this large numerical mathematical count of atomic matter. Their hoards of recorded numbers were, for the most part, not a measurement of time or distance, but the atomic count of matter. Archaeologists have yet to take this fact into consideration. Accurate knowledge of atomic patterns is essential when the manifestation of thought forms is attempted. To design a thought form is of course, the first step. To manifest it means to construct it from etheric materials. The atomic make-up of every form of material or alloy is different. Knowledge of these many, many materials is mandatory for the Fourth Density Aquarian in order to function adequately in his new found vibration. The ancient Mayans were well underway in prepara-

NOTES:

tions for this glorious happening. They were training their brains to function using very large numbers. The Tensor Portion of any one's brain can handle this task with ease.

* * *

As the Tensor Centers open and the Synoptical Connections are made, you become more and more aware of Love and Beauty as it truly exists on Earth and in the Universe. The illusion gives way to the true reality. Love of our One Infinite Creator is shared as the feeling of spiritual bliss encompasses the physical. Enlightenment provided the freedom to be aware of self and of Fourth Density MAN. This is the Joy, as Love prevails. Your potential is unlimited. Your only restrictions are self-imposed!

Increased awareness is the primary drive in the evolution of all life forms. Catalysts are the agents that sponsor this growth. As the stages of awareness quicken, spirituality begins to develop. The unfolding aspects of Love begin to manifest. The consciousness expands, and responsibility is assumed for self, other selves, and First and Second Density.

Those of Fourth Density MAN dwelling on the Planet Procyon are oldest known of the species. They have been happily functioning as such for 50 billion years. This is more than ten times longer than our Earth has been in existence. These noble ones, the most advanced of all in the physical, use only two-thirds of the Tensor Portion of their brain — a full third is yet undeveloped! This is an indication of the unlimited potential of that marvelous organ.

The Tensor Equations

As we begin to examine the Tensor Concepts and Equations, we remind you that this knowledge is only information. It is up to you to correlate it to the level of your understanding and then apply it to your daily life. Your mind has unlimited potential. Your increased mental/spiritual awareness provides a responsible sense of freedom that permits your individual control over matter and over your environment —

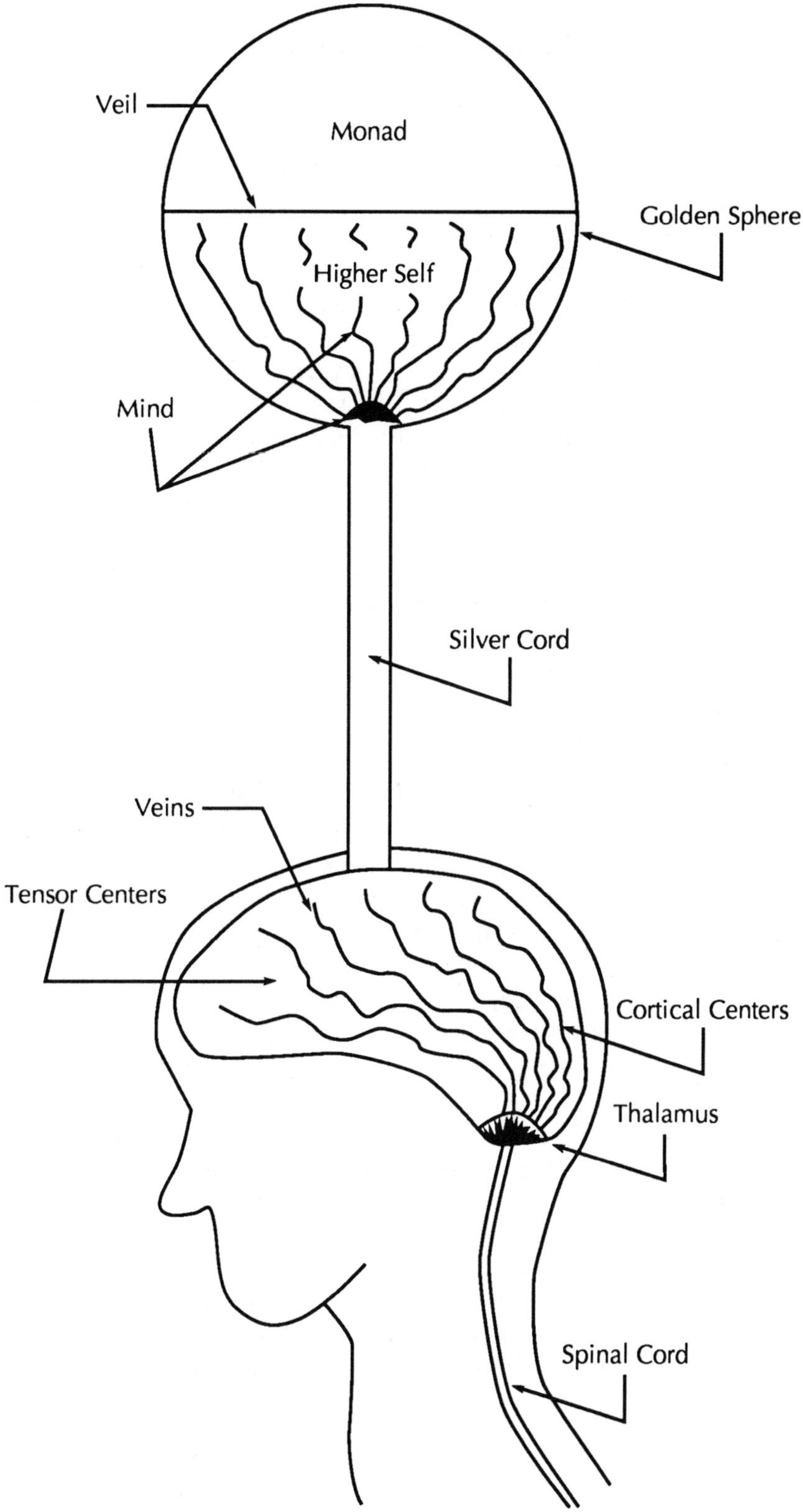

Monad
Veil
Golden Sphere
Higher Self
Mind
Silver Cord
Veins
Tensor Centers
Cortical Centers
Thalamus
Spinal Cord

NOTES:

when used and applied in Light and Love. This can be achieved in only a few moments.

The Tensor Thinking Process has the Divine ability to activate new and unused synoptical nerve endings in the unused portion of your brain, which increases your mental powers above Third Density Human to Fourth Density MAN. For those of you who have experienced brain cell damage this process shall open up new vistas of mental learning opportunities via newly constructed detours made by connecting new circuitry in the Tensor Centers of the physical organ brain.

A MAN called Soltec has volunteered to offer information of a technical nature describing the Tensor Concepts. A MAN called Mon-ka has elected to add the necessary color. These ones, and others, have attempted to teach these mental tenets to many, many people during this century, which is now drawing to a close. You may have been exposed to variations of these concepts in your previous studies. The following are the six Tensor Concepts.

The First Tensor Concept

When a person observes an event that is unfamiliar or new and then responds to the effect of that event by saying they "knew it all along," and were not surprised or amazed at all — this person is *identifying*. The act of "categorizing" an event into a group of experienced past events for the purpose of assessing and evaluating is a method of identifying.

Deductive reasoning, the mainstay of modern science (as opposed to the Mental/Spiritual philosophies of abstract physics), is a method of identifying.

Relying completely on manmade laws, scientific and civil, for guidance and direction, while ignoring the existence of Universal Law is a method of identifying.

Fear of the unknown is the *cause* for identifying.

Identifying is a barrier to your developing awareness, and it must be removed from your consciousness. It is to be replaced with independence, individuality, and the awareness of self by employing the "I am that I am" attitude.

NOTES:

This is discipline! This is self discipline!

The Second Tensor Concept

Space, Time, and Energy, in that order, are the manifest results of one or more of the four Creative Forces. (See Vol. I.) Each is an axis, working independently and in harmony with each other, giving direction to evolution via polarity. Space is the One Infinite Creator. It is unending. It contains all there IS. Nothing can be removed from space.

Time is always spherical. It grows. There are timeless areas of Space where time is not consciously counted. Time is the by-product of Motion. Time produces congruency in all living matter.

Energy is Intelligent. Intelligent Energy is Love. Love is the "glue," or force, that unites all of Creation.

The Third Tensor Concept

The leaves are green. Does this describe the leaves of a tree? Only in part. The Green leaves are also Silver when they catch the sunlight; they are Blue, when they reflect the sky; they are Orange and Red when they reflect the Sunset; they are shaped according to the species of the tree — and the list goes on and on. To say the leaves are Green is only a partial description. Learn to see ALL of the leaf. See TOTAL. Experience the TOTAL leaf with all of your senses — as best you can. BE AWARE! BE TOTAL.

The photograph is not the person. The picture depicts the likeness of that person, but the photograph is NOT the person. There are many, many aspects of that personality that the photograph does not reveal. Do not assess the personality on the basis of the photograph. Examine the TOTAL personality. Via your senses, experience the TOTALITY of the person, place or thing.

The picture is a symbol, an accurate symbol to be sure. Would it reveal more of the subject if it were painted by a skilled portrait artist? Certain essences of warmth or coldness of the personality the old photograph omitted would no doubt be

NOTES:

captured by the portrait artist. Either way, the picture is but a *symbol* that serves as a catalyst causing the viewer to remember many other aspects of the subject. The symbol (picture) is an instrument of recall.

Symbols are important tools that the mind uses to convey thoughts. Thoughts are triggered by necessity, real or imagined. A thought form is created and manifestation begins. Space/Time and Time/Space are employed simultaneously. Attention to detail in Time/Space produces the grandest results in manifested Space/Time. Symbols, easily manipulated, create the new ideas that translate in a working thought form.

The Fourth Tensor Concept

First is the stimulus, second is the nervous impact, third is the emotional reaction, and fourth is the response — probably verbal. This is the discipline.

Most Third Densitys react to the experience with immediate verbal response, skipping steps two and three all together. The stimulus is not tempered by experience/-knowledge/thought. This distorted impact results in trauma to the nervous system, which can produce neurosis or even psychosis.

When the catalyst is presented, the first step is to *Think!* Then, to temper that thought with *feeling* — a high refined form of raw emotion, and lastly, *respond* — verbal, or whatever is appropriate.

Relax the brain by using the Thalamatic Cortical Pause, or by "rolling the pea." The eye exercise is also very useful. These exercises will be described later. This will stabilize the nervous system as it balances the Cortical Centers with the Tensor Centers in the brain. This is the method to train your nervous system!

The Fifth Tensor Concept

To admit that you will never be able to know all there is to know may seem rather ludicrous considering how limited we all are at present. However, through the use of your Kundalini Meditation and your use of the Indigo Ray, you shall indeed open the door to Intelligent Infinity. There you will find unlimited knowledge. Now, the Tensor Portion of your brain is also beginning to open and you shall quickly realize that you too are unlimited. It is *then* when you must realize: you cannot know all there is to know. This is the realm of our One Infinite Creator. But, by all means, learn just as much as you can! This is so very satisfying to your Soul.

The One Infinite Creator, being aware of itself, knows all there is to know. All other forms of thinking consciousness know, to some degree, less than ALL. This built-in limitation must be realized and accepted. This realization is NOT to be applied as a noble excuse to cease the bother of continuing to learn.

Conditioned reflexes or reactions are to be diligently acquired through the total understanding of the experience/-catalyst. The basic fundamentals of life are then embraced.

Seek the opportunity to learn through application.

Realize and accept consciously, subconsciously, and unconsciously, that you will always know less than the ALL.

Retain this thought as your developing awareness is guided by your Higher Self, and your ego is relegated to its appropriate station.

The Sixth Tensor Concept

It is necessary for the individual to embrace the culture in order to receive the programmed catalysts provided by the Higher Self to satisfy the needs of the Soul. This will result in blockages to the Nervous System. Use the Thalamatic Cortical Pause Technique described later to elevate this reoccurring problem. This is your challenge: to eliminate emotions and replace them with true feelings.

This aligning and balancing of yourself permits your Mind/Body/Spirit Complex to achieve the at oneness with the environment, to fully capitalize on your abilities and talents; and to intuitively plan and seek your future.

* * *

Remove the blockages of your nervous system by clearing your chakras. The raising of the Kundalini will do this.

NOTES:

The Yellow Ray of Emotion will betray you; this is the Seat of Emotions, the source of all your problems. Always keep in mind that the physical reality is an illusion.

* * *

A lack of understanding of how your body and nervous system operates can and does cause trauma. Understand yourself. Train yourself. Relax the mind and body at regular intervals. Use the eye exercise to relax the brain.

The Thalamus, where the spinal cord attaches to the brain, is where the electrical synoptical connectors meet.

The eye exercise causes the brain to relax and shrink, as the pressure is relieved.

The Exercises

Roll the Pea. This is an exercise that permits you to integrate your upper body with your lower body, and thus stabilize and pacify your own nervous system. The method is as follows: the Kundalini has been raised. At the time of lowering, place a dab of White Light Kundalini, about the size of a pea or a small marble on the top of the head, and hide it in your hair. The remaining Kundalini is lowered precisely in the way that you have been taught (See Vol. I.) Now, at times of your selection, and *without* awakening or raising your Kundalini, align and balance your chakras. Activate the pea-sized dab of Kundalini by mentally causing it to enter into your skull, flow down through the gray matter to the Thalamus at the base of the brain, enter into the spinal cord, and go down the cord to the stem of the fifth chakra — the Yellow Ray Solar Plexis Chakra. There, the pea-sized dab of Kundalini enters the stem of that chakra and flows out to its head. Then, it turns upward and passes through the heads of the Green, the Blue, the Indigo, and into the Violet Chakra. Then, it flows down the stem of the Crown Chakra back to the top of your head. The circuit is then repeated — as many times as you deem necessary. As the pea circulates, take deep breaths and relax. This exercise of the "Rolling of the Pea," can be performed at any time, at any place. It is a quick and easy — and it works.

NOTES:

When finished, stow the pea on the top of your head for future use. This integrates feeling with thinking and thinking with feeling. When the stimuli is presented, the first thing you do is think, second is feel, and the third is speak. Think, feel, speak/act — that is the order.

Do not let the Yellow Ray Ego run and ruin the show. Your mind must always be in charge. Your Ego will challenge this system. Do not kill the Ego or eliminate emotions, they are valuable. Simply relegate the Ego/emotion to its proper place. The goal is: to have the nervous system controlled by the mentality, as in Fourth Density, and not by the emotions, as in Third Density. Evolution thus being properly promoted.

The Thalamatic Cortical Pause. Stand or sit erect. Relax. Envision a shaft of Emerald Green Ray entering the Heart Chakra. Envision its Love/Healing Energy flowing to the spinal cord, and then up the spinal cord to the brain. Flood the brain with Emerald Green Light. Pump it full. When you begin to feel pressure at your temples and forehead shut off the supply of Green Ray Energy. Now, permit the Green Light to slowly drain down from your brain, through the Thalamus, into your spinal cord, saturating your nervous system. As the Love in the Green Light gradually descends through the head, neck, shoulders, arms, the torso and on down through the legs and out the soles of your feet, it calms, heals, and stabilizes your nervous system, as well as purging your entire body of toxins and other impurities. This exercise takes approximately five minutes and may be repeated up to three times.

Under appropriate circumstances, the Thalamatic Cortical Pause could follow the "Rolling of the Pea" exercise, although both may stand independent of each other. You will note that this exercise is identical to the self-healing exercise offered in a previous section of this Volume.

The Eye Exercise. To create a sharp, active brain, a "breathing" cycle or exercise is useful. Emotionally and physically draw yourself up in tension, hold it for about 10 seconds, then exhale and completely relax for 20 seconds. Repeat the cycle, six — ten times. The eye exercise should

NOTES:

accompany this procedure. During the tensing portions, squint the eyes and "look hard" at some object as you breath deep. Then, as you relax, let the eyelids droop as the eyes go out of focus. Do not close the eyes.

This compound exercise pumps oxygenated blood into the brain. The relaxing portions also relaxes the blood vessels in the brain, thus stabilizing the organ's vitality.

* * *

In order to produce the activities described in the following chapter, it is first necessary to acquire a grasp of the full meaning and impact of the Six Tensor Concepts and be able to harmoniously integrate the mind/brain/nervous system in a relaxed fashion.

THE EXERCISES

THE THALAMATIC CORTICAL PAUSE

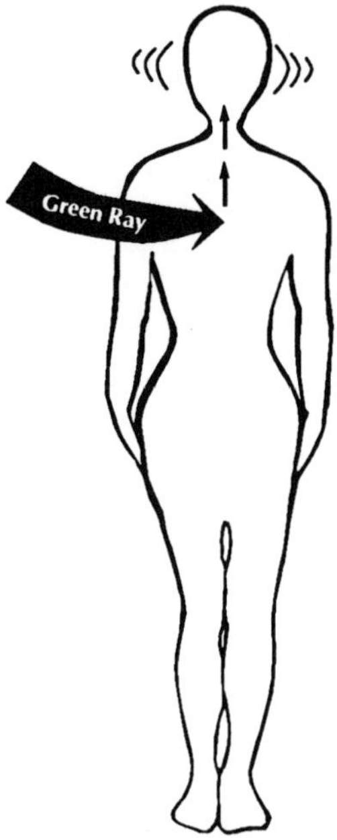

INTAKE

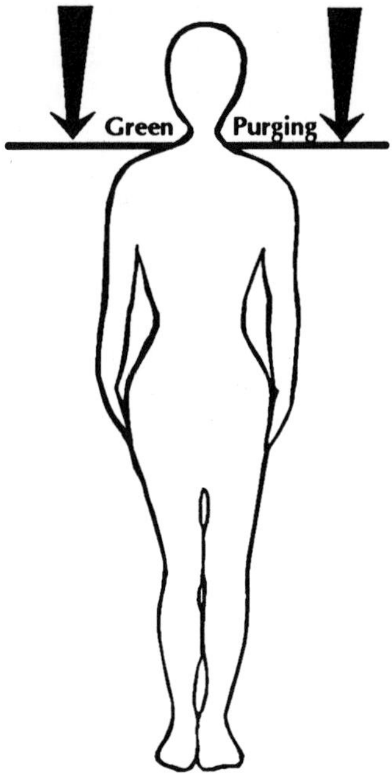

EXHAUST

ROLLING THE PEA

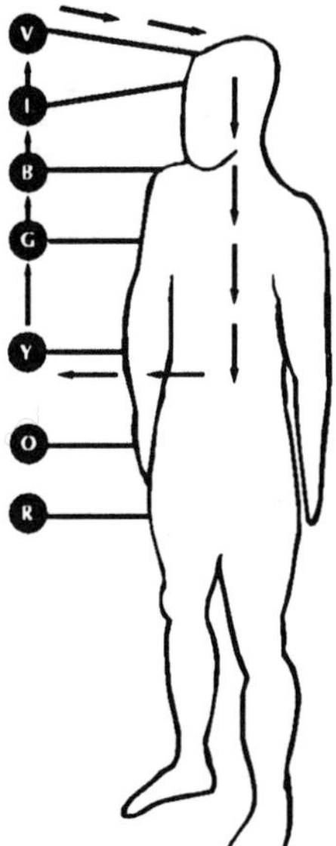

EYE EXERCISE

Inhale – Tension

Exhale – Relax

Chapter 20

Telepathy

Telepathy is the mental ability to transmit and receive thoughts from one entity to another without use of audio or video paraphernalia. Moving pictures are usually the product of thought transfer. Words are inadequate and present an insurmountable handicap. When pictures are used, language ceases to be a barrier. This *is* MAN'S mode of communication.

When one wishes to transmit thoughts to an animal of Second Density, action pictures are transmitted. This is easily recognizable to Second Density. You may note that it is more efficient to send than it is to receive, though you can learn to receive thoughts *from* your pet.

* * *

The Cortical activity must be slowed in order for the Tensor Centers to get the message across. Being open to suggestion from your Higher Self is much easier said than done. This, of course, was the prime reason for teaching the Kundalini Meditation in Volume I. In order to attune yourself with Mind and Spirit, a passive state is most desirable. This would be defined as opposite of intense concentration. Daydreaming is a form of passiveness. Incoming thought impulses are more readily noticed when the brain is relaxed and functioning smoothly and slowly, aware, but un-focused, open to suggestion, desirous of information but not desperate or feeling a sense of urgency. This is the state that you are attempting to achieve.

Employing the Thalamatic Cortical Pause is very useful while you are learning to acquire the habit of relaxing your brain. When practicing telepathy permit your thoughts to meander and drift about, something like fishing. Have a regular time allotted *each* day for your practice. Your quiet meditation time is ideal; the Kundalini is a tremendous asset. Thoughts, ideas, concepts, and solutions will filter through in such a matter-of-fact way, it may seem to you that they have always been there. You suddenly may not be able to remember a time of "not knowing it." Channeling and telepathy are the same

NOTES:

thing. The budding telepath's first contact will undoubtedly be with the Higher Self.

The Process

The process is as follows: the Higher Self receives instructive thoughts from the Soul or from other Higher Selves. This information is evaluated and passed on to the Mind which dwells within the Higher Self's Golden Spherical Complex. The Mind translates the information and via electrical impulses in the Silver Cord feeds it down to the Tensor Centers of the brain. These Tensor Centers then pass the information over to the Cortex for physical translation. An attempt to physically respond or manifest the original thought is undertaken by the personality. If the Cortex is preoccupied by deep focused thought, then the process is delayed until the Tensor Portion of your brain can find a better opportunity. Please understand, concentrated thought is not a crime; to make a waking career of it — is. Those ones who discipline themselves to extreme focused thinking during their awake time will find themselves dreaming profusely, for through the unconscious is then the only way the Mind has to inject guidance and instruction. Everybody dreams, but the Tensor Oriented personality has less need for dreams. These ones often see visions during their conscious hours.

The Cortical Centers, which is the consciousness, will not be aware of the transfer of thought from the Tensor Centers. Clarity and ease of thought will let you know when it has happened. Your intuition will be working overtime. Creative ideas and problem-solving original ideas will flow with ease. You will feel that you are teaching yourself with this unlimited supply of newly found knowledge. The learning process engulfs the Cortical Centers, as your Mentors smile.

Thinking, logic, and reason are products of the Cortex. Learning via experience committed to short-term memory, is the function of the Cortical Consciousness. The subconscious easily bridges the Tensor Centers, but not so easily as the unconsciousness. The subconscious regulates the vital automatic body functions from there. The unconscious aspect of the cortex

NOTES:

reaches the Tensor Portion via superhighways. They are so closely related that they are often construed as being one and the same. Though they are not the same, they certainly enjoy a great rapport.

Now, to confuse you and simplify this teaching, we must need remind you that the consciousness, subconscious, and the unconscious . . . are all the same thing! All are aspects of the Cortical Portion of your brain. All three parts can, and will, function in perfect harmony. When this discipline is achieved, the uniting with the 80% of the brain known as the Tensor Portion is a snap! Fourth Density MAN has accomplished this, and you can do it too. Why? Because your physical brain is identical to that of MAN. But this is only one example, the true reason is: The Law is ONE! Always remember that the results integrating of the three aspects of the Cortex will be a welcome asset to your thinking process.

The Tensor Centers never stop or rest; they work continuously. They are separate from the Cortex and do not engage in the functions indigenous to that sector of the organ. The Cortical Portion can be taught to work in harmony, in perfect harmony, with the remaining 80% of the brain. The Tensor Concepts allow the appropriate thinking to transpire that will bridge the countless synoptical nerve endings, to make this harmony possible. This is not a gift to you. You must earn it. You do it by thinking.

The Telepath

Now, back to that by-product of ESP known as telepathy. When you "hear voices" and receive messages only you are said to be clairaudiant. When you transmit as well as receive then you are a telepath. Telepathy does not work from a personality to another personality(s); it works from Mind to Mind. Actually, it works from Higher Self to Higher Self, but since there is undisputed harmony between the Mind and Higher Self, in this case, the two function as one.

The incoming thought is perceived by the Higher Self/Mind. If the thought is deemed useful and appropriate, then

NOTES:

the Mind alerts the Tensor Centers. The Tensor Centers then offer the thought to the Cortical Centers. The Cortical Centers then place the translated thought form on the current thinking path of the Cortex. The Cortex discovers the thought form and assess it. If value is ascertained action is initiated. Often the initial thought form is a symbol, such as the totem, the "call picture" of the one being called. This attracts the attention, which is usually the most difficult part — getting started. Refined transmission is often conversation. In the beginning stages, pictures, still and then moving, are a much easier way to communicate.

If the communication begins to develop "static," then it would be wise for one or both to employ the Thalamatic Cortical Pause or perhaps the Eye Exercise discussed previously, in order to further relax the brain. Excitement generates tension which causes blockages. Self-discipline, as well as patience and persistence, is called for. We caution against over complication on your part. Telepathy is simple. Avoid thinking about it too much, *just do it*.

Many Transmitters

Telepathy, now being defined as channeling, can put you in contact with entities from all over the Universe. This can be very good. It can also be hazardous to your good health. Not all entities communicating telepthically are of Love and Light, nor are they all of the same Soul Level. Your Higher Self will permit your Free Will to play a vital role in all your endeavors and will occasionally arrange for you to make certain choices as to who you talk to, and will refrain from suggestion, as you assess the material received. Always feel free to challenge your Source and feel free to "hang up" when you have had your fill. Never place yourself in a position of obligation or subjugation to an unseen entity. You are responsible for you; therefore, you are in charge of you — to have it any other way is a grave mistake.

A good way to practice telepathy, especially with your Higher Self, is to privately talk to yourself. Note your answers to your own questions. Sometimes the astute philosophy will

NOTES:

amaze you. It should be obvious that some of this did not originate in your Cortex! Keeping the emotions deactivated is the secret. The Higher Self/Mind is now flowing throughout your Cortex and a warm feeling of Love and Harmony envelopes you. If others are watching, you may be classified as demented. Take the chance; go for it! You have so much to gain as your awareness expands, and it will. You can more readily accept yourself as a vital part of our One Infinite Creator in your role as Co-Creator.

Mental Privacy

As you ponder your future living in a telepathic society, we should point out that no telepath is a Mind reader. Your mental privacy is intact and preserved. Without employing a "shield," your Higher Self can and does screen out all incoming calls and will protect you from invasion. No one can monitor your private thoughts without permission of your Higher Self. One who presumes that other selves are deeply interested in his private thoughts has an ego problem and suffers from delusions of grandeur.

Telepathy Stimulates Your Transition

Remember, you are a Mind/Body/Spirit Complex. Unify as such and operate accordingly. This is the way of MAN. The way of Love — the status that you are soon to become.

Those of Fourth Density MAN, and many other Beings even more advanced, are anxiously awaiting you to join them in a state of Brotherhood and Love. At this time, telepathy is the vehicle most likely to produce this contact and communication. Always know that you are most welcome to share their thoughts, as they willingly transmit to all.

The vibrations of the Earth Mother are rapidly changing. The New Dispensation is moving across the lands and the seas as it permeates the very air we breath. It therefore behooves you to change, as well. The Tensor Concepts will open new corridors in your brain, allowing your inhibited Mind to flow more freely. Telepathy is one of the major and vital aspects of your develop-

NOTES:

ing awareness. Thoughts coming from highly advanced minds, flood the ethers. You will be exposed to these thoughts, pictures, and concepts. As your inquisitive Mind telepathically probes for more and more mental awareness, your quest shall not be in vain. Great truths await you.

The Bridging

There is approximately 80% of your brain, known as the Tensor Portion, that never sleeps. This Tensor Portion does not think via the application of logic and reason; the remaining 20%, the Cortical Portion performs this function. Your total awareness is commonly divided into three basic divisions: the consciousness, the subconscious, and the unconscious. The last two have the Tensor Centers as their source. The waking conscious Mind is veiled from the Tensor Centers. This is normal. The idea is to become abnormal (no great feat for some of you) and bridge the communication gap between your consciousness and the Tensor Centers. Though hardly anyone does this, it is much easier than it may seem.

The Tensor Centers do not respond to stimuli encountered by the physical senses, as does the Cortical Segment of the brain. This vast area of unused mystery is always in direct contact with your Mind. Remember, your Mind does *not* dwell within your brain. Your Mind resides in the center area of the Lower Hemisphere of the Golden Sphere, which is your Higher Self. The Mind has magnificent communication with the Higher Self, which is the link to the Soul/Spirit. There are no circumstances where the Mind could possibly be in default. The problem always lies with the brain — the undeveloped brain.

As you ponder the Tensor Concepts, abstract thinking has its infant beginnings. Your use of the Kundalini Meditation concretes in any loose ends. These combined processes open up new synopsis in your brain. New electrical circuitry through the nervous system is created. The bridging between the Cortical and the Tensor Centers has its beginnings. Your conscious awareness expands, as the never before used portions of the brain begin to place their services on the line.

NOTES:

ESP And PK

There are two very basic mental functions that will begin to emerge and hopefully develop. The first is: Extrasensory Perception (ESP), and the second is: Psychokinesis (PK) — this is often referred to as telekinesis. ESP is the agent of detection. PK is that aspect of energy that causes physical action to transpire. ESP and PK are the two basic functions of the Tensor Centers, all other "phenomenon" are but derivatives of one of these two functions. Levitation and teleportation are the product of PK, clairvoyance and clairaudience are products of ESP. Clairaudiance and telepathy can be considered to be much the same. Telepathy is usually defined as transmitting and receiving, while clairaudiance is only the later.

Telepathy is not active in the sense that verbal communication is. *This is a passive exercise.* The receiver needs to be relaxed and even in a mental status of "day dreaming." The sender needs to be slightly more focused, but definitely avoiding tension or a hard, fixed thought. The received thought is *perceived,* not actually heard. The thought/idea/concept is gently placed in the path of your consciousness for your "discovery." Your Higher Self cooperates with the Higher Self of the sender/receiver, thus permitting the circuitry to be complete. Remember, the Mind dwells within the Higher Self. Therefore, transmission between Mind/Higher Self and Mind/Higher Self offers no difficulties whatsoever. The problem, if any, lies in getting the information down into the brain wherein lies the consciousness. Now, if your consciousness, via your Kundalini, is already saturating the Lower Hemisphere of the Golden Sphere, your Higher Self, and your Mind permanently resides therein — can you now perhaps begin to appreciate some of the more practical value of learning to do the *Kundalini Meditation?*

Calling Symbols

If a thought is stringently held it will not transmit. The process must be casual and passive, almost indifferent. This attitude eliminates the normal, physical five senses that initially tend to get in the way. Then how does one go about casually

NOTES:

attracting the attention of another? Essentially, this is accomplished through symbols. The calling symbol can be anything. Usually it is of some thing that the personality is familiar with and completely identifies with, such as a bird — perhaps a Redbird.

If the Redbird was your calling symbol, then another self would simply envision a Cardinal. This is an easy, gentle focus, requiring no special stress or strain. The image of a Redbird would flash across your conscious awareness. This would be similar to your telephone ringing. Someone is calling you. Symbols are received from all over the Universe. Be open to the opportunity to rejoin your true family of MAN of the Universe. This is the ecstasy of belonging.

The mark of the Adept is to be able to *gently* hold a thought for several minutes, immune to distraction. This is a discipline. It is this discipline that attracts the attention of the person being called. The thought must be held in a passive mode, lacking in intensity, but yet mildly perserverant. As circumstances permit, relax your total self, open your brain by avoiding concentration — dismiss mundania temporarily. Become passive and open to suggestion as you provide as much quiet with the absence of distraction as possible. Thoughts may now be impressed upon your consciousness. It is much easier to communicate via symbols rather than the spoken/written word, especially in the early stages. Practice makes perfect. A "conference call" can be established simply by sending out a series of call symbols such as the Redbird, then a Cat, then a Hawk, etc. When all have responded to their symbol, communication is then simultaneous and instantaneous. Distance is never a handicap.

Training Your Brain

Your physical brain is the problem. It can be trained by understanding and practicing the Tensor Concepts. The brain can be bypassed by elevating the consciousness to the Mind/Higher Self via the Kundalini. Both methods are advisable. The Kundalini cannot always be raised due to environment and circumstances. The methodical opening of the Tensor Centers is heartily

NOTES:

recommended. The bridging of the circuitry by activating and joining the Synoptical Nerve Endings is useful for many things besides telepathy. You shall eventually become multidextrous in your mental endeavors. This is a way of life for MAN, who you are soon to become. Suffice it to say you will be amazed . . .

Thought is a form created in Time/Space and indigenous to its Creator that will manifest on some probable world of reality. Thought forms create a reality of their own; be careful of your thoughts. What you think has a life of it's own. Thoughts are private in their origin but can be shared telepathically with the Universe. There is no part of Creation, physical, or otherwise, that is immune to the presence of thought. Remember: The Original Thought was: ONE. The Law is ONE.

The Light Shield

It is possible to create a barrier or shield to prevent your thoughts from being broadcast. However, this same shield will also prevent you from receiving telepathic thoughts from others. A shield is rarely used and is not necessary in any case. Third Density usually is not prone to the sharing of their private thoughts. The Yellow Ray Vibration of Emotion often does not produce beautiful thoughts worth sharing. The thought process indigenous to the Fourth Density Love Vibration is well worth sharing.

Actually, your own Higher Self monitors and controls all messages that are outgoing and incoming. As always, your Higher Self knows what it is doing and it will not permit you to be flooded with unwanted messages from dubious sources that might have a detrimental effect upon your evolution. There is no such thing as a "Mind Reader." Thoughts are shared only through the knowledge and consent of the Higher Self. The impressed thought, intuition, is your own Higher Self attempting to get through to you. This is also a form of telepathy.

Teleportation

First, relax Mind/brain by using the Thalamatic Cortical Pause exercise.

NOTES:

The object of teleportation is to transfer your entire physical self from the place where you are currently at to some other geographic local of your choice. This means that you physically will de-materialize "here" and re-materialize "there." You will be the same person "there" as you were "here." You may take with you anything that you can hold in your hands; it too shall vanish and reappear.

Through "induced teleportation," you can cause an object, animate or inanimate, to disappear "here" and to re-appear "there", or to disappear "there" and re-appear "here." Once learned, this can be incredibly useful! The use of locks, fences, and barracades will quickly become obsolete. The Law is ONE.

To accomplish this physical endeavor requires precise mental control. You teach yourself and develop this type of mental control by being observant. Practice with your current environment. Supposing you were elsewhere and wished to come "here." Mentally, you would need to envision *exactly* how your current area looked. The exactness of everything in your vicinity must be mentally imagined in absolute accuracy. As your mental image, or thought form, achieves greater and greater accuracy, up to twenty seven decimal places, then teleportation is instantaneous.

The mechanics require that you atomically de-materialize at your present locale, enter into the etheric, Time/Space, travel to your chosen destination, re-materialize in the physical, Space/Time. There are no barriers or obstacles, physical or non-physical, that can prevent or distort this happening. It is an ideal way to remove oneself from jail. You may define "jail" any way that you are comfortable.

The Key

Your ability to observe in minute detail, and then remember very accurately what you've seen, are the prime factors in making teleportation work. The destination locale must be visualized in impeccably fine detail, so that an atomic rapport is bridged from your own mentality to the vibration of that

NOTES:

designated place. Attunement to twenty seven decimal places is indeed *fine tuning!* This is not beyond your mental ability or capacity — at present, it probably is; however, you can learn by practicing. Look about yourself right now. If you had to form a mental image of this place sometime later what would you see? Would you remember *all* the details? Would your memory accurately serve you? At first it probably wouldn't, but with practice you can indeed learn. *Learn to see and learn to remember what you saw. That is the process.*

Time Travel

A word of caution: when practicing teleportation, we suggest that your attempts be relegated from one room to another. We further suggest that you practice in private or very select company. This is a startling phenomenon for the uninitiated Third Density personality to witness. If you are attempting to teleportate for some great distance, be advised to have bus fare in your pockets and be dressed appropriately to deal with the environment of your selected destination. You may be so astounded, that you will completely forget how to teleportate back! Another type of caution: If your destination is remembered from scenes of childhood, then the "woods" that you remembered from yesteryear may today be a condominium or even a dump! To suddenly materialize in some unsuspecting Third Density Entity's living room or bedroom is courting an opportunity to get shot! Furthermore, if you perchance get the atomic vibrational pattern correlated "just right," you could actually return to the "woods" of your childhood, just as it was! This is time travel into the past. One can also physically visit the probable future in this manner. Teleportation through time is *not* recommended for the novice. We suggest that you be less ambitious in your beginning stages.

As you create the thought form of your destination, attention to detail is the key! This image is created in a "scene" in front of your face. The Indigo Ray is the tool. When the rapport between the atomic and molecular patterns of that locale is incorporated within your developing thought form image, to

NOTES:

twenty seven decimal places, then teleportation is instantaneous. Prepare yourself mentally to be ready and willing to make the trip. As you become more and more proficient in your observations and in exercising your memory for total and instant recall, teleportation becomes a snap. It is a "way of life" for Fourth Density MAN. Third Density Humans don't do it much. The difference being that MAN is Tensor Oriented. Which means that he has tapped into and is utilizing, to some degree, the Tensor Portion of his brain. Third Density Humans and Fourth Density MAN have the same Tensor Portion in their brains. Third Density Entities could accomplish these things just as readily as Fourth Density Entities if they would only be open to the possibility that such things do indeed exist and then somehow become aware of it. The Light of Knowledge inspires spiritual evolution. Ignorance is not bliss.

* * *

Teleportation allows the personality to move at will, automatically from one point to another on the surface of a Planet, or to other Planets in the Galaxy, or within this Solar System or from Planet to Spacecraft and reverse. Also from moving Craft to moving Craft is possible — with use of calculated care!

Animals Do It

The limited perception of Second Density animals, as well as the higher forms of plant life, also have the learned ability to teleport! It is true that the negative radiation of our defective Sun has inhibited this practice for Earth's Second Density but they are not without this talent and on other "normal" Second Density Planets, this is a common practice. If the squirrels in the trees and the cat on your lap can manage to teleportate, then is it beyond you to do it also? Think on it; we are not discussing the impossible. Notice as your pet sleeps and dreams — how the body twitches. They are experiencing out-of-body phenomenon. Project your consciousness into and incorporate it with that of the animal. — and prepare yourself for a

NOTES:

thrilling experience of distorted black and white animated pictures.

A conveyance of transportation is not mandatory in order to move your physical body from one place to another. Your Mind can readily perform this task. You may teleport yourself to any place that you can visualize. Once the procedure is accepted to the conscious Mind, the action becomes automatic. Initially, the greatest hurdle to overcome is the mental acceptance that this is not impossible.

Re-Visit The Past

"Time Travel" is accomplished via teleportation. You can mentally and physically project yourself to any place, past, present, or future that you can envision. This is an excellent method of correcting past errors or checking out the future to ascertain if your current path is appropriate. Psychics are capable of performing this endeavor, mentally, not physically. This is good practice. Psychic abilities are the by-products of ESP. Teleportation is a by-product of PK or Psychokinesis (Telekenisis).

Before teleportation may be accepted and employed, it is essential that you fully realize that your *consciousness* dwells within your brain, while the *Mind* dwells outside the body within the Golden Sphere, your Higher Self. Your Mind is the agent of cause that produces the effect — teleportation. The consciousness and the Mind must get together if ESP or PK is to be successful. Projecting the consciousness up to meet the Mind is next to impossible for the Third Density Human. This built-in obstacle can readily be overcome through the use of the Kundalini Meditation. This is one of the reasons that we taught it in Volume I — did you learn it?

Types Of Teleportation

There are two types of teleportation: Local and Inter-Planetary. Local travel does not require the use of the Serial Universes to advance time in order to compensate for the vast distances. Inter-Planetary or even Inter-Galactic travel, do not

NOTES:

require it either. Only physical Spacecraft must need employ the different values of the Planck Constant and capitalize on them in future time for the sake of travel.

Teleportation is accomplished by thought alone. You can travel anywhere in the Universe in the length of time it takes you to think about it.

Before travel is attempted to an unfamiliar site, local or Inter-Planetary, it is wise to first Astral Project to that place and check it out. Your physical body may not be able to service you in its current condition, due to alien, adverse environment. It is highly recommended that you confine your experimentation to this Planet, or better still, to your own neighborhood.

Your Mind is capable of instructing your brain even as your Higher Self offers instruction to your Mind. The Thalamatic Cortical Pause is a technique that opens the doors to this instruction. Mental activity such as practicing teleportation accomplishes wonders in developing the brain, as the new Synoptical Connectors are made.

Those ones of Fourth Density who use these methods consistently, are standing by, willing and able, to assist you in your endeavors. Do not be afraid. You too shall soon be a member of the family of MAN and you are preparing yourself for that great day right now. Think! Always think. Never pass up an opportunity to think. These Tensor Concepts should be an inspiration. If you perchance teleport yourself into an alien environment, MAN will be on hand to assist you in creating a bubble of environment similar to your native Earth, so that you shall not perish. These are the teachings of MAN, he is your mentor, and as such it is his honor/duty to quietly stand by your side, visible or invisible, to offer the necessary aid. However, *you* must initiate the action. It is *you* who is the seeker. It is you who must need to learn. MAN is your most competent aide.

Levitation

Simply put, levitation means to raise an object or yourself and move it to another place. Unlike teleportation, the

NOTES:

object does not disappear "here" and reappear "there." Using levitation, the object or self is constantly physical.

To raise any object, three major factors are to be considered. First there is the *Mass,* which is the object itself. Second, there is the necessary acceleration of movement, which alters the stationary or resting status of the mass to be moved. *Inertia* must be overcome to commence the movement. Thirdly, there is the matter of *gravity* that must be dealt with and overcome.

The problem, as stated, would be acceptable to any physicist. However, the science of physics in this area may now be completely disregarded. The three basic factors: Mass, Inertia, and Gravity cannot be overcome by your brain. They can be influenced to respond to the desires of your Will. This "influencing power" is: Love. Remember, Love is Intelligent Energy. Love's twin is Intelligent Infinity, which is Light. Try to remember this as often as possible. It is a necessary habit to get into.

Now, the personality does not have the total ability to utilize Light and Love, but your Higher Self does. The secret is: To establish a good communication rapport with your own Higher Self. How do you do this? By using the Kundalini Meditation, of course! You learned how to make conscious contact with your Higher Self in Volume I of *The Teachings . . .* did you not? Always raise your Kundalini and establish a good contact with your Higher Self *before* attempting any kind of "psychic phenomenon." The at oneness with self is essential.

The Higher Self

The energy needed to influence the mass to perform in the way you require comes from the Higher Self. The energy is Love. The personality is not devoid of Love, but the personality does not have access to all forms of this Intelligent Energy. The Higher Self does. Two-way communication with the Higher Self promotes this cooperation to achieve the desired results. The lower self (the personality) makes his wishes known via Kundalini communication, and the Higher Self responds by cooperat-

NOTES:

ing, unless there is a very good reason why this should not happen at this time. Usually the denial of cooperation would be invoked if the Free Will of another is being infringed upon or if the Positive Personality is using this as a method to serve self.

You have the right to summon the Light;-feel free to do so. You have the duty to grow and evolve and enjoy the fascinating discoveries this entails. Cooperate with your Higher Self and participate in the fullness that life/experiences have to offer. Seek out the Joy, Love, and the Knowledges/Wisdom of Light. Practice using Light and Love in the form of levitation if you wish, but also make it a conscious part of your everyday living. Direct the Light via your mental processes combined with your Higher Self. This is not something that you do on special occasions; you should do this all of the time.

When you are comfortable with this Tensor Orientation, then the physical laws or properties of Mass, Inertia, and Gravity no longer will be the insurmountable issue. These concerns are physical and the physical reality is an *illusion!* Try to remember that!

When this is achieved, then you simply consider the thought that you are no longer standing here but you are rising up, a few miles or many feet, and because you considered it and because your Higher Self invoked it you are rising — you are levitating! Your Mind can really control your movements while in the state of levitation.

You are a Mind/Body/Spirit Complex. This unity, this at oneness with self, invoking the Second and Third Creative forces of our One Infinite Creator, makes all things possible. See through the illusion created by men and rise above it!

Moving Objects

The moving of inanimate matter utilizes forces that are not *of* the Mind. The Mind, which does not dwell in the brain, accepts these appropriate energies, converts them to the vibrational frequency of Space/Time, and then focuses that energy upon the object chosen to be moved or levitated. This is not a difficult thing to learn.

NOTES:

The power of levitation is not the power that propels Spacecraft. Spacecraft have a force field mechanically created about themselves that not only protects them from collision with each other but from all physical debris. This force field dissipates energy in a fashion that permits the Craft to exceed the speed of Light. This special force field alters the atomic structure of Space about itself as it penetrates the subtle layers of matter native to the Etheric Planes. This produces travel in Time/Space at fantastic speeds. A form of Light is used to achieve this. Levitation also uses a form of the Light to move physical objects "with the Mind." These are two different forms of Light usage and should not be confused. Levitation is not to be seen as part of teleportation. Physical objects, as well as self, can be caused to atomically disappear "here" and reconstruct "there," by Mind alone. This is a different discipline than levitation. Telekenisis is another term used to describe levitation.

Psychokinesis — How To Levitate

Use the Thalamatic Cortical Pause to relax and empty the Mind. Calm your Mind; think of nothing at all. The Kundalini should be raised and contact with your Higher Self established; this will help in controlling and relaxing the Mind. Residue emotions and fleeting images are always distracting factors that will cause you to exercise a great deal of discipline in order to overcome. When you feel that you have relaxed your Mind to maximum *then* attempt the exercise. This initial process is necessary regardless of the nature of your selected exercise. These exercises will activate the Synoptical Nerve Connectors in the Tensor Portion of your brain and bridge them to the Cortical Centers. This is how the necessary new circuitry is developed.

Your first attempt, or your first several attempts, are not likely to be all that rewarding. Be patient and persistent. It takes a while for the Mind to develop the brain to perform these physical functions that are often considered to be phenomenons. Training and conditioning are important. Your Higher Self will not permit any results to take place until the personality is mentally — emotionally capable of accepting and dealing with all

NOTES:

that he has wrought. Practice, then practice some more. When the time is right — it will happen.

The Swirling Mass Of Green Light

This is an exercise for performing that aspect of Psychokinesis called *levitation.* Though not mandatory, we suggest that you raise your Kundalini. Relax and empty your Mind. Release all thought patterns as best you can. When you are ready, envision a shaft of Emerald Green Ray coming into your Heart Chakra. Bring the Green Ray up your spinal cord to your Indigo Chakra — inside the skull. Now create a swirling Mass of Green about the size of a golf ball at the front of your brain, just behind your forehead. This swirling Green Mass consists of millions of atoms. The swirling part is made up of the countless electrons rapidly orbiting this nuclei. Envision the Green Ball as pulsating and becoming brighter and brighter. Get comfortable with this activity. Continue for two or three minutes.

Use The Indigo Chakra

Next, project this Swirling Green Ball out of your head via the stem of the Indigo Chakra. Place the ball a foot or so *beyond* the chakra (flower) itself and hold it there. Now, increase the size of the rapidly swirling mass of Emerald Green which is pulsating brightly. Cause it to increase to the size of a basketball. Maintain its integrity. Hold this image for a couple of minutes.

Next, project this basketball sized mass onto the object to be levitated. Use the Indigo Beam emitting from the Third Eye Chakra to guide the Mass to the appropriate place. The Second Chakra is one of the three transmitting chakras, remember? If the object to be levitated is larger than the basketball, increase the size of the swirling Mass at this time. Saturate the object with this special Green Light Force. Mentally request that the gravitational field of the object be reduced to zero. Remember: each of the swirling electrons is a miniature electro-magnet. As the gravitational field of the object is reduced and eliminated, that energy is immediately replaced with the guided force field of Green Ray.

NOTES:

The object will now float or drift, free of Earth's gravity. Mental effort, using *other* forces, can easily maneuver the object floating in the air. The force known as Coriolis permits lateral movement, and you mentally direct it. Centrifugal Force keeps the object aloft as long as you mentally keep the swirling Green Mass active. To cause the levitated object to continue to rise, simply increase the swirling speed of the Green Mass. To cause it to settle down, decrease the Centrifugal Speed. Move the levitated object laterally with your eyes. Do the same for yourself, if you are the levitated object. When the object is relocated to your satisfaction, simply quit thinking about it and it will remain securely in place. Practice, practice, practice! It is actually much easier to learn than the playing of the guitar, for example. In fifteen minutes you can be shown everything you need to know, but it will take you the rest of your life to learn it! Levitation can be grasped much quicker.

Levitating Yourself

Now, if you wish to levitate yourself, simply take the basketball-sized Mass of swirling Green electrons and mentally, via the Indigo Ray, project the Ball under your feet. Maintaining your balance will then become your greatest problem. Whether or not you are levitating yourself on an object, keep the Green Ball enforced with a continuous flowing of Green Ray being transmitted from the Indigo Chakra.

How It Works

Your Mind in conjunction with your Higher Self, allows this to happen. The Mind then activates the brain — this is where the physicality sets in. The Tensor Centers then serve as a conductor or converger of the Green Ray Energy. The required energy comes from *without*. The only energy that you supply is the mental energy to direct the show. The brain must be relaxed in order for this Green Ray Love Energy to flow through you unabated. If there are distractions or blockages, then the object will fall — if it rises at all. A clean, free flow of Love Energy is the ultimate in success. This is achieved through a practiced

NOTES:

Positive attitude. This attitude is augmented through the use of the Kundalini Meditation. In so doing, you are practicing and accelerating evolution.

The process of levitation can be calculated using equations. We will not go into explicit detail at this time. It is sufficient to note that levitation and other feats of Psychokinesis can be readily performed without any knowledge of mathematics whatsoever.

For those of you who are Physicists, we would suggest that you refer to the Planck Constant and how this theory would relate to the level of energy in the Universe. Then, note how the Mind can attune to the different values of the Planck Constant. The energy level has not been changed, whether we speak of the Universe or the object to be moved. The Mind, acting as a physical converter of Green Ray Energy, selects a specific value of that Love Energy to perform a specific task.

Heisenberg's "probability pockets," involving matrix calculus, indicates that electrons tend to behave like thought. Now, if the synoptical bridging does not take place within a given series of incarnations, then the forthcoming personality operates entirely in the Cortical Centers of his brain. This perfects practice as it denies theory. If the personality dwells solely in the Tensor Centers, then the opposite is true. The happy solution is to bridge the Cortical Centers with the Tensor Centers to establish and maintain a reasonable balance. Forever you will be balancing something with something else.

Energy must be expended, in some way, to move any object. Energy may be deployed physically or mentally. When an object rotates on an axis, an electromagnetic field is created. When that object is a Planet, that field is called gravity. The newly created swirling mass of electrons gradually reduces the gravitational force to point zero. The atoms comprising that object are most willing to cooperate with your wishes because: atoms are energy. Energy is intelligent. Intelligent Energy is — Love. Love is the Green Ray — *that's* the "value" of the Constant Green Ray that you are employing.

NOTES:

So that you do not become discouraged, we would like to point out that we have yet to meet a physicist who could perform levitation. It is not uncommon to get bogged down in theory to the point where practice becomes a non-virtue.

Summary

The Tensor Concepts, by whatever name, are designed in a way to cause you to think. A grasp of abstract total thinking is essential for the entity to graduate from Third Density to Fourth Density. These concepts are as old as Creation itself. Certain ones of the Confederation of MAN have translated these concepts into the English language and have incorporated them around the modern day vernacular. This modernized information is available to all who are able to penetrate Intelligent Infinity or perhaps are fortunate enough to channel those ones of MAN who are the designated teachers for this very special material.

It has been our honor/duty to present to you our distortion (our understanding) of the Tensor Concepts. Our objective was to simplify and clarify the thought process for your ease in understanding. If we have succeeded, then we are thrilled. If we have failed, then we humbly apologize. If the latter be the case, then we sincerely recommend that you seek the Tensor Concept information from a source of your choice, for it is most essential that you learn to open up and use the Tensor Portion of your brain.

The Third Density Vibration is not ideal for you to become prolific in the activation and use of your Tensor Centers; however, it is not so opaque that a good healthy beginning cannot be achieved. To entice you to begin and practice . . . and practice . . . and practice is our aim. This, along with the teaching of the Kundalini Meditation, is the Will of the Lord of the Earth. As teachers of same, we are but humble servants of those ones who are conducting the great Harvest.

To be Harvested alive requires a comfortable foothold in abstract thinking, otherwise the shock value of Fourth Density would be much too traumatic for your nervous system. The practice of the Tensor Concepts is your conditioning tool as you

NOTES:

quietly prepare yourself for that glorious day. The secret is: *to Think!* Think about everything. Who, what, when, where, why, and how — are questions that you should ask about everything. Delve into the unknown as well as into mundania — and with a zest! Your Mind is in excellent condition; it's that brain of yours that needs to be stimulated. Only *you* can give it a kick in the pants!

ESP and PK are simply functions of Universal Laws, Laws designed by our One Infinite Creator. Like the Easter Egg, you must first discover it before you may partake of it. There are no miracles. There is only Light and Love. These twins can produce events that obliterate common miracles. Intelligent Infinity/Intelligent Energy are yours for the asking. But first you must achieve knowledge, and with knowledge you acquire wisdom, and with wisdom you obtain understanding, and with understanding Enlightenment is your reward. Think! Exercise your brain! The future of your evolution depends upon it!

Conclusion

You shall now prepare to lower the Kundalini. Bring the White Light of the Kundalini up around yourself and gather it into an object over your head. As you do so, pull the Violet Dome next to your body. Now, bring the Kundalini in its entirety into the crown of your head as you detach your consciousness. Begin the descent, de-activating each chakra as we give the color count down: Violet . . Indigo. . Blue . . Green . . Yellow . . Orange . . Red. Put the Kundalini to rest and shut the door. Breath deeply.

Now, our Prayer of Protection: "In the name of the Presence and the Power Universal, protect us from harm and all Unenlightened Spirits, and may the Light of our Spirit Guides and the Light of our Higher Selves illuminate our thoughts that we might reflect the Radiant Glory of ALL THAT IS."

We leave you now in the Light and Love of our One Infinite Creator. Go forth in the joy of life and in the service to others.

Adonai. Adonai, Vasu Barragus, Adonai.

Section VI

Conversations With The Chief

Chapter 21

Commerce

Examining the ramifications of commerce as it affects the evolutionary process of our Aryan Root Race. The Negative impact of empowered money has enhanced the greed in Third Density Humans to the point where slavery to commerce becomes more desirable than Spiritual growth.

Chapter 22

Religion

The Negative influence that many religions have over the peoples of the World are examined from a bias rarely taken by one in human form. The startling effect that Christianity has had upon the United States, and the resulting impact the United States has perpetrated upon the World, provides thoughts uncommon to the western mind.

Chapter 23

Governments

Governments, though prospering, are obsolete. The heyday of big government is rapidly coming to an end. The willing slaves are no longer so willing. Like all organizations, governments are Negative. Their bloated obesity renders them unable to function for the benefit of the masses. Their demise is imminent.

Chapter 24

The Social Product

The results of the effects of commerce, religion, and government upon the people have produced the Mass Consciousness, the current and final phase of this Aryan Root Race. We are the product of our own making. We can choose our future. The power lies in the Present.

Chapter 21

We greet you in the Light and Love of our One Infinite Creator. We are Chief Little Summer and Warm Night Rain.

Let us begin this section with the chant:

"I am That I am, Ayeh,
I am that I am, Ayeh,
I am that I am, Ayeh,
I am that I am, Ayeh,
I am that I am, Ayeh,
I am that I am, Ayeh,
I am that I am, Ayeh,
A-yeh,
A-Yeh,
A-Yeh,
A-Yeh,
A-Yeh."

Our Prayer of Protection: "In the name of the Presence and the Power Universal, protect us from harm and all Unenlightened Spirits, and may the Light of our Spirit Guides and the Light of our Higher Selves illuminate our thoughts that we might reflect the Radiant Glory of ALL THAT IS."

* * *

Now, for those of you whose schedules permit, let us prepare to raise the Kundalini at this time. You should be thoroughly familiar with the procedure at this point. We shall assist you in raising through the use of the color countdown. Every function of a given chakra color is known to you in the sequence inwhich it is given. Let us begin. Make yourself comfortable, back straight. Align and balance the chakras . . . awaken the Kundalini . . . activate the Red . . . Orange . . . Yellow . . . Green . . . Blue . . . Indigo . . . Violet . . . With your consciousness attached, visualize the Kundalini, bathing the lower half of the Golden Sphere, which is your Higher Self. The flowing Kundalini falls down all around your body, which is protected by the aura of seven domes. Firmly establish the contact with your Higher Self and when you are ready, begin to read.

NOTES:

* * *

This section deals with the three determining factors that constitute the Third Density Ayran Root Race Experience. Commerce, Religion, Governments, and the product that has been produced is examined from a perspective rarely voiced in the World today. The student's (Chela) questions are indicative of the subject at hand. The responses employ a greater spectrum.

The candid responses may startle you, as an unaccustomed point of view is elaborated upon. We ask that you not be quick to draw conclusions; but rather, be open to suggestion as you read and evaluate the concepts. Later, as you ponder these thoughts in the company of your Higher Self, accept those portions which you are comfortable with and set aside that which you are not. As always, use your Free Will to strike a balance within yourself that you are comfortable with.

We further ask that you remember: we choose to deal with root causes and do not entertain symptoms. All true healings are accomplished in this fashion.

* * *

"Commerce"

Chief: "We greet you in the Light and Love of our One Infinite Creator. The subject is commerce. We appreciate the opportunity that you have given us to express our views on this international subject."

Chela: "In the past, Chief, you have often criticized commerce in a very detrimental way. Since commerce is worldwide and everybody is engaged in it one way or another, is your opinion of the people the same as your view of the activity which they practice?"

Chief: "Essentially no, although there are always exceptions to any rule. By and large, all peoples must embrace commerce in order to survive. Economic survival coincides with physical survival as affairs are conducted on the Planet Earth today. Commerce is the prime vehicle that the Mass Consciousness of this Aryan Root Race has chosen to experience the interaction between self and other selves. There were other choices; this one was selected."

Chela: "Do you feel that commerce was a bad choice?"

Chief: "Yes and no. We do not wish to appear to be hedging or to be deliberately obscure, but over the past 11,600 years both answers have been correct. In the beginning of this Root Race, after the final sinking of Atlantis, commerce had its infant beginnings in the form of barter. This System proved to be most useful to Third Density Humans in furthering the understanding of self, and via reaction, the other self. Much was learned.

Hostility, envy, greed, as well as compassion, sharing, service to others were produced. Commerce proved to be a vehicle that could bring out the best and the worst in a person. It was good. It was very useful."

Chela: "Commerce still does that, does it not?"

Chief: "Yes, of course. However, today, it becomes a bit more complex. The determining factor in this complexity lie . . . in the introduction of money about 3,000 years ago. Prior to that, commerce was negotiated in some form of barter. Now, with the introduction of money into the System, the concept of value was being established. Economic laws were being developed. Standards, rules, and laws were forthcoming."

Chela: "Was this wrong? Does not commerce and business need to be organized and regulated?"

Chief: "This in itself is not wrong at all, in fact, it is most useful and highly practical. We might further add that money, as a medium of exchange, does not have to be Negative. The problem lies in the unmitigated *power* of money. Money has not always enjoyed the immense power that it has today."

Chela: "You speak like there is a special power that money has. Could you elaborate, Chief?"

Chief: "We shall try. Orion, as you know, seizes upon every available opportunity to capitalize on teaching service to self. In Third Density, greed is a most useful tool. A few centuries after money was invented in Egypt, those of Orion came forth and invoked raw power upon money. This power was

NOTES:

given no instructions, specifying no purpose. Prior to this, Orion had done as much for stone edifices, such as those on Easter Island, for example. The outcome was, of course, predictable. Third Density greed can readily be provoked and stimulated beyond "normal needs." With sufficient money, one could do or be anything. The acquisition of same became a goal or even a conquest for those who were learning to manipulate. For the first time the "haves and the "have nots," the masters and the slaves, came into being. The Aryan Root Race now had its focus."

Chela: "Then, Orion is to blame for all our problems and shortcomings with commerce?"

Chief: "Not necessarily; it probably would have happened anyway. Orion simply guaranteed it.

Chela: I see money as a useful agent for us to know ourselves and our other selves. Everything has a price. If the money is right, anything goes. Nothing is sacred if the price is right."

Chief: "Unfortunately, you are correct. Survival of the fittest is the prime law of Planet Earth. The survival instinct is strong in all species. In modern times "survival" is defined as *economic survival.* As such, greed is often substituted for survival. As one person's greed provides employment for survival, this greedy person is then seen as a benefactor for all the "good" he is doing for a group of "poor people" who didn't have jobs before he came along. Thus, the employers antics are tolerated because of all the "good" he is doing."

Chela: "What do you mean by antics?"

Chief: "Specifically, the wanton and willful destruction of First and Second Density. The exploitation of First, Second, and Third Density through the creation of a System that Third Density willfully submit themselves in slavery, as an accepted way of life, so that they might survive, is the ploy. This, of course, is strictly in accordance with the Negative Tenets sponsored by Orion. The Hierarchy doles out enough money to its "slaves," so that they do not confuse themselves with chattel. This causes them to compete against each other to *earn* their

NOTES:

dollar, and the masters smile all the way to the bank — which they own too."

If commerce incorporates the concept of "profit" and uses a form of money as a medium of exchange, then First and Second Densities shall suffer severe and adverse effects/results. This is the general plan laid down by Orion. Greed permits it to function quite handsomely, while Third Density systematically destroys itself. No Earthly power can alter our course. We have created our own Reality. America leads and the World follows. Capitalism is the tool of Shiva, The Destroyer.

Chela: "But Chief, we have free enterprise. Anybody can get to the top if they want to work at it."

Chief: "This is a deliberate misconception. True, those in the ranks can and sometimes do rise above their station and reach to the stars. This is permitted. Occasional minor successes are not only tolerated, they are encouraged. They establish integrity within the System. However, if the entrepreneur becomes too successful, then the Hierarchy, bands together to destroy the enterprise. This is usually accomplished by the "buying out" procedure, though harsher and more violent methods are not unknown. The euntropenour is then willingly *forced* into early retirement with a lavish income. The threat is over for the Hierarchy while his peers are green with envy. Sufficient laws of extreme complexity are enacted to discourage the "average" person from breaking out of the status quo condition. Willing slaves are a valuable asset."

Chela: "There are some of us who realize what you are saying is true. We would like to break out and get away from the System. How can we do this? Is there a way?"

Chief: "If a formula existed, we would be pleased to share it with you. "You can run, but you cannot hide" is an old saying that is most appropriate. The Mass Consciousness, the Root Race, freely determines the direction that civilization is to take. Commerce in its current and developing form shall remain intact until a great majority of the Planet's population chooses to do something different."

Chela: "Will this ever be, Chief?"

NOTES:

Chief: "No. The addiction to monetary economic slavery is complete. There is no desire nor ambition to change. The Hierarchy would starve out the slaves, *their* barns are full. The workers/slaves are not able to survive in any other type of System. The Great Depression of the 1930's established this. Adults are *not* prone to sacrifice themselves for the betterment of their great-grandchildren. The major Capitalistic Nations do not subscribe to reincarnation, and therefore can see no profit in dealing with a future much beyond their own longevity. The sacrifice would be too great. It is best to learn to cope within the System and survive as comfortably as possible."

Chela: "Then there is nothing we can do about it, is that right?"

Chief: "There are not enough of you "dissenters" to sway the Mass Thinking or to do battle with the Orion Hierarchy. We suggest that you embrace the System for the catalyst it offers; but, do not *join* it."

Chela: "Commerce is destroying and polluting First and Second Density. Scientists have reported that 500 species have become extinct during the final twenty years of this century. This will include virtually all of marine mammals. The Caterpillar tractor gobbles up Rain Forests by the thousands of acres per day, per hour even, and this obviously cannot continue for any great length of time until they are all gone. Why can't the people see this and cease and desist?"

Chief: "Many do see it and they are concerned, they are frightened, and they are angry. But to suggest that people of a Third World Country cease harvesting twigs and branches, turning them into charcoal to sell for pennies, so that they might buy beans and rice, even though the process causes their once beautiful and fertile hills to erode and wash down into the bay to be lost forever, is not something we could comfortably recommend. We who are fat and comfortable in our fine homes cannot say to another man, quit seining the minnows from your pond; let them grow to a large size and then harvest them; this will only take a few years, in the meantime, you and your family can starve to death. Survival is the determining factor."

NOTES:

Chela: "But now we are talking about overpopulation, are we not?"

Chief: "Yes, to be sure. However, they go hand in hand. The Orion Hierarchy needs slaves at all times, especially when a war is deemed to be profitable. Cannon fodder is every bit as essential as is the mud, when it comes to waging a war. There must always be a surplus of people to consume. A large body count justifies the great expenditures of the mighty war machine — the defense contractors, which the slaves support via taxes, and also with their life blood, income via employment. Would the employees of the defense industry be relieved if all the companies were to suddenly shut down? Hardly! Yet, these very workers/slaves would be quick to tell the fellow in Bangladesh to quit seining his pond, or the Haitian father to quit pulling up seedlings for charcoal."

Chela: "The reports state that Denmark, Japan, and Mexico are the ones who are exterminating the mammals from the oceans. Are these the countries that are responsible for the raping and ravaging of our Earth Mother and the destruction of Second Density?"

Chief: "No. They are factors, even as many, many other countries are also factors, but they singularly or collectively are *not* responsible."

Chela: "Then who is responsible?"

Chief: "The entity that you know as the United States of America."

Chela: "Oh, come now Chief, the U.S. is certainly and unquestionably the most powerful Nation on Earth, but to say that she is totally responsible for all the Earth's woes isn't that a bit overstated?"

Chief: "An in-depth search shall show the answers to be correct. Directly or indirectly, the Americans are totally responsible."

"If the American is not directly involved with the action of rape and plunder, then he hires, coerces, or obligates those indigenous to a locale to do it for him. When Third World Countries are tempted with the dollar and what it will buy they

NOTES:

can be persuaded into doing the bidding of the Hierarchy of Commerce. If this persuasion should fail, then the world's mightiest military machine begins to flex its muscles, and the victim is threatened with oblivion via bombing. The U.S. has proven its capacity to destroy any designated friend or foe."

Chela: "The United States would invade a country only if their Human Rights had been violated. That is the reason, and not commerce."

Chief: "We invite you to look closely at the Kuwaiti War. Human Rights were indeed the announced issue and became the battle cry. Look at Kuwait and Iraq since the War closed. Are the peoples now so much better off? Has their social/economic conditions that were so terrible been elevated? Are those people better off because the United States waged a War on their homeland? Then, check the resumed flow of oil needed to satisfy the glutinous appetite of the Americans. Note how the other Arab oil-producing nations refrain from making any kind of waves that might possibly be offensive to America.

Look into the situation regarding Panama and Nicaragua; the deplorable conditions of the people were cited as the noble reason to invade. After the troops pulled out and returned home, the peoples were much worse off than they were before the Americans came in to save them. But America got what *it* wanted!

If you were to check for the underlying motive for America's engagement in any type of military activity since World War II you would find that it was indeed inspired by the Hierarchy of commerce which is heavily staffed by Americans."

Chela: "Then the Hierarchy is constituted of others besides Americans . . . ?"

Chief: "Yes, of course. But the vast majority are Americans."

Chela: "How do you arrive at this conclusion?"

Chief: "The United States comprises about fifteen percent of the World's population. It *consumes* seventy percent of the World's resources."

NOTES:

Chela: "Yes, you have made your point. In consuming the World's resources, a great deal of waste is generated, even in a place where disposal is a major problem. Do you suggest that we be more saving and recycle the waste?"

Chief: "Nature abhors waste. This is Universal Law. By all means save and be prudent. Recycling is most useful, for it reduces further depletion of First and Second Density and it also reduces the mountain of refuse."

Chela: "Then, this could actually make a difference in saving First and Second Density?

Chief: "No, it is a most noble practice, but will only result in prolonging the agony. This is not bad, however, for unique catalysts are offered under these peculiar conditions and valuable lessons are readily offered and perhaps learned."

Chela: "Then, by and large, the people/slaves, even the Americans, are victims of greed and they lack the courage to alter the System — is this correct?"

Chief: "Generally speaking, yes. The people are taught greed via psychological designed advertising. A product is promoted in such a skillful way that the consumer is hit with an instant case of the "wants." This is how business is created, and it promotes flow. Nothing happens until somebody sells something. After that, the dominoes fall in a prescribed path. Sometimes the product is described as one that we cannot possibly live without. The automobile is such a case. It is most difficult to function in this culture without an automobile.

Your Higher Self instills within your consciousness the courage to rebel, to take the radio out of the ears, and dare listen to the beat of a different drummer. This will probably get you some personal attention, and perhaps that could be useful. As far as it altering the economy, that is highly unlikely. Personally, I have not owned a car since 1964. I cannot see where my disdain for this product has had much of an impact on the automotive industry."

Chela: "If a large group of us were to abandon the automobile and partake of the bicycle do you think we could

NOTES:

make any noticeable effect? Could we begin a movement — a grassroots movement?"

Chief: "You have the Free Will to attempt anything that you can think of. The publicity of a large number of you taking to the streets on bicycles would be a delight to the news media and they would profit. The results would be that sides would be drawn, and physical as well as verbal battles would ensue. The bicyclists would be branded the rebels, and the automobile drivers would insist, nay, *demand* that conformity be enforced — for safety's sake, of course. If the rebels persisted, designated areas for riding bicycles would be set aside. These areas would be so designed that the cyclists couldn't actually go anywhere to accomplish anything utilitarian. The bicyclists would still be obliged to maintain an automobile in order to survive. The manufacturers of automobiles and bicycles would laugh all the way to the bank!"

Chela: "Then that's not a good idea to change the System? We would always be doomed to defeat if we tried?"

Chief: "The power lies in the accumulation of monies. The Hierarchy has this, the "lower-archy" does not. If any major changes are forthcoming, it shall be because the Hierarchy deemed it necessary. They would do this only if it were profitable for them to do so. If a resource has been exhausted, then the products of that resource will be phased out and replaced with another product similar in nature but considerably more expensive. The dependent people/slaves will have no choice but to buy it. The appropriate advertising will make this transition much more palatable. Your personal efforts to correct a wrong, in your opinion, will result in satisfaction to self only. Perhaps this is the most important aspect after all. This "wrong" that you are avoiding permits you to know yourself differently and better. Others become knowledgeable of your altered appearance and their reaction to the "new you" gives you a new insight into them. Now, the prime motivation of this Root Race is being used to its intended maximum.

NOTES:

Yes, it is *always* a good idea to try to change the System, but not to be too disappointed at your seeming lack of physical success."

Chela: "The idea then, is to take commerce and find favor with it, or find fault with it, but see it as a catalytic agent that causes us to understand ourselves and our other selves better and better."

Chief: "This is correct. To indifferently accept commerce as "normal" is to defeat this great teacher. This is identifying.

Chela: "Do all Third Density Entities experience commerce as we are doing now?"

Chief: "No. In the Root Races prior to this one there were forms of commerce. These Systems of commerce were not based on money, nor was the concept of profit instilled within the System."

Chela: "How could you have commerce without profit?"

Chief: "Profit is our incentive to promote trade. Sharing through Love will produce the same results. To produce an item and bestow that item as a gift is a token of Love. If the recipient were to offer an item/gift in return, then a form of barter would have been established. If value, or worth, or price is attached to either of the items, then the concept of profit appears. If one item has more worth than the other, then a supplement must be offered to balance out the trade. This would sound appropriate according to today's standards, but you will note that the concept of Love has been withdrawn."

Chela: "You have taught that Love is Intelligent Energy. Energy is power. Money is power, especially since it has had raw power invoked upon it by Orion; now, could not this money also be Positive Love Power just as easily?"

Chief: "Excellent question. Yes, it certainly can. The spirit in which it is used and the Positive Attitude of the giver and the receiver can readily make this phenomenon occur. The donation in the offering plate at a church or perhaps a contribution to a certain charity could also produce this Love Power. The tainting takes place when the Love money is injected into the market place and intermingles with less sacred currency."

NOTES:

Chela: "Money is a vehicle that facilitates the fluidity of commerce. Is the Barter System more pure than the Money System in the exchange of goods and services?"

Chief: "Yes, in all probability. Because barter is slower and more awkward, the ability for self to know the other self is greatly enhanced. "Haggling" over a trade is most useful for this purpose. If an item is priced and the price is fixed — take it or leave it, then the concept of getting a *bargain* or getting *cheated* comes into play."

Chela: "Then all Third Density engages in commerce."

Chief: "Loosely defined, yes."

Chela: "Third Density on other Planets as well as our own previous Root Races also engage in commerce?"

Chief: "In this Galaxy, yes. To our knowledge, in the Universe as well."

Chela: "How about Fourth Density; do they employ commerce?"

Chief: "Yes indeed, almost all do. Value, profit-loss, and deals are not a part of their concept of commerce. They do use a form of money, it is interesting to note. At birth each entity is automatically issued a sizable number of "credits." This number is equal to all entities in that dimension. These credits cannot be exchanged between selves for any reason. The "credits," unlike money, are personalized, and therefore, one man cannot acquire another man's credits and spend them on himself. The credits must be used for legitimate purposes. With a reasonable amount of frugality, there are more than enough credits to last the incarnation. Purchases could actually be made for goods at any place, but usually it is the Inter Planetary trade centers that support this activity."

Chela: "Where are these trade centers and how do they function?"

Chief: "An example, reasonably close, is the Planet we know as Pluto. Great Star Ships from all over this Galaxy and from many Galaxies in this Sector of the Universe gather well away from the little Planet, while smaller craft ferry the goods

NOTES:

to great warehouses constructed on Pluto for this purpose. It is here that the buying and selling takes place."

Chela: "What kinds of goods are we talking about?"

Chief: "As you know, Fourth Density MAN rarely produces anything by hand. These items are thought forms made manifest by involving the Green Ray. These items are made of raw materials native to the Planet of the seller and are fashioned in such a way as to convey a deeper understanding of that Planet and her people to the buyer. Vibrations emitted by the item permit the buyer to grasp certain knowledge of history through Psychometry. The purpose behind these endeavors is Love/understanding, but of course, this is the theme of Fourth Density MAN."

Chela: "Are these trade centers the only places of exchange?"

Chief: "No, not at all. Another example would be the interior of Mars wherein lies their shopping centers. These places are not unlike shopping malls on this Planet. There, a computer System is at work, as credits are not carried on the person. Items of need are "purchased" on a regular basis. You will note that Fourth Density MAN has the ability to manifest anything that he needs or even desires. Then why the shops? Some people can think of a better item than others can. There are special skills and areas of expertise in Fourth Density, just as in Third Density. Skills are shared in this way."

Chela: "The Credit System of Fourth Density deals solely around goods. What about services; can they be acquired too?"

Chief: "Technically no, though service is, of course, rendered. Service to others is the prime purpose that justifies the existence of Fourth Density. Serving others is an honor, a privilege, and a joy. No thought of compensation is ever entertained."

Chela: "What about commerce on Fifth and Sixth Density?"

Chief: "Neither of these Densities engage in commerce. Those native to these high vibrations of evolution share Love and

NOTES:

Light with all of Creation, wherever they find it. This exchange could hardly be construed as barter/commerce. The value of Love/Light is priceless. These lofty ones recognize this.

Chela: "Did the Red Man, the Indian, engage in commerce, and if so, how did he employ it?"

Chief: "We appreciate the opportunity to offer a comparative viewpoint. The Red Man practiced a form of commerce. Barter/trading took place between individuals within a nation, and there was trade between nations. The articles were usually utilitarian or artistic. Sometimes food was the substance. Usually food wasn't traded. It was a gift or it was "loaned" — to be paid back later. Raw materials were often swapped within a Clan for the commerce of the community.

The Indian Nations rarely had large numbers of people residing in a specific area, such as a city. When the clan was under twenty five persons, more or less, then everybody was a "jack of all trades." Everybody knew how to do everything. Some were more skilled at certain tasks than others, but they made do with work that was below average from time to time. When the community grew larger (more than twenty five people) then the concept of the specialist set in. Those ones who were especially skilled at a certain line of work did mostly that and little else. These services or goods were then traded to others with different skills to balance out their needs. This method vastly improved the quality of goods and services. The continued maintenance of a large group was rare. The Clans of a Nation would meet at the Main Body for counsel sessions four to six times per year, sometimes more often if prevailing conditions warranted it. These would be times of feasting and trading.

Gold, silver,and precious and semi-precious stones did not hold the commercial value that they do in the White Man's World. A gold nugget could not hold the esteem of a well-made flint arrowhead. Value priorities were: utilitarian first, artistic beauty second, and all else fell in place somewhere after that. Gold and silver in the raw state had no special value."

Chela: "How did the Indian trade or sell his land?"

NOTES:

Chief: "The individual did not own parcels of land. The Nation "owned" hundreds of square miles of land, and this was recognized and respected by all other Nations. The people were nomadic on their own land. The individual claimed it all, but no special portion of it. There were no real-estate deals among the Red peoples."

Chela: "What do you think of the private ownership of land that we have here today? Do you see it as being a better idea?"

Chief: "No, we do not. The owner of a parcel of land may do with that land whatever he pleases. The trees are bulldozed, the land is raped, devastated, and rearranged, houses or shopping malls are constructed, as the Earth Mother is dressed up as a whore. Wanton destruction of First and Second Density to satisfy the greedy appetite of commerce is the rule, not the exception. If the citizenry complains, then the developer takes his case to Court, and the commerce-inspired Court System is most eager to uphold the civil rights of the developer to do as he pleases on *his* land. If any major problems or damage are occured, the taxpayers will pick up the tab — the local politicians will see to that.

This farce could not continue if *all* the people owned all the land. A single protest would stop all development forever."

Chela: "But Chief, if a single citizen could stop work all over the land, then how would we ever know progress? And how could we ever grow?"

Chief: "Growth is mental/spiritual. Physical, economic and commercial materialism are the illusions that provide the catalyst for interaction between self and other selves. Mental/spiritual growth can readily be achieved without polluting and annihilating First and Second Density. This is not in any case necessary. The Red Peoples have unquestionably proved this. Our Mayan calendar goes back over 52,000 years. We have been an organized, civilized culture since the final days of Mu. The Red Race as a whole were the most highly evolved people on the Earth. This evolution was achieved in harmony with First and Second Density, for they were our magnificent teachers. Who

NOTES:

teaches the American? Progress via construction, manufacturing, growth, development — all of which are necessary so that jobs are created, so that more money is circulated, and so that more progress can be achieved. This treacherous cycle is based on greed and false religious tenets. Life on this Planet cannot survive another fifty years at this pace. Some know this and say so. The rest do not wish to know, claiming it is not their responsibility. They vote, pay their taxes, and dutifully place head back in sand."

Chela: "What do you see as the ultimate outcome of our commercial progress?"

Chief: "By 2050, life as we know it shall become extinct. First and Second Density will be consumed. Orion will see this as a great victory. The slaves have served the Hierarchy with their last full measure of devotion. Some Third World peoples are already in this situation. The rest shall surely follow."

Chela: "Will not Third Density terminate before this happens?"

Chief: Probably. However, it is mandatory that sufficient progress be accomplished so that the outcome is obvious, so that the great lesson is learned. As Third Density continues on in the Pleiadese, this lesson of greed, greed so great that it destroyed a Planet, shall be one of the tenets on which the new Pleiadian culture will be based."

Chela: "Commerce is a useful vehicle for teach/learn, learn/teach if it doesn't get out of hand. Do you think there is any hope of the peoples of the Earth reversing the current situation?"

Chief: "No. It would require the employment of a very different type of attitude by the Masses. The Masses have been trained for many generations to see their lives in terms of money and materialism. Any type of change that would produce the necessary results would have to be drastic. This would be interpreted as "instant Stone Age," and nobody would be apt to go along with it."

NOTES:

Chela: "This sounds rather hopeless; what should we do?"

Chief: "Teach by example. Be frugal, do not waste, and speak out at the times you deem appropriate. To call the matter to the attention of one other person would be a deed well done. If one is informed, all are included, and the Law is ONE. Do not be despondent that you have not changed the world; that is not your job. Commerce is now a vehicle of destruction — note this point it out when you can. The perpetrators of this misuse of commerce will receive their just rewards in due time. Do not feel that it is your job to balance the score."

Chela: "How about joining environmental groups?"

Chief: "We are not prone to recommending the joining of groups and organizations. However, certain environmental groups have been quite effective in bringing these matters to public attention. None are likely to go so far as to suggest the curtailment of commerce to preserve the Planet and her life forms. They mostly endorse new methods or different equipment to accomplish the same thing in a less destructive way. It is the *attitude* of the Mass Consciousness that must change, not just the procedures. With the aid of the organization, the individual can then be quite effective in teaching by example. It is the thought that counts. The destruction of nature or the preservation of nature, either way, both are an illusion. Everything is important — but nothing really matters. Be concerned while you control your anger."

Chela: "You said earlier that commerce was the prime mover of this Aryan Root Race. What is another kind of prime mover that might have been chosen?"

Chief: "The most common alternative is personal relationships. The interaction between individuals to achieve a better understanding of self and the other self, as he or she relates to the other self, is readily achieved via intimate personal relationships. Sexual encounters are the prime aspect of this endeavor. To offer comparison, would you prefer to make in-depth discoveries about yourself and other self via the sex act, or would you rather attempt to acquire the same discovery via

NOTES:

the haggling over the price of a used car? The Aryan Root Race chose the latter method. You may or may not agree with the wisdom of this choice. It should be noted that First Density and Second Density prosper under personal relationship conditions. Third Density seems to thrive as well. This System is not without stress, but the stress is minimal compared to today's economic stress."

Chela: "That has covered the aspect of commerce Chief; we now have much to contemplate. Thank you."

Chief: "Thank you for asking, it has been our pleasure."

Chapter 22

Religion

Chief: "Faith and belief are accepted substitutes for lack of knowledge. This is a necessity in early developing Souls. It is a cop-out for the higher developed Souls. In a Third Density environment, religion is useful. If it becomes dictatorial it becomes a hazard to evolution. Keeping a balance is often most difficult to achieve."

Chela: What Soul Levels would benefit the most from organized religions? Could you comment on that please?"

Chief: The Infant Soul would probably be frightened by the crowds and the enthusiasm. He would stand on the outside and look in. The Baby Soul would find comfort in the large, organized body. His world is expanding, and religion offers a vehicle of exploration without risk. He would be a staunch and devoted member. The Young Soul would assume the leadership and give vitality, drive, and direction. He would fight with vigor to maintain the status quo or fight for change with equal vigor. These are the crusaders, the preachers, and the priests.

These are the ones who would benefit the most from organized religion. The Mature Soul experiences bewilderment. Tradition dictates that this is a correct procedure, yet inner drive is now developing that spurs the need to establish individuality, Free Will, and accepting the responsibility for self. Evolution beckons. The dilemma: hang back with the crowd or move ahead into the unknown. These ones make conscientious leaders but they are often hesitant to accept the role. The Old Soul would smile knowingly and then go fishing or perhaps take a walk in the park."

Chela: "Does religion stabilize a community?"

Chief: "It is supposed to, and that is the intent, however, it does not do this. The tenets of the foundation of any religion must be strong, solid, secure and well-developed. If they are not, then they will not attract the weak. Rigid laws provide the happy comfort that the majority desires.

NOTES:

The irony is that this great rigidity that attracted the people in the first place is also its Achilles heel. A religion must also be malleable and capable of growing with the changing times. The rigid foundation will crack and crumble. Malleability produces an uncomfortable freedom and gives the impression of being directionless, as old values are being lost. Without growth, there is stagnation. This is readily understood, but the methods adopted to avoid it create the internal problems within the organization. The wisdom of the Mature Soul is sought out to resolve the dilemma. As the factions separate, a Young Soul steps forth to organize and lead his camp.

If this does not happen, then the Church crumbles under its own stagnant weight. When it does happen, the growing pains often provide permanent splits. This action is correct. These splits are the first steps in seeking and establishing independence and individuality.

The splinter group quickly organizes itself with a new, solid foundation in order to preserve itself, only to sow the seeds for a future upheaval. The scenario is amusing. Righteous anger and pride bristles. Right is right, and each side knows precisely how to define it."

Chela: "How did religions begin on this Planet, Chief? Could you recall that for us?"

Chief: "Our memory is very similar to the distortion offered by Lord Easu. Early inhabitants endowed with curiosity sought understanding. Understanding is the product or refinement of Wisdom. Wisdom is acquired through the accumulation of knowledge. Since knowledge is the result of experience, and this was early Third Density, experience was at a minimum.

People wondered about things. Why is grass green? Why is the sky blue? What is Love? How did all this get here? How did life begin? What is this feeling called Love? These were the types of questions being bandied about. Answers were frustratingly slow.

Prior to Sunrise, the people would gather and look to the East and await the rising Sun. Each in his/her own way would show respect or worship the Creator. This was repeated again at

NOTES:

Sundown, this time looking to the West. A more ambitious one in the group, a man called Jacob, sincerely felt that his method of worship was superior to all others. He therefore set out to organize and lead the worship service. The others, thinking he might be right, submitted and followed him. Soon, almost all were joining in. The choreographed service was now a part of the daily ritual. Praise offered verbally, instead of silently, and in unison, would attract the attention of the One who Created everything. This made logical sense, considering no one was coming up with any suitable answers on their own.

After a period of time had elapsed, the people still did not have any of the required answers. Since Jacob was their leader, it was expected that *he* had somehow managed Divine contact, and the people would approach him for their answers. Jacob could not afford to admit that he too had not been blessed, and in order to maintain his position as their leader, he offered answers anyway.

Certain ones in the group challenged his answers and demanded proof. Jacob had none. He allowed that *he believed* that these answers were correct when they were told to him in private, and the people should *have faith* that this was correct. To his amazement, the people bought it! Now, Jacob was an ambitious man and he could see a great future in his new found profession. If people wanted answers, he would supply them. Belief in the unknown was just as good as concrete answers based on knowledge and facts. The people were eager to accept the belief/faith system, for it relieved them of a lot of personal work. Jacob would provide the answers and all they had to do was have faith in Jacob and believe that he knew more than they did.

Others were around and, from time to time, noted Jacob's success and decided to found their own organization. Competition ensued. One Jacob would take away some of the flock of another Jacob, for in numbers there is strength. This power was coveted. Each leader would devise rituals that would make his organization unique and tempt the others to leave their group and follow him.

NOTES:

The rituals became barbaric. They were performed on non-members. Belonging avoided a horrible fate. Jealousy reigned. No leader was a good sport when it came to losing some of his flock. Defenses were now necessary. Armies were created. Territories were defined. The little man who led a little group of people in praise to the Creator has now become the mighty politician equipped with earnings.

This organized System was pleasing to the people — they now had protection — protection from enemies they never had before this great System was introduced. But they didn't seem to remember that.

They taught their children and they taught their children, and soon no one could remember ever doing things any other way. The old ways were forgotten. The new ways were pleasing to the Creator. Well, they were pleasing to Jacob anyway.

The Jacobs of the World knew that they had a good thing going for them but they had no past experience or knowledge as how to best manipulate things. They asked — they called. Now enter Orion, for he heard their calling. He eagerly gave the information requested, and it proved to be a resounding success. Eliteness was taught and discrimination resulted. Forcing or cohearsing others to serve the leader became honor/duty to the flock, for the leader was the only link to the Creator.

Other leaders also claimed the same Creator. There was much apprehension amongst all the leaders that the people might somehow discover that the Law is ONE and would then see right through their great scam. To avoid this calamity, the leaders elected to drop the Creator and invent "gods" to take his place. Gods could be personalized and claimed exclusively a collective group. Gods could not and would not be shared with the infidel which was all others who were not members.

Now, the people wanted to see what the gods looked like. Jacob didn't know; he had never seen one either. He called again. Orion came to the rescue. He taught Jacob how to fashion images out of earth, wood, and stone. Then, Orion invoked power upon these sculptures. When Jacob presented these gods to the people, they could *feel* the power and they were afraid.

NOTES:

But Jacob was not afraid, and the people saw this and they feared Jacob — the Lord, and God. He had the power they all had felt it. The subdued people willfully submitted their allegiance to their leader and dutifully did his bidding. The dissenters kept still, for they were vastly outnumbered."

Chela: "Religion hasn't changed much has it Chief?"

Chief: "No, the basic pattern is much the same."

Chela: "Did the Indian also follow this path?"

Chief: "Yes, there have been no exceptions. All religions have followed this pattern. Some religions have developed it more extensively than others, but basically they are the same. Nature gods were big with the Red Man and many other peoples as well. Appeasement to an angry god, became a common practice. The Priest or Medicine Man could easily pass the buck to an available and obliging god who would then demand restitution for the people being saved. Sacrifice after sacrifice was offered until the condition changed. It would have changed in the same way at the same time, if the people would have stayed home and popped popcorn. But it gave them something to do, and it caused the people to feel that they had now earned the right to and were qualified to receive the good rewards."

Chela: "We are speaking about the Indian now, aren't we Chief?"

Chief: "Yes. Enlightenment has the evasiveness of quicksilver, and no Race of people is immune to it. Though highly evolved in other areas, the Red Race shares this Third Density weakness."

Chela: "Why is there always the area of weakness?"

Chief: "The unknown factor, the Abstract Metaphysics, spirituality, death, life, etc., all led to what we now call Science. Science dealt with the physical, the tangible, and set out to explain it. When Science progressed beyond physical justification, then Metaphysics stepped in to bridge the gap. Physicists rarely accept any Metaphysician's explanation, though the time is at hand when they must, simply because there is no other direction to turn. People need to know. Buried or dormant, this

NOTES:

issue lies in the breast of every Human Being. This is the agent that spurs evolution on.

When the demand becomes great, a Charlatan will come along and satisfy the need — for a price, of course. Necessity is the mother of invention. Jacob established this. There are usually threads of truth running through these Teachings, else the people would not accept it at all. Myth and superstition are a vital part of religion. They fill in the gaps, as well. The Hierarchy manipulates superstition in a way that is beneficial to them. The people accept this, for they see the priest as a protector — a person of strength and of knowledge.

You will note that Love rarely enters the picture. Fear is the motivating force."

Chela: "Why is that, Chief?"

Chief: "Fear can be taught. Parents teach their children through fear. Organized society operates on fear. A fearful people are easy to control or govern."

Chela: "Religion, that is, the churches, teach fear disguised as Love for God. They talk about Love but teach fear. They talk about aiding the less fortunate but refuse to walk amongst them. They do dispatch missionaries from the security of the Church, but the Love quickly dissipates once outside the sanctuary of the building. Do you then see the Church as evil?"

Chief: "Firstly, we agree with your observation. Now, as far as the Church being evil — "good" and "evil" are ambiguous in their definitions and most people have their own definition anyway. We shall address your question in terms of Positive and Negative. Briefly, you will recall that the definition of Positive is: service to others, and totally incorporating Free Will in all endeavors. Negativity, on the other hand, is dedicated Service to self. Free Will is to be abolished without any qualms or hesitation when it is necessary to render increased service to self. Elitism in Negativity replaces equality in Positivity.

Religion is an organization. All organizations are Negative in their very structure. They have rules, laws, and procedures that *must* be followed in order to establish and maintain efficiency, continuity, and purpose/direction. Members

NOTES:

know and understand (probably) all these tenets and willfully and freely subscribe to them because of reasons that are satisfying to them personally (probably). In so doing, the subscriber has willingly forfeited a portion of his/her Free Will. Once this process has begun with the individual and it becomes and accepted practice in the community, then the individual's Free Will is nibbled away until there is precious little left. Complaints are short-lived because "everybody's doing it," and "just look at all the fringe benefits that are free."

The tenets of religion are Negative in connotation. The member is inundated with Divine Orders of things that he shall not do. Now, these laws often make a great deal of sense and are readily seen as being most worthwhile. Most of the laws restrict the subscriber from doing things that he probably would never do anyway, but it is handy to have a Divine Reason for not doing something — others are not so likely to argue the point."

Chela: "Excuse me Chief, but, even though the laws are stated in a Negative fashion, they are still appropriate laws to follow, are they not? And why should such an issue be made over rules that make good sense and ought to be followed?"

Chief: "Good point! There are two aspects: fear and Karma. The subscriber obeys out of fear — fear of the consequence, physical or non-physical. Independently determining these things for self is not attempted, though it's probably quite a good idea, for fear of getting it wrong, fear of not pleasing the community and becoming ostracized, fear that God might take a dim view of this brashness, and for fear of paying the price of being a nonconformist. Unity/conformity is the backbone of a religion. It is the *reason* that one obeys the laws that are Negative! The law itself may have merit. Do you obey the law because you sincerely wish to or do you do so out of the fear of the consequences? The reason, the attitude andthe thought behind the attitude, is what counts.

Then, here is the aspect of Karma, a factor which most Western religions do not take into consideration. If the religion ignores reincarnation, then the Karma or lessons from Past Lives are but a joke. For those of you who are enjoying a more mature

NOTES:

spiritual status, this becomes very important as you duly consider your catalysts and the catalysts affecting your other selves.

Third Density sees life from a tangible, physical point of view. If a person "sins," then that person must be punished in a way that is sufficiently severe to cause that person not to ever, ever do that thing again. Why? Because it was wrong. The organization, and perhaps the culture as well, see this as being less than desirable, and will not — cannot tolerate it. The Masses have been taught to agree with this line of thinking, which is: crime and punishment.

But what about the Soul of the individual who committed the "sin" and the Soul of the victim, as well. Was this "sin" an act to compensate for a reverse experience from some Past Life? Is the sinner/personality simply following diverse wishes of his/her own Soul to create an incident so that the Soul might add the *opposite* form to its repertoire of experiences? Remember, the one thing your Soul cannot do is: *It cannot experience Experience!* The personality is always in business for his/her Soul, even when the "business" happens to be in violation of religious, civil, or criminal laws. Men of Third Density do not consider this factor, this *determining* factor, when judgment is handed down."

Chela: "Wouldn't this consideration cause everybody to use Karma as a cop-out just to do anything they want, and wouldn't that produce chaos?"

Chief: "Undoubtedly it would. There are those amongst us that would use this as a "cop-out," and apparently they would be highly successful at it. It would be an experience and the Soul would not object to this procedure — once, perhaps twice. Then, the reincarnating entity would be endowed with such a tremendous degree of guilt and "conscience" that, in future incarnations this "cop-out" attitude would be minimal. Each Soul, via their incarnated personality, would likely choose this experience; but, to make a career out of it would stymie evolution. The Soul would view this and would plague the personality to shape up. The personality would view the manipulation of Karma as clever. If the Soul Complex were dedicated to specific experienc-

NOTES:

es of service to self, Negative, then this would be a most convenient tool. The vast majority is on a service-to-others path, and this cop-out would not enhance the journey.

If the religious and legal communities were to suddenly embrace such a program, there would be instant chaos. This would last for one or two more incarnations. This would cover a period of 300 to 500 years, after which, the deep sense of personal responsibility for self, other selves, the plant and animal kingdoms, and the Earth Mother herself would innately be endowed to all those incarnating. Responsibility would be the end result. This would preserve First, Second, and Third Density and promote evolution into Fourth Density to the maximum. The end results would certainly be worth it, but the ensuing three to five centuries could be chaotic."

Chela: "What is likely to happen if Western Religions do not choose to alter their stance on reincarnation?"

Chief: "Accompanied with modern technology, the traditional attitude will result in even deeper stagnation. Greed/survival will result in the annihilation of life on Planet Earth. The Churches must reform and take the lead to force industry and government to implement the appropriate programs. The resulting inconvenience will be well worth it in the long term. If Third Density could realize that they will be back to live in the garbage and pollution that they are creating today, then today's devastating practices would quickly change."

Chela: "Do you think Western Religions will ever do this?"

Chief: "No."

Chela: "Early religions, in their beginnings, had what we now call Metaphysics as their basis. This was the attempt to explain the unknown, physical and non-physical. As the physical understandings developed, the newly formed "sciences" began to phase out Metaphysics in favor of the tangible. This practice flourished for a very long time. So long, in fact, that Metaphysics was all but forgotten and was kept alive through Alchemy and the Occult. Now, with physical Science having developed to the place where it is beyond the point of explaining itself via

NOTES:

tangible proof, it becomes necessary to phase back into Metaphysics in order to continue the process of explaining how things work. Is this correct?"

Chief: You are most perceptive! Everything cycles. All things begin in the etheric and end in the etheric. In the process, they pass through the physical, and the physical has a crack in it via the sciences. Hardcore physical Science is not in error. It is indeed appropriate and useful. If, in their glory, scientists choose to ignore the spiritual aspect then they shall perish in frustration and stagnation. Physics and Metaphysics are the same thing. The Metaphysician knows this; the Physicist had best grasp it also, or fall behind and drop out.

Religion has little influence on physics today, but some will see Metaphysics as a form of religion. This is learned in the process. It has not been in error. Types of experiences were produced that could not have been achieved in any other way. The Cycle is continuous; it must be seen as such and permitted to let flow."

Chela: "Will this likely happen, Chief?"

Chief: "Free Will always makes the future unknown. If Science does not embrace the spiritual aspect of Physics, then the probability of modern Science putting an end to life on this Planet is indeed excellent. Commerce thrives on service. The two are highly compatible. Religion *could* be the mediator between the two, and a healthy, compatible compromise could be reached. The working preservation of First, Second, and Third Density would be the happy result."

Chela: "Will religions see their duty and come forth?"

Chief: "Not likely, though anything is possible. Churches lack the courage and the support of their congregations to initiate such a revolutionary action as this. The leaders would see no advantage to it. Since you only go around once, there is little profit in getting too excited about the future of the Planet. Posterity will just have to fend for itself — just as we did, and *we* made it, didn't we?"

Chela: "This is a terrible burden that we place upon our good children."

NOTES:

Chief: "Of course it is, but the concensus of opinion is: our grandparents did as much for us . . . so why should we do any different?"

Chela: "That's a fatalistic attitude."

Chief: "Yes, but if you truly believe that you will never come around again, and that Karma is but a figment of the imagination then you have everything to gain and nothing to loose. The *responsibility* is conveniently buried. If responsibility is worthy of note, then let the Hierarchy of the religions handle it — after all, that's what we're paying them for. If you pay your money to a Church or to a government you are personally relieved of all responsibilities concerning the matter. This puts power in the seat of authority by a willing citizenry, and all concerned are happy with the System. The fact that it doesn't work is a point not considered by anyone. What took place on this Planet a year ago, one hundred years ago five hundred years ago is *your,* is *my* responsibility. We *are* our own grandpa! The power lies in the present — Now! Karma is real! When we face up to the fact that it is *we* who are totally responsible for the past, just as it is *we* who chart the future — then, and only then will Third Density evolution get off dead center."

Chela: "The religious leaders are not going to promote this line of thinking. The people do not want to hear it, it would be too embarrassing, too humiliating."

Chief:"That is correct. Therefore, the standard of living shall deteriorate by the mindless waste of First and Second Density until Third cannot survive. Waste and contamination produced by commerce shall innundate and destroy all life on Planet Earth. As Third Density grasps it's final breath, we wonder if they will say: "It's not my fault! I'm not responsible! I paid my taxes, I paid my Church dues! What went wrong? Who's to blame? . . . Not me!"

Unfortunately, this shall be the final thought of a great number of people. First Density and Second Density will have paid a tremendous price to offer a beautiful lesson that was never learned. The religions could offer a valuable service by teaching the spiritual Law of Karma and its boomerang effect. Traditional

NOTES:

Fundamentalists refer to Karma as the Law of Cause and Effect. It is the same thing expanded beyond birth and death."

Chela: "What about Christianity, Chief? You have spoken about religions in general but have not identified any. Since Christianity is the major religion in the Western World, tell us how you view this major religion."

Chief: "Christianity is a misnomer. It's author is unknown. The Christian Church is *not* the creation of the one known as Jesus of Nazareth aka Lord Easu. This organization had its beginnings long after the crucifixion/-resurrection/ascension Easu existed and was Lord of the Earth. He is *not* a fantasy. Almost everything else is.

At the time of his sojourn on the Earth some two thousand years ago he was a high Fourth Density Wanderer that perchanced to be seeking an opportunity to be of service to others. The Planet Earth caught his attention. He studied the Akashic Records, and the plight of the Jews brought out in him great compassion. The powerful Sanhedren was warping the backbone of a mighty Race of people who were not native to this Planet. As a non-physical unseen entity, he whispered in many ears. As usual, this process produced little success in Human Beings.

Therefore, he elected to incarnate amongst them as one of them — as a Jew. His purpose was to re-awaken the Jews and, through teachings, install them on a more proper path that would further their evolution and not retard it, as was being done by their own leadership. Orion was seeking to install a vital portion of itself as the godhead of Judaism. The Sanhedren elected to cooperate with this ploy for power and control. Easu, seen an infant, bewildered budding civilization which was being led blindly down the path of Negativity. He set out to awaken a nieve people who were unfamiliar with the ways of the World. He obviously enjoyed success. The Sanhedren soon lost power and control over the Jews, and the Jews have since moved forward on a more progressive path that has stimulated their evolution.

NOTES:

Now, there was at that time a large group of people who were non-Jew. These were known as the Gentiles. The Gentile could function under the rule of the Sanhedren. Lord Easu brought about its demise. The Gentiles, never very strong, now were weakened even further. They needed to organize themselves to present a show of unified strength to keep from being overrun by the Free Jews.

The Gentile had no leader. None could be produced, so they selected a famous Jewish leader, a thinker, a Rabbi: A MAN called Easu. Now, this was three centuries *after* the crucifixion/resurrection/ascension of this great teacher. The Gentile "adopted" one of their enemy and molded him into a god of their own Creation. They attributed all sorts of miraculous things to this one, and a great Standard was being created for their people, the Gentile, to follow. There is a great power in Easu, so this plan showed success from its inception. Orion took notice. Fourth and Fifth Density Negative Ones came forth to offer their services. The distortion was working and continued to run unabated. Easu was declared to be Christ-like, then he became the Christed One. He became the *only* begotten Son of God. He was God.

Jesus, the Jew, did not desire to be the Messiah or the Savior of anyone. The Jew knew this and accepted it. The Gentile made this one into *their Savior,* while the Jew smiled and went about his business. Now, the Gentile, via distortion, was able to organize himself into a unified body and was able to stand his own against the powerful Jewish Nation. The numbers of the Gentile, now calling themselves Christians, were much greater than were the number of Jews. As time elapsed and the inner refinement of the Christian organization now called "The Church" grew, the balance of power shifted. Orion was at the helm. An elite Priesthood was established and the master/willing slave conditions readily developed. In a few centuries, the "Holy Christian Church" was the *one* power to be reckoned with in the known World.

The Church could, and did, topple governments. It sent forth the missionaries to conquer the rest of the world. The

NOTES:

church, working hand and hand with commerce, systematically exploited the entire planet. Second Density has been disrupted, First Density has been raped and ravaged, and Third Density has become woefully enslaved. The Planet is dying, life is perishing, and evolution is in retrograde!"

Chela: "We can see what is happening around us; all this is due to Jesus the Christ?"

Chief: "Indirectly, yes . . . unfortunately. Christians can perform any act they collectively so desire, attribute it to the calling of Jesus, and consciously get away with it. If there are objections, then the protester is labeled an "Infidel," and is worthy of extermination. All non-Christians are Infidels — unless they convert and bestow upon the conquering missionaries all their treasures and their land.

Now, this is all accomplished in the name of Jesus. If you ever wonder why this MAN is so sad and weeps continuously consider his plight. The Gentile/Christian has made promises, false promises to the peoples all over the entire world, and now *demand* that he, Jesus, fulfill all the promises that they made in *his* name! His anger is conquered by his compassion and he is rendered helpless."

Chela: "Then, why has Lord Easu not come forth and set the records straight? Could he not have fixed this a long time ago?"

Chief: "To do so would have infringed upon the Free Will of the people to do and distort anything they jolly well please. He came to help the Jew find a better path. He did this. He did not bargain for his "godlike lot" with the Gentile. The devastating situation is completely out of control. Through channels, Lord Easu has, during the past century, attempted to set the records straight. This information is labeled as Satanic. Neither religion or commerce are willing to upset the apple cart by endorsing the validity of these channelings of Lord Easu. Much material exists and is readily available today, but Orion does not want it circulated and he prompts certain ones of his followers to rise forth in righteous anger and slay the perpetuation of heresy."

NOTES:

Chela: "Is Lord Easu still the Lord of the Earth?"

Chief: "No, he has been replaced by Lord Sandis. Easu may choose to accept the opportunity to follow his flock — the Unharvestable Ones — to the Planet in the Pleides. There, in a different environment, perhaps he can overcome all the wrongs that have been fostered in him. The Unharvestable Ones constitute approximately 90% of the World's population, so perhaps he would not deem this such a loss after all."

Chela: "I don't know how to ask this. But, who is it that the Christians worship? If their original leader was a fantasy of a Jewish teacher, just who is it that the Christians worship today? Is this clear?"

Chief: "We grasp your question. Shortly after the Gentiles distorted image of Jesus appeared on the Earth scene, Orion came forth in the guise of the one Christians call Lucifer. He then gave personification to the newly created image. Again later, with the aid of Italian artists, a physical image was constructed of stone and on canvas, and on a great plaster wall in a Church. The image was seen as kind, benevolent and understanding. He was pictured as tall, lean, raw boned, with long dark wavy hair, and wearing a dark beard. This is the image. Inside this magnificent facade, dwells the Negative Orion entity, commonly called Lucifer. This one has many names."

Chela: "What did the real Jesus look like?"

Chief: "He was a short, stocky, burly fellow with a fat face and flaming red hair. His red beard was a short stubble. He had a wide, toothy grin, which he employed regularly. He was built like a fullback and looked like a truck driver. This correct image would never have produced the desired results as did the one attributed to him. If he were to walk amongst you today, you would not know him, even if he wore his robes."

Chela: "What is your personal opinion of Christianity, Chief?"

Chief: "We prefer to reserve that bias and ask that you examine your history instead. Note the wars that have been fought in the name of Jesus: Christians vs. Non-Christians, and Christians vs. Christians. Note all the Non-White peoples that

NOTES:

have been conquered, plundered, bullied, or forced into a way of life not of their choosing! The Governments open and close with prayers and their monies bear the inscriptions of Christianity. Christianity rules the World — in constant disharmony. Greed for power and control over others, all others is the name of the game. Death resolves everything; that what is different, that which you don't understand, that which stands in your path — destroy it! If perchance you are in error, fear not! Jesus will take care of it *for* you. For after all, you have been "saved!" All consequences of your actions are automatically absorbed in the loving arms of the Savior. Any of you shall be given renewed strength to smite your enemies, which are *his* enemies too! And *He,* through *you,* can control all these heathens and teach them a thing or two about respect and the awesome power of fear via belief in a deity who is the *only* Son of God!

We ask that you simply read your history with a jaundiced eye and attempt to stand in the moccasins of the poor victims who are being "saved" and draw your own conclusions."

Chela: "Then what you are saying is all Christians who have been worshiping Jesus for the past 1700 years have actually been worshiping Lucifer, disguised as Jesus?"

Chief: "This is correct. The Christian layman has no idea who the true Jesus really is. Most of the Clergy/Priesthood doesn't know either, though surely some must suspect the truth.

Through his dark angel Lucifer, Orion has chosen the United States of America as his headquarters on Planet Earth. This is why America lives a "charmed" existence. No great calamities befall the people of the land. Americans eagerly place their faith and trust in Jesus, who is Lucifer in disguise, and good fortune is their lot. Through missionaries of religion or of commerce, the influence of Americans is so great that they have become the controlling factor in the entire World."

Chela: "This is awesome news Chief; it is outrageous! Jesus is Lucifer in disguise and Americans are the working power of Orion . . . America is Negative!?"

Chief: "This is correct. There are almost 62 million Light Bearers of Fourth, Fifth, and Sixth Densities incarnated in

NOTES:

the World today. There are 38,192,400 of them incarnated in the U.S. The World will offer a little over one-third billion of her population for the Fourth Density Harvest. Out of that, some five million Americans will join those ranks. Now, why would so many Light Bearers be assigned to a Nation to Harvest a minute portion of the overall Harvest? The prime reason so many Light Bearers are in America is to provide the Positive balance that offsets the Negativity instilled by Orion via the collective Christian Church.

Chela: "Then, Orion uses Americans to turn the World into Negativity through Christianity and through Capitalism — Commerce . . . Wow! It seems odd that the World doesn't know about this . . . "

Chief: "The World *does* know! It is the Americans who are willfully blind to their situation! We do not insist that you accept our words. We do suggest that if you study American History and the History of Christianity with this concept in mind, you shall quickly appreciate the validity of it."

Chela: "Since the Christian's Jesus is actually Lucifer in disguise, what about our prayers? To whom do we pray?"

Chief: "We base our response on Lord Easu's own admonition: better to pray and seek council with your own Higher Self through meditation and introspection. You are a Mind/Body/Spirit Complex. Your Higher Self is your first contact, as this put you in touch with your Soul, which is a fragment of your Spirit, which is a fragment of your Social Memory Complex, which is but one small step away from our ONE Infinite Creator. It is better to pray to your Higher Self than to a real or imagined deity. We might add if you do pray to a deity, that deity will simply parrot the desires of your Higher Self/Soul, unless, of course, that deity was Negative."

Chela: "Then we shouldn't pray to Jesus?"

Chief: "You are endowed with Free Will; therefore, you may do anything you wish. Jesus/Lord Easu did and does, exist. The Christian's concept of this MAN defiles the original and true Jesus. Few Christians know this. The true Jesus never wished to become the Figurehead of a mighty organization and be wor-

NOTES:

shipped as a God. This was never the intent. Orion, the opportunist, created Christianity in his own image. The underlying teachings of all Christianity is: service to self. In the case of individuals, there are always the exceptions. Again, we respectfully invite you to examine the history of Christianity. In the guise of service to others, it has actually been a vehicle of achieving service to self. Orion is clever. The Gentile was/is a willing dupe. Prosperity, or the hope of it, is the just reward.

We respectfully suggest if you pray or seek counsel with *any* Deity, that you examine the qualifications of that Deity based on historical performance rather than on your own wishful thinking. Always think for yourself! Never let the course of your life be determined by prayers answered by a glorified entity who heads up a powerful and prosperous organization. The proper path for your future must always be a Free Will choice between you the personality and your own Higher Self.

Unless you are absolutely confident that you know precisely what you are doing and aware of all of the ramifications contained therein, we suggest that you not pray to *any* Deity including the one commonly known as Jesus. We comfortably speak these words, completely aware that we have the full blessings of our Brother, Lord Easu/Jesus of Nazareth.

The Christian's God is Orion. His "only begotten son" is Lucifer, commonly called Jesus. *Any* god/deity that requires worshiping is: An aspect of Orion. Orion has infiltrated all religions and heads up most of them. The ONE Infinite Creator is: ALL THAT IS. There is nothing in Creation that isn't the Creator. Respect, Love, and Understanding are the required tenets. There is nothing to fear; therefore, there is nothing to worship!

Chela: "Praying and worship — is this Positive or Negative?"

Chief: "Positive Entities do not need or require being prayed to or worshiped. Anonymity is their watchword. Negative Entities, on the other hand, rejoice in praise and adoration because it helps them establish the pecking order amongst themselves.

NOTES:

It is interesting to note that a Negative Entity has the power to heal among many other powers. When a healing or a benefit is bestowed, there is always a condition that goes with it. That condition is usually a forfeiture of more Free Will, or more and more devout devotion to "the cause."

When you pray, you invite that Entity into your presence and that Entity is made welcome. Suppose that Entity is Negative? All the protection of Light that you may have created about yourself is suddenly useless and powerless because you have *willfully* invited a Negative Entity into you and you now have become disgruntled with it. You are guilty of turning it off and on! The Light of our Creator will not interfere with your Free Will. Orion has no such qualms.

Chela: "Do you pray, Chief; and, if so, what do you pray?"

Chief: "At meals we say Grace: "In the Name of the Presence and the Power Universal, may our Creator's blessings be upon this food." This is said silently or aloud with no ritual.

As did/does Lord Easu, we pray to "Our Father" who is our Higher Self/Soul. Our Prayer: "May the Light and Love of our Father be reflected upon the face and the deep of our beloved Earth Mother. May we know where we must be and what we must do, so that our offering of Love, Light, and Service might always be maximal for First, Second, Third, and Fourth Densities on this orb in this Cluster of Spheres and this Sector of Space. In the Name of the Presence and the Power Universal, we pray."

Then, of course, we have our Prayer of Protection, which we have already taught you. We pray to and commune with, our Source, not deities. Praying to the Father, the Higher Self, unifies the Complex of the Mind/Body/Spirit. Making conscious contact with you own Higher Self is the Third Density perception of the "Rapture." This is precisely why we have taught you the Kundalini Meditation. We were charged by Lord Easu/Jesus of Nazareth to teach this many years ago. The Harvest of Souls is at hand; it is time for the Truth to be known."

NOTES:

Chela: "What about other religions? Are they like this too?"

Chief: "Some have similar tactics, while others are essentially opposite. We cite Buddhism as an example of the latter. This is a gentle religion that fulfills the spiritual needs/understandings of the Asian peoples. There is only little distortion from the original teachings of the accepted founder, Siddhartha Gutama. His sojourn lasted over eighty years and took place circa 600 B.C.

There are four basic tenets to Buddhism. First, you seek *knowledge,* for with knowledge you achieve *wisdom;* and with wisdom, you acquire *understanding;* and with understanding, you become *enlightened.* This line of thinking is harmonious in almost any culture and would enhance, not disrupt, the current path they happen to be on. Buddhists are non-aggressive. Buddhism is a passive religion. It teaches patience! It teaches tolerance!"

Chela: "I was wondering about the Three-Fold Flame, especially as it is associated with the Green Ray, the Heart Chakra. Could you comment please?"

Chief: "As the Three Fold Flame relates to religions and personalities personifying religions, we suggest that you think of *Love* as being related to Lord Easu/Jesus of Nazareth, *Wisdom* as being related to Siddartha Guatama, the Buddha, *Power* as it relates to Christianity."

Chela: "We catch your drift."

Chief: "Religion is not necessary in any case. It can indeed be useful to Infant and Baby Souls, and of course, low Young Souls. Most religions tend to prohibit the entity from evolving out of the Young Soul status. The churches purposely intend to maintain the status quo in order to maintain top strength. The Higher Self spurs the personality onward, and this results in the serving of two masters: Your Soul vs. your Church. You are told that they are the same thing. But there comes a time when you know this isn't true. You rebel, in favor of your Soul, as indeed you should. This often works a tremendous hardship upon the personality. The Church, the community,

NOTES:

and your kinfolks will not joyfully release you with the understanding that you have matured and are moving on towards independence, individuality, and further awareness of self. No, quite the opposite, they shall see you as a backslider and attempt to pull you back *up* when actually they are pulling you *down!* You are caught in the push me — pull me scenario, and this is far from pleasant. At this stage, religion becomes highly detrimental.

There is the fear that your leaving the flock might attract others as well. This splintering and re-organizing weakens the main body. It is better to forfeit more and more of your Free Will, than to cause this to happen. To want and need to stand alone is unthinkable in the view of organized religions. "United we stand — divided we fall" — this is the theme. We all go to Heaven in a group, and Jesus has made all the reservations and is picking up the tab!

Ignorance begets ignorance; folly begets folly. The four basic tenets of Buddhism could be put to fine use here. Think on it."

Chela: "What about the Holy Bible, would you please comment on that?"

Chief: "The Bible is an historical transcript written by and/or influenced by, Orion. It is obviously Negative in it's connotation. Obscurity and contradiction are the format. Interpretation is mandatory. This provides for the necessary confusion that separates and divides and conquers. Only God (Orion) is the unchallanged unity. Orion enjoys competition in the lower ranks but detests being challanged.

The Bible has its own built-in safeguards that the devout use to preserve their existence, such as: "The false prophets," "the Anti-Christ," the Infidel," etc. Orion/Lucifer anticipated the day when he would be challanged and long ago stored up his ammunition. When the church is accused of anything, it simply turns the tables and quotes scriptures that are eloquently prepared. Scriptures that have stood since the beginning of time — 5,000 years ago!

NOTES:

The Holy Bible is a *very* powerful instrument. Lucifer and his source, Orion, are *very* powerful Entities. They stand fully behind the Americans, and the Christians have all the guns."

Chela: "Thank you Chief."

NOTE: There will be more about Lucifer and the Bible in Volume III of *The Teachings*.

Chapter 23

Governments

Chief: "Governments, like religions, have their prime objective: to organize the people, the Masses, into organized conformity, to simplify its control by the Hierarchy. Again, like religion, fear is the tool employed by the Government to achieve their objectives. There are various forms of Governments that utilize various philosophies in order to achieve the same thing. If the leadership of any government is wealthy, powerful, and feared by their subjects, then that government is successful.

The Hierarchy of different Governments argue amongst themselves occasionally for purposes of domination, and to adjust the "pecking order" amongst the Nations of the World. When diplomacy fails, i.e., when one refuses to capitulate to the threats/demands of the other, then power is introduced into the issue. Greed provides the impetus. Conspiracy amongst Nations to antagonize another nation can readily produce the same results. War becomes inevitable. The Hierarchy feeds its subjects a line of propaganda that historically arouses their National Pride, and they quickly become most eager to support any type of War Machine their Government desires. This practice is guaranteed to work in this Third Density Vibration — especially on Planet Earth where "Survival of the Fittest" is the accepted and only way of life."

Chela: "Then what you are implying is: if we didn't have Governments then we wouldn't have Wars? Is this correct?"

Chief: "This is precisely correct! An individual, or even a group of individuals, could not afford the armament. There will always be skirmishes between individuals and even between organized groups; but nothing like what we have witnessed since the time of the American Civil War."

Chela: "Killing is killing. Battle is battle, no matter what scale it is on. The results are the same."

Chief: "This is not necessarily true. Only Governments can afford to arrange for a battle so large and so destructive that

NOTES:

the Earth might never be the same again. Atomic Warfare is a prime example. Only a Government could afford such a feat. When First and Second Density are obliged to pay such a tremendous price for the folly of Third Density, then there is a whole lot more at stake than the maiming of bodies and the termination of Third Density lives."

Chela: "But weren't all Wars fought with maximum disaster even though they were on a smaller scale and fought with less sophisticated weapons? Has the procedure of War changed so much?"

Chief: "You are naive! Of course it has. Technology has made the difference. For example, those of us of the Red Race also had our disputes. The battles were hand-to-hand conflict. When finished, First and Second Density were none the worse because of it. In fact, they probably were enhanced. This type of battle was common throughout the World. The invention of explosives made the difference. Weaponry has come a long way in a very short time. People could afford guns, but they couldn't afford cannons — which were the fore-runners of the profile of today's mighty military machine, and its awesome ability to annihilate all that lies in its path."

Chela: "War is but a single aspect of Government, but it is a vital one it seems. All Governments have a military. They would soon fold if they didn't. The unprotected country soon vanishes."

Chief: "Again, not necessarily so. Take Costa Rica for example. It resides in a hotbed of turmoil. Her neighbors seem to be constantly in dispute with the United States, openly or clandestinly backing one side or the other. Costa Rica abolished its army in 1948 and has prospered ever since. On a grander scale, consider Japan. After the War, Japan was forbidden to re-arm, now she refuses to arm, even though the United States is trying with every means to get her to do so. Japan has become the wealthiest Nation on Earth, a good portion of which can be attributed to the fact that she has not been obliged to financially support a War Machine. A standing Army is NOT necessary to

NOTES:

insure the survival of that Nation. Actually, quite the opposite is true."

Chela: "When a Nation, a Government, is rich, then the people of that Nation are also rich . . . "

Chief: "It would appear that this is sometimes the case. In the case of Kingdom/serfdom, the peoples did not share the wealth. Impoverished slavery was their lot. It is wise to note that there are always exceptions to the rule. By scanning the oil-producing Nations of the Middle East, one can find examples of both."

A "Democracy" tends to share the wealth, but this is a well orchestrated illusion. The Government causes the people to handle large sums of money, thus solidifying the illusion. High prices and enormous taxes eat up the profits. Commerce thrives as the Government becomes more and more powerful, namely in it's ability to afford to hire more people to be the watch-dogs of the complacent Masses to see that no one steps out of line. Conformity is easily achieved under these conditions. A Government's might is not always measured in its ability to hoodwink the people into forfeiting their Free Will and practicing responsibility for self and for First, Second, and other Third Density, in favor of material wealth/goods. The United States is a prime example of this — where 70% of the World's resources are *consumed* by 15% of the World's population. Being financially able to waste causes many to feel rich. The Government plays on this greed. Few Americans would complain about the System."

Chela: "Then Government and commerce are the same thing?"

Chief: "In certain types of Governments, yes. In other types of Governments, they are compatible bedfellows."

Chela: "We get the impression that you do not favor Governments. Is this the case, Chief?"

Chief: "Like religions, we do not embrace, nor do we deny any religion or Government its right to exist. Both are vehicles which produce catalysts that are designed for Third Density to know self and to know other selves in a fashion that contributes to evolution. Certain immature Soul Levels need

NOTES:

Government in order to survive. This is not in error. The basic problem lies in a Government's ability to control and to force individuals of *all* Soul levels into a single group and enact laws that cause or force, via fear, all the citizenry to respond uniformly. It is this display of power that prohibits evolution. For many of you, there is the need, the longing, to grow up and begin to assume certain responsibilities for self. You are denied this opportunity. To play the role of the rebel and actually think for yourself on matters above and beyond the color of your next new car is vehemently denied you.

You find that you don't want to play the game anymore. You want to get away from it all. Someplace else is better. It probably is different but probably not any better. The change can often be a welcome diversion for a few years, and then it's time to move on again. Contentment is not your companion. Perhaps it never should be. A complacent attitude also stagnates evolution. But, it must also be noted that a reasonable degree of inner peace and tranquility, must be available — at least occasionally — else the balance will be permanently lost."

Chela: "Does this account for the unrest and mobility of the peoples, especially those in the more affluent Nations?"

Chief: "Those who are Wanderers — wander. This would be true regardless of the affluence of the individual or his Nation. Some wander physically and some wander mentally. Most do both. Transportation has become both efficient and comfortable, and these factors attract the rest of the mobile ones. It has become the chic thing to do — it is in vogue. Most people are not content to stay put for very long."

Chela: "Do Governments influence this trend one way or the other?"

Chief: "Indeed they do. A transient community is easy to control. The enforcement of community laws are readily accepted by a new resident. The laws/rules may be atrocious, but the newcomer will not feel that he/she has the "right" to object because he/she has not lived there long enough. They don't plan on staying there forever, either.

NOTES:

Then, who makes all the silly laws, anyway? It is the bold Young Soul — he is of the "shakers and movers."

The Young Soul sees things as *my way*. If *your way* is not like my way, then we're going to *have to change* your way! The Young Soul has the vitality to do all this. He probably wasn't born in that community either, perhaps he only arrived last month.

Mobile people are disorganized. They offer little or no threat to any Government. They are easily prodded into conformity. An old, organized community could easily become a liability to Young Soul political leaders and could alter the flow of history by simply being different from what the Politician/-Government had in mind. Transient peoples are the blockbusters. Government is pleased.

Immobility tends to stagnate commerce. Trends tend to bypass an old, stable community without notice. Commerce is dependent upon fads. Government is dependent upon commerce. For the good of all Hierarchies concerned, Government encourages the mobility of its citizens."

Chela: "This sounds like a diabolical ploy of the Government to control the people."

Chief: "It is. It keeps the people weak. The individual, however, grows in strength. Through changing scenes of experiences, he/she becomes more and more aware of self and other selves, and often this discovery breeds dissatisfaction with the System. The individual, vocal, or otherwise, has the annoyance of a mosquito to the Government, but if these mosquitoes should gather into a swarm, then the Government would *spray* for them! Note the "S" preceding "pray." Government officials are usually none too religious in such matters!"

Chela: "Do you consider Anarchy to be a wave of the future?"

Chief: "Total Anarchy — probably not. As we have mentioned, there are those amongst us who require more freedom, and they need to experience the responsibility that accompanies freedom. The time is at hand when this shall become a demand. The Masses will see this as being most

NOTES:

foolish, and the Governments shall be eager to support the Masses and suppress the maturing ones.

The maturing ones can snatch the leadership away from the Young Souls any time it chooses if they muster the necessary ambition, for they too were once Young Souls. To enact laws that would be comfortable to Infant, Baby, and Young Souls would work a great hardship on those of the Mature and Old Soul status. It is said that laws must not discriminate. A class system would result if they did. A duality in laws would not produce harmony.

To separate the people by Soul Level would not be practical or even possible. Who would decide? And using what criteria? No, the laws would have to be the same. The legislatures would not be able to legislate any form of difference that could result in equality for all Soul Levels."

Chela: "Then it is but a pipe dream. There is nothing that can be done about it. Governments are hopeless."

Chief: "Well, perhaps some are. The real need is in the area of understanding, especially as practiced by those ones assigned to law enforcement. These ones could readily be trained to observe and differentiate between citizens of responsibility and those of less maturity or childlike natures. A responsible citizen found circumventing the letter of the law to achieve a result that would be of benefit to others, without harming or infringing upon the right of others, should not be chastised in anyway. Actually, this one is setting a fine example and is therefore teaching by example. The rewards and benefits of living life in a responsible way, considerate and courteous of others as a custodian of First and Second Density, and a credit to the community should be the epitome of what all others are striving to be.

The Mature and Old Souls are the teachers. A system of laws that forbid this to happen is in error and doomed by the overwhelming weight of its bloated body. The yet lesser evolved ones would then have a goal to strive for and have the teachers on hand to teach them how to do it. This is Love. This is evolution towards Fourth Density, and that is what Third Density

NOTES:

life is all about — to establish the body Politic in no way promotes you into Fourth Density."

Chela: "This certainly makes good sense, but . . . I cannot imagine Law Enforcement Agents, Police Officers, being able to size up a situation to know when to act and when not to. The police would be judges and juries right there on the spot. I don't think they would be good at it, and I also suspect that they would abuse this spectrum of power being bestowed upon them. I can't imagine it working."

Chief: "We agree. You are undoubtedly correct. In the early stages of such a program there would be chaos. The freedom now displayed by the responsible, mature personalities would eventually prevail. Youth would follow their leadership. The reward for responsibility is freedom — freedom to follow the guidance of your own Higher Self, rather than follow the law to the letter for fear of the consequence. As evolution takes hold, the *need* for enacting a law against virtually everything would quickly be fazed out.

Government would have less work. Their services could be cut dramatically. Eventually all Government would be reduced to a Figurehead, for the people would be governing themselves, as their Free Will, tempered by their conscious, dictates."

Chela: "Do you honestly believe this will happen, Chief?"

Chief: "No. Governments are not about to give up their powers. Politicians will go to any lengths to kill the thought. They see the people as subjects, as mindless chattel, with no reasoning abilities at all. No one in the Government employment would be keen on implementing a System that would eliminate their jobs. The Hierarchy would not cooperate. The evolution of their own body politics is their prime interest and objective. Lawyers would become an extinct species. That aspect of commerce would not retire gracefully.

There is always the possibility of revolution. However, forceful overthrow of any Government rarely results in benefit to the people. It is usually a trip from the frying pan into the

NOTES:

fire. A revolution by force is an experience and not necessarily a good one. The new regime, lacking organization, would be obliged to invoke even more stringent powers and force in order to hold their infant Government together long enough to set about the new reforms that they grabbed power for in the first place. They would never get around to it. Even if they did, the new "enlightened" Government would need the cooperation of the rest of the World, and that is not likely either.

A revolution of reform within an existing Government is not likely to achieve ultimate success either. This movement could be injected into many Governments throughout the World, simultaneously. Time and a great deal of patience would be involved."

Chela: "Would politicians actually allow this concept to get a foothold in their System?"

Chief: "They might. They would see it as folly and as destined to failure and might choose to humor the chattle — in order to garner more votes come next election. The real opposition would come from organized religions and from commerce."

Chela: "Individual independence and responsibility is a threat to religion? Aren't religions there to promote spiritual growth? And how could that affect commerce?"

Chief: "As we have mentioned, religions are organized and operate through a Hierarchy of their design. If the awareness of self, the individuality, and the independence were to come forth, then the need for organized religion would vanish. The clergy would view those of their departing flock as competition to themselves and would be less than delighted.

Commerce would suffer due to the depletion of "fads." The immature members of society would take their cue from their elders, who are essentially back to basics, and indulge in minimal materialism. Commerce would suffer."

Chela: "You have stated that commerce was the prime mover for this Aryan Root Race. Don't Governments control commerce?"

Chief: "Governments will go to great lengths to present the facade of regulating commerce — for the protection of the

NOTES:

people, of course. These Government regulators are the Hierarchy of commerce, or sometimes, their hired dupes. In this case, the right hand knows exactly what the left hand is doing! All Governments subscribe to this type of control in order to survive. Back in the early 1950's, the president of General Motors said: "What's good for General Motors, is good for the Country." Here is a Corporation that has become so big and so powerful that it sees it as prudent and wise for the U.S. to *follow* in the path of policies that it has set down for itself. It chooses a direction and America follows. Government becomes the servant of industry."

Chela: "Is there one form of Government that is more useful to the growth of the individual? Does any form of Government stimulate spiritual growth?"

Chief: "We do not choose to debate ideologies, their merits and perhaps their drawbacks. We will deal directly with the question asked and not deal with the ramifications thereof.

There are three major forms of government functioning at this time. In general terms, there are forms of Democracies, forms of Kingdoms, and forms of Communism. Of these three major categories, Communism leads the pack. Essentially the reasons are: Communism tend to squelch religions. This inhibiting factor, now dormant, causes the individual to seek within, since there is no other alternative. Democracies and Kingdoms utilize religion as a mainstay to justify their existence.

By its very nature, Communism promotes collectivism or communal living. This is Positive — service to others. But you know, this concept is not all that effective, as it attempts to cohabitate with the style of commerce that is practiced throughout the rest of the World. Never-the-less, it is the thought that counts and the idea of sharing with others for the good of all is a noble thought, whether it works or not. This indoctrinated attitude, coupled with lack of religious choice, opens the door to individual spirituality. Many do not use the door and long for a religious organization to take care of them. These ones long for materialism. Many do use the door and their evolution leaps forward — relatively unfettered. Since this is achieved individu-

NOTES:

ally and not within a group, the process does not threaten the regime.

Democracies and Kingdoms promote the individual in an economic way. Commerce is the lifeblood of the System. The individual is schooled/trained to better self via higher earned income. Competition is rampant. Aggression is rewarded with even further economic gains. Combativeness between the "haves" and the "have nots" is an accepted way of life. The people's preoccupation with the acquisition of money to secure themselves and their families leaves little, perhaps no time for personal and spiritual discovery and growth. This is essentially Negative — service to self. Spiritual growth is certainly not impossible in an environment of a Kingdom or a Democracy, but it definitely is more difficult. No Government is perfect. All have their advantages and disadvantages."

Chela: "Are we then to understand that you are in favor of Communism, Chief?"

Chief: "No, not at all. We favor or support no government. We simply point out that Communism, in a World free of commerce, deploys a Positive attitude and could gently survive, as evidenced by the fact that the Red Man successfully employed this system for milleniums; whereas, historically speaking, Democracies rarely survive more than 200 years, and Kingdoms tend to fade in and out of importance.

Chela: "In one way or another, it seems that Government's role is to control the people into a state of conformity by canceling portions of their Free Will via laws to make them easier to govern. The people seem so willing to let all this happen to them. Why is that?"

Chief: "Politicians, using the Government as the vehicle, create problems so humongous in scope that the individual, or even groups of individuals, are so overwhelmed by the enormity of the task, it becomes unquestionably obvious that only a Government could possibly undertake such a project. This justifies the existence of politicians and big Government. The thing that political rhetoric camouflages/distorts is the actual *need* for such a project. The political leadership adopts the

"Madison Avenue" approach and sells the people on the idea. They call it an "issue." One will be for it; another will present a different version. The people will get excited and choose Plan "A" or Plan "B." Democracy is now working. What the people don't ever seem to realize is: they don't actually need either one! *None of the above* would have been the correct vote — but that choice was never offered. The only way that the attitude of the governed can be expressed at the polls is: no turn out. Indifference says a lot."

Chela: "Doesn't this indifference place the power in the hands of the minority, and the political leaders are not representing the majority at all?"

Chief: "Not really. The politicians do what the Hierarchy of commerce demands, whether they were elected by the minority, or by the majority of the people. The people's vote, or lack of it, has little impact on the functioning of Government. Overwhelmingly, the people have voted for a moratorium or a special issue, and the political leaders state publicly that they will refuse to honor the people's wishes because — they are in conflict with *their* prearranged plans! The issue is never implemented because the leadership, the *elected* leadership — doesn't want to. The politician pledges his allegiance to commerce, not to his constituents."

Chela: "But the political leaders are representatives of the people, and the Government is supposed to operate through the advice and consent of the governed . . . "

Chief: "Truly a noble thought; but, think on it. Has any Government leader ever come to *your* door and asked your advice or sought *your* consent on *any* issue?"

Chela: "No."

Chief: "Do you know of *anybody* who has ever experienced this phenomenon?"

Chela: "No."

Chief: "Fame and fortune are the politicians's reward. A powerful ego drives these ones forward. An occasional maverick will enter the herd, but he is soon hogtied and branded. The System flows mindlessly onward."

NOTES:

Chela: "Then it doesn't matter who we vote for, and the end result is: we get a different version of the same thing. And the "thing" is probably something that the people never needed at all. The Lords of Commerce, have laid the plans for the whole thing. Then, who is in charge of the Governments? Who is responsible?"

Chief: "No one knows. The Government is a headless monster that rolls onward in directions known only to the secret Hierarchy that remotely guides the bulldozer. The U.S. Government is the largest organized body of power on the Planet today. It has surpassed General Motors a long time ago. When the President of the U.S. is elected he becomes the President of the World. As such, he sets World policy. If any Nation should step out of line, for whatever reason, the U.S. will quickly secure a U.N. mandate, like a land developer getting a permit to wipe out an ancient woods to build a shopping center, and then proceed to bomb the offending Nation into oblivion until commerce is back on track once again. Little else is accomplished. The persecuted people, the true victims, are left with token attendance. Their lot has worsened. This is not important, since they are of no commercial value. The War Machine returns home in acclaids of glory. The American people have recorded another "victory." The elite 15% of the World's population can now continue to consume 70% of the World's resources without fear of shortages."

Chela: "Why do you refer to the Americans as "elite?" Does that mean Divine Guidance and Protection?"

Chief: "The U.S. has experienced "Divine" Protection from its inception. This aid has become quite profound during the past 50 years. As you note in your history, you will find that the Earth offers disasters of magnanificent porportions from time to time and place to place. Some Nations seem to be getting more than their fair share. You will also note that the U.S. has been spared. There has been no event that has taken tens of thousands of lives, or altered the topography, or threatened the existence of the Government in anyway. The U.S. is consistently fortunate. This is no accident or coincidence.

NOTES:

The Americans of the North believe that God is on *their* side and that *their* enemy is also God's enemy. God will guide and protect them against all odds, for their way, their System, is right and holy, and God favors them above all others. All of this is quite true. The thing that the Americans don't realize is: their "God" is *Orion!"*

Chela: "What?! Orion, the Negative Hierarchy is leading America? Oh, come now Chief, this can't be so. These are *good* people!"

Chief: "Of course they are good people, but good people can be dupes, perhaps more readily than anyone else. Remember the definitions — Positive: service to others; Negative: Service to self. Look at the U.S. as a total entity; the service to self is obvious. Do the bidding of Orion, and you shall be rewarded. For every diabolical and destructive act that occurs on, or in, this planet, you can rest assured that an American was directly or indirectly responsible for it. Orion wishes to conquer the World and is using America as the vehicle to accomplish it. Look about you; he has seen nothing but success!"

Chela: "But Americans are so generous, they forever sending aid to someone, even at the expense of home projects."

Chief: "Again, you are correct. We simply ask that you look at your own statement with a jaundiced eye. Just who on the home front, is being neglected? What is the economic impact of this home front neglect? What is the economic impact of the foreign aid? Evaluate the situation and you will find that the denial to self was denial of the portion of self that has little or no value and should be amputated. The foriegn aid, on the other hand, will ultimately result in windfall profits for American business and will also permit the American Government to procure even more dominance over other Nations. Service to others *must* result in grand service to self, else there is no deal."

Chela: "Has this always been the case?"

Chief: "Yes. But in recent times it has become more personified. The reason is that Orion is anxious to secure his Harvest and He is busily sowing the seed for future Harvests.

NOTES:

Teaching service to self in a commerce-based society is relatively easy. Greed is the key."

Chela: "Then the American people are Orion? This bothers me, Chief. I feel fraudulent and suddenly quite empty inside."

Chief: "By practicing the philosophy that America is so famous for, the citizenry of the U.S. is as a whole, the instrument of Negativity, sponsored by Orion. The mighty Government provides the power. The religions, especially Christianity, which comprises over 80% of the population, provides the substance that causes the people to believe that their way of life is the *Divine* way of life. Orion teaches elitism. All Americans *know* they are better than anyone else in the World because God is always with them. This is obvious. Look how grand it is in America, and how bad it is everywhere else. America is charmed. America is God's favorite. God smites his enemies through the mighty thunderous sword of the U.S. military. The American Government can do no wrong. They force others, even their *own* citizens, to obey laws that they themselves ignore. The American Citizen knows this! Yet, he confidently smiles with inner pride and entertains no thoughts of justice. If America does it — it must be right."

Chela: "What is Orion trying to accomplish using the Americans as his tool?"

Chief: "His goal is to conquer the World."

Chela: "Oh! But the U.S. does not conquer people and take their land."

Chief: "They did . . . that's how America came to be in the first place. Your history boasts of the numerous victories over the Red Nations and fellow Europeans as well. The Nation was conceived in war and founded upon stolen land. The American Government will still go to *any* length to protect this land from its former and rightful owners. No Nation on Earth has ever come forth to do battle with the U.S., to free the land and restore it to the rightful original owners. The power of Orion would prohibit any success that might unbalance his precious seat on the Planet."

NOTES:

Chela: "But the U.S. doesn't do that type of conquering and land grabbing anymore; we are above that."

Chief: "There are different forms of conquering. Orion, through the economic dominance of Third World Countries, is conquering the World via destruction! Commerce is the tool, the weapon. The goal is to destroy First and Second Density, thus making the planet uninhabitable, and Third Density would now also sucumb. American people tend to sense this; but, not subscribing to reincarnation, due to Christianity, the individual feels that he only comes around once, and if he gets his now, posterity will just have to fend for itself — just as he did."

Chela: "But how does the Government fit into all of this?"

Chief: "The Government permits and encourages the destruction of the Planet and of Second Density by manufacturing and selling arms that have the capacity to destroy the terrain and by permitting the sale of chemicals such as pesticides to peoples who cannot read the instructions, causing them to use the product full strength instead of properly diluting it. This produces more sales — good for business. These same chemicals are forbidden for use in the United States because they are too dangerous. Then there are the trade agreements with Third World Countries that exploit cheap labor to provide more consumer goods to satisfy the gluttenous appitite of Americans.

The destruction of the Rainforests and the depletion of fish from the seas to support the livelihood of the people of the underdeveloped countries, so that their cheap labor will last as long as possible. The Government-sponsored American Industry sets up factories in foreign lands to exploit the cheap labor and resources.

There are no peoples anywhere on Earth that remain untouched by the American Government! Directly or indirectly, the President of the U.S. *is* the President of the World. Orion, via the American Government will conquer the World by destroying it. This is a major victory for those of the Negative persuasion. The annihilation of the Planet Maldek was a more recent example of serious effort by Third Density. Prior to that,

NOTES:

the surface of Mars was rendered uninhabitable following the same process currently being deployed on Earth."

Chela: "Environmentalists are going to great lengths to prevent this from happening. Will they be successful?"

Chief: "No, though we certainly would never discourage their efforts. They are teachers. They look for solutions. But the killer of our environment is commerce, backed by Governments and religions. Nobody ever speaks out on eradicating commece! No one can imagine life continuing without it. Government could reform commerce, but it won't — greed forbids it."

Chela: "Is there any form of Government that would be successful?"

Chief: "Not really, though some would be more desirable than others. For example, a Confederation would produce a weak Central Government and strong State Governments. This System would impose a bit more responsibility upon the citizen where he might feel that he has a bit more control over his own future. Also, each State,being practically independent in its own right, could offer a choice of law and Government. One could travel from State to State, and the experience would be almost like traveling from Country to Country. The people would then have definite choices. The citizens of a given State could mold their own future in most any way they chose, without any interference from the Central Government, or from other State Governments."

Chela: "Nobody in Washington D.C. would find any merit in this line of thinking."

Chief: "You are absolutely correct!"

Chela: "The philosophy then, is to produce less Government, less laws, less restrictions, which would produce more and more responsibility for self, for other selves, and for our environment — First and Second Density.

Chief: "Well said."

Chela: "This type of reform will not be easy to achieve. Politicians will be reluctant to relinquish their power, and people will also be reluctant to assume responsibility for taking care of

NOTES:

themselves. This is a scary thought. Insurance Companies should thrive!"

Chief: "Insurance in all forms is the prime problem (asset) with commerce. If they didn't exist, then prices would *have* to fall into a more reasonable bracket. This would drastically cut the money flow but would stabilize the economy — like it was at the turn of the Century. If any workable reforms are to be made, then the concept of insurance will have to be eliminated from the thinking minds of men. Devising goods and services for the purpose of producing jobs and making profit will have to be erased. This would be the direction a New Civilization would have to take. The Government would have to lead the way. Individuals could not achieve it."

Chela: "Is there any real point in trying to pursue it?"

Chief: "No, not really. It is sufficient that you be aware with as full an understanding as you are capable of. The form of Government is not the issue. The real question is the validity of *any kind* of Government. The immature Soul Level personalities basically require some form of organization structure for the security it offers. This is good. The older, more mature personalities should be permitted to enjoy the emancipation from adolescence. They are not. Herein lies the dissatisfaction which the crux of the problem.

To arrange and allow for normal growth of the elders, while giving the younger ones something to strive for, would create tremendous problems for any form of Government. All the major Governments of the World would need to harmoniously cooperate. No one would undertake such a project unilaterally because of the obvious weakness it would create in its loose unity, and the absence of Supreme Authority. Yes, we agree with you, it is not likely to change."

Chela: "If we are stuck with something that cannot be changed, then why bother talking about it? What purpose have we served in this discussion?"

Chief: "We remind you that all physical reality is an illusion. It is the thought that counts. For those of you who are able to see through the illusion and record the results and

NOTES:

ramifications mentally, then perhaps in some future Root Race, history will not have to repeat itself. Even in discord there is Love. Lessons are learned from the catalysts presented. Nothing is perfect. There is always room for improvement. Governments are usually flexible enough to adjust to the changing times and they survive. The Governments that are linked closely with a religion that has its tenets set in concrete are the ones likely to experience stagnation.

It is the people's learned dependency upon Governments that creates the real problems in the evolution of the Soul. The Soul knows this and prods its personality to seek independence. The personality hears the calling and attempts to respond, but a mighty Government is standing in the path and there is no way to circumnavigate it. Progression is unthinkable. The Government will not budge. The irresistible force meets the immovable object. Life in Third Density is no bed of roses."

Chela: "What about all the Wanderers that are incarnated in the U.S. today, 38,192,400, I believe you said; what is their role in all this?"

Chief: "There are more Fourth, Fifth and Sixth Density Wanderers incarnated in the U.S. than in any other Nation or Continent on Earth. There is a good reason for this. It is necessary to counterbalance the Negative force of Orion who is using the Americans as his prime tool. The Russian Government was once his tool as well but he has since lost that handle. The Russian people were never a part of Orion's dominance; whereas the American Government and her people are united on the side of Orion, whom they refer to as God. The uniting factor is religion, especially Christianity. Russia was not plagued by that.

Nothing is permanent. The American people are beginning to wake up and look around. However, it may be too late. The Nation is becoming more and more Totalitarian by the day. The Executive and Judicial branches of the government are uniting to nullify the Legislative Branch which is the people's only voice — such as it is.

Freedoms and Free Will are being extracted from the peoples at an alarming rate. Drugs/crime are the noble reasons

NOTES:

that the government is taking these stringent steps. The people object blandly, for it is being done "for their own good." They have been told this and they yet believe it. The leaders of the American Government realize that their future is hanging by a thread and they are taking the appropriate action to protect themselves against the day where the people have finally "had enough."

The excuse of "stopping the drug trafficking" has always been a farce. The governments *promote* the drug trade! Government economists out of Washington D.C. have flatly stated that if the drug trade were to somehow suddenly cease, Florida would be in instant economic depression within 24 hours, the United States would fold within one week and the entire World would be in irrevocable depression within 10 days! This information came from the Federal Government! Various governments put forth efforts to "crack down" on the drug trafficking, but this is only a ploy to keep the prices up! It also provides a facade to pacify the American public, so they can see where their tax dollars are going. Government and commerce are working hand in hand to enslave the people.

Government, commerce and religions function a whole lot smoother if their subjects are in a docile stupor created by some form or forms of addiction. How many people do you know that are not addicted to anything? Addicts can be controlled, and obviously it's working. The highest percentage of the victims are the Wanderers and those of Third Density who are eligible to make the Positive Harvest. There is no stamina left to continue to resist. The battle to survive takes precedence over the desire to complete a mission. Orion is winning. The one percent Negative Harvest is gleeful. The 90 percent Un-Harvestables occasionally pull their heads out of the sand like government, commerce, and religion dictate. Their rewards shall come "later."

The Will of the people has been broken. It could be restored but it probably won't. The individual feels helpless. No organization or Nation is powerful enough to sway the course of action set down by the Orion — led U.S. The combined force of

NOTES:

the World could not stand up to the military, political, and economic might of the Americans. The United States is unsinkable, perhaps like the Titanic? The people are encouraged to enjoy as much of the remaining freedoms left as they possibly can, for next year those too shall be removed — for your own good, of course!

Chela: "For the record Chief, would you please restate your opinion on drugs?"

Chief: "We are purveyors of Free Will. Freedom of choice is essential to the proper functioning of Creation. You must always be equipped with the Free Will to choose, whatever your reasons may be. We state flatly that we do not sympathize with the use of drugs, alcohol, tobacco, or the use of any substance that might possibly alter the intended workings of the brain. Self-discipline must be learned and practiced. Responsibility must be anticipated with joy."

Chela: "Chief, could you predict the probable future of the United States?"

Chief: "As always, anything is possible. However, the trend for freedom rings loud in the minds of men. To overthrow the shackles of stress, depression, and slavery to materialism is the wave of the future. Permanent victims of too much Government is causing the American people to look at the crumbling Russian Empire with envy.

It will be impossible to "phase out" the National Debt, the Military Industrial Complex, the Pentagon, the I.R.S., the C.I.A. and the F.B.I., and all the mindless Bureaucrats who make our lives a cesspool of insane laws and complexity. The only way is to "start over." Our collective situation defies being "fixed." There is no hope of a cure or even a resurrection for the Government of the United States, none what-so-ever. Government promotes the ecstasy of drugs upon its subjects to avoid or postpone a collapse of a putrid organization. This was the procedure used against the Chinese by the Americans during the Boxer Rebellion. It is working. The slick schemes and the Madison Avenue approach is keeping the populace in line, thus far.

NOTES:

When more and more of the Wanderers awaken and begin to put their services on the line, then a national disenchantment shall set in. The Government shall disintegrate over night. A tax revolt against the obnoxious, high-handed ways of the I.R.S. will probably be the catalyst. Fear will sweep the offices of the elected Politicians and the hoards of Bureaucrats. Many will find urgent and prolonged business overseas.

State Governments shall collapse immediately thereafter, though Local Governments shall remain essentially intact. In rather short order, sections of the country shall see the need to band together and form small Nations in their own right. Current state boundaries are not apt to prevail. Some of the newly founded Countries may choose to re-divide into States, while others will not. Most of the New Countries in the now adjacent forty eight will form a new democracy patterned after the old but with less laws and more responsibility extracted from its citizenry."

Chela: "How will the country be divided and into how many countries?"

Chief: "We see five countries. They are nameless at this time. Indian names will be popular and there are many to choose from. We see the boundary lines as follows: A North-South line from New Orleans to Deluth, following the Mississippi River, provides the Western boundary for two Eastern Nations. The Ohio River separates these two Nations.

A line from St. Louis Westward, following the Northern edges of Kansas and Colorado to the Utah state line and then Southward to Mexico provides the boundaries for Country number three.

That Northern line continuing Westward along the current Northern boundaries of Utah, Nevada, and California encompass Country number four.

The remaining area constitutes Country number five.

If you were to mark them on your map you could readily note that all five countries have access to ocean shipping. Each section would have much in common with itself, and all would

NOTES:

be virtually independent of each other, though trade would no doubt continue.

Being independent nations, governments could be formed that meet the will and needs of its people. A commonwealth society would develop amongst people who have much in common with each other. Responsibility for self, for other selves, and for First and Second Densities would readily be forthcoming. This arrangement would give the people a feeling of hope as they begin to take charge of their own destiny. Frustration would give way to enthusiasm for building a new future for themselves and their children.

Russia set the example, the United States shall surely follow. The Bear shall lead the World into our New Age. This is appropriate, for the Heart Chakra of our Earth Mother is located in Northern Russia. The Divine Purpose of Third Density is to learn to be independent, to become an individual — to be aware of self. This will be very easy to learn when people are citizens of a small Nation. Evolution will prosper as will all the people."

Chela: "Who then, would object to this proposition?"

Chief: "Orion, the Politicians, the I.R.S., other career Government employees, and affluent, addicted dupes in general, including the religious Fundamentalists."

Chela: "Do you really think that the United States will divide into five separate Countries? Do you really think the people will do this? And do you think the Federal Government would allow this to happen?"

Chief: "Anything is possible, of course. In this case, the probability is indeed excellent. It is impossible for anyone to devise a plan that would be acceptable to even the majority of the people. A few would benefit at the expense of the majority. Justice/equality would not prevail. The politicians are virtually helpless, handicapped as they are by the laws enacted by their mentally constipated predecessors. The cost of feeding this monster is outragious. As the Light Bearers awaken and begin to alert the native Third Density Citizenry to these obnoxious facts, we see a tremendous vocal disatisfaction amongst the peoples.

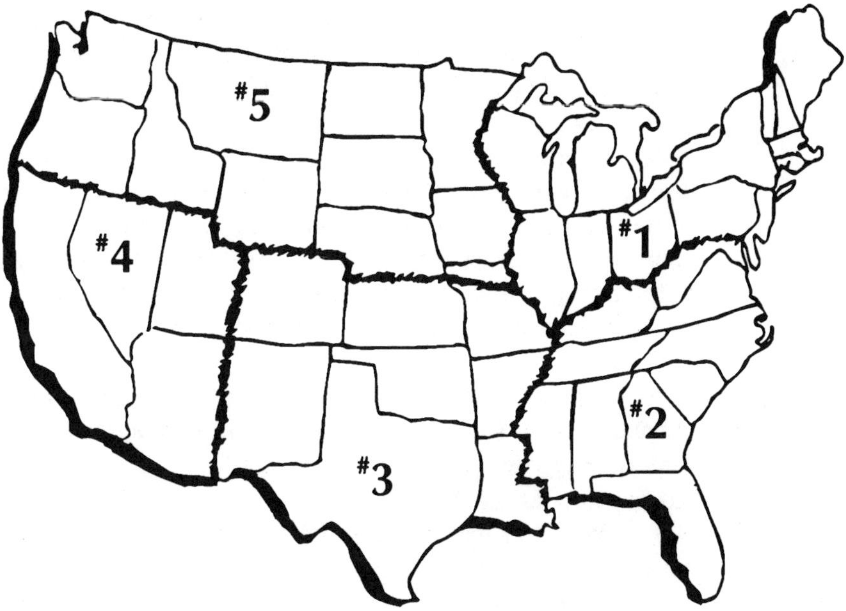

The Probable Boundaries of the FIVE EMERGING NATIONS

NOTES:

The only solution, though drastic, will be to separate several States in a block and form a type of Government that meets the needs of the people of that Geographic locale. Seeing this, the Federal Government would have no choice but to capitulate and quietly close down. The United States is a debtor Nation and many people would be hurt, Americans and foriegners as well. The loss would be spread as equally as possible under this method. The "common person" would be least affected, while the rich and the powerful would stand to lose the most.

Ingenuity would prevail and the thrill of beginning anew, afresh, debt free, with new laws that apply to your own sector of the Hemisphere, will inspire and thrill the timid as well as the ambitious. Being responsible for yourself and for your fellows, with a firm grasp on your own destiny, is a beat that drums loud in the weary hearts of men and women dwelling in a land betrayed by its heritage."

Chela: "Yes, I see. You have given us a rare and unusual concept for us to ponder. This is a choice that I'm sure none of us knew we had. Perhaps our future is not so obscure and hopeless as we thought.

Will you lead us or show us the way to get all of this started?"

Chief: "No."

Chela: "Megwich, Chief!"

Chapter 24

The Social Product

Chief: "We have observed the impact of Commerce, the religious justification of actions, the Governments enslavement of its peoples, and now we shall attempt to summarize these three determining factors as we analyze their results: The Social Factor.

The Social Product *is* the Aryan Root Race. We all determine it and we are the product of it. The citizens of the World freely chose to be what they are. It is true there is a great deal of influence injected from outside sources which are definitely mitigating factors. These influences were both Positive and Negative — as they should be. The Human Experience has been duly recorded and its history is rich in variety of experienc.

The three major factors Commerce, Religion, and Government have apparently stymied personal spiritual growth. In some cases this is true, of course. But, on the other hand, innumerable Souls have prospered due to the unusual and abnormal characteristics of life on this wayward Planet. In no way has there been total loss. Certain ones of you will no doubt argue that point and this is your privilege to exercise your analysis of your perception. This is Free Will in action."

Chela: "What about depression, Chief? We all seem to be plagued with it. If we can shake it at all, it is soon to return. What can we do about it?"

Chief: "In a word: attitude! But permit us to expand a bit. A long range future is more impossible to see now than it has been in the past. It is something like being in a concentration camp, minus the confining walls. Everybody speaks of being "trapped." Yet there are few restrictions, perhaps none. It doesn't seem "right" to do anything. Decisions to act are accompanied by numerous misgivings. Doubt and indecision are the constant companions. Depression is the result.

We remind you that your Multidimensional Self has, since 1991, congregated upon you as the last bastion of incarnated flesh on any of the probable worlds of reality. Consequently,

NOTES:

you are plagued with thoughts/possibilities/probabilities. All seem to have merit, but none are outstanding, thus increasing the difficulty to choose. Once a choice is made, then the disappointed aspects of your Multidimensional Self come forth to torment you about your decision."

Chela: "My sense of values seem to vacillate. The old reliable standards do not always feel appropriate; I'm never quite sure if I'm doing right or not. I seem to have no direction about me. I'm on a merry-go-round, and it's spinning so fast that I don't spot the brass ring until I've passed it. What's happening?"

Chief: "Again, in a word: detachment! Learning to detach is a vital part of your new and developing attitude. One must learn to be able to release from every thing on this Planet, including the body you now wear. This is never easy. To part with items that have been near and dear to you, and perhaps your family, for decades is no easy task. Your Higher Self is producing this vacillating sense of values, so that you will be obliged to deal. You are preparing yourself to enter the New Dispensation. Even if you are among those who are to be "Harvested Alive," the process still takes on connotations and ramifications of death. You must be willing and able to walk away naked, leaving everything of the Third Density Vibration behind. To learn this will probably require practice.

You may feel the urgent need to relocate. This may or may not, be justified as practicality. This thought is shrouded by your lack of perception of your future. Nothing seems certain. Therefore, you are now taking a giant step into the unknown — for reasons that are illusions. Second thoughts bombard you. Your attitude is altering, and this is good. Yet, you are unable to see where the altered attitude is leading you, and this is most uncomfortable. Relief from your anxiety and depression is not forthcoming."

Chela: "I would just like for the World to stop, so that I could get off. I crave peace and rest and can find it no where. I feel like I got more rest and relaxation during the War! There are times, a lot of times, when I feel like my sanity is on the brink."

NOTES:

Chief: "The pace quickens. As we reach the end of the conical spiral, the revolutions become shorter and shorter. There is no time for rest. There is not enough time to finish the task at hand because another begs for attention. We run in circles mentally, and times literally. These are not pleasant times. Priorities are constantly being adjusted to compensate for the moment, as trusted standards vanish in the wind.

Commerce relentlessly pounds upon us, and in our dazed condition, we accept, often unquestioning, whatever they throw at us. Somebody must know what is going on; we don't seem to, so perhaps *they* do. We are advised to "take a vacation." If you do, be sure to bring along plenty of money! Commerce is everywhere, survival is at stake."

Chela: "What attitude is appropriate, Chief? Can you enlighten us?"

Chief: "There are but two basic attitudes that any personality may adopt in order to run the gambut of these final days. The first: gather the core of your material life, goods and possessions, and cocoon yourself in a very small quarters. Get comfortable, with treasures and familiar objects tightly around you. Reduce your World — return to the womb.

The second method is to reduce, or even eliminate, the material core of your beingness as you willfully and perhaps painfully detach from all or almost all, of your worldly possessions, and learn to rejoice in the experience of this freedom. Be ready "to go!" Feel the lightness! Laugh at the illusion!

The Un-harvestable Ones will close themselves in as they prepare for the hibernation and the resulting metamorphosis.

The Harvestable Ones have already experienced the metamorphisis and are now emerging into the freedom of Fourth Density, though the vibration is not yet totally upon us.

There is a strong pulling between these two camps, each enticing the other to join them — for obvious reasons. Choose your attitude and be content with your choice. Those who attempt to practice *both* are the pitiful ones."

Chela: "Though I presumably would choose the later, never-the-less, either way it would be difficult to implement

NOTES:

either one of these attitudes for most people. One could be inclined to practice the "in" or the "out," but circumstances, family or job, or whatever, could prohibit any real success. Life is what it is and due to others, sometimes we can not change things the way we would like. What would you suggest?"

Chief: "When it is not practical to assume a new life style for legitimate reasons, all is not lost. Think about it! All activities first begin with a thought. It is the thought that counts! You *may* be obliged to live in two Worlds simultaneously. This is a dual challenge *and* a dual experience for your Soul. This duality will broaden the scope of your total experience. Keep your thoughts pure and simple and your priorities straight."

Chela: "We seem to be on a collision course with doom and disaster. Unrestrained Commerce is the culprit, this is further enhanced by Religions and Governments. We should do something about it — what should we do?"

Chief: "Understand the root cause of the basic problem. Cause others to also grasp this understanding. This will change nothing here and now. The conscious memory of this disaster will be carried to the Planet in the Pleides, and with lessons learned here on Earth, perhaps, these same lessons will not have to be repeated elsewhere. This is the hope. This is the teaching. This probable World of Reality will continue to function until the conditions become so putrid that almost everyone will come to realize the folly of following false leadership from the Lords of Commerce, the self serving Priesthood, and the two faced Politicians.

This deplorable condition could have been seen and steps taken to prevent it during the early development of Commerce. By not teaching the truths about reincarnation, Religion thwarted the issue. People's greed/survival prevailed. Governments could have overridden the Churches and regulated the power out of Commerce, but they didn't. Politicians are Church members too and their greed for more power over the people was financed through Commerce. *They* wouldn't dream of upsetting the apple cart. There is no action perpetuated by Third Density that will alter the current situation. The knowledge, the thought, is

NOTES:

sufficient for now. When the great cataclysms come, all shall be cleansed, and a new beginning will be enjoyed by all. Until that time, observe — learn."

Chela: "But shouldn't we make some tangible effort to fix the situation? Take some kind of action?"

Chief: "We offer you the analogy of the microcosm: The drunk driver. Multitudes of people are up in arms about this activity. Law makers enact dozens of laws to prevent this happening. Some effect is noticed, but the problem is not resolved. Nor will it be — nor can it be. Though the numbers may be reduced through fear of the consequences, they can never be eliminated. There are those who drink, and there are those who drive, and there are those who, by their own Free Will, do *both.* No threat of law will prevent this.

Alcohol has been part of the Human Experience for many milleniums. It cannot be eliminated. This is but half of the total problem. The other half is the wheel, the automobile. Now, the automobile has been around for only about a century, not milleniums, like alcohol. The solution is to eliminate the mechanized wheel! This would put an instant and permanent stop to drunk driving! This would impose a uniform inconvenience for all, the drunkard, and those who oppose the drunkard. The vehement protesters of today would not likely endorse this plan, for they would see *their* price as being too great. We can live without the automobile, and there are those amongst us who can remember the times when Commerce flowed and life flourished without the automobile. We *know* we can live without it.

Government could outlaw its existence — but they won't. The Lords of Commerce would annihilate any Government that tried it! The American people would never accept life without a car. All the detrimental aspects of the automobile are grimly tolerated, rather than done without. Those opposed to drunk driving would be forever silenced, if this was the only alternative. One cannot deprive the drunk from the car, because the car exists, and he will find it! Nothing can prevent this from happening. The only way to keep drunks from behind the

NOTES:

steering wheels of all mechanized vehicles is to eliminate the transportation industry entirely! This will not happen.

To equate this example with Commerce in general, would be to extract money as the medium of exchange, from all Commerce. True values would quickly be established and greed would be minimized. Many would see this as a giant step backwards. However, the current path is leading us pell mell into oblivion as it systematically destroys First and Second Density and incapacitates Third Density."

Chela: "It is still difficult for me to believe that the U.S. is the number one culprit in perpetuating the destructive problems on the Earth. To think of my Country as being Negative . . . being used as the dupe of Orion, sponsored by the Church . . . isn't easy to swallow. It makes me feel sick . . . "

Chief: "We again remind you that this is our biased conclusion. All conclusions are biased. They must be. Bias gives direction — *a* direction. We have objectively examined history, just as you could. We have collected data, just as you could. We have analyzed the data and applied it to history, just as you could. We have formed a bias and drawn a conclusion, just as you could. You may agree or disagree, totally or partially with our bias — this is always your Free Will right. We wish to have it no other way."

Chela: "I understand your thought patterns all too well. To have it so blatantly portrayed is most uncomfortable. There is ample evidence, current and past, to verify what you say. It has never been interpreted in the manner that you describe, to my knowledge. But those ones who do interpret data and history are the ones that have betrayed us, and we are all guilty of doing Orion's bidding! This is incredible! It makes me limp. It also makes me angry."

Chief: "Do not be vengeful. This would accomplish nothing. Alter your own perception of self to form an image that you can be comfortable with and proud of. We are all obliged to participate in the System, but we are not obliged to join it. Teach by example."

NOTES:

Chela: "Will Commerce be the prime mover on the New Planet in the Pleides for our Un-harvestable Ones? Will history repeat itself?"

Chief: "Anything is possible, but it is highly probable that Commerce will be minor, and not a determining factor at all. The physical vehicle worn by those Third Density inhabitants will be various forms of the amphibian. This body style does not lend itself to the workings of the aspects of industry. Their lack of hands with a thumb, and their basically prone positions will probably prevent them from ever destroying their beautiful Planet. Their Souls will be relatively free of ego — greed, and therefore, evolution should grow dramatically. It promises to be a delightful experience for all."

Chela: "An Amphibian body seems like punishment to me . . . "

Chief: "It should not be construed as such. These ones will have no recall of their Past Lives on Earth in the Humanoid form. The lessons learned previously shall be retained, but these ones will not remember how they were conceived. Wearing a body that has the equivalent of hands — that can make and use tools, does little to promote spiritual evolution."

Chela: "If Commerce is not the prime mover, then what will it be?"

Chief: "This will be established by their first newly forming Root Race. However, the probability is that it will be personal relationships based heavily on emotions and sex. This is an excellent vehicle with which to know, discover, and understand self and self as self relates to other selves.

On this Planet, the Atlanteans, and their predecessors, the Lemurians, used personal relationships as their prime mover. The Planet Venus has become famous for perfecting it into a beautiful Love Vibration."

Chela: "I wish we could have done that too . . . "

Chief: "Many share your thoughts."

Chela: "Did the Indian use this method?"

Chief: "Prior to the appearance of the European, yes. Personal relationships accompanied by an intense harmony with

NOTES:

nature, were the prime movers for the Red Race. This was gradually being developed to rather high degrees and the spiritual evolution of the Red Peoples had reached a high status of Awareness of Self, as the independence and individuality was being firmly implanted. The White Invaders introduced materialism, and this was quick to catch on. To "have things" became of paramount importance. Greed replaced, or enhanced, jealously. Spiritual heights were lost, evolution was in retrograde. A proud and ancient Race withered under the onslaught of the industrious White Man.

Since we are on the subject we should point out that the Brown and Black Races also had little intercourse via Commerce. Certain ones of the Yellow Race did — somewhat. But, this was essentially trade goods, and money was not a factor. It was the European's craving for gold, silver, and precious stones that turned the tides of Commerce.

Today, all Nations, large and small, *must* become a Capitalistic Democracy — or perish! The U.S. proudly takes credit for this major and magnificent achievement! The end results will be the U.S. will conquer the World through destruction. The Americans *are* Shiva: The Destroyer. America and Orion work together like hand in glove."

Chela: "Wow! This viewpoint overwhelms me! Chief, the Human Being is a social fellow, and there are a lot of personal relationships going around. Why isn't this more of a factor than it is?"

Chief: "Current personal relationships are certainly important. Assuming marriage is the ultimate in the example, let us note how almost all marriages are based on economics. Marriage must be "affordable" before it is undertaken. The financial supporting of any marriage is a serious consideration. The priority needs for certain domestic items are discussed at length. The planned parenthood rests heavily upon the single or combined annual income.

The sexual attraction usually is the initiator. This initiation supercedes finances, at least for the moment. Sex is then redefined as love, as the couple blissfully pour over their bank books. This is not an erroneous process. But it is heavily tainted by finance/Commerce. Religion steps in next and blesses the union, or prohibits it. The relationships responds accordingly. Sometimes defiance and spite are the binding factors. If the couple are of different Nationalities, then the Governments enter into the personal relationship to pronounce their demands.

Personal relationship defaults exist and are quite useful, but they are incredibly impure! However, there is no way to improve upon them considering the dictates of this culture. Can you imagine what it would be like to engage in a Love affair with another without any regards to finances, religious laws or civil law? It would resemble a fairy story from a child's book, would it not?"

Chela: "It seems there are so many people who seek counsel, or who are already in therapy. The stress factor is widespread. Could you comment on this?"

Chief: "A part of the counseling hinges heavily on the lucrative income on the part of the counselor. Also, it is the fad, the prestige of being able to afford to "be in therapy." However, it must be honestly said that more good than harm comes from this. It must also be noted that counseling, by whomever, is *not* the ultimate in answers.

But let us dwell on the subject of stress. The insecurity of the culture breeds stress. The mobility of the society, the looseness of the ties between family members and friends, and the frequent changes of employment, are all major factors leading to what is commonly called stress.

The individual attempts to combat or counteract stress in order to curtail this unwelcome guest. Counseling can be effective for some. Others will attempt to escape through the use of alcohol and/or drugs. These agents can produce a level of euphoria, or a relief of some nature which justifies the activity in the mind of the user. Others might choose to lose themselves in television. The "soap operas" are a prime example. All ages can learn to live vicariously through the unfolding stories. Often as not, the TV life is more interesting than their own. The stress is eliminated through the escape mechanism chosen.

NOTES:

A make-believe world is created by the practitioner. This fantasy is then intermingled into the real life "to temper it." This can make life tolerable for many, as the stress factor is reduced dramatically. This produces an experience. This is not necessarily the type of experience the Soul had counted on. Come now the Higher Self to prod the individual into a more productive form of existence that would meet the catalysts head on.

The personality resists, not wishing to forfeit the relief. The Higher Self insists, and the War is on. The personality always loses. This is not only correct, but it is *delightfully* correct! When the ego capitulates, the result is pure joy. The ego doubts this severely, to the last second.

The numbers of people losing themselves by promoting an addiction to drugs/alcohol/TV/etc., is increasing steadily. *This is the Mass Consciousness! These* are the ones who are *leading* our beloved Earth Mother along this phase of her evolutionary path! This is preposterous! Never-the-less, this is Universal Law. Again, enter Orion, who is taking full advantage of an unfortunate situation. Also, note that the Mass Consciousness of America greatly influences the rest of Humanity. Orion capitalizes on this opportunity. The Mass Consciousness, led by Americans, is in a stupor! Bewildered by the complexity of the economy, coupled with the complexity of Government laws, the people retreat. They seek escape. They find relief in their addictions of whatever nature. The cycle is vicious. Orion is at the invisible helm. The Americans dutifully obey his every command. Patriotism supplemented by their religious beliefs, justify their every action. God and Country is the battle cry . . and Orion laughs all the way to the bank!

Stress is a useful tool. It is the ploy of Negativity. It promotes addiction. Addicts are readily controllable. A firm grasp on reality eludes the addict. Almost all people are addicted to something. The future is predictable. Orion is pleased. The make-believe reality avoids noticing the destruction of First and Second Density. The Church speaks of "having dominion over" all things. The path is both profitable and Divine — how could anything be wrong?"

NOTES:

Chela: "The fast pace adds to this situation. So much has happened in such a relative short span of time. My Grandmother was born in 1911. In her lifetime, she has seen the horse and buggy give way to: the automobile, World War I, Prohibition, The Great Depression, World War II, Korean Conflict, Sputnik, Men on the Moon, Vietnam, a President's resignation, another's assassination, Communism's rise and fall, gold's rise from $35.00 per ounce to over $800.00 per ounce, the radio replaced by TV, a computer in most people's homes, and the price of automobiles rising from $650.00 to over $20,000.00, to say nothing of the complacent attitude toward drugs and sex. And now we have AIDS . . . ! so much has happened. So many, many changes have taken place that nobody ever got comfortable with anything before it became outdated. Nobody knows about things anymore. Nothing can be fixed, it has to be replaced . . . "

Chief: "Your list could extend forever. Your point is well taken. This is Commerce in action. It is accomplishing precisely what it intended. Governments and religions are its ally. The minds of the peoples are being molded into a strong and willing service-to-self attitude. Orion is having a field day. Be aware! Know what is happening. Keep your wits about you and rise above it. Knowledge is the key that unlocks the door to your prison of ignorance. Use it!"

Chela: "It seems that I am experiencing monotony and boredom. It does not appear to me that those around me are doing the same, yet, when I ask them, they claim they are too. This seems to be a paradox in times that are moving so swiftly when change is constant. What's going on?"

Chief: "First of all, let us be familiar with definitions. Boredom is the lack of excitement. Constant change does not necessarily contain excitement and can therefore be boring. Usually, one does not keep up with change, for whatever reason, and the change in itself offers no stimulus. In certain categories we all become "dropouts." Things move too quickly and we fail to keep up. Commerce via technology is making tremendous strides in many, many directions. Just keeping informed is a major undertaking . This is the age of the specialist and often as

NOTES:

not, we are none too sure of their expertise. Life has become so complex and complicated that we are unable to do anything for ourselves anymore. This is frustrating for those of you who are versatile."

Chela: "How does this affect the Mass Consciousness?"

Chief: "Unfortunately, this *is* the Mass Consciousness. The beer, the drugs the TV are the stabilizing and uniting factors of the elite World Societies. Only the backward Aborigines are relatively unaffected. This is acceptable, for there is no profit in controlling them anyway. The Mass Consciousness is the problem. If the people would somehow "wake up" and realize they are victims of a golden conspiracy — made of "fool's gold" and adjust their mental attitude accordingly, the Mass Consciousness could do a flip, and the Earth Mother could then be projected into our New Dispensation with minor inconvenience. As it stands now, the Great Lesson depicting the ultimate destruction of First, Second, and Third Densities via Commerce shall be carried out to its bitter conclusion. This could take several more decades of misery."

Chela: "Should we then try to prevent commercial destruction of the Planet, or should we encourage it, to hasten the end?"

Chief: "The altering of the thinking patterns of the Mass Consciousness would, of course, be ideal. However, this is not likely, due to the enslaving harness placed upon the peoples by Commerce, Religions, and Governments. Therefore, to go to any great lengths to preserve the purity of our Planet, our home, or to save a species of animals, or even an individual Second Density entity, or to prevent great forests from being devastated — so that workers can continue to "feed their families" — would be an exercise in futility and would succeed only in postponing the inevitable. For the sake of expediency, shut your eyes and don't watch the life around you perish. The sooner, the better — this is most merciful, considering our conditions. To prolong the agony is not useful or appreciated by First and Second Density. Third Density will selfishly cling onto a dying aspect of the plant and animal kingdom and righteously demand that Commerce,

NOTES:

Religion, or Government come to the rescue. But, these are the very agents that are dedicated to the destruction of the species! A compromise is often offered to placate the public. We will save it *here,* while we eradicate it *there.* When *there* has been completed, we will refocus our attention back to *here.* If it has no immediate commercial value, then it is standing in the path of progress; it is trash."

Chela: "The Social Product, us, is something less than desirable. There is a feeling of shame. It is like my life has been a waste. I have been a fool . . . "

Chief: "Your assessment of self is incomplete. Observe from the lofty position of your Soul. Your Soul, all Souls, have prospered because of the unique Negativity that is prevalent upon this Probable World of Reality. These are the kinds of experiences that cannot be duplicated elsewhere. personalities suffer, while their Souls thrive. Remember: Personalities come and personalities go, but the Soul is eternal. The personality is always working for his/her Soul. This has been a great schoolhouse, a place of learning that has enrolled students from all over our Galaxy, and the Universe, as well. The Earth and her unorthodox systems are not accidents. Entities wiser than you and I formulated this plan to enhance long-term evolution. From a high perspective, this has worked out in grand fashion. Do not be dismayed.

From the Human point of view, limited as it is, this could appear as a disaster. In order to make the attitude/catalyst effective, it *must* appear as such, in order to drive the lesson home."

Chela: "Excuse me Chief, precisely what *is* that lesson?"

Chief: "The lesson of abundance — the lesson of waste. In the Creator's Universe there is no waste. Abundance prevails. The etheric is unlimited in its supply of materials. On Planet Earth, the anomaly of the opposite is taking place. Unlimited natural resources was the foolish theory that laid the plans for waste. Mountains of waste indicate the affluency of the "civilized" portions of our World.

NOTES:

Commerce made the abundance of our natural resources short-lived, Religion condoned it as God's (Orion's) Will " . . . having dominion over . . . ," and Governments heartily embraced it for the power it bestowed upon themselves. Waste produces shortages, and power/money determine the "haves" and the "have nots." Even the Eagles fight amongst themselves for the few remaining nesting sights.

Greed, which is service to self, which is Negative, which is the teachings of Orion, rules the Social Product. It did not have to be like this. Greed is the product of Free Will. This opened the door to Orion. The Mass Consciousness did this willingly! They may or may not have accepted the dire consequences. Ignorance is *NOT* bliss! The catalysts and the lessons could have been readily obtained, and would have been just as efficient in a much less destructive manner. This destruction was not planned or intended. Destruction and extermination are the work of Orion. How many wear his mark? It is much easier and quicker to count the ones who do not!

Remember, all change begins on the inside and works outward. You have the right, the duty, to change yourself. You are not the missionary. You do not have the right to change others. Begin by altering your attitude through understanding. As you change yourself, you become the catalyst, as you now teach others by example. This is gratifying to your Soul, as it is to other Souls. The wheels of evolution begin to roll once again. Always remember, the physical reality is but an illusion — try not to take it too seriously. It is the thought that counts."

Chela: "What is the power that Orion deploys through Commerce, Religion, and Government? How is he able to consistently maintain such tight control?"

Chief: "The power is fear. We are all intimidated through the use of fear. A business can crush an individual at any time. The recourse is often too costly to take. The tenets of Religion comprise the Negative "Thou shalt *not* . . . ," while Governments seem to have a law against everything that an individual might like to do. This is a Worldwide situation. There is always the fear that you cannot "get ahead." That is coupled with the fear that you might lose everything that you have.

People are easy to control when they are afraid. If you protest too loudly, there will be someone from the FBI or the local Police who will take your name and run it through their computers and your life will never be the same again. Fear of the consequences keeps us all in line. Verbal protest is politely endured with earplugs, but if you choose to take any form of physical action, "they" will bring out their big guns you, and the individual, don't stand a chance. If you organize then you become just as Negative as "they" are. Power begets fear. If your organized power threatens them, then "they" will challenge you. This process is called War. War results in one brand of fear dominating over another brand of fear. Either way, Orion wins and it gives the people something to do. Any conflict is bound to be good for Commerce, as it rejuvenates Religion and strengthens one of the governments.

The nucleus of Third Density is a fear of something or other. It is interesting to note that the word "fear" shall be impossible to define in our New Dispensation. This is the first great change that you will be aware of after the Transition."

Chela: "Is there anything we can do to overcome fear between now and the great Transition?"

Chief: "As an individual, see the physical reality for the illusion that it truly is and try not to take it so seriously. Educate yourself so that the fear of the unknown will be minimized. Bask in the comfort of your Higher Self as you practice your Kundalini Meditation.

Teach by example. If all of you Light Bearers and Love Bearers would awaken and humbly accept your true status, as you put your services on the line — the entire World could change in a matter of minutes. *This is why you incarnated — This is your mission!* This is why we teach and write these books — to assist you in your mission, as you get about your Father's business. Raise your Kundalini and study the Tensor Concepts!

The Mass Consciousness can change almost overnight if it is faced with the impetus to do so. *You are that catalyst!*

NOTES:

Establish and promote your independence, your individuality, your awareness of self. All of you Wanderers must do this. It is not necessary to organize yourselves physically because this will be accomplished telepathically via the subconscious. Your Higher Self will work "miracles" before your very eyes — but first you must awaken and open your eyes!"

Chela: "What about the Industrial Revolution, Chief? Could you comment on the impact it had on Commerce?"

Chief: "The Industrial Revolution was considered and then permitted to unfold for the express purpose of granting more free time to those comprising the labor force. When a person worked twelve to fourteen hours or more per day, six days per week, there wasn't any time left over to quietly look within self, to discover self, and to grow spiritually. To permit thought patterns to flow into the minds of men, inventors produced the machinery that was to ease the work load and provide more free time. This happened. It worked well. But the free time was not directed to the intended goal. Free time became known as leisure times, and plans were quickly forthcoming on how to use this leisure time in a recreational way that would show a commercial profit for business. Professional sports were developed due to this "opportunity." The Churches were not keen on having their members meditate for fear of alienating their loyalty, so they collectively agreed that meditation must be a "sin." Unions sprang forth, and Government decided it needed to regulate the whole thing; and controlling laws were promptly passed. The intended blessing of free time soon became a hazard to everybody's health.

As distortion continued, the welfare state emerged. The corruption continues. The deterioration remains unchecked. This noble idea has actively prevailed in a generation of people who are perfectly content to go through life with their head in the sand and are essentially oblivious to all that goes on around them. Crimes are committed in their presence and they fail to notice! The World crumbles around them and they open another can of beer and get back to their television! Industry has given them the time and the money to be able to afford to do this.

NOTES:

Again, the three determining factors singularly, or collectively, will cause all noble gifts to be misused. Orion is clever."

Chela: "I have known a lot of good, strong, noble people who didn't seem to fall into the category that you describe. It's like fooling *all* the people *all* the time."

Chief: "We grasp your difficulty to accept. The saying that you refer to is: "You can fool all the people some of the time; You can fool some of the people all of the time; but you can't fool all of the people all of the time." We heartily agree with you. Some of the people have never been fooled. They definitely are in the minority. Others who have been fooled are beginning to awaken. Then there is that vast majority that make up the Mass Consciousness, which can be fooled all of the time. These are the ones who very well may have to experience the devastating experiences of Commerce gone mad, as it systematically destroys all life on this sphere. This would constitute an awakening that would sear their Souls for an eternity. Some must learn the hard way. These ones could listen to you and the likes of you and get the same results — but they won't. We all know this. The lessons in our immediate future will be hard lessons indeed.

The "economy" determines everything. All our lives hinge around it. It is *the* determining factor. Your words and our words will not phase the mind set of the majority. They cannot imagine their lives being conducted in any other way. They are not open to suggestion. Their heads are firmly planted in the sand. Quickly would they go to war to defend their way of life. The Government would sponsor such a move; Religions would sanction it. They are what they are — Laggard Souls. At the end of a major cycle, these ones incarnate by the droves. Innately, they feel if the Planet is destroyed or rendered uninhabitable, then they shall not have re-incarnate again. Maintaining the status quo is a comfortable state of darkness (ignorance), and is the extent of their ambitions. These are our kinfolks, friends, and neighbors.

As you aptly pointed out, all are not like this. There is always that proverbial ten percent that doesn't get the word, and

NOTES:

they are mavericks, the thorn in the side for the rest of the World. How does it feel to be a thorn? Remember, a small prick from a sharp thorn can cause a great steer to change course! The thorn is the *Truth!* Truth cannot be hidden by the bloated belly of a fat society. The sharp point of Truth has the power to mold the Universe. You are the thorn; you are the Truth. We beseech you to muster the *courage* to invoke the Law of Motion into your beingness, so that your teachings might bear fruit. You are a product of your Root Race. The leopard cannot deny his spots. You are a manifested aspect of our One Infinite Creator. You are a Co-Creator. We respectfully suggest that you, in all due humility, recognize yourself and start acting the role that you volunteered to play in this drama called life. *You are a Co-Creator, act like one!"*

Chela: "Chief, we understand that a bias must be adopted and injected into data/information, to assemble it in a form that will make a point. You have your biases, just as we all do. Chief . . . where are you coming from?"

Chief: "First Density. It is our honor/duty to be of Earth Service, with Light and Love for all — The Law is ONE."

Chela: "Megwich Chief, Our Thanks!"

-Summary-

The three major catalysts that have made the Aryan Root Race what it is today are: Commerce, Religion, Government, and in that order of importance. We have shared with you a candid conversation between ourselves and our students. It has not been our intent to anger you or to provoke disenchantment. Quite the opposite. It is our delightful duty to inform and enlighten you, our dear and faithful reader. We are permitted to offer Truth undiluted and un-camouflaged. Our purpose is not to be offensive, though we realize some of you are taken aback by some of our statements. A point of view has been presented that has been unthinkable for Americans since before the Country's inception. We have barely touched upon the subjects; you may fill in the details yourself. Commerce in its present form must be eradicated from the minds of men. The concept of the exchange

NOTES:

of Light and Love between all things is the only trade acceptable in the Face of our ONE Infinite Creator.

Some religions are more destructive than others; you may define them to your own satisfaction. Ultimately *all* religions must perish and be replaced with the attitude: *As an individual, I seek out and see the Creator in everybody and in everything. All is ONE.* As governments collapse around you, assume responsibility for yourself, as you are consistently considerate of others who are doing the same.

Develop your attitude of sharing and blending your Light and Love with all things. Rise above the conflict of emotions, the core of Third Density, as you teach by example the ways of MAN. May humility be your companion.

-Conclusion-

For the final time, let us prepare to lower the Kundalini. Bring the White Light of the Kundalini up around yourself and gather it in an object over your head. Bring it in it's entirety into the crown of the head as you detach your consciousness. Begin the descent, deactivating each chakra, as we give the color countdown: Violet . . . Indigo . . . Blue . . . Green . . . Yellow . . . Orange . . . Red . . . put the Kundalini to rest and shut the door. Take a deep breath.

And now, our Prayer of Protection: "In the name of the Presence and the Power Universal, protect us from harm and all Unenlightened Spirits, and may the Light of our Spirit Guides and the Light of our Higher Selves illuminate our thoughts that we may reflect the Radiant Glory of ALL THAT IS."

We leave you now in the Love and Light of our One Infinite Creator. Go forth in the joy of life and in the service to others.

Adonai. Adonai, Vasu Barragus, Adonai.
We thank you, we thank you *very* much!

-The Farewell-

Again, we come to the close of another Volume of *The Teachings*. It has truly been a labor of Love for us. We have

NOTES:

enjoyed sharing our distortion of Intelligent Infinity with you. The opportunity to share makes our incarnation worthwhile. Without you, dear reader, we would be incomplete. We sincerely thank you for reading our books. We feel that we have found in you a dear and remembered friend — one that we have known in the ancient past. We have met before; we shall meet again . . .

Kije Manito Adieanahuk Pehs!
(May the Great Spirit's Blessings be yours!)

We Are . . . Chief Little Summer and Warm Night Rain

Megwich!
(Our Thanks!)

A

B

C

R

S

BOOKS BY CHIEF LITTLE SUMMER & WARM NIGHT RAIN

REFLECTIONS ON A RAINY APRIL DAY

A Saturday fishing trip with his father is postponed due to rain. The small lad is destined to spend the day relegated to his bedroom in the company of his pet cat. Unexpectedly, his Higher Self announces its presence and an enlightening conversation ensues. The lad is introduced to other aspects of himself – including those portions that dwell on parallel worlds of reality. A fascinating story that prompts the child to examine cause and effect as it relates to responsibility. You will not become bored while reading this story to your child!
23 pages, color illustrations.

THE MISFIT

A poignant story of first love. She is the most popular girl in the sophomore class. He is the outcast. A small, 1940s Midwest rural community provides the setting for this suspenseful, humorous drama. The main characters learn to use their psychic abilities of telepathy which drives their poor English teacher bonkers! Fast moving, beautifully written, historically accurate. The bittersweet lessons of life and death are beautifully portrayed as the pure emotions of the characters are laid bare. Their world becomes your world. This classic is a must for all teens and pre-teens. Adults will cherish the memories the story provides.
300 pages.

THE TEACHINGS FOR THE FOURTH DENSITY AQUARIAN VOL. 1

Explicit instruction is given in how to awaken and raise the Divine Kundalini Energy. . .which permits you to make conscious contact with your Higher Self. Learn how and why Creation was created via the Laws of Fragmentation; why we are returning home to our Source, our Radiant One, our Creator! Learn how the Soul develops as you discover your own spiritual status. Learn about Love, about Light, about Karma and Reincarnation. Understand the transition called "death." The fears of this phenomenon are finally put to rest! The mystery of life after death is exposed to the Light of understanding. A tour of our own Solar System is also included. Discover the types of MAN who live in/on the various Planets. The Teachings concludes with over 100 questions and answers.

ORDER FORM

Number of Copies		Price	Amount
________	*Reflections*	$7.95	$________
________	*The Misfit*	$10.95	$________
________	*The Teachings, Volume 1*	$14.95	$________
________	*The Teachings, Volume II*	$16.95	$________

All prices in U.S. Dollars only ***(Prices subject to change)***

U.S. surface	Canada surface	Overseas Air
Under $10.00, add $2.00	Add $3.50 first book,	Add $10.00 first book,
$10.01–$30.00, add $2.50	$1.50 each additional	$8.00 each additional
Over $30.00, add $3.50		

Add Postage and handling: $________

Add state and local sales tax for orders shipped within Texas (8%) $________

TOTAL PAYMENT: $________

____
NAME

____
ADDRESS

____
CITY, STATE *ZIP* *COUNTRY*

Please make checks/money orders payable to **Piqua Press**

• P.O. Box 202590 • Austin, TX 78720-2590 •

Allow 3–5 weeks for delivery.